*f*P

BLAMING
THE
BRAIN

THE TRUTH ABOUT
DRUGS AND MENTAL HEALTH

ELLIOT S. VALENSTEIN, PH.D.

1998

THE FREE PRESS

New York   London   Toronto   Sydney   Singapore

THE FREE PRESS
A Division of Simon & Schuster Inc.
1230 Avenue of the Americas
New York, NY 10020

THE FREE PRESS and colophon are
trademarks of Simon & Schuster Inc.

Designed by MM Design 2000 Inc.

Manufactured in the United States of America

10 9 8 7 6 5 4 3 2 1

Library of Congress Cataloging-in-Publication Data

Valenstein, Elliot S.
    Blaming the brain: the truth about drugs and mental health /
Elliot S. Valenstein.
        p.   cm.
    Includes bibliographical references and index.
    1. Mental illness—Pathophysiology.   2. Mental illness–Etiology–
Physiological aspects.   3. Brain—Effect of drugs on.
4. Psychotropic drugs—Marketing—Moral and ethical aspects.
5. Medical misconceptions.   6. Deceptive advertising.
7. Pharmaceutical industry—Moral and ethical aspects.   I. Title.
RC455.4.B5V35   1998
616.89'071—dc21   98–27346
                                                        CIP

ISBN 0-684-84964-X

To Paul and Marcia, Carl and Susan, Clara and Helen,
Max and Laura—
just in case I don't write another book.

Contents

Acknowledgments

When you have been working in a field for almost a half century, it is impossible to know the origin of most of your ideas. There have been uncountable conversations with colleagues and students, lectures attended, and books, articles, grant applications, unpublished manuscripts, and research proposals read, or at least perused. All of these experiences have influenced my ideas, where they did not completely originate with them.

I should note that while working on this book I wrote to many colleagues, some I had never met, and all of them responded to my inquiries with helpful information and often with copies of articles and books they had written and preprints of articles not yet published. Not infrequently, these colleagues suggested other articles, or other people, that might be helpful, and in a number of instances I was made aware of issues or literature that I might have overlooked. More colleagues were helpful than would be practical to list here, but I would like to mention several individual who patiently and collegially responded to several requests for additional information. I am indebted in this way to Seymour Fisher of the Department of Psychiatry & Behavioral Sciences of the University of Texas Medical Branch in Galveston, to David Healy of University of Wales College of Medicine, and to Andrew Herxheimer, Chairman of the International Society of Drug Bulletins. I want to also acknowledge the help provided by Leopold Hofstatter of the Mental Health Systems Research Unit of the University of Missouri at Columbia and Patricia Goldman-Rakic, of the Yale University School of Medicine.

I want especially to express my appreciation to Randolph Nesse of the Department of Psychiatry at the University of Michigan. Randy regularly forwarded information to me through campus or electronic mail that was most helpful either in developing my ideas or in illustrating them with interesting examples. Randy also provided encouragement as well as advice during several conversations over coffee. Giorgio Bignami of the Istituto Superiore di Sanità in Rome was similarly helpful. During the several months I spent in Rome, Giorgio left articles in my mailbox almost every morning. Giorgio had a good sense of the direction I was heading in my writing and the articles and newspaper clippings that he brought to my attention as well as the many conversations we had were enormously useful. I am also most grateful for his friendship, hospitality, and thoughtfulness during the time I spent in Rome.

I want to thank Julius Axelrod for providing me, over a pleasant lunch in Washington, D.C., a fascinating firsthand account of his Nobel Prize–winning research on catecholamine metabolism and for his comments on how early clinical investigators and neuropharmacologists, especially those at the National Institute of Mental Health, were thinking about drugs, brain chemistry, and mental disorders during the 1950s and 1960s.

I am also greatly indebted to colleagues in the Biopsychology group at the University of Michigan. Terry Robinson read much of an early version of the manuscript and offered many helpful suggestions, several of which forced me to give more thought to issues that I probably had discussed too superficially. On a number of occasions, Aldo Badiani helped me locate specific neuropharmacological information that I needed and he was also most kind in preparing the illustrations of drug-brain interactions.

Although his field is pathology, my son Paul Valenstein was able to make a number of quite helpful substantive suggestions on the contents of several chapters, usually while we were walking his dog. I also suspect that Paul may have especially enjoyed improving my literary style, perhaps as a way of reciprocating for all of my much earlier comments on the papers he wrote for high school assignments.

I have to single out my Biopsychology colleague, Kent Berridge, for special thanks. I am not sure that I could conjure up a more thoughtful and helpful colleague. Despite being extremely busy with his own work, Kent read several versions of the entire manuscript and made many insightful comments that greatly improved the final version. Not only did Kent's suggestions help clarify the way the ideas were expressed, but he constantly pushed me to develop them further and to consider implications that I had not addressed. Moreover, depite being considerably younger than I am, Kent has a talent for providing the gentle encouragement I needed when I might otherwise have been inclined to let something short of my best effort slip by.

While all of the above were enormously helpful, they are, of course, not responsible for the ideas expressed in the book. Colleagues always made suggestions in the spirit of helping me develop my own ideas and express them more effectively, regardless of whether they agreed with them or not.

I would also like to acknowledge the help of Susan Arellano, my initial editor at The Free Press, who made several suggestions that helped to make the manuscript clearer and more accessible to a wider audience. After Susan Arellano left The Free Press, Philip Rappaport took over the editorial responsibilities and carefully read several revisions of the manuscript, making a large number of valuable comments and suggestions that I am certain improved the book enormously. I am also greatly indebted to Celia Knight and Sean Devlin for the painstaking effort they obviously expended in improving the style of the manuscript, checking every detail, and in eliminating errors.

I received considerable help from the research librarians at both the University of Michigan's Taubman Medical Library in Ann Arbor and the National Library of Medicine in Bethesda. The Psychology Department of the University of Michigan provided support in numerous ways while I was working on this book.

My agent, Katinka Matson (president of John Brockman, Inc.), was most helpful in consummating all the arrangements with The Free Press, so that I could concentrate on the writing.

I also want to express my appreciation to the Rockefeller Foundation for inviting me to do some of the writing at the Villa Serbelloni in Bellagio, Italy. Despite spending too much time gazing at the snow-peaked Swiss Alps across Lake Como, I managed to complete quite a bit of work while being pampered in this magnificent setting. I want also to thank the Fulbright Foundation for a Fellowship that made it possible for me to spend a very fruitful period talking to colleagues in Italy.

Chapter 1

INTRODUCTION

American psychiatry is said to have changed from blaming the mother to blaming the brain. It was not so very long ago that the cause of mental disorders was thought to be rooted in early experiences within the family, but now it is widely believed by most authorities and the public alike that the cause is a chemical imbalance in the brain. Today, schizophrenia is commonly claimed to be caused by an excess of the neurotransmitter dopamine and depression by a deficiency of serotonin, while anxiety and other mental disorders are attributed to other neurotransmitter abnormalities. Brain chemistry is believed to be not only the cause of mental disorders, but also the explanation of the normal variations in personality and behavior. How did these radical changes occur within the span of a few decades and does the evidence really support these new theories? Whose interests are served by promoting drug treatment and biochemical explanations and how are these interests advanced? What are the long-range implications of the biochemical theory of mental disorders and the growing reliance on drugs to treat all psychological and behavioral problems? This book attempts to answer these questions and to provide a long-overdue examination of the assumptions fundamental to current biochemical theories.

From about 1945 through 1960, most people had very different ideas about the cause of mental disorders. Although orthodox psychoanalytic therapy was practiced by only a small percentage of mental health professionals, psychoanalytic explanations of the causes of different mental disorders and the best way to treat them dominated the field. In 1950, it was rare that someone not committed to psychoanalytic theory would head a major psychiatry department.[1] Psychotherapists in private practice often spent years trying to discover the repressed causes of their patients' mental disorders. The value of this approach and the theory underlying it is now widely questioned, if not totally rejected, by most mental health professionals. Today, the disturbed thoughts and behavior of mental patients are believed to be caused by a biochemically defective brain, and symptoms are not "analyzed," but used mainly as the means of arriving at the diagnosis that will determine the appropriate medication to prescribe. Almost all current chairmen and the majority of the staffs of psychiatry departments are committed to a biochemical approach to mental illness.

How radically our ideas have changed is indicated by the fact that most psychiatric residents no longer receive any instruction in intensive psychotherapy, and many complete their training without meeting regularly with a single patient in psychotherapy sessions.[2] During the 1950s, any research on schizophrenia was considered unethical if it included a control group given drugs without complementary psychotherapy. By 1970, however, the situation had reversed, and it was considered unethical to have a group that received only psychotherapy and no drugs.[3]

These changes started in the 1950s, following the accidental discoveries of several drugs capable of altering mood and mental states. When tested on mental patients, these drugs alleviated some symptoms of mental illness. Many patients became calmer and less of a problem for those responsible for their care. Initially, psychiatrists in private practice were highly skeptical of drug treatment, but in the large institutions, where there was a pressing need to reduce costs, drugs were widely adopted. By 1965, over 50 million prescriptions had been written for Thorazine (chlorpromazine), the first of the new psychotherapeutic drugs to be marketed for schizophrenia, and there were many other drugs available for treating depression and anxiety as well. At first, psychiatrists in private practice were willing to try these drugs only as an adjunct to psychotherapy, but gradually they began to rely more on drugs and less on intensive psychotherapy. Today, it is not uncommon for a psychiatrist to rely almost exclusively on drug treatment, and the annual sales of quite a few psychotherapeutic drugs are in the billions of dollars.

The many recent books on the so-called "pharmacological revolution in psychiatry" are another indication of how much our prevailing notions of mental illness have changed. These popularly written books use such phrases as "molecules of the mind" and "chemistry of mood" to convey the idea that all the important aspects of mental life are determined by brain chemistry. Chemical imbalances are believed to be the cause not only of depression, schizophrenia, anxiety, and obsessive-compulsive disorders, but also of much maladaptive behavior, such as eating disorders, violence, alcoholism, excessive gambling, and compulsive shopping. Moreover, personality traits ranging from shyness to assertiveness, from passiveness to aggressiveness, from risk aversion to sensation seeking, and from the capacity to delay gratification to requiring immediate satisfaction all are claimed to be caused by abnormal activity of only a couple of brain neurotransmitters, or even only one. Brain serotonin level, for example, is claimed to underlie self-confidence, and all pleasurable experiences are said to depend on brain dopamine activity.

Many recent books exaggerate and distort the connection between brain chemistry and psychological states. A University of Washington psychiatrist recently described a "world-wide epidemic of depression" caused by the "serotonin depleting times" we are living in.[4] Actually, there is not a shred of evidence of any worldwide decrease in brain serotonin. In another book, a Pulitzer Prize–winning science writer describes the "revolutionary" finding that major personality and behavioral traits are regulated by the balance between norepinephrine and serotonin.[5] There is really no convincing evidence supporting this view, but by describing some weak trends as established facts and by failing adequately to acknowledge contradictory evidence, many popular writers make it appear that complex personality variables are completely dependent on the balance between two neurotransmitters. It is not surprising that so many people now believe that drugs are able to produce "cosmetic" changes in personality. We have almost reached the point where there will be no limits to what people will believe brain chemistry can explain and where the slogan "Better living through chemistry" could well be changed to "Better lives through chemistry."

Today, physicians are routinely informing patients with mental disorders that their condition is caused by a biochemical imbalance that can be corrected by drugs in the same way that insulin treats diabetes. While many physicians are apparently convinced that this is true and that it has been firmly established by scientific investigation, others may not be completely convinced, but they have found the insulin analogy useful in overcoming the reluctance of some patients to take psychotropic drugs. Pharmaceutical companies have an enormous influence in promoting this message both to physicians and to potential consumers of drugs. Patient advocate groups also play a prominent role in this area. In order to encourage people in need to seek professional help for a psychological problem, various support groups, often funded by large grants from the pharmaceutical industry, exaggerate and sometimes distort the effectiveness of drug treatment and what is known about the relationship of brain chemistry to mental illness. Patients with psychological problems and their family members are usually more than willing to believe that the problem is biochemical, as this interpretation does not convey the stigma of mental illness that is unfortunately commonly associated with many traditional psychological theories.

Throughout this book I will argue that the evidence and arguments supporting all these claims about the relationship of brain chemistry to psychological problems and personality and behavioral traits are far from compelling and are most likely wrong. The claim that psychotherapeutic drugs correct a biochemical imbalance that is the root cause of most psychological problems also rests on a very shaky scientific foundation. These ideas are simply an unproven hypothesis, but for reasons that will be explored, they are heavily promoted as a well-substantiated explanatory theory. Because these ideas have enormous implications, there is a great need to examine the evidence and basic assumptions much more critically than has been done up to now.

It may surprise you to learn that there is no convincing evidence that most mental patients have any chemical imbalance. Yet many physicians tell their patients that they are suffering from a chemical imbalance, despite the reality that there are no tests available for assessing the chemical status of a living person's brain. While there are some reports of finding evidence of an excess or deficiency in the activity of a particular neurotransmitter system in the brains of deceased mental patients, these claims are controversial, as other investigators cannot find any such relationship. At best, such claims are trends that result from averaging the data from many patients. As the brain chemistry of many patients in these studies was found to be perfectly normal, it is hard to argue that their mental problems were caused by a chemical imbalance.

Moreover, the brains of some "normals"—people with no history of any mental disorder—may show signs of some excessive or deficient neurotransmitter activity. It needs to be recognized that even if a chemical abnormality were eventually found to be highly correlated with the incidence of a particular mental illness, it would not be clear how such a finding should be interpreted. It might well be that the chemical "abnormality" was caused by the stress or some behavioral peculiarity commonly associated with a particular mental illness, rather than having been the cause of that illness. It is also well known that psychotherapeutic drugs can be the cause of chemical abnormalities. The "cause" and the "effect" of a mental illness are routinely confused.

When the first psychotherapeutic drugs were accidentally discovered we knew so little about brain chemistry that it was not possible to even propose a biochemical theory of mental illness or to offer any explanation of how drugs were acting on the brain. Our initial chemical theories of mental disorders emerged after it was realized that the first drugs introduced seemed to be acting on the few neurotransmitters then known to exist in the brain. It is now estimated, however, that the number of substances that act as brain neurotransmitters may be over one hundred, and we have learned that most psychotherapeutic drugs affect many more neurotransmitters than initially suspected.[6] Yet the theories have changed very little over the years despite much evidence that they cannot possibly be correct. The theories are held on to not only because there is nothing else to take their place, but also because they are useful in promoting drug treatment.

There is a tendency to confuse the giant strides that have been made in our knowledge of brain chemistry and neuropharmacology with our still primitive understanding of the causes of mental illness and knowledge of how drugs can produce psychological changes. Stimulated to a great extent by the discovery of psychotropic drugs, the advances in our knowledge of brain chemistry and neuropharmacology have truly been remarkable. We now know not only that there are a great many more neurotransmitters in the brain than were suspected, but also where in the brain these different "chemical communicators" are located. We have learned how a neuron can use enzymes to make neurotransmitters from chemical precursors and how the different neurotransmitters act on their respective targets ("receptors"). We also know how the action of the different neurotransmitters is normally terminated and how, under certain conditions, the action may be prolonged. The science of neuropharmacology has contributed enormously to our understanding of the ways that drugs can modify all of these neuronal processes. However, all of this new knowledge has revealed critical exceptions to *every* chemical theory that has been proposed to explain mental illness, and the task of integrating all this new information and relating it to mental states grows more, rather than less, formidable.

Scientists, clinicians, and pharmaceutical companies have predicted that our new knowledge of brain chemistry and neuropharmacology will make it possible to develop drugs capable of acting like "smart missiles" that can correct the precise biochemical error responsible for each mental illness without any of the adverse side effects commonly seen with the drugs now marketed. The history of the neurotransmitter serotonin illustrates why we should maintain a healthy skepticism about these predictions of pharmacological "magic bullets" for treating mental illness. When serotonin was first discovered in the brain, it was thought that it acted on only one receptor target. We now know that there are at least fifteen different serotonin receptors. While technical advances may soon make it possible to develop drugs that act on only one of those receptors, we have little idea what these receptors do or how they may be related to any psychological state. There are good reasons for believing that every psychological state is influenced by different neurotransmitters and by brain circuits distributed widely throughout the brain that undoubtedly involve a number of different neurotransmitters. Furthermore, all information available should lead us to conclude that every neurotransmitter and every receptor target plays a role in different behavioral and psychological phenomena. There is no good reason to believe that there will be a simple and unitary relationship between a particular neurotransmitter or receptor target and any psychological state.

Most proponents of drug therapy use the fact that certain classes of drugs seem to be most effective in alleviating a particular mental illness as a strong argument for a biochemical cause. However, the relationship between the cause of an illness and the claimed effectiveness of a treatment can be quite misleading. The history of medicine is rife with examples of treatments that alleviated the symptoms of an illness without addressing its cause. Prefrontal lobotomy, insulin coma, and other treatments that are now totally rejected were claimed, in their time, to be just as effective in treating mental illnesses as it is now claimed that drug treatment is. Many current studies also have shown that electroconvulsive treatment (ECT) of depression may be more effective than drugs and there is good evidence that several of the briefer psychotherapies are at least as successful as drugs in treating some mental disorders. The tenuous relationship between what is judged to be effective in treating an illness and what has caused that illness in the first place is discussed in later chapters. Also discussed is how the judgment of improvement is made and how political and economic factors can influence that judgment. The success that is claimed for drug treatment is often exaggerated, while adverse side effects are commonly minimized.

Contrary to what some readers may conclude, I did not write this book because I am opposed to using drugs to treat mental illness. I believe that drugs are often useful in treating mental disorders. I should also make clear that I do not treat patients and have no reason to be for or against drug therapy, psychotherapy, or behavior therapy or to take any side in any disagreement between nonmedical therapists and psychiatrists. Furthermore, I am definitely not opposed to biological explanations of mind and behavior. In fact, I have spent over forty years working as a biopsychologist studying how the brain and other biological factors such as hormones and drugs influence behavior. I am certain as a scientist that biological factors have an important influence on behavior. In short, my motivation for writing this book was not that I was for or against anything. The book had a completely different origin.

I am convinced that biological factors may predispose some individuals toward developing a mental illness, but there is more to biology than neurotransmitters and brain chemistry. While I believe in the importance of biological factors, I am equally convinced that the way all biological factors are expressed in behavior and mental states depends equally on social and psychological variables. There is nothing startling about this statement, and there are probably very few who would not agree that biological and environmental factors interact to produce their effects. However, in their everyday practice physicians are increasingly being pressured to neglect everything but drugs and chemical explanations in treating patients with mental disorders, and therein lies a great danger.

For a number of years, I have been interested in how scientific ideas and explanations arise and change. My plan when I started this book was to trace the accidental discoveries of psychotherapeutic drugs that led to the revolutionary changes in how we think about mental disorders. Today, mental disorders are so widely believed to be caused by chemical deficiencies or excesses in the brain that even some psychotherapists are jumping on this biochemical bandwagon by suggesting that the "talking cure" works because it changes brain chemistry.[7] While it may be true that every mental change must be accompanied by some change in the brain, the claim has little substance behind it, as almost nothing is known about what brain changes take place during psychotherapy or how they may relate to any improvement in a patient's condition.

I was aware at the outset that this would not be a simple story of scientific progress. When the first psychotherapeutic drugs were introduced there were groups that opposed them, while other groups had a considerable interest in promoting their use and a different way to think about mental disorders. At the time that chlorpromazine and the other early drugs used to treat mental illness were discovered, little was known about brain chemistry or neuropharmacology. In the early 1950s, the field of psychopharmacology did not really exist. The discipline developed and matured together with the increased use of drugs to treat many different mental disorders. All of this background had convinced me that there was a fascinating story to be told about how serendipity, science, and psychosocial and economic factors interacted to bring about the changes in how mental disorders are conceptualized.

Starting with the discovery of the first psychotherapeutic drugs, I let the literature lead me backward and forward in time, learning more about early theories of mental disorders, brain physiology and chemistry, and how these changed over the years. I chose not to work from an outline, because I wanted the conclusions to emerge from the literature rather than the other way around. This made my progress much slower, but it had the advantage of leading me to some literature that I knew little about when I began. Besides, when working closely from an outline it is all work, without the joy of discovery. As I read more of the experimental and clinical literature and examined the social and intellectual context in which much of the evidence and theories was embedded, the purpose of the book gradually changed. Although I still wanted to describe the history of how all these changes took place, I decided that it was equally important to evaluate the evidence and arguments that are claimed to justify the biochemical theory. My own views were not well formed when I started the book, but as they became firmer I wanted to state them as clearly as possible so that others could challenge them in a way that I hoped might start a long-overdue dialogue about what is being claimed and what we really know about drugs and mental disorders.

Chapter 2 describes the fascinating story of how the major classes of psychotherapeutic drugs were discovered. This history provides the intellectual and social context that is necessary for understanding how drug treatment became widely accepted and how the effects of drugs revolutionized our theories about the causes of mental illness. Chapter 3 discusses the emergence of chemical theories proposed to explain how the drugs worked and what could be inferred about the causes of the different mental disorders. The evidence and arguments for the biochemical theories that emerged are presented as clearly and as convincingly as possible in this chapter to make it clear why so many came to accept these theories as having a sound scientific foundation. Chapter 4 examines the evidence and arguments for the chemical theories much more critically. This chapter documents the fact that much of the evidence that was described as convincing and compelling was often difficult to replicate, based on a very limited knowledge of brain chemistry and neuropharmacology, and often subject to other interpretations than the one offered.

Chapter 5 raises issues and arguments that go beyond an examination of the reliability of the empirical evidence. Included in this chapter are discussions of such topics as the confusion of the cause and the effect of a mental illness and, in general, what can be inferred about the origin of an illness from the effects of a treatment. Also discussed in Chapter 5 are the limits of reductionism, how much of psychology and behavior can be explained by genetics, whether drugs act as specifically on different mental disorders as claimed, and the role that science and politics have played in the classification of mental disorders. Chapter 6 and 7 examine the various ways that economic and psychosocial factors and special interest groups have promoted the "biochemical theory of mental disorders." These chapters discuss the enormous influence of the pharmaceutical industry in promoting drugs and the many different ways this influence has been exerted. The chapters also discuss how psychiatrists, medical insurers, and patient support groups promote drug treatment and the chemical theories of mental illness. The conflict between medical and nonmedical mental health professionals in interpreting the effectiveness of various treatments is also discussed in these chapters. Chapter 8 reviews the major arguments presented throughout the book that are believed to justify the conclusions reached. This chapter also attempts to anticipate and answer some of the criticisms likely to be raised and discusses some of the implications of the path we are now following.

So much for introduction. It is time to begin at the beginning with the discoveries that set the stage for all that followed.

Chapter 2

DISCOVERIES OF PSYCHOTHERAPEUTIC DRUGS

She [Helen of Troy] cast into the wine they were drinking a drug [Nepenthe] to quiet all pain and strife, and bring forgetfulness of every ill.

Homer

Or have we eaten of the insane root
That takes the reason prisoner?

William Shakespeare, *Macbeth*

Canst thou not minister to a mind diseased.

William Shakespeare, *Macbeth*

In the absence of a coherent understanding of the pathological basis of a disease, only serendipity can provide effective drugs for its treatment. Nowhere is this more evident than in an examination of the history of psychotherapeutic drugs.

Walter Sneader (1990)[1]

We know from a large body of evidence that mind-altering substances have been used throughout much of human history.[2] Paintings, sculptures, and other artifacts have been found— some several thousand years old—that depict the opium poppy, coca plants, various hallucinogenic mushrooms, cacti, and other plants containing psychotropic substances. This evidence, along with the findings of

very old vats for fermenting fruits and grains into alcoholic beverages, testifies to the ancient and widespread knowledge of substances capable of
altering emotion, mood, perception, and thought.[3] In all probability, these
psychotropic substances were discovered accidentally while searching for
edible plants, and their use was later often incorporated into religious and
mystical ceremonies.

Yet, despite this long history and the likelihood that people must
have noticed that the mental states induced by these hallucinogenic substances sometimes resembled insanity, it was not until relatively recent
times that anyone seriously pursued the implications of this similarity.
There were occasional statements throughout the years that suggested that
insanity might be caused by some humors or chemical substances acting
on the brain, but without sufficient knowledge of brain chemistry these
suggestions could not be pursued.[4] For example, statements attributed to
the Hippocratic school (c. 460–360 B.C.) suggested that mental illness
was the result of some abnormal "humoral" state of the brain, and much
later, in 1852, Heinrich Laehr, a physician in Halle, Germany, speculated
that "an extremely small chemical and physical change in the brain . . .
will suffice to produce a mental disorder."[5] About thirty years later,
Thudichum (1829–1901), the founder of modern neurochemistry, wrote
that:

> Many forms of insanity are unquestionably the external manifestations
> of the effects upon the brain substance of poisons fermented within the
> body, just as mental aberrations accompanying chronic alcoholic intox-
> ication are the accumulated effects of a relatively simple poison fer-
> mented out of the body. These poisons we shall, I have no doubt, be able
> to isolate after we know the normal chemistry to its uttermost detail.
> And then will come in their turn the crowning discoveries to which our
> efforts must ultimately be directed, namely, the discoveries of the anti-
> dotes to the poisons and to the fermenting causes and processes which
> produce them.[6]

Thudichum's remarks were advanced for the 1880s, but the knowledge and
technical skills required to pursue his ideas would not be available for more
than a half century. Moreover, Thudichum was speculating about toxins
formed in the body that could disturb normal mental functioning much
as alcohol did. He was not referring to the action of neurotransmitters. The
German psychiatrist Emil Kraepelin actually coined the term "pharmacopsychology" in the 1890s,[7] but he was not referring to any treatment of
mental illness. Early in his career, Kraepelin worked in the laboratory of
Wilhelm Wundt, the acknowledged founder of experimental psychology,
and he used "pharmacopsychology" to refer to the use of chemicals to help
in the study of normal mental processes.

Even Sigmund Freud's prophetic remarks, made as late as 1930, did not encourage anyone to search for a chemical basis of mental disorders:

> ... it is a fact that there are certain substances foreign to the body which, when present in the blood or tissues, directly cause us pleasurable sensations, but also so change the conditions of our perceptivity that we become insensible of disagreeable sensations. ... But there must be substances in the chemical composition of our bodies which can do the same, for we know at least one morbid state, that of mania, in which a condition similar to this intoxication arises without any drug being absorbed. ... It is greatly to be regretted that this toxic aspect of mental processes has so far eluded scientific research. (Sigmund Freud, *Civilization and Its Discontents*, 1930)

And the same year, in a letter to Maria Bonaparte, Freud once again commented that he believed that chemistry would eventually provide us with an understanding of the mechanisms underlying the neuroses and psychoses and that chemical therapy, while still far in the future, will be possible some day:

> We know that the mechanisms of the psychoses are in essence no different from those of the neuroses, but we do not have at our disposal the quantitative stimulation necessary for changing them. The hope of the future here lies in organic chemistry or the access to it through endocrinology. This future is still far distant, but one should study analytically every case of psychosis because this knowledge will one day guide the chemical therapy.[8]

Although Freud did become interested in the effects of cocaine on the mind, he did not incorporate any of his rudimentary speculation about chemistry into his theories about the causes of mental illness and the way to treat them. While many European psychiatrists believed the cause of psychosis would be found in the brain, they were searching primarily for structural, not chemical, abnormalities. This is not surprising in view of how little was known about brain chemistry, and, as will be described later, most neurophysiologists still believed that communication between nerve cells in the brain was electrical rather than chemical.

Work earlier in the century by Henry Dale and others had demonstrated that in some synapses in the peripheral (outside of the brain and spinal cord) nervous system norepinephrine was used to transmit signals between neurons and between neurons and muscles. Otto Loewi had also demonstrated that the vagus nerve slowed the heart by releasing a chemical "vagus stuff," later identified as the neurotransmitter acetylcholine. However, this work was not generally considered to apply to the brain, where transmission between neurons was considered an electrical induction, rather than a chemical, process. In the 1930s, several psychiatrists actually attempted to treat schizophrenia with acetylcholine, but not because acetylcholine was accepted as a brain neurotransmitter. A. M. Fiamberti, the Italian psychiatrist who developed the surgical approach that Walter Freeman later modified into the transorbital lobotomy procedure, used acetylcholine to produce a vascular shock that he hoped would benefit schizophrenic patients.[9] At the time, there were various anecdotal reports that seizures and traumatic brain injuries sometimes produced remarkable improvement in schizophrenic patients. The 1930s was a period when almost anything that might conceivably alleviate otherwise intractable mental disorders was considered worth trying, and there were few restraints on psychiatrists wanting to experiment.

Between 1930 and 1950, more was learned about brain chemistry, but compared to the accelerated interest in the subject that was to follow, the advances were relatively modest. In 1956 Wolfgang de Boor, a professor at Cologne, wrote the first textbook of psychopharmacology, but he, like Emil Kraepelin earlier, was mainly interested in using drugs to answer questions about normal mental functioning raised by experimental psychologists, rather than as a means of studying or treating mental disorders.[10] As will be described, the pharmacology industry played a major role in research on brain chemistry, and the first president of the International College of Neuropharmacology was Ernst Rothlin, director of Sandoz Pharmaceuticals.

The Discovery of LSD and the Events That Followed

The discovery in 1943 of lysergic acid diethylamide (LSD) by a Sandoz chemist played a major role in interesting psychiatrists and neuropharmacologists in how chemical substances might produce mental illnesses. LSD is an extremely potent hallucinogen that produces hallucinations and delusions that resemble, at least superficially, the perceptual and thought disorders of schizophrenia. However, the discovery of LSD did not immediately lead to the development of a chemical theory of psychosis. The 1940s was a period when psychoanalytic ideas were dominant and much of the early interest in LSD involved its use as an adjuvant to psychotherapy in the hope that it might facilitate access to the unconscious mind. This was not an unusual quest. The noted psychoanalyst Harry Stack Sullivan, for example, occasionally plied his patients with alcohol for "three to ten" days in order "to loosen them up for psychotherapy."[11] In 1954, the active ingredient in LSD was identified, and it was determined to have a chemical structure similar to serotonin. At this point, a number of people proposed that psychotic hallucinations were caused by abnormal serotonin activity.[12]

As would occur a decade later with all the early psychotherapeutic drugs, the discovery of LSD was accidental. LSD was initially obtained from an ergot fungus *(Claviceps purpurea)* that grows as a parasite on rye, wheat, and some other grasses. Ergot is a poison in high doses and it was responsible for deaths, convulsions, and a gangrenous condition known as St. Anthony's Fire in the Middle Ages.[13] Despite its toxicity, it was widely used through much of the nineteenth century by midwives and obstetricians to induce labor and to stop bleeding after childbirth.[14] In the 1930s, chemists at Sandoz Pharmaceuticals in Basel discovered that ergonovine was the active substance in ergot that produced uterine contractions, and Albert Hofmann, a Sandoz chemist, developed a method for producing large quantities of ergonovine for use in obstetrics. In the course of this work, the chemical structure of ergonovine was modified a number of times. One day in April 1943 while working on LSD-25 (the twenty-fifth modification), Hofmann was exposed to a minute amount of the drug and was forced to lie down because of dizziness.[15] In a memo to his supervisor at Sandoz, Hofmann wrote that: "in a dreamlike state with eyes closed I perceived an uninterrupted stream of fantastic pictures, extraordinary shapes with intense, kaleidoscopic play of colors." Hofmann suspected that LSD-25 was responsible, so he undertook what he thought would be a conservative test of this hypothesis by ingesting only twenty-five milligrams of the drug. It actually turned out to be a massive dose, as LSD-25 is extremely potent. Most drugs are measured in milligrams, thousandths of a gram, but LSD is measured in micrograms, millionths of a gram. Hofmann recorded his experiences following the ingestion of the drug:

> Everything in my field of vision wavered and was distorted as if seen in a curved mirror. . . . Pieces of furniture assumed grotesque, threatening forms . . . the lady next door, whom I scarcely recognized, was no longer Mrs. R but rather a malevolent, insidious witch with a colored mask. . . . Even worse than the demonic transformations of the outer world were the alterations that I perceived in myself, in my inner being. Every exertion of my will, every attempt to put an end to the disintegration of the outer world and the dissolution of my ego, seemed to be a wasted effort. A demon had invaded me, had taken possession of my body, mind and soul. I jumped up and screamed trying to free myself from him, but then sank down again and lay helpless on the sofa . . . I was seized by the dreadful fear of going insane. I was taken to another world, another place, another time. My body seemed to be without sensation, lifeless, strange. Was I dying? Was this the transition? At times I believed myself to be outside my body, and then perceived clearly, as an outside observer, the complete tragedy of my situation.[16]

It took fourteen hours before Hofmann returned to a normal mental state. Several of Hofmann's colleagues at Sandoz also tried LSD with similar experiences. Although there was little basis to speculate about how LSD might affect brain chemistry or what might be inferred about schizophrenia from this drug's action, Sandoz started exploring possible therapeutic and commercial applications of LSD. The company began to supply LSD and funds to psychiatrists willing to investigate potential clinical applications of the drug. The psychedelic experiences induced by LSD soon caught the imaginations of a whole subculture of people wanting to open up the untapped creative and artistic sides of their personalities. Aldous Huxley, who had earlier experimented with several hallucinogenic drugs, claimed that these drugs induced a mystical and religious experience that made it possible to enter the mental world of poets, artists, and saints.[17] A 1959 issue of *Look* magazine contained an article entitled: "The Curious Story Behind the New Cary Grant," which reported that LSD had transformed the actor into a stronger personality capable of really loving a woman and making her happy. Grant told the gossip columnist Joe Hyams that he had taken LSD over sixty times in therapy and that as a result of the drug "young women have never been more attracted to me."[18] Such reports and many other fascinating, but not necessarily reliable, anecdotes encouraged all kinds of uncontrolled "experimentation," sometimes resulting in irreparable damage to the lives and minds of people taking the drug.[19] In 1963, Timothy Leary, who had been fired from Harvard for inducing students to experiment with LSD, started a crusade to get people "to turn on, tune in, drop out." Eventually severe restrictions were placed on all LSD research.

From about 1955 through much of the 1960s much of the clinical research with LSD amounted to not much more than "playing around" with the drug. Nonetheless, several international conferences were convened to discuss the therapeutic applications of LSD.[20] A 1958 article in the *Journal of Nervous and Mental Diseases,* which has always had a biological orientation, illustrates the extent to which Freudian concepts influenced the way psychiatrists thought about mental disorders at the time. LSD was described as a "primitivizing agent" that caused "a loss of ego boundaries and the breakdown of ego defenses, giving rise to depersonalization, derealization, oceanic feelings and transcendental experiences, assisting in the emergence of archetypal images and a return to the Freudian primary process."[21] It was believed that LSD could speed up the psychotherapeutic process, and in Europe, the use of LSD to shorten psychotherapy was called *psycholytic therapy.* Several psychotherapists claimed that large doses of LSD produced psychedelic experiences that sometimes frightened patients into sobriety, but many more proposed psychoanalytic explanations of how the state induced by LSD helped patients gain the insight they needed to stop drinking. The psychologist Abraham Maslow argued that LSD research on alcoholics confirmed his belief in the therapeutic value of "peak experiences."[22] There were also claims that LSD helped relieve intractable pain. John Lilly, who was studying dolphins, reported that LSD profoundly altered the way these animals relate to humans.[23] There was also a great amount of questionable and potentially dangerous exploration with LSD, and in 1963, Sandoz restricted the supply of the drug to the National Institute of Mental Health, the Veterans Administration, and state commissioners of mental health. However, by this time LSD was readily available on the "street" through illegal channels.

Despite all the "research" with LSD, more than a decade elapsed from the time of its discovery before there was sufficient knowledge to develop theories about how the drug acted on the brain. While Albert Hofmann believed that LSD somehow altered nerve conduction and synaptic connections, he did not pursue this topic. Although he speculated that LSD might, in some unspecified way, help us understand psychosis, Hofmann seemed to emphasize that hallucinogenic drugs, like meditation and religion, helped us understand our place in the universe: "I see the true importance of LSD in the possibility of providing the material aid to meditation aimed at the mystical experience of a deeper comprehensive reality. Such a use accords entirely with the essence and working character of LSD as a sacred drug."[24]

It was John (later Sir John) Gaddum, who played a major role in providing the key to the idea that many drugs might influence mental state by modifying the activity of brain neurotransmitters. Gaddum, who was at the time Professor of Pharmacology at Edinburgh, had discovered in 1953 that LSD blocked serotonin's effect on the uterus of experimental animals. After Betty Twarog, a young Harvard Ph.D., discovered that serotonin was present in the brain, Gaddum suggested that LSD might produce hallucinations by blocking brain serotonin.[25] Gaddum hypothesized in 1954 that sanity might require brain serotonin. It was the first clear statement that mental states might depend on the action of a neurotransmitter, and that psychotropic drugs, and by extrapolation also psychotherapeutic drugs like chlorpromazine, which had recently been discovered, might modify mental states by acting on brain neurotransmitters. This was a major step leading to the theories that would soon be proposed to explain the action of the newly discovered antipsychotic and antidepressant drugs.

Three Early Chemical Treatments of Mental Disorders

Before the introduction of chlorpromazine (Thorazine) and the early antidepressants in the 1950's, clinicians used various chemical substances to alleviate their patients' symptoms. However, none of these treatments led to a chemical theory of the origin of mental illness. For some time, sedating drugs such as opiates and barbiturates had been used for calming patients and relieving the staff of difficult management problems, but these drugs were considered only palliatives, not a cure of mental disorders. There were some theories that hyperexcitable nervous systems might cause mania and that nervous "exhaustion" might underlie depression, but these ideas could not be pursued, as there was no way of measuring these hypothesized abnormal nervous system states. Throughout much of the latter half of the nineteenth through the first half of the twentieth centuries, sedating drugs were commonly mixed in "cocktails," consisting of various combinations of scopolamine, atropine, chloral hydrate, bromides, barbiturates, and morphine. These cocktails were used mainly to quiet agitated and manic patients.

Sedating drugs were also used in prolonged sleep therapy that was believed to be an effective treatment for some psychotic conditions and also for drug addiction. The treatment is believed to have originated with a Scottish physician who was asked in 1897 to transport an acutely manic woman from Japan back to her family in Shanghai. Not having nurses available to help him with his uncontrollable charge, the physician put the woman into a deep sleep with bromides and had her transported to the ship in a hammock. During the five-hundred-mile trip the woman was kept in a bromide-induced sleep state most of the time. When the patient was awakened in Shanghai she was reported to be without "a trace of mental disturbance."[26] A number of similar anecdotal reports followed and in the early 1920s the Swiss psychiatrist Jacob Klaesi popularized sleep therapy. Klaesi used various combinations of different barbiturates to maintain patients in a prolonged sleep state—except for brief semiawakened periods for food and bowel movements—in the belief that this treatment could cure schizophrenia. The treatment was adopted throughout much of Europe—less so in the United States—with many claims of success with psychotic patients. Eliot Slater, a psychiatrist at the Maudsley Hospital in England, recalled that sleep therapy "was the one treatment we had in the early thirties which was of any avail with acute psychotic illness."[27]

There were two other chemical treatments of mental disorders that were widely used just before the beginning of the modern era of psychotherapeutic drugs. Metrazol and insulin treatment were introduced in the mid-1930s, and within a few years they both had been widely adopted in much of the world. Initially, metrazol was used to treat virtually every type of mental disorder, but after several years of experience it began to be used primarily to treat depression. Insulin, on the other hand, was used almost exclusively to treat schizophrenia. These chemical treatments of mental illness helped to pave the way for the acceptance of chlorpromazine in the early 1950s.

Metrazol (the chemical name is pentylenetetrazol and the trade name used in Europe was Cardiazol) is a synthetic drug that is chemically similar to camphor, the active ingredient in certain plants that had been used as "tonics" for many centuries in the Far East. It was known that at higher dose levels, metrazol produces violent convulsions. Joseph Ladislas von Meduna, a Hungarian psychiatrist and brain researcher, was pursuing the then commonly held idea that epilepsy and schizophrenia rarely coexisted in a single patient. This hypothesis originated in a number of anecdotal reports that seizures sometimes alleviated the mental symptoms of schizophrenia. Meduna reported that schizophrenics improved after camphor-induced convulsions, but later he agreed with others that it was actually most effective in treating depression.[28] Meduna had first used camphor, but later switched to metrazol (Cardiazol), and metrazol treatment was widely used throughout the late 1930s and the early 1940s despite the fact that the drug produced violent convulsions that frequently caused bone fractures.

Patients hated and feared metrazol shock treatment and they sometimes had to be chased around the ward as they tried to escape the injection. Electroconvulsive shock treatment was introduced in the late 1930s, and during the 1940s it completely replaced metrazol treatment because it was considered easier and safer to administer. During the 1950s, there was speculation that convulsive therapies were helpful because they broke up the perseverative neural activity hypothesized to be responsible for the persistence of the disturbing thoughts that caused depression. At the time, it was thought that memories might be stored in reverberating neural circuits and that these were disrupted by brain seizures. Today, the idea that memories depend on the persistent activity in certain neural loops is no longer considered feasible.

While metrazol is a synthetic drug, insulin is a natural hormone that is needed to get glucose out of the blood and into cells. A deficiency of insulin is the cause of one type of diabetes. Moderate levels of insulin are known to produce hunger, presumably because it drives most of the blood glucose into the cells of the body and consequently lowers the amount of glucose reaching so-called "glucose detectors" in the brain. When brain glucose levels are low, these glucose detectors send out signals that result in hunger and the motivation to eat. High doses of insulin, on the other hand, deprive brain cells of almost all glucose, disrupting their functioning to the point that convulsions and coma occur.

Working in a Viennese sanitarium in the 1930s, Manfred Sakel had been giving drug addicts low doses of insulin to stimulate their appetite. One day, he accidentally induced a convulsion by administering too much insulin.[29] After recovering, the patient's craving for drugs seemed to have been diminished, so Sakel started to purposely induce insulin convulsions as a treatment for drug addiction. One of the drug addicts happened also to be schizophrenic, and following an insulin-induced convulsion, Sakel thought that the patient's mental condition had improved. Pursuing this observation, Sakel developed a complex schedule of daily insulin injections that produced comas and convulsions, and he became convinced this was an effective treatment for schizophrenia. Sakel emigrated to the United States in the mid-1930s and the Sakel Insulin Treatment was adopted around much of the world. By 1940, over 50 percent of the psychiatric institutions in the United States were using insulin to treat schizophrenia. Despite the introduction of chlorpromazine and other drugs for treating schizophrenia in the 1950s, there were still more than one hundred "insulin wards" in mental hospitals in the United States. Eventually, insulin treatment was abandoned as psychiatrists became more willing to use chlorpromazine and other drugs and after several well-controlled studies demonstrated that the effectiveness of insulin treatment was actually much lower than commonly reported.[30]

The theories proposed to explain how insulin treatment worked illustrate the way many psychiatrists thought about mental disorders at the time. Sakel tried to present a physiological explanation of insulin treatment, but his theory was vague and impossible to test. He speculated, for example, that schizophrenia injured the phylogenetically younger (most recently evolved, like the neocortex) parts of the brain in such a way that the older, more primitive parts of the brain became dominant. Sakel suggested that his insulin treatment selectively "muffled" the older parts of the brain that he hypothesized were abnormally active in schizophrenia. In some unspecified way, Sakel suggested, a healthy balance between the phylogenetically older and younger parts of the brain could be restored by insulin treatment. Sakel's physiological theories about the origin of schizophrenia or how his treatment worked were never taken seriously and he sometimes admitted that he really did not know how insulin worked.

In general, psychoanalytic concepts were employed in most attempts to explain how insulin treatment worked. The speculation of the prominent psychiatrist Smith Ely Jelliffe is representative of the ideas of many psychiatrists about insulin treatment and schizophrenia.[31] Jelliffe attempted to blend some extremely crude and vague ideas about developmental neurology with his own variety of psychoanalysis. Thus Jelliffe proposed that insulin coma:

> brings the subject practically into an intra-uterine bath of primary narcissistic omnipotence . . . one sees complete release from the more superficial layers of the tyranny of the superego. The world becomes a loving, not a threatening, world and early erogenous zones are permitted a certain freedom of functioning . . . [this] form of psychotherapy can be, it seems to me, of great value in synthesizing a fragmented ego.[32]

Jelliffe proposed that a more lasting cure might result if at the end of the treatment a slower-acting and more lasting form of insulin, such as protamine insulin, was used to keep the patient in just the right balance "at the edge of the death threat." Such "theories," which reflect the intellectual climate at the time, were never formulated in a way that could be pursued scientifically.

While both metrazol and insulin were chemical treatments of mental illness, neither of these treatments resulted in any chemical theory of mental illness. The effects of metrazol and insulin on the brain were much too crude, causing violent convulsions and unconsciousness. These massive effects on the brain did not readily lend themselves to physiological theories. It was like banging a watch on the table to get it going for a while. What was needed for a chemical theory of mental illness to emerge were drugs that acted on specific chemical processes in the brain. This did not happen all at once, but the foundation was laid in the 1950s. This early history does reveal, however, that with no effective treatments available, psychiatrists were willing to try almost any physical treatment that might help their patients.

Physical treatments also helped psychiatrists gain respectability within the field of medicine and enabled them to compete more successfully with neurologists, who often treated patients with so-called "nervous disorders." Psychiatrists were held in particularly low esteem by most other physicians, who quite generally regarded their theories as strangely metaphysical and unrelated to "scientific medicine." There were few separate psychiatry departments in medical schools. Neurologists commonly treated patients suffering from what today would clearly be called a psychiatric disorder. Such somatic treatments as metrazol, insulin, and electroshock made psychiatry seem more like the rest of medicine. Perhaps only partly tongue in cheek, Louis Casamajor, a New York psychiatrist, commented that insulin and shock treatments succeeded in "shaking neurology from the saddle," adding: "One may question whether shock treatments do any good to the patients but there can be no doubt that they have done an enormous amount of good to psychiatry."[33] One psychiatrist, reflecting on the indoctrination he received around 1980 in medical school and during a psychiatric residency, wrote:

> I was taught that psychiatry has become much more modern and scientific since the introduction of the neuroleptics [antipsychotic drugs] in the 1950's, and the enthusiasm of psychiatrists for biological explanations of mental illness was presented as being based on a solid scientific foundation . . . I also saw how badly biological psychiatrists want to be regarded as doctors and accepted by the rest of the medical profession.[34]

The Beginning of the Modern Era

The psychotherapeutic drugs are grouped according to the conditions they are thought to alleviate most effectively. Thus, there are *antipsychotics* (also referred to as antischizophrenics, neuroleptics, and major tranquilizers); *antidepressants; anxiolytics* (also called antianxiety drugs or minor tranquilizers); and *mood stabilizers* such as lithium and several other newer drugs, which are used primarily to decrease large mood swings between mania and depression.[35]

All of the initial discoveries of drugs in these four groups were typically stumbled on during the course of an investigation that had an entirely different purpose. There was really no other way it could happen with so little known about brain chemistry and virtually no agreement about what caused mental illness. This pattern is not unique to psychiatry, as many important discoveries in science have been made accidentally. In most instances, theories that emerge to explain accidental discoveries evolve and change as new information become available and accommodated. However, the theories that were first proposed to explain how drugs alleviate mental illness continue to be promoted as though they are true, despite all that has subsequently been learned. As will be described, these early theories are held on to not only because there are no other theories available that can replace them, but also because they are useful for advancing the interests of various groups.

Discovery of Drugs for Treating Schizophrenia

Chlorpromazine: The Drug That Ushered In the New Era

The discovery of chlorpromazine is generally considered to mark the beginning of psychopharmacology in the modern era, although this was not immediately apparent. At the time, psychiatrists believed that schizophrenia resulted from either a brain disorder or traumatic psychosocial experience. The possibility that a drug could repair a defective brain or undo the effects of life experiences seemed unrealistic and to some, absurd. For psychoanalysts, who believed that the root of mental illness was to be found in the repressed wishes, fears, and fantasies in the unconscious mind, the idea of a drug cure was both simplistic and threatening to their most basic tenets. Nor did drug treatment make much sense to those who believed that schizophrenia was a degenerative brain disease. Even in France, where chlorpromazine was first developed and tested on mental patients, psychiatrists were not optimistic about its prospects. French psychiatrists had seen too many "cures" that later proved worthless to take seriously the initial claims made for chlorpromazine.

There were at least three important factors that eventually overcame this reluctance of psychiatrists to try chlorpromazine. First, there were simply no effective alternative treatments for schizophrenia. Second, the drug was endorsed by several influential psychiatrists. Third, the pharmaceutical industry coordinated a massive promotional campaign, as will be described in Chapter 6. Initially, chlorpromazine was adopted primarily by hospital psychiatrists. Psychotherapists in private practice were generally opposed or, at best, unenthusiastic. Later, many psychotherapists were persuaded by reports that chlorpromazine was proving useful in making schizophrenics more accessible to psychotherapy and more willing "to discuss their deep-seated emotional problems spontaneously."[36]

Chlorpromazine belongs to a group of chemical compounds called phenothiazines, which were being investigated as potential synthetic dyes. During the middle of the nineteenth century, German chemists working in the coal-tar industry were collaborating with organic chemists in universities to develop synthetic organic compounds that could substitute for the natural dyes extracted from plants. The rapid growth of the textile industry had created an enormous need for good synthetic dyes. In 1856, William Perkin, an eighteen-year-old English chemist, had accidentally discovered that dyestuffs could be made from a phenothiazine-like compound that he had distilled from coal-tar, a byproduct of illuminating gas. A major advance occurred in 1883, when August Bernthsen, a research chemist in Heidelberg, synthesized phenothiazine. It was learned that phenothiazine's chemical structure was essentially the same as Lauth's violet and methylene blue, both valuable dye products.

Many of the major pharmaceutical companies actually got their start as chemical companies working on synthetic dyes, and for a number of years, drug research was supported by the sale of synthetic dyes. Geigy's first pharmaceutical operation in Great Britain was started in 1948. It was located in a house at the end of a row of mill workers' cottages in Rhodes, a mill town outside Lancaster. Before this time, Geigy in Britain had only made dyestuff for the mills, and its start in pharmaceuticals was quite modest, mostly packaging a few drugs received from the parent company in Switzerland.

In the course of doing research on phenothiazines and synthetic dyes, it was discovered that some of these compounds also had biological properties potentially useful in medicine.[37] The property of phenothiazines that proved most relevant to the discovery of chlorpromazine was their ability to antagonize the action of histamine, that is, to act as an antihistamine. Interest in the role of histamine can be traced back to the early 1900s, when Sir Henry Dale, working on an ergot fungus, had isolated a substance, identified as histamine, that played a critical role in allergic reactions and anaphylactic shock.[38] It became apparent that an antihistamine that could ameliorate the action of histamine could be a highly profitable pharmaceutical product.

In the 1940s, the Rhône-Poulenc Pharmaceutical Company in Paris was investigating the physiological effects and potential medical applications of various phenothiazine compounds. It was discovered that some of these compounds had antihistaminic activity. It was learned that the phenothiazines had a great many other interesting physiological effects including hypothermia (loss of temperature regulation), a decrease in muscle tone, a reduction of nauseousness, a potentiation of the sedation produced by barbiturates, and, in some instances, a mild euphoria. Initially these effects were considered unwarranted "side effects" in the search for a marketable antihistamine drug, but later some of them were pursued for their potential to treat various medical problems. The decrease in muscle tone, for example, led to clinical trials on Parkinson patients and to several reports that phenothiazines reduced tremors and facilitated spontaneous movements. A few French psychiatrists were even using antihistamines to calm agitated and manic patients as early as 1943.[39]

It was the French surgeon Henri Laborit who first convinced psychiatrists to try chlorpromazine. Laborit, in collaboration with the anesthesiologist P. Huguenard, was trying to reduce postsurgical shock, a neuroendocrine reaction to stress that could at times be fatal.[40] Laborit's goal was to develop a preanesthetic compound—he called it a "lytic cocktail"—that could reduce the life-threatening responses that occasionally are triggered by the shock of surgery. ("Lytic" refers to the capacity to loosen or to relax.) The antihistaminic action of some phenothiazines, plus their capacity to enhance barbiturate sedation, to relax temperature regulation, to induce a kind of catalepsy (a state of "waxy flexibility" in which patients could be shaped into any position, which they held for long periods), and to suppress nausea all seemed to be potentially useful properties for a lytic cocktail that could be administered before surgery.[41]

When Laborit began to think about the desirability of a lytic cocktail he was a surgeon in the French navy working in the Maritime Hospital in Bizerte, Tunisia. It was the period immediately following World War II. Soon after, Laborit relocated to the Val de Grâce Military Hospital in Paris. One compound, promethazine, seemed to have effects that were close to what Laborit was looking for, and he obtained permission from the Rhône-Poulenc Pharmaceutical Company to try it on some patients.[42] Laborit observed that when promethazine was added to the other ingredient in his lytic cocktail, surgical patients experienced a peculiar kind of analgesia, a reduction of pain that sometimes made it unnecessary to administer any morphine. Laborit described the "analgesia" induced by promethazine as a "euphoric quietude . . . patients are calm and somnolent, with a relaxed and detached expression."[43] At this point, Laborit asked an army psychiatrist to watch him operate on some of what he called his "tense, anxious Mediterranean-type patients."

After surgery, he agreed with me that the patients were remarkably calm and relaxed. But I guess he didn't think any more about his observations, as they might apply to psychiatric patients.[44]

It was well known by this time that antihistamines produce drowsiness, and a state of detachment or indifference had also been reported by several physicians who had prescribed these drugs to treat allergies. One physician described a taxi driver on antihistamines who received a ticket for going through a red light, which he admitted having seen, but did not "care enough to stop."[45]

At this point, Laborit asked the Rhône-Poulenc chemists if they had any analogues of promethazine with even greater central nervous system effects.[46] As it turned out, some of the company chemists had been studying the central nervous system effects of phenothiazines, and they had synthesized other compounds similar to promethazine.[47] The Rhône-Poulenc investigators suggested to Laborit that their experimental drug RP4560 (the compound later named chlorpromazine) might be just the compound he needed.[48]

In November 1951, Laborit tested chlorpromazine for toxicity on a young female psychiatrist at the Villejuif (Jewish City) Mental Hospital. The drug was administered intravenously, and when the psychiatrist got up to go to the bathroom, she fainted. The head of psychiatry at the Villejuif decided he did not want any more experimentation with chlorpromazine, but Laborit continued to explore the properties of the drug at the Val de Grâce hospital. Laborit's first report on chlorpromazine was published in 1952, but by that date the Rhône-Poulenc company had already observed a number of physiological properties of chlorpromazine, including some that were potentially relevant to psychiatry. Chlorpromazine had been explored as an adjunct to sleep therapy (see page 16) and was being tried together with electroconvulsive shock treatment.[49] There had also been claims before Laborit's first report that chlorpromazine provided relief from severe depression and anxiety. There was even one claim that it reduced the salience of hallucinations and delusional thoughts. When schizophrenics were given chlorpromazine and asked whether they still heard voices when treated with chlorpromazine, they usually said that they did, but the "voices" no longer seemed to command the same attention and patients were able to ignore them. According to one interpretation, chlorpromazine "suspended" rather than removed the hallucinations.[50] Most of the psychiatric effects of chlorpromazine that had been explored before Laborit's first publication on the subject were mentioned only in the internal reports of the Rhône-Poulenc company, but some were published as early as 1951.[51] Actually, chlorpromazine had so many different physiological effects that the Rhône-Poulenc company attempted to cover all possibilities by naming the drug Largactil—a drug of many actions.

Published in 1952, Laborit's first article on chlorpromazine was a brief account of this drug's usefulness in surgery. He reported that patients seemed to suffer less after surgery and that it was often unnecessary to administer any morphine for pain. Although the paper was written from an anesthetic perspective, a psychic effect, described as "detachment," was briefly mentioned.[52] In a following paper, published later that same year, Laborit described his surgical patients under the influence of chlorpromazine as calm, relaxed, detached, and uninterested in what went on around them. He suggested that the drug might prove useful in any field that could benefit from a dampened "autonomic" (visceral or emotional) reactivity, and he noted also that the relaxed mental state might have an application in psychiatry. In a public discussion, Laborit noted that a colleague had commented that chlorpromazine produced "a veritable medicinal lobotomy."[53] On another occasion he emphasized the drowsy, uninterested state induced by the drug.[54]

Laborit encouraged the psychiatrist J. Hamon, at the Val de Grâce Hospital in Paris, to try chlorpromazine on some patients. In February 1952, Hamon reported that an uncontrollable manic patient was made calm and was eventually discharged after chlorpromazine was administered together with barbiturates and an analgesic.[55] Hamon clearly recognized the potential psychiatric value of the drug, but his report was difficult to evaluate because chlorpromazine had been used in conjunction with other drugs and also following electroshock treatment, in some instances.

The French psychiatrists Jean Delay and Pierre Deniker at the Hôpital Ste-Anne in Paris are generally credited with introducing chlorpromazine into psychiatry. Although theirs were not the first reports, between May and July of 1952, Delay and Deniker published six papers describing the results of trials with chlorpromazine. These papers did not mention Laborit's observations.[56] What distinguished Delay and Deniker's reports was that chlorpromazine was used alone, and they had concluded that "although this product [chlorpromazine] is generally used as a potentiator of anesthetics, analgesics, and hypnotics, it seems to us more rational to use it by itself."[57]

While Delay and Deniker initially emphasized that chlorpromazine reduced the excitation and agitation of manic patients, as others had, they also noted that the drug alleviated the confusion and paranoia of psychotics.[58] They also mentioned that chlorpromazine retarded movement, and under its influence patients often remain motionless and silent, but they do respond to questions appropriately, indicating that they are capable of attention and reflection. Chlorpromazine was said to produce an attitude of indifference, separating patients from their environment "as if by an invisible wall." Delay and Deniker also confirmed the observations of others that chlorpromazine had little antihistaminic action and appeared to act "centrally," referring to the brain.

Chlorpromazine was called a "neuroleptic," a term Delay introduced to imply that the drug somehow took hold of the nervous system and depressed its activity. The central nervous system action of chlorpromazine was inferred from the fact that the drug produced motor effects resembling the movement disorders seen in Parkinson's disease, which were suspected of being caused by a brain abnormality. However, Delay and Deniker had no direct knowledge of where chlorpromazine acted in the brain.[59] These motor effects of chlorpromazine are called "extrapyramidal signs," by neurologists, in contrast to "pyramidal signs," which refer to gross impairment in the capacity to control movements of skeletal muscles. The name is derived from the pyramid-shaped cells in the "motor cortex" of the frontal lobes, which control the gross movement of muscles. The "extrapyramidal system" in the brain is responsible for the fine motor adjustments controlled by subcortical brain structures, particularly those in the basal ganglia. Impairment of the extrapyramidal system results in tremors and jerky, uncoordinated movements, and chlorpromazine seemed to produce similar effects.

By the end of 1952, Delay and Deniker began to mention the possibility that chlorpromazine might alleviate psychotic thinking and confusion, and they reported that the drug was helpful in some cases of schizophrenia and catatonia. Their emphasis, however, continued to be placed on chlorpromazine's capacity to reduce excessive emotional states and to improve mood. A tense paranoid patient, for example, was said to have a pleasant, docile mood after some days on chlorpromazine. Initially, however, none of these observations had much impact on psychiatrists, and Deniker later recalled that once when he was giving a report on chlorpromazine at a meeting, few psychiatrists attended, and the chairman asked him to hurry as time was short.[60]

In 1952, Rhône-Poulenc had started to make chlorpromazine (under the name Largactil) available for clinical trials, sending samples to over 115 investigators in nine different countries.[61] Because of its many physiological effects, chlorpromazine was being explored for different applications in medicine—as an anesthetic, to induce "hibernation" during surgery, as an antiemetic for seasickness, and as a treatment for burns, stress, infections, obesity, Parkinson's disease, and epilepsy, among other potential medical uses. By 1953, Delay and Deniker, along with others in Switzerland and in Great Britain, were reporting that chlorpromazine was transforming the atmosphere of locked wards, and it almost completely eliminated the need for any restraint. Gradually, because of the experience of Delay and Deniker and other European investigators in France, Switzerland, and Great Britain and the reports by Heinz Lehmann in Montreal and N. William Winkelman, Jr., in Philadelphia, the clinical trials of chlorpromazine became centered on psychiatric applications.[62]

The various clinical trials resulted in close to a consensus that chlor-promazine produced feelings of detachment, relaxation, and indifference, which made agitated patients and disruptive wards much less a problem for the staff. Most reports emphasized that chlorpromazine was especially effective with manic and overly excited patients. There were reports that chlor-promazine produced euphoria in some patients, but this was not observed consistently. Walter Freeman, one of the leading proponents of prefrontal lobotomy, and others as well, often referred to the effect of chlorpromazine as a "chemical lobotomy."[63] The two treatments were used somewhat inter-changeably in controlling difficult patients. In his history of the somatic treatments used to treat mental patients in California during the first half of the twentieth century, for example, Joel Braslow reported the following from the 1955 notes of a psychiatrist at the Stockton State Hospital:

> This is a 38-year old woman, hospitalized for ten years, who was seen today for consideration of a second possible lobotomy after a trial on Thorazine [chlorpromazine] . . . When seen at clinic today the patient was quite agitated, disturbed and had difficulty finding her landmarks. She established a very autistic and bizarre relationship with the examining group. Psychomotor activity was rather under pressure, sweeping and at time uncontrolled. . . . The patient was considered to be a suitable candidate for a trial on Thorazine. It may be necessary to use a parenteral [feeding tube] approach when her negativism precludes all medication. After an adequate trial on Thorazine a second lobotomy may be considered, since it is apparent from the record that results of the initial lobotomy performed in 1949 were not successful.[64]

In this instance, chlorpromazine treatment was considered adequate and the second lobotomy was not performed.

Following both prefrontal lobotomy and chlorpromazine treatment, psychotic thought processes were claimed to be diminished and hallucinations and delusions, while not eliminated, seemed to be less real and compelling, and patients complained about them less. There were also reports that obsessive thoughts lost their imperative character, and anxiety, depression, and melancholia were reduced. Later reports, however, tended to agree that chlorpromazine was not particularly affective in alleviating depression. So little was known about how chlorpromazine worked that psychiatrists who wanted to distinguish the effects of this drug from a lobotomy made a point of noting that unlike lobotomy, chlorpromazine did not produce mental confusion, hyperactivity, or the incontinence commonly observed immediately following a surgical lobotomy.

By the end of 1952, Rhône-Poulenc had made arrangements to start marketing chlorpromazine in a number of countries in Europe. Chlorpromazine was marketed in Great Britain through Rhône-Poulenc's subsidiary,

May & Baker, Ltd. In Italy, Largactil was marketed through Farmitalia and in Germany, the Bayer Pharmaceutical Company marketed it under the name Megaphen. Samples of the drug were also sent directly to psychiatric clinics in other countries, and in November 1953 more than fifty Swiss psychiatrists gathered in Basel to report their results with chlorpromazine. The Basel Symposium was the first conference devoted exclusively to a psychopharmacological drug, and the reports on chlorpromazine were generally positive.[65]

Although he was not actually the first in North America to report that chlorpromazine alleviated psychiatric symptoms, Heinz Lehmann, a psychiatrist working at the Verdun Hospital in Montreal, is generally given credit for introducing the drug on this side of the Atlantic.[66] Lehmann, who was born and educated in Germany, came to Canada as a refugee psychiatrist in 1937. He was able to get a position at a large psychiatric institute in Montreal (the Verdun Protestant Hospital, now the Douglas Hospital), where there were only a few physicians for over sixteen hundred psychiatric patients. Lehmann described the conditions as "pretty horrible." Being convinced that psychosis and the major depressive disorders had a biological cause, and because there were no effective treatments available, Lehmann later recalled that he was willing to try anything—very large doses of caffeine, sulfa injections, typhoid antitoxin to produce fevers similar to those produced by malaria treatment of "general paresis," (see p. 205, Chapter 7). Even turpentine was applied to the abdominal muscles to produce sterile abscesses that would increase leukocytes. If there was any theory at all underlying some of these "heroic treatments," it was very weak and strained. For example, in the case of the trials with turpentine, the hope was that this treatment would increase leukocytes, which might combat some infection that had caused the mental disorder. Although there were plenty of claims of "promising results," nothing really helped for very long.

In the spring of 1953, a Rhône-Poulenc detail man left a sample of chlorpromazine with Lehmann's secretary with the message "that this stuff is so good that the literature alone will convince him." Lehmann later commented that at the time "no one in their right mind in psychiatry was working on drugs. You used shock, or various psychotherapies."[67] Nevertheless, he became interested in the drug after reading the literature left for him, and he tried chlorpromazine on several volunteers from the hospital staff. Lehmann then invited a psychiatric resident to collaborate on a clinical trial on mental patients. They chose seventy-one patients, most of them selected following Delay and Deniker's report that the drug worked best on excited states. Lehmann's report described chlorpromazine as "a new drug which seems to possess specific properties for the psychiatric management of excited states," and he noted that the drug made manic patients amenable to reason, and they didn't even object to bed rest. However, Lehmann did not limit chlorpromazine's value to mania, as he commented that it appeared to be a drug "of unique value in the symptomatic control of almost any kind of severe excitement. This includes catatonic schizophrenia, schizoaffective conditions, epileptic clouded states, agitation occurring in lobotomized patients immediately or several months after surgery, and organic-toxic confusional states."[68]

Overall, the results were considered good, and in some instances exceptional. Some patients became drowsy, but this tended to subside as the treatment continued, and in a paper sent off for publication, Lehmann reported that despite the fact that some patients appeared heavily drugged and seemed indifferent to what was going on around them, their consciousness was not impaired and they remained accessible when approached. However, Lehmann described limitations to the effectiveness of chlorpromazine:

> The new drug should not be considered a cure-all in psychoneuroses. If moderate oral doses of 100 to 200 mg per day do not give satisfactory relief from tension, higher doses will usually be of no avail. If traumatic factors cannot be excluded from the environment and major conflicts persist, chlorpromazine can only be considered an adjuvant to psychotherapy.[69]

Still, Lehmann had given chlorpromazine a major endorsement, and even before his paper was published, the Rhône-Poulenc company circulated Lehmann's results, and he was flooded with requests for copies of the unpublished manuscript.

Lehmann's paper was entitled "Chlorpromazine, New Inhibiting Agent for Psychomotor Excitement and Manic States." Although the drug did produce significant improvement in manic and agitated patients, the few chronic schizophrenics included in the study did not improve. However, after the paper was published, Lehmann discovered that several chronic schizophrenic patients, who were accidentally left on chlorpromazine, did seem to improve. In retrospect, Lehmann later commented that no one at the time believed a drug could alleviate chronic schizophrenia, but he decided, nevertheless, to pursue this lead in a second study and found that 20 to 25 percent of chronic schizophrenics "could be salvaged" if chlorpromazine treatment were prolonged. Lehmann considered this to be nothing short of "miraculous." A third study with acute schizophrenics was then undertaken despite the fact that several colleagues questioned whether the patients "didn't first deserve a chance with insulin coma therapy." Lehmann concluded that chlorpromazine also had a dramatic effect on acute schizophrenia. He described chlorpromazine as just as effective as either insulin or electroshock treatments.[70] This conclusion is more than a little ironic, as a well-controlled study would soon indicate that the effectiveness of insulin treatment had been grossly overstated, and today, few people believe that electroconvulsive shock is an effective treatment of schizophrenia. While there had been several earlier reports that the confused thinking pattern and paranoid ideas had been alleviated by chlorpromazine, these reports were not particularly convincing, as they tended to be casual observations that were added to reports about the value of this drug for treating agitated and manic patients. Lehmann's reports of successful chlorpromazine treatment of schizophrenia played a major role in extending the drug's usefulness to a condition thought by many to be a progressive and virtually hopeless disease.

There were adverse side effects of chlorpromazine treatment. Patients were made drowsy, especially during the early period of drug treatment, and they also developed a pallor, because blood pressure was reduced, sometimes markedly. When a patient failed to respond, Lehmann increased the dose level several times above what was recommended in the literature. Some patients became jaundiced, and Lehmann later recalled that he had been frightened when a neurologist noticed that Parkinson's symptoms began to appear. Ironically, chlorpromazine had been tried as a treatment for Parkinson's disease, widely called "paralysis agitans" at the time. There were earlier reports that chlorpromazine produced Parkinsonlike motor effects. Delay and Deniker were convinced that there was a "parallelism" between the motor and psychic effects of chlorpromazine. While they did not believe that there was a causal relationship between the motor and psychic effects, Delay and Deniker thought the two effects were inseparable, and they routinely increased the dose level of chlorpromazine to get the motor effects, believing that this reflected the dose level required to achieve the desired psychic effects. Deniker continued to believe this and as late as 1983 he wrote that "it remains true that in each of the chemical groups, the compounds with neuroleptic characteristics [defined as those that produce motor effects] are antipsychotic and the others are not."[71]

Although Delay and Deniker did not seem particularly concerned about the adverse motor effects produced by chlorpromazine, others were. In 1954 the Swiss psychiatrist H. Steck reported that continued treatment with chlorpromazine (and also the drug reserpine) produced Parkinsonism and other extrapyramidal movement disorders. This report and the confirmation by others contributed to a growing concern over the sometimes permanently disfiguring side effects of the antipsychotic drugs.[72] The motor impairment, called "tardive dyskinesia" (from the same root as "tardy," because the symptoms are slow in developing and usually seen only after prolonged treatment with antipsychotic drugs), can involve grotesque mouth movements and ticlike tongue protrusions. Tardive dyskinesia is now considered distinguishable from Parkinson's disease, but some of the same neural circuits in the basal ganglia are thought to be involved.

Early in the 1950s, the Rhône-Poulenc company had been searching for a pharmaceutical company willing to market chlorpromazine in the United States. Several companies had been contacted, but none of them were interested in gambling on a drug that did not have a clear marketing direction. However, Smith Kline & French, which was at the time a small drug company that mainly sold "over the counter" medicines, was beginning to expand into the "ethical" (prescription) drug market. When Francis Boyer, the new president of Smith Kline & French, obtained the U.S. rights for chlorpromazine in 1952, it was not clear how the drug would be marketed. Initially, Boyer believed he had purchased an antiemetic possibly useful for preventing nauseousness. There was apparently some awareness that the drug might be useful in psychiatry, but a Smith Kline & French memorandum dated February 13, 1953, noted that studies of chlorpromazine applications to psychiatry "are still limited at this time," and a memo written a month later mentioned exploring four areas (nausea and vomiting, itching and skin diseases, general sedation, and psychiatric states). The memo recommended "widespread distribution to encourage investigation in all fields."[73]

By fall 1953, Smith Kline & French apparently had narrowed down the list of possibilities of marketing chlorpromazine, as they sponsored Henri Laborit and Pierre Deniker's visits to a number of surgical and psychiatric centers in the United States. An internal company memorandum dated July 1953 mentions that "we had sent our clinicians to Europe and so had decided to bring Laborit and Deniker here. We hoped that they would convince the American 'high priests' in surgery and psychiatry to evaluate chlorpromazine."[74] Laborit's demonstrations at surgical centers were generally unsuccessful, as the experimental dogs' hearts often began to fibrillate and several dogs became anoxic and died. Besides, it became clear that American anesthetists and surgeons had little interest in artificial hibernation, and, in general, they were not enthusiastic about any of the properties of Laborit's "lytic cocktail" or the way he conceptualized shock. Smith Kline & French's interest in marketing chlorpromazine to surgeons or anesthetists cooled rapidly.

At the same time, Deniker was visiting a large number of prestigious psychiatric centers on the East Coast of the United States and also in Cleveland, Chicago, and Montreal. Deniker's presentations convinced many psychiatrists to try chlorpromazine, and Smith Kline & French began to concentrate their efforts toward marketing chlorpromazine as a psychiatric drug. According to an internal memorandum dated November 1953, the company had already sent supplies of the drug to more than six hundred physicians and to about twenty "top rate mental institutions." By May 1954, the company was marketing the drug for use in psychiatry under the label Thorazine. By today's standards, it would be impossible in such a short time to move from acquiring a drug, through testing it in the laboratory and then in clinical settings, getting FDA approval to market it, working out production problems, and to the stage of marketing and promotion.

There was limited psychiatric experience with Thorazine in the United States when Smith Kline & French started to market the drug. There had been some clinical trials in state mental institutions and in Veterans' Hospitals, but they tended to be small-scale trials, some with only nine or ten patients. Henry Brill of the New York Psychiatric Institute tried chlorpromazine on patients after receiving one of the advance copies of Heinz Lehmann's unpublished manuscript from Rhône-Poulenc. Brill agreed that patients and wards became quieter and more manageable after chlorpromazine and that delusions and hallucinations were less disturbing to the patients. A Smith Kline & French report (dated July 10, 1953) on the status of clinical investigations noted: "In psychiatry, a study is underway by Dr. N.W. Winkelman, Jr., at the Sidney Hillman Center in Philadelphia; plans for major studies at Western Reserve by Dr. Bond and at Tulane by Dr. Heath are being drawn up; and Dr. Overholser expects to start his study at Saint Elizabeth's Hospital by September 1, 1953." An internal Smith Kline & French memo dated November 5, 1953, stated: "Thorazine already supplied to over six-hundred physicians, which is the largest group ever to receive an investigational use drug from SK&F. Expect distribution in the near future to reach monthly rates of 3,000 ampules and 10,000 tablets."[75]

In May 1954, the same month that the marketing of Thorazine began, the results of Winkelman's clinical trials were published. This was the first publication of a chlorpromazine study performed in the United States. Winkelman had received Thorazine from Smith Kline & French, and shortly after beginning the clinical trials he had written to the company that the effects were remarkable, particularly with anxious and agitated patients. Winkelman commented in the introduction to the published paper that he had regarded the report of Simone Courvoisier (a Rhône-Poulenc physiologist) that chlorpromazine abolished conditioned reflex responses as "provocative from a psychiatric standpoint."[76] Actually, Courvoisier had given few details of her experiment, and her conclusion that chlorpromazine interfered with the ability of rats to make a conditioned avoidance "rope climbing" response was difficult to interpret.[77]

Winkelman's clinical trial was unusually prolonged, as he administered Thorazine continuously for periods up to eight months. The subjects were a heterogeneous group of 142 patients, including 65 psychoneurotics, 15 schizophrenics, 5 with psychophysiological disorders, 27 agitated senile patients, 10 agitated manic patients, 6 epileptics, and a group of neurological patients used to determine appropriate dose levels. Assessment of improvement was based on Winkelman's subjective evaluation plus input from patients and their families and friends. He concluded:

> Although it [Thorazine] should never be given as a substitute for analytically oriented psychotherapy, it must be considered a true therapeutic agent with definite indications. The drug is especially remarkable in that it can reduce severe anxiety, diminish phobias and obsessions, reverse or modify a paranoid psychosis, quiet manic or extremely agitated patients, and change the hostile, agitated, senile patient into a quiet, easily managed patient.[78]

Although Winkelman had extended the required homage to "analytically oriented psychotherapy," he had essentially concluded that Thorazine was useful in treating just about any type of mental disorder a psychiatrist might confront, with the exception of depression. Considering the dominance of psychoanalytic theory at the time, Smith Kline & French could not have asked for a stronger endorsement. The decision to market Thorazine as a psychiatric drug was strongly influenced by the Winkelman trial in Philadelphia as well as by the reports by Heinz Lehmann in Montreal and by the psychiatrist John Vernon Kinross-Wright at the Baylor University College of Medicine in Houston.[79] Smith Kline & French made a careful appraisal of who would be most favorably disposed to drug treatment and who would be opposed and then planned a three-stage unprecedented marketing campaign that eventually overcame almost all opposition. All of this brought a return that exceeded even the most optimistic predictions of Smith Kline & French's marketing people. Within a year from the start of marketing, over 2 million prescriptions had been written for Thorazine.

Initially, even those psychiatrists who were reporting that chlorpromazine was producing a remarkable transformation in hospital psychiatry usually qualified these remarks by stating that the drug should not be considered a general cure capable of wiping out mental illness and replacing all other treatments. Most psychoanalysts were critical of chlorpromazine and commonly made remarks like Jules Masserman's comment that the drug was nothing more than a "glorified sedative." In spring 1955, however, *Time* magazine took psychoanalysts to task for their criticism of the institutional psychiatrists who used chlorpromazine:

> The ivory-tower critics argue that the red-brick pragmatists are not getting at the patient's "underlying psychopathology" and so there can be no cure. These doctors want to know whether he [the patient] withdrew from the world because of unconscious conflict over incestuous urges or stealing from his brother's piggy bank at the age of five. In the world of red bricks, this is like arguing about the number of angels on the point of a pin.[80]

Interest in chlorpromazine was growing by leaps and bounds. In October 1955, The First International Colloquium on Chlorpromazine and Neuroleptic Drugs was held in Paris. In 1957 Henri Laborit, Pierre Deniker, and Heinz Lehmann were awarded the American Public Health Association's prestigious Albert Lasker Prize for their introduction of chlorpromazine to psychiatry and the "demonstration that a medication can influence the clinical course of the major psychoses." By 1965 chlorpromazine had been the subject of about ten thousand publications worldwide. By 1970, Smith Kline & French's Thorazine sales totaled over $116 million, a significant proportion of the company's total sales.

Despite the phenomenal growth of Thorazine's sales in the United States, there was a need for a well-controlled study of chlorpromazine and the other phenothiazines.[81] Few of the earlier studies used double-blind procedures, placebo controls, or randomly assigned patients who had not been exposed to other treatments. After several years of discussion, controversy, planning, and testimony before several different congressional committees, money was allocated to the National Institute of Mental Health (NIMH) for a six-week study that would incorporate all the appropriate controls. The study began in April 1961 and was designed to compare chlorpromazine and two other phenothiazines with a placebo treatment in nine hospitals.[82]

The NIMH study ended with a strong endorsement of phenothiazine treatment, confirming the results of the earlier uncontrolled studies. It was concluded that 75 percent of the patients were either "much improved" or "very much improved" and 50 percent were judged to be no longer even "mildly ill." In total, 95 percent of the patients on phenothiazines were reported to have shown some improvement. Moreover, no patient was said to have become worse after drug treatment. There did not appear to be anything unique about chlorpromazine, as the other phenothiazines tested were equally effective. This was encouraging to drug companies that hoped to get a share of the now huge and still growing market for chlorpromazine. The report, however, may have been too uncritical in its enthusiasm for the phenothiazines. For example, the fact that no "serious" aversive side effects were found is clearly surprising, considering that contemporary reports from others indicated that up to 61 percent of the patients on phenothiazines suffered from extrapyramidal side effects (parkinsonism, dyskinesia, and motor restlessness).[83] Furthermore, almost 50 percent of the patients given placebos showed some improvement, even though their improvement was said to generally have fallen short of the qualitative improvement of patients receiving drug treatment.

The conclusion of the NIMH study that phenothiazines alleviated a wide range of symptoms of acute schizophrenic psychoses contributed to the growing speculation that these drugs might be specific "antischizophrenic agents," not just tranquilizers. Thus, in a little more than a decade, chlorpromazine went from an "autonomic stabilizer useful in surgery," to a "new type of sedative" or tranquilizer for treating psychomotor agitation and anxieties, to being considered a specific "antischizophrenic agent."[84] Although chlorpromazine continued to be used for agitated and manic patients, it increasingly was perceived as a drug for the treatment of schizophrenia. It was also reported that phenothiazine treatment could be used safely and effectively in many settings besides psychiatric hospitals, including psychiatric services in general hospitals, and for nonhospitalized ambulatory patients. The 1964 publication of the results of the study sponsored by NIMH had a major influence in overcoming much of the resistance to drug treatment among psychiatrists, although some expressed their reservations about the effectiveness of the phenothiazines.[85]

The phenothiazines were widely adopted, as the huge sales figures indicate, but how these drugs worked remained a mystery. The discovery of chlorpromazine had been accidental, and its use in psychiatry was based solely on the evidence that it was effective, although the opinion of what it was most effective for kept changing. In his foreword to the publication of the proceedings of a 1958 conference of "experts on pharmacotherapy in mental illness," Dr. Robert Felix, Director of the NIMH, wrote that "in my opinion, the conference served—if the editors and participants will forgive me—as an 'exchange of ignorance.' I think everyone would agree that we really know pitifully little about the effects of drugs on behavior and maybe even less about their use in mental illness."[86]

Delay and Deniker did not offer an explanation of how chlorpromazine alleviated mental illness, other than to assume that extrapyramidal brain structures were somehow involved. Even this conclusion was only an inference made from the fact that the drug produced motor effects resembling those seen when the extrapyramidal structures are damaged. The early "theories" about how chlorpromazine alleviated mental illness were just speculation, often hidden behind a thin veil of pseudoneurology. Laborit, for example, speculated that chlorpromazine produced a "relaxed indifference" by reducing the impact of stimuli through its ability to reduce neural transmission from the thalamus to the cerebral cortex.[87] There was absolutely no evidence for this speculation.

Winkelman initially believed that chlorpromazine acted on the frontal lobes of the brain because the "drug produced an effect similar to frontal lobotomy." Later, Winkelman changed his mind, and in a 1957 paper he speculated that chlorpromazine produced an "indifference" because it inhibited the reticular formation. The reticular formation is a phylogenetically old neural system, which courses through the center or core of the brain and is believed to play an alerting or arousal role. Its name is derived from its netlike appearance, as the Latin reticulum is the diminutive for net. Winkelman's speculation that chlorpromazine acted on the reticular formation seems to simply reflect the great interest in this part of the brain at the time. Different investigators claimed that the reticular formation played a critical role in motivation, memory, learning, attention, and so much more that it led the neurologist Sir Geoffrey Jefferson to remark that it was like a giant international cartel that was taking over everything in sight.[88] Today the reticular formation is rarely mentioned in the neuroscience literature.

The pioneers in this field cannot be faulted for being unable to explain the action of chlorpromazine, as there was no scientific basis for any credible theory. Even in 1966, the best statement on the action of psychotherapeutic drugs that could be made by two well-informed psychiatrists was:

> There was hope that the newer compounds might eventually lead to an understanding of the pathophysiology of some behavior disorders since the drugs either resemble or influence the metabolism of endogenous substances, which in unexplained ways influence mood and behavior. The few but sometimes surprising biochemical links with neurobehavioral mechanisms that have already been established emphasize our ignorance of what may lie ahead in research.[89]

Haldol: A New Class of Antischizophrenic Drugs

Despite the ignorance about how the chlorpromazine worked, the enormous financial rewards of the marketing of this drug led other pharmaceutical companies to try to modify its chemical structure in order to develop and patent similar drugs. Among the other more successfully marketed phenothiazine drugs were thoridazine (Mellaril) and thifluoperazine (Stelazine). In the meantime, another class of antischizophrenic (antipsychotic) drugs was accidentally discovered by Paul Janssen and his young colleagues.[90] During the latter part of the 1950s, Paul Janssen was working in Belgium at a small pharmaceutical company started by his father. The company did no research and held no patents of its own, but it was modestly successful in manufacturing and marketing some generic drugs. There was little hope the firm would be able to expand unless it developed its own drugs. Janssen had spent much of his time during his compulsory military service studying medicinal chemistry and pharmacology, and he developed considerable skill in modifying the chemical structure of existing drugs. After completing his military service, Janssen planned to modify drugs sufficiently so they could be patented and marketed as the company's own product. They had some initial success with a few drugs and were able to move to larger quarters in Beerse, where the discovery that established the company as one of the leaders in marketing antipsychotic drugs was made.

In Beerse, Janssen and his colleagues stumbled on a promising drug that had opiate-like analgesic properties, but it was also observed that this drug produced sedation, calmness, and muscular rigidity similar to that produced by the existing antipsychotic drugs. With further chemical modification designed to increase the antipsychotic properties of this new compound, they inadvertently produced a butyrophenone, a completely new class of drugs. At the time, new drugs thought to have some potential for treating schizophrenia were routinely tested for their ability to inhibit the reaction to the psychomotor stimulant amphetamine. It was known that people who took large amounts of amphetamine would often hallucinate and have delusions and other symptoms that were commonly mistaken for acute schizophrenic episodes. An animal model based on amphetamine's capacity to evoke hyperactivity and stereotyped behavior was used to test potential antipsychotic drugs.[91] In 1957, haloperidol (Haldol), the name given to the first butyrophenone marketed, was found to be many times more effective than chlorpromazine in blocking amphetamine-induced stereotyped behavior in animals.

Confirmation of haloperidol's potency and evidence of its clinical efficacy were obtained in clinical trials at the Psychiatric Clinic of Liège University. There was great interest in haloperidol, and soon after the completion of the clinical trials, the drug was being widely used in Europe and a little later in the United States. Janssen has estimated that in the decade after its discovery over a thousand articles on haloperidol were published. Haloperidol, like the other available antipsychotics, often produced the motor impairment known as tardive dyskinesia, and at the time Paul Janssen agreed with Delay and Deniker that the effectiveness of antipsychotic drugs was somehow tied to the tendency to produce tardive dyskinesia. Even though tardive dyskinesia can be a permanently disfiguring condition, it was generally not considered too high a price to pay to alleviate a crippling mental disorder.

There are, today, newer antipsychotic drugs that target other neurotransmitters, but that part of the story is best left for the following two chapters, which discuss the biochemical theories of schizophrenia and the mechanisms proposed to explain how antipsychotic drugs work.

Discovery of Drugs for Treating Depression
The Monoamine Oxydase Inhibitors

It was only a few years after chlorpromazine was first tested on psychiatric patients that the drug iproniazid (the proprietary name in the United States is Marsilid) was reported to be an effective antidepressant. The events leading up to the discovery of iproniazid were just as fortuitous as those that led to the discovery of chlorpromazine. During World War II, the Germans had developed the V-2 rocket, which had been used to bomb English cities. One of the fuels used for the V-2 rocket was hydrazine. When the war ended, drug companies acquired much of the large stock of hydrazine at a negligible cost. Although hydrazine is explosive and toxic, when it is combined with other chemicals and otherwise modified, new compounds were formed, and some of these were found to have properties that seemed as if they might be useful in medicine. As tuberculosis was still a major medical problem, many of these new compounds were routinely tested for effectiveness in combating the tubercle bacillus. In 1951, researchers working for the Hoffman–La Roche company in Nutley, New Jersey, found that two hydrazine compounds, isoniazid and iproniazid, were effective inhibitors of the tubercle bacillus, and after some clinical trials, both drugs were marketed for treating tuberculosis.[92]

By Easter 1952, newspapers described TB patients dancing with joy in hospital corridors after treatment with iproniazid and isoniazid. Initially, the euphoria was considered an annoying side effect, but it was soon realized that this property might make these drugs useful in treating depression. Several groups, including one headed by Jean Delay, the same French psychiatrist who had reported chlorpromazine's effectiveness as a psychiatric drug, began testing iproniazid and isoniazid on psychiatric patients. These initial tests were abandoned after a short, unsuccessful trial. It is now known that these drugs usually take several weeks before they begin to have an antidepressant effect.

Several years elapsed before clinical trials produced clear evidence that iproniazid alleviated depression. Everyone who tested the drug agreed that it had psychological effects, but the effects reported were quite variable. The results of a study published in 1954, for example, indicated that in a series of forty-five patients given iproniazid, five developed manic psychosis, there were two instances of paranoid states, and there were three cases of marked euphoria.[93] Not everyone agreed that iproniazid was an effective treatment for depression. Even by 1959 there had been only two controlled studies of the effectiveness of iproniazid as an antidepressant, and both found that the drug was no better than a placebo.[94] Although they did not conduct a "controlled" clinical trial with a placebo comparison group, Nathan S. Kline and his collaborators J. C. Saunders and H. P. Loomer tried iproniazid in 1956 on a heterogeneous group of patients at the Rockland State Hospital in New York. Unlike earlier clinical trials, in this one the patients were maintained on iproniazid for at least five weeks, and toward the end of this period a number of patients, particularly the depressed patients, seemed to have improved. Kline called iproniazid a "psychic energizer" useful for treating depression, and in another report he claimed that some of the depressed patients in his private practice had "a complete remission of all symptoms." Kline later remarked that "it was the first drug cure in all of psychiatric history to act in such a manner."[95]

Kline, who died in 1983, was the research director at Rockland State Hospital, and he held many prestigious positions in psychiatry.[96] Kline was a gregarious man with many influential contacts, and he took steps to assure that his results received a great amount of attention. A summary of Kline's results with iproniazid was even inserted into the 1957 *Congressional Record*.[97] Kline later wrote that in only one year after the publication of his first report, Marsilid (iproniazid) had been used on four hundred thousand patients.[98]

Nathan Kline later won the prestigious Albert Lasker award for discovering the antidepressant action of iproniazid, but there is an unsavory side to this story. J. C. Saunders, one of Kline's collaborators, claimed that the original idea was his and that he had actually initiated the studies with iproniazid.[99] Saunders sued and he was initially joined by H. P. Loomer (another collaborator on the original study) for a share of the Lasker prize. After a protracted legal battle, Saunders was eventually awarded one-third of the prize money.

Iproniazid was effective in alleviating depression in a number of instances, but there are some serious side effects of this drug and all monoamine oxydase inhibitors (MAO-I) The enzyme monoamine oxydase normally helps metabolize the amino acid tyramine, and when MAO inhibitors decrease the availability of this enzyme a dangerous level of tyramine can accumulate in the body. As high levels of tyramine are present in many common foods such as aged cheeses, wine, pickled foods, and other gastronomic delights, patients who eat such foods may develop dangerous levels of tyramine and experience throbbing headaches, jaundice, a precipitous rise in blood pressure, and, possibly, lethal hemorrhaging. Patients on MAO inhibitors must restrict their intake of foods rich in tyramine. Because of these potentially dangerous side effects, several of the MAO inhibitors (including iproniazid) were temporarily withdrawn by the FDA. Since 1964, iproniazid can only be used under close medical monitoring. Nardil and Marplan are two of the MAO inhibitors currently being marketed. Although not the most frequently used antidepressants, MAO inhibitors are still believed by some to help certain classes of patients who do not respond to the more commonly used tricyclic antidepressants.

The Tricyclic Antidepressants

At approximately the same period when iproniazid's effectiveness was being demonstrated another class of antidepressants was discovered. This new class of antidepressant drugs are called tricyclic antidepressants (TADs) because of their three-ring chemical structure. The discovery of the tricyclic antidepressants was also made by accident, this time while researchers were attempting to improve sleep therapy. It was mentioned earlier that bromides and barbiturates had been used to induce a prolonged "sleep therapy" that was believed to be an effective treatment for some psychotic states. Although not practiced today, sleep therapy was still in use in the 1960s at a number of European institutions. When, for example, the author visited psychiatric institutions in the Soviet Union and East Germany (GDR) in 1961, so-called electro-sleep (unconsciousness induced by passing an electric current through the brain) was commonly used to treat mental patients.

In the 1950s, Roland Kuhn, a Swiss psychiatrist, was trying different drugs in an attempt to improve sleep therapy. Among the drugs being tried were some that were similar to the phenothiazines, because, it will be recalled, these drugs tend to make people drowsy. One such drug made by Geigy, a Swiss pharmaceutical company, was imipramine, which has a chemical structure closely related to that of the phenothiazines. Much to his surprise, Kuhn observed that the drug did not induce sleep, but quite the opposite. Imipramine seemed to energize patients and to elevate their mood. Following this observation, Kuhn treated more than five hundred psychiatric patients with imipramine over a three-year period. When he reported the results late in 1957 at the International Congress of Psychiatry in Zurich his presentation received a mixed reception: "Our paper was received with some interest, but with a great deal of skepticism. This was not surprising in view of the almost completely negative history of drug treatment of depression up to that time."[100]

Kuhn reported that imipramine dramatically alleviated the symptoms of patients with deep depression, but it tended to exacerbate the symptoms of patients with agitated depression, mania, and schizophrenia. In a speech later given at the Galesburg State Hospital in Illinois, Kuhn concluded that imipramine was not simply a stimulant or "euphoriant," because stimulants such as amphetamine do not relieve depression. Kuhn's description of the effects of imipramine on depression was enormously compelling:

> The patients get up in the morning of their own accord, they speak louder and more rapidly, their facial expression becomes more vivacious. They commence some activity on their own, again seeking contact with other people, they begin to entertain themselves, take part in games, become more cheerful and are once again able to laugh. . . . The patients express themselves as feeling much better, fatigue disappears, the feeling of heaviness in the limbs vanishes, and the sense of oppression in the chest gives way to a feeling of relief. The general inhibition, which led

to retardation, subsides. They declare that they are now able to follow other persons' train of thought, and that once more new thoughts occur to them, whereas previously they were continually tortured by the same fixed idea. . . . Instead of being concerned about imagined or real guilt in their past, they become occupied with plans concerning their own future. Actual delusions of guilt, or loss, or hypochondriacal delusions become less evident. The patients declare "I don't think of it anymore" or "the thought doesn't enter my head now." Suicidal tendencies also diminish, become more controllable or disappear altogether. . . . Fits of crying and moaning cease . . . the sleep is felt to be normal and refreshing, not fatiguing and forced. . . . Not infrequently the cure is complete, sufferers and their relatives confirming the fact that they had not been so well for a long time.[101]

Kuhn noted that this improvement can occur suddenly after two to three days of treatment, but it usually takes from one to four weeks and then it may occur either gradually or suddenly. Although Kuhn stated that the patient can seem completely cured, he made clear that the action of imipramine:

is always purely symptomatic. As soon as the medicant is discontinued the illness breaks out again, usually with undiminished severity after a few days, and it can be cured again by repeating the medicant. It is thus possible experimentally in suitable cases to provoke or to cure the illness.[102]

The Geigy Company started marketing imipramine (Tofranil) in 1958, approximately a year after the first antidepressant, iproniazid, had been introduced. Other tricyclic antidepressants, such as Elavil and Anafranil, were introduced by other pharmaceutical companies, and they also have had huge sales. By 1980, approximately 10 million prescriptions for antidepressant drugs were being written annually. Most of the prescriptions were for the tricyclic antidepressants because they are usually (but not always) more effective and have less serious side effects than the MAO inhibitors. However, imipramine and the other tricyclics also have some adverse side effects, and a number of depressed patients do not improve when treated with these drugs. As the tricyclics inhibit the reuptake of norepinephrine, dopamine, and serotonin, although not all these drugs affect all three neurotransmitters equally, it is hoped that some of the adverse side effects might be eliminated by drugs that are more selective in their action. For reasons that will be discussed in the following two chapters, interest began to be focused on drugs that were more selective in potentiating the action of serotonin, and new drugs with these properties have been adopted with great enthusiasm.

Discovery of Lithium Treatment for Mania and Other Mood Disorders

The discovery of lithium as a treatment for mania and other mood disorders was also fortuitous. In this instance, there was at least a continuing investigation of the cause of mental disorders, but the use of lithium was completely accidental. Lithium, as will be explained, was used only because it was a conveniently available solvent, not because it was suspected of having any therapeutic value. Nevertheless, lithium does have an interesting history, and for a number of years before it was discovered to alleviate manic-depressive illness, it was thought to have various other medical applications.

Lithium is a metallic element that was first extracted from stone in 1817 by the Swedish chemist Johan August Arvedson. Its name is derived from "lithos," the Greek word for stone. It is commonly found in the sea along with other minerals, and in natural springs, but it is also present in animal and plant tissue. Because lithium is both light and strong it has many industrial applications in metallurgy, ceramics, and batteries, and as a coolant and a dehumidifying agent.

Lithium had in the past also been used to treat many different medical problems, mostly with questionable results. Lithium bromide, for example, had been used experimentally to treat epilepsy because it was thought to depress neural excitability, and lithium salt was used extensively to dissolve kidney stones, urate deposits in cartilage, and as a treatment for gout. In time, more and more ailments were thought to benefit from lithium, and large numbers of lithium tablets, as well as an enormous quantity of bottled water from so-called lithium springs, were consumed. The water, which was advertised as a treatment for gout, rheumatism, kidney and bladder stones, dropsy, diabetes, eczema, and neuralgia, among other conditions, was sold in the United States under many names, including Farmville Lithia Water, Buffalo Lithia Water, Tuckahoe Lithia Water, and Londonberry Lithia Water. Many of the European spring waters currently on the market, such as Vichy, Apollinaris, and Perrier, had earlier been advertised for their high lithium content. Therapeutic levels of lithium were advertised to be in the waters of many popular spas, such as the one in Lithia Springs, Georgia. By 1910, however, there was evidence that most of these "waters" contained so little lithium that it was ruled by the Supreme Court of the District of Columbia that:

> For a person to obtain a therapeutic dose of lithium by drinking Buffalo Lithia Water he would have to drink from one hundred and fifty thousand to two hundred and twenty-five thousand gallons of water per day. ...Potomac River water contains five times as much lithium per gallon as the water in controversy.[103]

There was also some early speculation that lithium was an effective treatment for mania and other psychiatric disorders. Although not too much weight should be given to some of these stories, it is interesting, nevertheless, that Caelius Aurelianus, a fifth-century African physician from Numidia, is said to have recommended drinking "natural waters, such as alkaline springs" for the treatment of mania.[104] During the Middle Ages, some believed that drinking the water from particular European wells could cure mania. As we know nothing today about the minerals in those wells, this part of lithium's history is highly speculative and these stories probably should be considered "medical anecdotes."

Around the middle of the last century there were physicians in England and in Scandinavia who were recommending lithium to treat mania or depression.[105] At the time, lithium was being used quite extensively for treating rheumatism and gout, and the English internist A. B. Garrod was one of several physicians who believed that a relationship existed between these joint disorders and mania. The assumption was that whatever was causing the inflammation of bodily joints might also produce a brain inflammation. In fact, mania was commonly called "brain gout," and Garrod recommended that it be treated by a daily intake of lithium at a dose not dissimilar to what is used today to treat mania. About twenty years later, the Danish neurologist Carl Lange—well known in psychology for a theory of emotion (the same theory independently proposed by William James)—described the symptoms of "periodic depression" as a rheumatic condition and recommended a prophylactic treatment of lithium. There were other physicians who had similar ideas, perhaps most notably the English physician Alexander Haig. The six editions (1892–1907) of his book *Uric Acid* made note of the association of "melancholia" with gout. By 1910, however, the earlier meaning of gout and rheumatism had changed and its association with psychiatry was forgotten.

Ideas can be too early for their time. William A. Hammond, a prominent neurologist at Bellevue Hospital in New York and a former surgeon general of the United States, recommended lithium as a treatment of mania as early as 1871:

> Latterly I have used the bromide of lithium in cases of acute mania, and have more reason to be satisfied with it than any other medicine calculated to diminish the amount of blood in the cerebral vessels and to calm any nervous excitement that may be present. The rapidity with which its effects are produced renders it specifically applicable in such cases. The doses should be large and as high as sixty grams or more should be repeated every two or three hours till sleep be produced, or at least till half a dozen doses be taken. After the patient has come under its influence, the remedy should be continued in smaller doses, taken three or four times in the day.[106]

During the 1940s, lithium was widely sold as a substitute for table salt (sodium chloride). It had been known for some time that lithium chloride has a salty taste, and during the 1940s when it became known that hypertensive patients should be on a low–sodium chloride diet, lithium salt was marketed as a substitute for common table salt. In 1948, there were four main brands available in U.S. grocery stores—Westsal, Foodsal, Salti-salt, and Milosal. There had been several reports of toxicity associated with the consumption of large numbers of lithium tablets, but these had not generated much attention until 1949, when Dr. A. M. Waldron of Ann Arbor, Michigan, noted in a letter published in the *Journal of the American Medical Association* that four of his patients using Westsal as a salt substitute had tremors, disturbed gait, weakness, and blurred vision, and one became critically ill.[107] This letter triggered other reports, one from the Cleveland Clinic, of fatalities believed to have been caused by Westsal.[108] *Time* magazine ran an article, "Case of the Substitute Salt," that reported cases of lithium toxicity, and Morris Fishbein, editor of the *Journal of the American Medical Association*, asked newspapers and radio stations to warn people of the danger. The FDA issued a stern warning: "Stop using this dangerous poison at once!" combining it with the recommendation that the interstate distribution of these salt substitutes should be discontinued. Actually, it was never clear how many of the deaths were caused by lithium rather than by a severe sodium depletion, but lithium-induced cardiac depression may have placed some people with congestive heart conditions at risk.

During World War II, John Cade, a physician in the Australian Medical Corps, was captured by the Japanese and spent three and a half years in a military prison. During the period in the Japanese prison, Cade began to wonder if the mania that he observed occurring in some of his fellow prisoners was caused by an excessive accumulation of some breakdown product (a metabolite resulting from a natural chemical reaction in the body), which had a toxic effect on the brain. The idea was little more than a hunch, as Cade had no idea what that metabolite might be, if indeed it existed. Nevertheless, Cade was committed to the idea, and shortly after the war, he started to pursue his hunch.

The research idea was not only conceptually simplistic, but Cade had to conduct his research in a pantry with almost no equipment available. Cade was working at a psychiatric hospital in Bundoora, a suburb of Melbourne, but most of his experimental guinea pigs had to be kept in the backyard of his home. As he had no idea what metabolite might be accumulating in the body, Cade cast his net as widely as possible. He started by collecting urine from manic, depressed, and schizophrenic patients early in the morning, a time he thought the metabolites should be most concentrated. After storing the urine in the family refrigerator, he injected it into the abdomen of guinea pigs, speculating that any differential accumulation of the hypothesized metabolite in the urine of the patients might be reflected in the reaction of the animals.[109]

Although all the guinea pigs died after the urine was injected, Cade convinced himself that the animals injected with urine from manic patients had died more rapidly. Cade decided that it was the urea that had killed the guinea pigs, but it soon became evident that this hypothesis had two major problems. First, in all cases the urea concentration was found to be below the lethal dose, and secondarily, the urea concentration was determined to be the same in the urine from the different patient groups. Cade then speculated that the urine might contain differential amounts of some other substance—a "quantitative modifier"—that enhanced the toxicity of urea when injected into animals. He found it necessary to postulate several modifiers of urea toxicity. Cade hypothesized that uric acid potentiated the toxicity, creatinine protected against urea toxicity, and an unidentified substance was thought to be present that canceled the protective effect of creatinine. As the research continued, Cade's "theory" became increasingly Byzantine and ad hoc.

In a small book published in 1979, Cade reconstructed what was on his mind when he discovered lithium treatment:

> In view of the utter uselessness of psychotherapy based on psychopatho-
> logical theories in either treatment or prevention . . . a medical model
> seemed more attractive as an explanatory hypothesis. After all, manic and
> melancholic patients seemed to be truly sick in the medical sense. Were
> there, however, any medical conditions that would provide some sort of
> analogy?
>
> . . . Was it possible, therefore, that mania was due to some metabolic
> substance circulating in excess and could melancholia be explained as
> the corresponding deprivative condition?
>
> But even so, how to demonstrate it, knowing nothing whatever of its
> properties? An obvious thought was that if mania were due to the circu-
> lation of some substance in excess, some might be excreted in the urine
> and demonstrable therein. The best initial approach seemed to be to use
> an extraordinarily crude differential toxicity test to discover whether any
> differences could be detected between urine samples from manics and
> depressives. And crude the experiment was. It involved the injection into
> the abdominal cavity of guinea-pigs of samples of concentrated urine,
> in varying amounts, from manic, melancholic and schizophrenic
> patients; "normal" controls were also involved. Although the mode of
> death of the animals was the same in all cases, suggesting the presence of
> the same toxic agent, the urine from some manic patients had a far more
> toxic effect than that from any other group. Urea proved to be the guilty
> substance, but why was it so much more toxic in these manic cases?

It was at this point that Cade began to postulate that there were substances such as creatinine that protected individuals from the toxic effects of urea, while other substances, such as uric acid, enhanced the toxic effects. Cade found it difficult to test uric acid because he had difficulty getting it into solution. He used lithium urate as a substitute only because it was easy to get into solution and it happened to be available in the pharmacy. To Cade's surprise, lithium had just the opposite effect from the one anticipated. As Cade described what happened:

> Surprisingly the toxicity was far less than anticipated. Contrary to expectations it, like creatinine, was protective. So it became important to determine the effects of lithium salts by themselves. It was quickly evident that they had a powerful calming effect on the guinea-pigs. The animals remained fully awake, but after about two hours they became so calm that they lost their "startle-reaction" and frantic righting-reflex when placed on their backs. It was this observation which prompted the trial of lithium salts in that over-excitable state of mania.[110]

Nathan Kline later expressed his belief that Cade's guinea pigs may have appeared to have been quieted because the amount of lithium administered was close to toxic levels.[111] Mogens Schou, the psychiatrist eventually responsible for gaining acceptance of lithium therapy, reached essentially the same conclusion:

> Seen from a distance of forty years, Cade's discovery contains strange elements. The word serendipity has been used repeatedly, for he himself saw the development as a series of logical steps. However, the reasoning behind his experiments was far from clear (why would a compound counteracting the effects of intraperitoneal urea be of psychiatric interest?), and it is my belief that the lethargy observed in those guinea pigs was in fact caused by a toxic overdosage rather than a specific tranquilizing action of lithium. I have at least not been able to produce such an effect myself in guinea or rats with anything but strongly toxic doses. Nevertheless—and that is the marvel of the thing—an idea flashed in Cade's questing mind, and he performed the therapeutic trial that eventually changed life for manic-depressive patients all over the world.[112]

In any case and to his credit, Cade experimented first on himself to determine the safety of lithium carbonate. After remaining on lithium for a few weeks and convincing himself of its safety, he began the first clinical trial on patients. He tried a lithium regimen on nineteen patients, ten of whom were described as suffering from either chronic or periodic manic psychoses. In his initial report published in the *Medical Journal of Australia* in 1949, he described a striking reduction in psychotic excitement in all ten manic patients treated with lithium.[113] As reported by Cade, the very first manic patient (Case 1, WB) treated with lithium was fifty-one years old and in a state of chronic manic excitement for over five years:

> He was amiably restless, dirty, destructive, mischievous and interfering. He had enjoyed pre-eminent nuisance value in a back ward for all those years and bid fair to remain there for the rest of his life. He commenced treatment with lithium citrate 1200 mg thrice daily on 29 March 1948. On the fourth day, the optimistic therapist thought he saw some change for the better but acknowledged that it could have been his expectant imagination (It was April Fool's Day!). The nursing staff was non-committal but loyal. However, by the fifth day it was clear that he was in fact more settled, tidier, less disinhibited and less distractible. From then on there was steady improvement . . . he was kept under observation for a further 2 months.
>
> He remained perfectly well and left hospital on 9 July 1948, on indefinite leave, with instructions to take a maintenance dose of lithium carbonate 300 mg twice daily.
>
> The carbonate had been substituted for the citrate as he had become intolerant of the latter. He was soon back working happily at his old job.
>
> It was with a sense of the most abject disappointment that I had admitted him to hospital 6 months later as manic as ever but took some consolation from his brother who informed me that Bill had become overconfident about having been so well for so many months, had become lackadaisical about taking his medication and had finally ceased taking it about 6 weeks before. Since then he had become steadily more irritable and erratic. His lithium carbonate was at once recommenced and in 2 weeks he had again returned to normal. A month later he was recorded to as completely well and ready to return to home and work.[114]

Cade reported that the six schizophrenic patients became less excitable, but their basic pathology, principally hallucinations and delusions, was unchanged. The three chronically depressed patients included in the initial group were described as unchanged, neither better or worse.

The results were certainly dramatic and might have encouraged many psychiatrists to try lithium treatment had it not been for the fact that Cade was virtually unknown and because of the skepticism about drug treatment of mental illness. John Cade's initial report of lithium's success in treating "psychotic excitement" was published in 1949.[115] He later commented that this report "could not have occurred at a less propitious time and circumstances." Not only was the report published in the midst of the lithium scare in the United States, but also, as Cade wrote about himself: "An unknown psychiatrist, working alone in a small chronic hospital with no research training, primitive techniques and negligible equipment was hardly likely to be compellingly persuasive, especially in the United States. And so it turned out."[116]

The reports of lithium toxicity certainly scared away many psychiatrists who might otherwise have been willing to try this drug. Cade also may have been concerned about lithium's safety, as his first patient (Case 1, WB, referred to above) died, a fact he never mentioned in any of his publications. According to Neil Johnson, who had access to Cade's unpublished clinical notes, WB's mental state deteriorated whenever he stopped taking the drug, and he had to be rehospitalized several times.[117] About two years after the beginning of treatment, WB started to have myoclonic twitches, his heart slowed, and he lost consciousness and expired. Johnson concluded that Cade had purposely minimized the adverse side effects of lithium in his publications. According to Samuel Gershon, who was in Melbourne at the time, Cade was apparently concerned about lithium's safety and stopped using it at one point.[118] Actually, the year following Cade's initial report, two notes appeared in the *Medical Journal of Australia*, each describing a fatality that appeared to have been caused by lithium.[119] In the five years following Cade's initial publication, only eight papers describing lithium treatment were published, and two of these mentioned fatalities, so it is not surprising that psychiatrists were hesitant to try the treatment.

In addition to the reports that lithium depressed heart activity, there were also reports of goiters resulting from lithium treatment. The following two statements from authoritative sources certainly would not have encouraged psychiatrists to try lithium treatment:

> Such measures as the treatment of manic patients by lithium (poisoning) seem quite unjustified and are to be deplored on humanitarian grounds. (Abraham Wickler, 1957)[120]

> The lithium ion has no therapeutic applications and, so far as is known, no biological function. Indeed, the only pharmacological interest in lithium arises from the fact that the ion is toxic. Even this would be only of academic interest were it not for the fact that lithium salts have been employed as flavoring agents in low-sodium diets and have caused poisoning. (*The Pharmacological Basis of Therapeutics*, 1958)[121]

The concern over lithium toxicity led to the development of techniques that eventually made it possible to keep lithium levels within safe limits. In Australia, several researchers began to monitor serum lithium in order to determine the minimum dose that was both safe and effective, but it was John Talbott at the University of Buffalo who had the most influence in demonstrating how lithium treatment could be given safely.[122] In 1950, after conducting a number of tests on animals and on humans, Talbott developed a technique for monitoring serum levels of lithium that laid the foundation for the routine monitoring of lithium levels in the blood that would eventually make the treatment safe.

Besides the concern about lithium toxicity, there was by no means a consensus that lithium treatment of mania was effective. There were reports confirming Cade's results and others that failed to replicate his success. There was more interest in the treatment in Europe than in the United States. Psychiatrists in France, in particular, were interested in lithium treatment, perhaps due in part to the openness of the French to the medicinal properties of natural waters. Lithium treatment received its biggest boost, however, from the studies of Mogens Schou, a young Danish psychiatrist working at the Aarhus University Psychiatric Hospital. Schou had been monitoring the literature on manic-depressive illness for personal reasons, as his brother had suffered for many years from severe bouts of a recurring mood disorder. When he came across Cade's report, he decided to try lithium, using a more carefully controlled research procedure. Schou's 1954 paper confirming the therapeutic value of lithium may have been the first "double-blind" pharmacological study in psychiatry. (A "double-blind" study is one in which neither the patient nor the person evaluating the outcome knows what drug or placebo was given to any individual.) When Schou switched the patients from drug to placebo and back again to the drug it seemingly provided convincing proof of lithium's effectiveness as a treatment of mania. Even though he used flame spectrophotometry to monitor blood levels of lithium, Schou acknowledged that there was a potential danger in lithium treatment. Schou continued to investigate lithium treatment, and in 1959 he reported an 80 percent success rate with more than 150 patients.

Schou and his collaborators had carefully followed all the patients on lithium, and they concluded that not only was the treatment effective for mania, it also prevented the recurrence of the depressive episodes in manic-depressive disorder. Other investigators, particularly G. P. Hartigan, a psychiatrist in Canterbury, England, had noticed that lithium treatment seemed to inhibit mood swings in both directions in manic-depressive patients. Hartigan proposed that the drug might be an effective stabilizer of all moods. Schou visited Hartigan and encouraged him to publish his observations.[123] Schou later reported in 1981 that his brother's recurring bouts of depression, some of which had lasted many months, had been under complete control for the fourteen years he had been on lithium and that, functionally, he was completely cured.

While lithium treatment was rather widely taken up by psychiatrists on the continent, there remained considerable skepticism in England and in the United States. Samuel Gershon was one of the earliest proponents of lithium treatment in the United States. Before coming to the Ypsilanti State Hospital in Michigan in 1960, Gershon, as noted earlier, had worked in the same hospital in Australia as John Cade. Gershon and Arthur Yuwiler's 1960 review article describing the effectiveness of lithium treatment increased awareness of lithium treatment in the United States, but there still was considerable hesitation to adopt the treatment.[124]

It did not help that in the late 1960s, *Lancet* published several critical letters by Barry Blackwell and Michael Shepherd of the Maudsley Hospital in which they claimed that lithium was a "therapeutic myth" based on uncontrolled studies, faulty statistics, subjective criteria for assessing improvement, failure to consider the role of spontaneous remission, and a biased selection of patients, some of whom were claimed not to have been chronically ill.[125] Shepherd, who was a well-known epidemiologist and Aubrey Lewis Professor of Psychiatry at the Maudsley, considered lithium "dangerous nonsense."[126] Although Schou's studies were innovative in design features and much better-controlled than most drug studies in psychiatry, the inevitable result of the exchange of letters that followed was to raise the level of skepticism.

Schou and his collaborators finally published the results of a study that put most of the reservations to rest. First, however, they had to grapple with the ethical problem of having to satisfy the skeptics by both withholding effective treatment from manic patients in the control group and withdrawing patients from a treatment that was apparently working. What was finally done was to use a sequential design in which eighty-four patients on lithium were withdrawn from treatment and given a placebo. The research was conducted in a double-blind procedure so that neither the patients nor those rating their condition knew whether the placebo or lithium had been administered. Those patients who were clearly relapsing when on the placebo were placed back on the lithium treatment. Furthermore, it was decided in advance that the study would be ended when the data reached an acceptable level of statistical significance. The results, published in *Lancet* in 1970, were unequivocal. The experiment was ended after six months, by which time more than one-half of the patients switched to placebo had relapsed, while none of the patients on lithium had recurrences of their illness.

The U.S. Food and Drug Administration (FDA) had hesitated to approve the use of lithium because of the toxicity scare and the controversy over its effectiveness, but by 1970 the drug was finally approved, though only as a treatment for mania. The FDA refused to approve lithium treatment for recurrent depressive episodes: "The sole indication for the use of lithium carbonate at this time is for control of manic episodes of manic psychosis. Evidence for efficacy in other indications is not yet available."[127]

The psychiatrists Samuel Gershon, Nathan Kline, and Ronald Fieve each in his own way played an important role in getting lithium treatment accepted. Early on, Gershon's review article served to make psychiatrists at least aware of lithium treatment, even if they were hesitant to try it. In 1968, Nathan Kline, who at several international meetings had described successful treatment using lithium, wrote an influential editorial in the *American Journal of Psychiatry* entitled "Lithium Comes into Its Own." In the editorial, Kline stated that "lithium, the 20-year old Cinderella of psychopharmacology, is at last receiving her sovereign due."

In the early 1970s, the psychiatrist Ronald Fieve, who was never known to shun the limelight, appeared on many national television talk shows with Joshua Logan, the famous playwright and director-producer of *Charlie's Aunt, Mister Roberts, South Pacific,* and *Camelot.* Logan had been one of Fieve's patients, and he described his thirty years of devastating mood swings before starting on lithium. Logan noted that for the four and one-half years since he started on lithium he had had no highs or lows and was more productive than ever and currently working simultaneously on two musical comedies and an autobiography. Fieve invited Logan to participate in a televised panel discussion organized by the American Medical Association, and afterward both of them were interviewed by the press. Logan's success story made millions aware of dramatic changes that could be brought about by lithium.

In 1975, Fieve's popularly written book *Mood Swing: The Third Revolution in Psychiatry* was published and was soon translated into four languages. By 1980, the English edition alone had sold over a million copies.[128] The book described a great number of eminently creative people (William Inge, Sylvia Plath, Balzac, Van Gogh, Handel, Schumann, Rossini) and political figures (Abraham Lincoln, Theodore Roosevelt, Winston Churchill) as victims of periods of crippling depression alternating with "high" periods of great productivity. These productive "highs" were referred to as "hypomania," a state of high energy and productivity that was said to be related to manic psychoses, but was distinguishable by being less extreme, more realistic, and socially appropriate. Fieve described case histories of patients who had been transformed "in one to three weeks from the terrible throes of moodswing to normalcy":

> I believe that depression is terrifying; and elation—its nonidentical twin sister—is even more terrifying, attractive as she may be for the moment. But as she goes higher, man is even more dangerous than when in the depths of depression. However, I'm sure that the thing that is almost as much of a menace to the world today is the stupid, almost dogged ignorance of these illnesses; the vast lack of knowledge that they are able to be treated and the seeming ease of the cure, the simplicity of bringing them under control.[129]

Fieve stressed the ineffectiveness of psychoanalysis and all other talking therapies and made it clear that he was convinced that manic-depressive illness was a metabolic disorder: "The term metabolic indicates that the depression is caused by an abnormality in the body's chemistry, or metabolism, and not by stress or problems in living."[130] In ruling out environmental factors, Fieve clearly indicated his conviction that this disorder was inherited, although his logic was not above reproach: "Mania and mental depression must be due to biochemical causes handed down through the genes since they are correctable so rapidly by chemical rather than talking therapy."[131] Of course, that lithium treatment may be more effective than psychotherapy does not, by itself, prove that the manic-depressive disorder is genetic.

It has been claimed that pharmaceutical companies refused for quite a while to invest much money promoting a drug that might not be profitable.[132] When no drug company seemed interested in marketing lithium, the American College of Neuropharmacology considered applying for a New Drug Application (NDA) in its own name. By 1970, however, the Rowell Laboratories and Charles Pfizer & Company had become interested in marketing lithium, and the FDA approved applications for Eskalith, Lithonate, and Lithane, three lithium preparations. Nevertheless, it is still claimed that even now, when its value is widely acknowledged, the marketing of lithium has not been nearly as vigorous as that for more profitable drugs.[133]

It is also claimed that some resistance to accepting lithium as a treatment for depression was attributable to the "biogenic amine theory" of mood disorders. This theory will be explained in the next chapter, but briefly it postulated that biogenic amine neurotransmitters (norepinephrine, dopamine, and serotonin) were overactive in a manic state and underactive in depression. It was difficult, therefore, for people to believe that a single drug could be effective in both enhancing and inhibiting the same neurotransmitters. As the psychiatrist Joseph Mendels commented:

> It has long been my impression that the dominant hold of the biogenic amine hypothesis of affective disorders, with the view that there was an aminergic excess in mania and a deficiency in depression, led many of the leaders in the field to rigidly resist the notion that a single pharmacological treatment might be effective in both depression and mania. Given that lithium had clearly been established to be effective in the treatment of acute mania, there was considerable reluctance to seriously consider the possibility that it might have an antidepressant effect. I recall many discussions and arguments around this point in the late 1960s when we were beginning our work on the project. There was also considerable resistance to funding this type of research because many of the people who were involved in making decisions about grant support were heavily invested in the classic amine theory and appeared to resist the ideas that we (and others) were beginning to advance.[134]

Today, the effectiveness of lithium and some more recently developed "mood stabilizers" is widely accepted. Recently, the popularity of Kay Jamison's book *An Unquiet Mind: A Memoir of Moods and Madness* has done much to make people aware of lithium's effectiveness against destructive mood swings.[135]

Jamison, a psychologist who has written extensively about manic-depressive disorders, has this condition herself, and she has given a vivid account of what it is like to suffer from this disorder and how she was helped by lithium. When lithium proves not to be effective, one of several anticonvulsant drugs such as carbamazepine and valproic acid are sometime helpful, either as an alternative to lithium or as an adjunct complementing lithium treatment. As will be discussed, however, there is still a significant number of people suffering from manic-depressive disorders who do not respond to any of the available "mood stabilizers."

The Discovery of the Minor Tranquilizers: The Antianxiety Drugs

The first antianxiety drug was discovered accidentally by researchers looking for drugs that were effective against infectious gram-negative microorganisms. (This was quite similar, it will be recalled, to the accidental discovery of the antidepressant iproniazid, which when used to treat tuberculosis, produced euphoria in some patients.) Gram-negative microorganisms are not detected by the stain developed by the Danish physician Hans Christian Gram. Not long after penicillin become available in 1945, it was learned that this antibiotic, although enormously valuable for treating many infections, was not useful against gram-negative microorganisms.

Frank Berger played a major role in the discovery of the first antianxiety drug. Berger was born in Pilsen, Czechoslovakia. In 1937, shortly after completing his medical training in Prague, he left the country for England. In 1945, after the war, Berger went to work as a bacteriologist for a British pharmaceutical company, where he collaborated with the chemist William Bradley in searching for drugs effective against gram-negative organisms. They became interested in Phenoxetol, a drug claimed to be useful against gram-negative organisms, but they found its effectiveness left much to be desired. Bradley began developing new drugs by modifying Phenoxetol, and one of them appeared to be an improvement. This new drug, mephenesin, was tested by Berger for its safety by administering it to mice, rats, and other small laboratory animals. Unexpectedly, the drug produced a muscular paralysis and a loss of voluntary movement. If the animals were placed on their backs they were not able to right themselves. Their muscles were limp, yet they seemed fully awake and their heart rate and breathing were normal, as were other "vegetative" (visceral) signs. The animals completely recovered in a few hours.

Mephenesin proved to be a most interesting drug. When it was administered in low doses, animals were quieted without any obvious effects on their muscles. Moreover, there was no initial period of excitement as commonly occurs with so-called "hypnotic" drugs.[136] Mephenesin was tested on patients, and in 1946 Berger and Bradley reported that symptoms of anxiety were eased, patients being less tense, but consciousness did not seem to be impaired.[137] These effects were called "tranquilization," a description Berger and Bradley had used seven years earlier to apply to the properties of the drug reserpine.[138] Mephenesin had a serious shortcoming, however, as it was rapidly metabolized and as a result its duration of action was too short.

Shortly after discovering mephenesin, Berger moved to the United States, taking a position as an assistant professor of pediatrics at the University of Rochester Medical School. While at Rochester, Berger consulted for the pharmaceutical company Carter Products, which was known mainly for "Carter's Little Liver Pills," an over-the-counter drug. In 1949, Berger left the University of Rochester for a position at the Wallace Laboratories (a Carter Products subsidiary), where he began working to improve mephenesin. Although the short duration of action of mephenesin might be a useful feature for a muscle relaxant, it was a serious limitation for a drug to be used for reducing anxiety. With the collaboration of chemists at Wallace Laboratories, similar drugs were screened for effectiveness on animals. In May 1950, the drug meprobamate was tested, and it appeared to be far superior to all other compounds, especially in its ability to reduce the viciousness typically displayed by rhesus monkeys housed in laboratories. A film was made of the calmed monkeys, and this generated considerable interest in meprobamate.

In clinical trials on humans, meprobamate was reported to reduce anxiety without any drowsiness. Wyeth Laboratories obtained a license from the Wallace Laboratories to market meprobamate, and as soon as FDA approval was obtained, Wyeth began marketing the drug as "Equanil," while Wallace marketed it as "Miltown." (The name "Miltown" had been adapted from the New Jersey town of Milltown where the Wallace Laboratories were located.)[139] Miltown and Equanil were promoted through huge advertising campaigns, and they were soon enormous financial successes as tranquilizers and, in a slightly modified form, as a centrally acting muscle relaxant for relieving spasms after injury. Sales exceeded $100 million a year, and Berger became president of Wallace Laboratories. The name Miltown became a household word, helped in part by the numerous magazine articles with titles such as "Happy Pills," "Peace of Mind Drugs," and

"Happiness by Prescription." The comedian Milton Berle referred to himself as "Miltown" Berle and the humorist S. J. Perelman called his 1957 book *The Road to Miltown.*

It was a propitious time to introduce meprobamate, as serious concern had developed over the safety of long-acting barbiturates, such as phenobarbital, which had been used up to this time to treat anxiety.[140] Miltown and Equanil were advertised as safe nonbarbiturates, which were not habit-forming. This claim turned out to be as true as the Bayer Company's promotion of heroin in 1898 as a safe, nonaddicting cough syrup in contrast to cough preparations containing codeine. While meprobamate had a greater safety margin than barbiturates, it was not completely safe and, moreover, it was habit-forming. With chronic administration, a tolerance was developed and higher and higher doses were required. As with the barbiturates, when people stopped taking meprobamate they often became hyperexcitable and intensely anxious, and sometimes they even had convulsions. This class of drugs was eventually replaced about a decade later by the benzodiazepine drugs—for example, Valium—which are thought to be more effective and which produce less drowsiness.

Serendipity also played a major role in the discovery of the benzodiazepine drugs. The huge financial success of Miltown and Equanil motivated other pharmaceutical companies to search for drugs with similar properties. It is a common practice of pharmaceutical companies to search for chemically similar drugs (analogues) that they can patent and market as competing products. The hope is that a drug can be found that is at least equally effective, and can be claimed to have fewer undesirable side effects, but it must be just different enough so that it can be patented as a separate drug. This practice has been referred to as "searching for the least patentable difference."

The serendipity involved in the discovery of the benzodiazepine drugs occurred when an unexpected chemical reaction produced a completely different class of drugs. It will be recalled that this is how the antipsychotic haloperidol was discovered. In the early 1930s, the chemist Leo Sternbach was doing postdoctoral research at the University of Cracow, Poland. He had synthesized some quinazoline compounds that he hoped would be useful as dyes. At the time, he had no interest in any biological properties of these compounds. With the rise of Nazism and the German army on the march, Sternbach left Poland, securing a position at Hoffman–La Roche Pharmaceutical in Basel. In 1940, however, it was feared that the Germans might invade Switzerland, and the company transferred Sternbach to one of its smaller branches in Nutley, New Jersey, where there was an interest in developing drugs with properties similar to those of meprobamate. Sternbach systematically tested the forty quinazoline compounds that he had previously worked on in order to determine if any were useful as a sedative, muscle relaxant, or anticonvulsant. All of these compounds, however, were found to be inactive for these purposes, and Hoffman–La Roche decided to abandon the project.

Shortly afterward, as Sternbach described it, in the process of cleaning up the clutter in the laboratory he came across a quinazoline compound that had not yet been tested. More in the way of tying up loose ends than expecting any positive results, this last compound was sent over to Lowell Randall, head of pharmacology, to be tested. The report from the laboratory was that the compound was far superior to meprobamate as an anxiolytic (anxiety-reducing) drug and as a muscle relaxant. Vicious monkeys, for example, seemed tame at low doses of the drug, which did not reduce alertness. It also was found to have some of the properties of chlorpromazine in animal laboratory tests. The obvious question was why this one drug had these effects while the forty previously tested quinazoline drugs did not. The answer was found in the chemistry—a chemical reaction had followed a different pathway, and this compound was not a quinazoline, but rather was the first of a new class of drugs now known as benzodiazepines. It was named chlordiazepoxide and further tested as a potential "minor tranquilizer" to distinguish it from the antipsychotic drugs sometimes called "major tranquilizers." Another term that is used to refer to any drug that produces some tranquilization is "ataractic," a word derived from the Greek *ataraktos,* implying "peace of mind," "perfect composure," and "without confusion."

Chlordiazepoxide and other minor tranquilizers thought to be potentially useful for treating anxiety were first tested on animals in an experimentally induced conflict situation. The test involved training hungry rats to press a lever for food. After the animals were pressing the lever at a steady rate a light was turned on randomly for a few minutes. If the rats pressed the lever when the light was on they received a mild shock in addition to the food. Not surprisingly, even though the rats were hungry they were quite hesitant to press the lever for food when the light was on. The rats also displayed signs of nervousness (defecating and excessive grooming) whenever the light came on. However, when the rats were given benzodiazepine drugs such as chlordiazepoxide, they tended to press the lever even though they received a shock and they did not appear to be as nervous. As morphine and other analgesics did not have the same effect, it was concluded that the change in behavior did not occur because chlordiazepoxide had reduced pain sensitivity, but because the drug had reduced the animal's concern about the shock. Although it might be questioned whether this test is a good model for anxiety in humans, it was believed to be a reasonably good predictor of which drugs would reduce anxiety in clinical trials on humans.[141]

Hoffman–La Roche's medical director persuaded some psychiatrists to test chlordiazepoxide on patients. The initial clinical trials were not encouraging, as the drug was tested mainly on geriatric patients who developed ataxia and slurred speech. However, following further testing on some sixteen hundred patients, it was concluded that the initial disappointing results were due to a case of the "wrong patients" and the "wrong dose." The drug was judged to fill a clear need. Meprobamate was used primarily with the "walking psychoneurotics," while chlorpromazine and other phenothiazines were used primarily to treat psychotic patients. There were many "intermediate" patients for whom meprobamate was too weak and the phenothiazines too strong.

A United States patent for chlordiazepoxide was filed in May 1958, and in 1960, the FDA granted approval for the sale of chlordiazepoxide. Hoffman–La Roche began marketing the drug under the proprietary name Librium. Simpler analogues were produced, the most notable being diazepam (proprietary name "Valium"), which has had enormous sales as both an antianxiety drug and a muscle relaxant. Similar drugs, such as oxazepam (under Wyeth Laboratories' proprietary name "Serax"), were marketed later. The benzodiazepines have been among the most financially successful drugs ever produced. It is estimated that in 1975, 100 million prescriptions for benzodiazepine drugs ("benzos") were filled in the United States alone, and about 15 percent of the population had taken one of these drugs, many for the minor stresses of everyday life. About one woman in five and one man in thirteen were estimated to be taking minor tranquilizers at this time.

Some serious problems began to develop with the benzodiazepines. While often successful in reducing anxiety, the benzodiazepines are habit-forming, and according to one estimate, there were about 10 million Valium addicts in the United States. Some investigators now believe that the abuse potential of Valium and the other benzodiazepine drugs may have been exaggerated.[142] There is no doubt, however, as in the Rolling Stones's song "Mother's Little Helper," far too many women had the habit of "running for the shelter" of the pill that would help them get through their day.[143]

The active metabolites of benzodiazepines remain in the body for days, and this creates the possibility of an interaction with alcohol and other drugs. There is a clear danger and Judy Garland's death in 1969, for example, has been attributed to the synergistic action of alcohol and a benzodiazepine. A U.S. Senate investigating committee headed by Edward Kennedy conducted investigations, and the public hearings led to a marked decrease in the prescriptions written for Valium and other benzodiazepines. In 1975, the FDA put the benzodiazepines and meprobamate on their list of "Schedule IV" drugs, requiring pharmacists to report all prescriptions filled and recommending that these drugs be used only for relatively brief applications. Despite these restrictions and some reduction in sales, antianxiety drugs are still among the most often prescribed drugs, and the current estimates are that almost 7 million prescriptions are written annually in the United States. Among the more popular antianxiety (anxiolytic) drugs currently in use are Valium, Librium, Xanax, and Ativan.

We have seen that all the early psychiatric drugs were discovered accidentally. Despite virtually no knowledge of how they actually worked and some serious adverse effects, the drugs were readily adopted. With no effective treatment of mental illness, the need was great, and almost anything that held out any hope was considered worth trying. It soon became clear that there were enormous profits to be made in drugs to treat mental illness. At first, the market for psychiatric drugs was mainly in public mental institutions, where there were too many patients, too few staff, and no effective treatment. The drugs were promoted as a way to decrease costs and to lighten the load on the staff caring for the patients. Later, when the concept of what constitutes a treatable psychological problem was greatly expanded, an increasing number of people starting seeking professional help, and the market for drugs, especially antidepressants and antianxiety drugs, was greatly expanded. Pharmaceutical companies and government funding agencies began to invest huge sums of money in basic and applied research on psychiatric drugs. A new field of psychopharmacology arose as researchers in different disciplines began to focus their efforts on learning what the drugs were doing and what could be inferred about how the brain normally regulates psychological states and what might go wrong when mental illness occurs. Biochemical theories to explain drug action and mental illness emerged, but as will be seen they were initially based on the very little knowledge of brain chemistry that was available at the time. These theories became firmly entrenched, and despite their clear inadequacies and much contradictory evidence, the theories have been defended, propped up, and heavily promoted, for reasons that will be discussed at length in later chapters.

Chapter 3

THEORIES OF DRUG ACTION AND BIOCHEMICAL CAUSES OF MENTAL DISORDER

No twisted thought without a twisted molecule.
Attributed to Ralph Gerard[1]

The claim that drugs could treat mental disorders was initially met with considerable skepticism. Many psychiatrists found it difficult to believe that a drug could remove the repressed conflicts that were thought to underlie most mental disorders. It was conceded that drugs might temporarily alleviate some symptoms, but these would soon be replaced by other symptoms. Most psychiatrists believed that patients had to be made aware of their unconscious fears, desires, and conflicts before any lasting help could be achieved and this could only be accomplished through psychotherapy.

After a while, however, these criticisms began to have a hollow ring. Drug treatment did seem to alleviate the symptoms of some seriously ill patients, while the claim that psychotherapy was successful in treating these same difficult patients was increasingly being challenged. Furthermore, even when psychotherapy worked, it was much too slow and labor intensive to have a significant impact on the large numbers of people with mental disorders. Drugs, on the other hand, could decrease patient management problems and reduce the escalating costs of caring for institutionalized mental patients. Furthermore, the potential market for psychotherapeutic drugs was huge. This factor, and the intellectual challenge of explaining how the drugs worked, attracted many into the new field of psychopharmacology.

Some Historical Background
Resistance to Chemical Explanations

The early psychotherapeutic drugs were all discovered accidentally, with no, or at least no relevant, theory guiding the work. Scientists who wanted to understand how the drugs worked started to search for what the drugs that alleviated the same disorder had in common. While the logic of this approach was clear, there were some serious drawbacks that prevented investigators from proceeding in this fashion. At the time of the initial discoveries of psychotherapeutic drugs, little was known about brain chemistry. What was known about neurotransmitters was gained from studies of the peripheral nervous system, but it was widely thought to apply only to the peripheral nervous system and not to brain neurophysiology. Leading neurophysiologists were convinced that communication between neurons in the brain, if not in most of the nervous system, was electrical, not chemical. The evidence for chemical transmission in the peripheral nervous system came primarily from studies of the sympathetic nervous system. The sympathetic nervous system refers to the nerves that act on those visceral organs and glands that produce the responses that prepare an animal to meet emergencies—the "fight or flight response." It had been reported in 1899 that activation of the sympathetic nervous system produced effects almost identical to those produced by extracts from the medulla (core) of the adrenal gland.[2] The adrenal gland extract was named epinephrine, and when commercially available it was called adrenaline. In 1904, T. R. Elliott, a student at Trinity College, Cambridge, speculated that the sympathetic neurons released adrenaline when they were activated: "Adrenaline might be the chemical stimulant liberated on each occasion when the [neural] impulse arrives at the periphery."[3] The eminent British neuropharmacologist Henry (later Sir Henry) Dale offered Elliott a position in his laboratory even though he was skeptical of the chemical transmission theory. Dale eventually accepted the idea and furthered the concept by demonstrating that it was norepinephrine, not epinephrine, that was responsible for the similar effects produced by adrenal gland extract and the sympathetic nervous system.[4] However, this work remained isolated from the mainstream of thinking of most neurophysiologists.

The War Between the "Sparks and the Soups"

Throughout the 1940s and well into the 1950s when chlorpromazine was discovered, leading neurophysiologists insisted that transmission across the synapse separating neurons was electrical, not chemical. Influential textbooks, such as John Fulton's *Physiology of the Nervous System,* included such statements as:

> There is no evidence that synaptic transmission of nerve impulses differs fundamentally from conduction along fibres. Recent investigations suggest that the concept of acetylcholine as a "synaptic transmitter" in its original form has to be abandoned. The release of acetylcholine appears to be intrinsically connected with the nerve action potential, thus playing an essential role in the mechanism of conduction of nerve impulses along fibres as well as across synapses.[5]

And in a later edition of the same book, Fulton concluded: "The idea of a chemical mediator released at a nerve ending and acting directly on the second neuron or muscle thus appeared to be unsatisfactory in many respects."[6]

In the 1950 edition of their widely adopted physiological psychology textbook, Clifford Morgan and Eliot Stellar described how transmission across the synaptic gap separating two neurons occurred when the electrical changes in the first cell depolarized the membrane of a second cell, and they rejected the proposal that transmission might be chemical.[7] The idea of chemical transmission gained acceptance slowly, and even in the 1953 edition of Stephen Ranson's classic textbook, *The Anatomy of the Nervous System,* the idea of chemical transmission was considered, at best, only an alternative hypothesis to the electrical transmission theory.[8]

Although the issue was still being debated, by the mid-1950s, many "neuroscientists" (the term was not yet in use) were convinced that chemicals mediated transmission between at least some neurons in the brain, but there remained eminent neurophysiologists who continued to argue that "synaptic electrogenesis" was the most common mechanism of transmission across a synapse.[9] The sometimes heated controversy between the proponents of electrical and chemical transmission was referred to as "the war of the *sparks* and the *soups.*" Henry Dale was the major spokesman for the chemical transmission position and John Eccles played that role for the electrical transmission position.[10]

With so little being known about brain chemistry in the 1950s when the first antipsychotic and antidepressant drugs were being discovered, there was virtually no way of explaining how the drugs might be working. The French psychiatrist Pierre Pichot had trained with Delay and Deniker at the time they reported their initial results with chlorpromazine. Pichot recalled that at a 1955 meeting only chlorpromazine's therapeutic effectiveness could be discussed and nothing could be said about how it might act:

> . . . At that time the biochemistry of the brain, as it exists now, was unknown. It was only at the beginning of the 1960s, that we began to

speak of the role of the neurotransmitters in the action of both neuroleptic drugs and antidepressants and of their potential abnormalities in
the disease process.[11]

In the early 1960s, researchers began to speculate about the action of
psychotherapeutic drugs on brain neurotransmitters, partly because of the
work of a group of Swedish histochemists and pharmacologists. These
investigators had discovered that when thin slices of brain are exposed to
formaldehyde vapors, the biogenic amines fluoresce different colors. Thus,
norepinephrine fluoresced as bright green and serotonin as yellow. This
made it possible to locate norepinephrine, serotonin, and later dopamine in
the brain, yet apparently there remained some uncertainty about what
these amines were doing in the brain.[12] But once it was clearly demonstrated that these neurotransmitters accumulated at nerve endings and
were discharged into the synapse when the nerve fired, the "electrical theory" holdouts found it difficult to deny any longer that transmission in the
brain was chemical.[13] Even before that time, however, several pharmacologists, biochemists, physiologists, and biological psychiatrists were providing evidence that hallucinogenic drugs produced their effects by acting on
neurotransmitters. This led to speculation that psychotherapeutic drugs
might also modify neurotransmitter activity and that mental disorders
might result from either an excess or deficiency in the activity of some neurotransmitter.

A Parallel Development:
The Emotional Brain

During the second half of the nineteenth century, a number of European
investigators developed techniques for electrically stimulating or ablating
("lesioning") parts of the brain and observing the effects on behavior. Most
of these brain-behavior studies were restricted to the cerebral cortex
because there were few techniques available for exploring the parts of the
brain that were hidden below the surface. Around the turn of the century,
however, several investigators began to insert stiff wires (electrodes) into
structures located deep within the brain, which provided a way of stimulating or ablating subcortical brain structures. A major advance occurred in
1908 when the eminent British neurosurgeon Victor Horsley and his collaborator, the physiologist R. H. Clarke, developed a device, now called a
stereotaxic instrument, that made it possible to place electrodes accurately
into virtually any part of the brain.

Several European investigators began stimulating the hypothalamus, a
region at the base of the brain, just above the back of the roof of the mouth.

Most notable were the series of investigations by J. Karplus and A. Kreidl at the University of Vienna. Published between 1909 and 1928 under the title *Gehirn und Sympathicus (Brain and Sympathetic Responses)*, the research of Karplus and Kreidl reported that stimulating different areas of the hypothalamus of animals produced all of the autonomic (visceral) responses associated with emotional states. Thus hypothalamic stimulation could produce such changes as pupillary constriction or dilation, blood pressure and heart rate changes, sweating, glandular secretions, and much more.

Another major advance came with the demonstration by Walter Hess of Zurich of a way to stimulate deep regions of the brain in fully awake and relatively unrestrained cats. Hess, who started this work in the 1920s and was awarded the Nobel Prize in 1949, was able to evoke various behavior, including voracious eating, rage, and other emotional responses, by stimulating different regions of the diencephalon (mainly the thalamus and hypothalamus).[14] Hess's studies encouraged a number of researchers throughout the world to adopt and to modify his methods, and in the ensuing years there were many reports describing the different behavior that was evoked by electrical stimulation of subcortical brain sites. Stimulation of the hypothalamus, in particular, evoked a number of biologically significant behaviors such as eating, drinking, rage, aggression, predatory behavior, sleep, and sexual behavior. By 1950, substantial evidence demonstrated that the hypothalamus played a critical role not only in integrating the visceral responses associated with emotional states, but also in motivating animals to engage in such biologically adaptive behavior as seeking out food, water, or sexual opportunity, or engaging in aggressive behavior.[15]

The Discovery of a Brain Circuit for Pleasure and Reward

Few discoveries in this field aroused as much interest as did the 1954 report by James Olds and Peter Milner, psychologists at McGill University, that rats seemed to be experiencing something that resembled great pleasure when electrical stimulation was delivered to parts of the hypothalamus and other closely connected brain areas. Olds and Milner found that rats were highly motivated to press a lever or to repeat any behavior that was followed by electrical stimulation of these brain regions.[16] They reported that rats would press a lever ("self-stimulate") over and over again in order to stimulate their own brains, provided the electrode was located in what came to be called the brain's "pleasure" or "reward" circuit. Because the rats were highly motivated to obtain this stimulation their behavior could easily be "shaped" by providing "rewarding brain stimulation" whenever they did something that brought them closer to a preselected response. Under the guiding influence of brain stimulation, animals readily played the "getting hotter or colder" game, and once they had made the correct response they kept repeating it as long as the rewarding brain stimulation was delivered.[17]

It was soon found that "self-stimulation" was not just a rat phenomenon. Every mammal studied responded in the same way, and there was even some suggestive evidence that humans might also respond similarly to stimulation at comparable brain sites. There was enormous interest in the implications of the "rewarding brain circuit" and there were many theories that this circuit had evolved to provide the "fuel for motivation"; the pleasure and reward that is derived from satisfying any appetite, whether for food or sex; the system that maintains goal-directed behavior; and the way of "tagging" experiences that are sufficiently important to be stored in memory. These ideas led directly to the speculation that much of the impaired functioning seen in different mental disorders, such as the loss of interest in food and sex or the inability to experience pleasure or to maintain a logical sequence in thinking, might be the result of some deficiency in the "brain reward circuit."

Chemical Stimulation of the Brain

During the early 1960s it was discovered that not only electrical stimulation but also chemical stimulation was capable of evoking pleasure and reward. There had been several earlier reports that chemical stimulation of different brain areas could modify behavior in predictable ways. The chemicals were inserted into subcortical areas through cannulae (fine tubes) that had been inserted into the brain. The Scandinavian researcher Bengt Andersson, for example, reported in 1953 that when a hypertonic salt solution was injected into the hypothalamus of goats, the animals start drinking water almost immediately. Moreover, this drinking did not seem to be simply a reflexive response, as the goats were clearly motivated to learn any response that was rewarded by access to water.[18] Other investigators began to use similar techniques to explore what behavior could be evoked with other chemicals, including natural hormones. In 1956, the psychologist Alan Fisher reported that when certain "sex" hormones were injected into particular regions of the hypothalamus, rats began to display maternal behavior such as nest building and retrieving pups. When testosterone was injected into other hypothalamic regions, the sexual activity of male rats became unusually vigorous and persistent.[19] These reports were interpreted as evidence that different regions of the brain were particularly sensitive to chemical substances, such as salt and hormones, and that when these critical brain areas were activated they triggered natural motivational states. Hypertonic salt solutions and hormones were thought to be blood-borne signals of an animal's biological needs.

None of these early brain chemical studies used neurotransmitters to stimulate the brain. It probably had not occurred to anyone to try neurotransmitters because, as already described, it was still not widely accepted that the neurons in the brain used chemicals to transmit signals across a synapse. Between 1955 and 1957, however, there were separate reports by José Delgado and Paul MacLean, both at Yale University at the time, that acetylcholine and chemically similar synthetic compounds could evoke various responses in cats, such as rage, pain, sleep, purring, and other manifestations of pleasure, depending on the brain area stimulated.[20] Although acetycholine was widely accepted as a neurotransmitter in the peripheral nervous system, the emphasis in these early studies was on finding an alternative to electrical stimulation, as it was thought by some to be too crude a technique to reveal precise localization of function within the brain. The closest any of these early reports came to a discussion of brain neurotransmitters was a brief and isolated statement in 1957 that the hippocampus was chosen as a site to inject acetylcholine because the high levels of the enzyme choline acetylase suggested that acetylcholine "might play a role in neural transmission."[21] This was still an era of uncertainty about chemical transmission in the brain, and authors of scientific articles commonly expressed this uncertainty by referring to the acetylcholine, serotonin, and norepinephrine found in the brain as "putative" neurotransmitters.

The psychologist Sebastian "Pete" Grossman was the first researcher to report that different behavior could be evoked from the same brain area, depending on which neurotransmitter system was activated. This research was Grossman's 1960 doctoral dissertation at Yale University, and he and his faculty mentor, Neal Miller, were aware of the earlier work of José Delgado and Paul MacLean using acetylcholine to stimulate the brain.[22] Grossman tapped either norepinephrine or acetylcholine crystals into fine tubes ("cannulae"), which he inserted into the hypothalamus of rats. Grossman reported that cholinergic (acetylcholinelike substances) stimulation at certain hypothalamic sites evoked drinking in nonthirsty rats and decreased eating even in hungry animals, while adrenergic (norepinephrinelike substances) stimulation at the same brain sites did just the opposite, causing food-satiated rats to eat, while decreasing the drinking of even thirsty animals.[23] Moreover, in later work, Grossman found that such drugs as atropine, which blocked the action of acetylcholine, made thirsty animals drink much less than they normally would, while drugs that blocked the action of norepinephrine, such as dibenzyline, decreased food consumption even in hungry animals.[24] These results suggested that there might be overlapping but functionally distinct systems in the brain that could be distinguished by the different neurotransmitters that activated them.

In a seminal article published in 1965 in the journal *Science*, Neal Miller reviewed experiments that he interpreted as demonstrating that much behavior might be regulated by different brain neurotransmitters. Miller relied heavily on Grossman's findings that norepinephrine and acetylcholine stimulation or blockade had differential effects on the motivation to eat or drink. It seems strange today that Miller still had to justify the idea of brain neurotransmitters, but as late as 1965 he needed to remind readers that acetylcholine and norepinephrine were now accepted as neurotransmitters at some peripheral nervous system synapses, and he then asked:

> Does similar coding of transmission occur in the brain, and if it does, is it related to specific forms of behavior? Biochemists have shown that the hypothalamus is especially rich in both acetylcholine and norepineph-rine. What are they doing there?

Miller's conclusion at the time was restricted to certain biologically essential behaviors such as eating and drinking.

> Evidence is accumulating that a general homeostatic system, with both overt behavioral and internal physiological components, may use neural circuits that are chemically coded in the same way in at least certain different regions of the brain.[25]

The idea that different neurotransmitters could be regulating different motivational states gradually gained acceptance, and before long many behavioral neuroscientists were claiming that particular neurotransmitters in the brain were responsible for regulating hunger, thirst, aggression, and much other behavior.

In the 1960s, chemical stimulation of the brain was also used in combination with rewarding electrical stimulation as a way of investigating what neurotransmitters might be responsible for regulating pleasure and reward and what implications such findings might have for understanding how psychotherapeutic drugs worked and what caused mental disorders. The psychologist Larry Stein was responsible for much of the initial research in this area. The theory behind this research began to be expressed as early as 1962:

> It is common knowledge that insufficient positive reinforcement or reward depresses behavior and mood. Normal people become depressed after the loss of a loved person or desired goal and, in general, during periods of low "pay off." Even a rat's learned behavior is depressed or extinguished if the reward is no longer presented.
>
> Unlike the normal person or rat, the depressed patient despairs even when the environment supplies a normal amount of rewarding stimulation. This failure of rewarding stimulation to produce its usual energizing effect suggests that the neural reward mechanism of depressed patients is somehow deficient or pathologically hypoactive. In "primary" depressions, the deficiency may arise from within the reward system itself.[26]

Not only did Stein speculate that the "reward system" was involved in depression, but he and others even suggested that some impairment in this brain circuit might be the reason that schizophrenics had difficulty sustaining goal-directed behavior and why their thought processes drifted from topic to topic. A number of investigators began to demonstrate the effect that different drugs, including antidepressants and antipsychotics, had on the self-stimulation rate of rats pressing levers for "rewarding brain stimulation." Arguments later developed over whether it was norepinephrine or dopamine that was responsible for reward and pleasure. Despite such differences in the details, it became widely accepted that the "brain reward system" depended on biogenic amine neurotransmitters, a category that included both of these neurotransmitters.[27] This conclusion was supported by the demonstration that animals would self-stimulate in order to receive minute brain injections of drugs that released biogenic amines. Moreover, after Swedish investigators described the location of the neurons that made norepinephrine, serotonin, and dopamine in the brain, it became apparent that there was a close correspondence between the location of the biogenic amine neurotransmitters and the places where electrical and chemical stimulation were rewarding. These same brain areas were also the sites where stimulation could evoke much of the behavior, such as eating, drinking, sexual activity, and sleep, that is often impaired in mental disorders.

Biochemical Explanations of Psychotherapeutic Drugs

All these observations contributed to the acceptance of the idea that psychotherapeutic drugs alleviated mental disorders because they corrected an impairment of some brain neurotransmitter system. While the electrical and chemical stimulation studies just described were continuing, neuropharmacologists were finding evidence of how various psychotropic drugs affected neurotransmitter action. Almost none of this early work was done on the brain. So, for example, after it was discovered that serotonin caused the uterus to contract, it was found that small amounts of LSD could completely block this effect. Later, when serotonin was found in the brain it raised the possibility that LSD produced its psychological effects by blocking brain serotonin, a small step away from the speculation that schizophrenia is caused by a serotonin deficiency. As will be explained shortly, there was further support for this line of speculation when it was found that reserpine and the other early psychotherapeutic drugs also acted on the biogenic amine systems. The discovery that dopamine was a brain neurotransmitter led to the theory that schizophrenia was caused by an impairment of the dopamine rather than the serotonin system.[28] How this happened will be described in the next chapter.

Theories of Depression and the Action of Antidepressants

The first antidepressant, iproniazid, was accidentally discovered after it was observed that some tubercular patients became euphoric when treated with this drug. The first lead that biogenic amine neurotransmitters might be involved was provided by Albert Zeller, a chemically oriented bacteriologist in the Department of Biochemistry and Bacteriology at Northwestern University Medical School. In 1952, Zeller was studying iproniazid and isoniazid's effectiveness against tubercular bacilli. It was known that certain antibiotics and synthetic antitubercular drugs were effective because they inhibited bacterial enzymes, and Zeller, together with his colleagues, determine that isoniazid and iproniazid also inhibited mammalian enzymes. They found that iproniazid, which was the more effective antidepressant of the two, was also more effective in inhibiting the mammalian enzyme monoamine oxydase.

> Since monoamine oxydase is considered to be an important agent in the inactivation of adrenaline and noradrenaline [now commonly called epinephrine and norepinephrine], this strong inhibition of the enzyme may be connected with some side reactions produced by the drug, indicating a sympathetic stimulation.

As iproniazid was more effective in blocking monoamine oxydase than isoniazid and it was also a more effective mood elevator, Zeller and his colleagues considered the possibility that prolonging the action of the biogenic amines might explain how antidepressant drugs alleviated depression.[29] This hypothesis was given a big boost by some research on reserpine, a drug that had only just begun to arouse interest among western physicians and pharmacologists, despite its long history of use in India.

Reserpine—India's Miracle Drug

Reserpine, or at least an extract from the plant *Rauwolfia serpentina* (the root of the plant resembles a snake) was introduced into western psychiatry in the early 1950s, about the same time that chlorpromazine was being tested on patients. An extract from the plant had been used medicinally in India for more than one thousand years. It was considered to have a calming effect and to be useful to quiet babies and to treat insomnia, high blood pressure, snakebite, insanity, and much more. There were many legends about reserpine, including the apocryphal story that the mongoose chewed the plant before attacking a cobra. In the West, the curative powers attributed to the plant were mostly dismissed as unreliable anecdotes until western-trained Indian physicians began publishing reports of successful treatment of violently disturbed patients with *Rauwolfia*. The earliest scientific reports appeared in the 1930s, but because they were published in Indian medical journals they had little impact in the West.[30] By early 1950, however, the Squibb Pharmaceutical Company became interested in testing *Rauwolfia*'s reported capacity to lower blood pressure. Other pharmaceutical companies were also interested in different properties of *Rauwolfia*, and in 1953 chemists at Ciba isolated the active ingredient from the plant, determining that it was an alkaloid. The active ingredient was called reserpine, and Ciba marketed it as Serpasil, while other pharmaceutical companies used different proprietary names for the same drug.

In 1953, some people at the Squibb Pharmaceutical Company noticed a report in *The New York Times* that a Dr. R. A. Hakim of Ahmabad, India, had been awarded a gold medal for treating more than seven hundred schizophrenics with *Rauwolfia*.[31] Shortly afterward, Nathan S. Kline, a psychiatrist at Rockland State Hospital in Orangeburg, New York, contacted a friend at Squibb to try to obtain funds for a new research project. The two of them worked out an arrangement whereby Kline would be able to siphon off enough money to do his own project if he agreed to test reserpine on some of his psychiatric patients.[32] Kline tested reserpine, which Squibb called Raudixin, on many of his patients. Although the results were highly variable, Kline reported several instances of dramatic improvement following treatment with reserpine. A few patients, who were described as crippled by anxiety, were reported to have become relaxed and able to get on with their lives. Some delusional schizophrenic patients, while not cured, were able to think about other things besides their delusions. Kline did not believe, however, that reserpine altered what he called "the schizophrenic process" in chronic patients. Most patients became sedated to varying degrees, and like patients treated with chlorpromazine, they seemed to be indifferent to much around them. Kline also reported some favorable results both with assaultive patients, who became quite tractable, and with several obsessional patients. Despite this report, which implied that the effectiveness of reserpine left much to be desired, Kline was soon promoting it as an "effective sedative for use in mental hospitals," and he played a major role in stimulating enthusiasm for the possibility that this drug could alleviate the overcrowding in state mental hospitals.

After the psychiatrist Paul Hoch was appointed commissioner of mental health in New York state in 1955, he recommended that reserpine be given to all 94,000 patients in the state psychiatric hospitals. Averell Harriman, who was on the governor's staff, arranged a meeting with the governor. When Hoch estimated that it would take about $1.5 million to treat all the patients in the state mental hospitals with reserpine, Harriman, an investment banker, is reported to have responded that there would be no problem getting the funding. Not long afterward, reserpine was routinely administered at the New York state psychiatric institutions.[33] Reserpine had serious side effects, such as permanent movement disorders ("extrapyramidal symptoms") similar to those produced by chlorpromazine and the other phenothiazine drugs being used to treat psychoses. Despite this, reserpine was heavily used throughout the late 1950s and early 1960s. Its use was discontinued only after it was generally agreed that chlorpromazine and the other phenothiazines were more effective drugs, although they too had some of the same serious side effects. While reserpine is rarely used today, studies of its pharmacological properties laid the foundation for the theories of depression and mania that have dominated our thinking to this day.

The Neuropharmacology of Reserpine: An Important Model

It was the neuropharmacological studies of reserpine that proved critical for the development of the biochemical theories of depression. In 1955, Bernard "Steve" Brodie and colleagues at the National Institutes of Health in Bethesda, Maryland, reported that reserpine reduces the level of serotonin in the brain.[34] This was the first clear demonstration that a psychotherapeutic drug produced changes in the activity of a neurotransmitter. Brodie's work was stimulated by an earlier report by John Gaddum (see p. 15) that LSD also reduced serotonin activity. LSD, however, was not a psychotherapeutic drug. Brodie's report had an enormous impact partly because his laboratory was generally acknowledged to be at the frontier of neuropharmacology, attracting researchers from all over the world. Arvid Carlsson, for example, was in Brodie's laboratory at the time of the discovery of how reserpine affected serotonin, and after returning to Sweden he, together with his colleague Nils-Ake Hillarp, demonstrated that brain norepinephrine levels are also reduced by reserpine.[35] When dopamine was later recognized as a distinct neurotransmitter in the brain, Carlsson and Hillarp reported that reserpine also decreases this neurotransmitter. Thus, it was established that the three major biogenic amines in the brain, norepinephrine, serotonin, and dopamine, were all decreased by reserpine.[36]

Reserpine and the Biogenic Amine Theory of Depression

The breakthrough in understanding the neuropharmacology of reserpine stimulated a large number of animal studies with this drug. Researchers worldwide studied the effects of reserpine on behavior ranging from simple reflexive movements to complex conditioned emotional responses.[37] It was observed that animals administered reserpine showed a short period of increased excitement and motor activity, followed by a prolonged period of inactivity. The animals often had a hunched posture and an immobility that was thought to resemble catatonia. This second stage might last several days, during which time the animals appeared to be depressed. Further studies of the neuropharmacological action of reserpine were able to explain the dual action (excitement followed by immobility) of this drug. It was discovered that amine neurotransmitters are normally stored in little protective "pouches," called synaptic vesicles, which are located at the terminal endings of neurons adjacent to the synapse. Reserpine causes the biogenic amines to leak out from the protection of the vesicles, and this stimulated neighboring neurons and was responsible for the initial excitatory effect. Soon afterward, however, the biogenic amines that had leaked out were broken down ("degraded") by the enzyme monoamine oxydase. This breakdown process resulted in a long-lasting deficiency of biogenic amine neurotransmitters and it was this deficiency which is believed to have caused the prolonged period of inactivity and apparent depression.

Our understanding of the different ways that drugs could affect neurotransmitter activity was greatly enhanced as a consequence of the completely surprising observation of what happened when the antidepressant drug iproniazid was given to animals before the administration of reserpine. Under the influence of both drugs, the animals become very active, almost hyperenergized, and the second stage of inactivity that reserpine normally produced did not occur. Iproniazid by itself, however, did not produce any increase in activity. These surprising results were explained by investigators at the National Institutes of Health who learned that iproniazid blocks the production of the enzyme monoamine oxydase, which breaks down and terminates the action of the biogenic amine neurotransmitters, while reserpine causes biogenic amines to leak out from their protection in the synaptic vesicles. However, when animals are treated with iproniazid before being given reserpine, there is little monoamine oxydase available to inactivate these neurotransmitters, and the period of excitation is prolonged and not followed by any depression of activity. The knowledge gained from these experiments was extremely helpful in understanding the neuropharmacology of antidepressant drugs, and this soon led to what was called the "biogenic amine theory of depression."

Guy Everett and J. Toman extended the rat experiments with reserpine and iproniazid to monkeys, and in a 1959 publication, they compared all that was then known about how different drugs modify biogenic amine activity with the ability of these drugs to elevate or depress mood. Everett and Toman then presented one of the first explicit statements that the level of biogenic amine activity determines mood:

> One may speculate on the possible role of centrally active amines present in the brain in the normal activity and general responsiveness of an individual. An excess of these might result in irritability, restlessness and aggressiveness. In the opposite direction, a deficiency of these substances would result in depression and general lassitude. The favorable response to iproniazid therapy would in this scheme result from the increase in central catecholamine amines after inhibiting monoamine oxidase, an enzyme that metabolizes these amines.
>
> It would be presumptuous to expect that so simple a scheme would account for all the variations of motor behavior and reactivity in health and disease, but the evidence thus far obtained in animals has been highly reproducible and suggests that we may indeed be dealing with a biochemical area of major importance in the understanding of animal and human behavior. The way in which these substances are acting centrally is unknown.[38]

Everett and Toman did not implicate a specific neurotransmitter, but they were among the earliest to propose that depression was caused by a deficiency and mania from an excess in biogenic amine activity. The biogenic amine theory relied heavily on the fact that the effectiveness of drugs to alleviate either spontaneously occurring depression or what was called "reserpine-induced depression" seemed to be determined by their capacity to elevate biogenic amines. While Everett and Toman explicitly cautioned that there was no direct evidence that there was a deficiency of biogenic amines in depressed patients or an excess in manic patients, their review gave a big boost to the idea that the biogenic amines regulated mood.

However, the drug imipramine and the other tricyclic antidepressants seemed to contradict the biogenic amine theory of mood disorders. The tricyclic antidepressants (TADs) do not inhibit monoamine oxydase, and at the time it was thought this enzyme was the only way that biogenic amine action was terminated. Erik Jacobsen, another early proponent of the biogenic amine theory of depression, acknowledged that there were several problems with the theory. Jacobsen was puzzled by the fact that caffeine and amphetamine, two drugs that elevated the biogenic amines, were not effective antidepressants. Moreover, Erikson could offer no explanation of the action of the tricyclic antidepressants, and in autumn 1959 he stated that there was no known pharmacological effect of imipramine which can explain how this drug alleviated depression: "Where the effect of imipramine stands in this matter is still a complete riddle which must await elucidation. Here our present ignorance is such that not even a preliminary hypothesis can be offered."[39]

Jacobsen, unable to explain why the tricyclics acted as antidepressants but caffeine and amphetamine did not, suggested that these drugs might have a different affect on norepinephrine and serotonin. Jacobsen stated that when norepinephrine activity is increased it stimulates the central nervous system as a whole and elevates mood and "increases mental energy." He concluded that norepinephrine was more important than serotonin in elevating mood, because it had been reported that injection of serotonin into the brains of animals produced somnolence, not activation. The arguments about whether serotonin or norepinephrine activity level is the most critical for depression continue to this day, and many current antidepressant drugs tend to act on both of these neurotransmitters. While both serotonin and norepinephrine are biogenic amines, they can be further subdivided, based on chemical differences, into the indole amines, which include serotonin, and the catecholamines, which include norepinephrine, epinephrine, and dopamine. Thus, those who believed that norepinephrine was more critical for regulating mood began to call their theory a "catecholamine theory" of depression to emphasize their belief that a norepinephrine deficiency was more important as a cause of depression than serotonin.

The Puzzle of Tricyclic Antidepressant Drugs is Explained

Julius Axelrod and his colleagues rescued the catecholamine theory of mood disorders by solving the problem of the tricyclic antidepressant drugs. Axelrod, who received the Nobel Prize in 1970 for his many contributions to our understanding of biogenic amines metabolism, had in his own words a completely "unexpected life in research."[40] He had applied to several medical schools after completing his undergraduate studies at the City College of New York in 1933, but was not admitted to any of them. Axelrod was able to get a twenty-five-dollar-a-month job as a technician in an industrial hygiene laboratory where he tested vitamin supplements added to food. Although he managed to earn a master's degree in chemistry, attending New York University at night, Axelrod expected to remain in this laboratory for the rest of his life. However, his talent for chemistry, both as a bench worker and as a problem solver, began to be recognized around the New York City area and he started to receive other offers.

Axelrod joined Bernard "Steve" Brodie's group at New York University's Goldwater Memorial Hospital. With Brodie's encouragement, Axelrod experienced the excitement of research, studying how various compounds were changed in the body. In 1950, Axelrod moved with Steve Brodie to the National Heart Institute in Bethesda, but despite the growing recognition of the importance of his work, he was not promoted because he lacked a doctoral degree. So in 1955, at the age of forty-two, Axelrod took some time off from work to get a Ph.D. from George Washington University, which accepted a subset of his now many published articles on the metabolism of biogenic amines as his doctoral dissertation. Axelrod was finally given a small laboratory of his own in the National Institute of Mental Health. Most of his research at the time was involved in tracing the metabolic transformation of "sympathomimetic drugs," that is, drugs such as amphetamine and mescaline, which mimic the physiological effects of norepinephrine in the peripheral nervous system.

There were at the time two much-discussed theories of schizophrenia that seemed to involve norepinephrine or epinephrine metabolism. Both theories attributed the cause of schizophrenia to a toxic chemical that is formed as a result of an abnormal chemical process that breaks down (or metabolizes) a natural substance in the body. Robert Heath, a psychiatrist in New Orleans, claimed that he had isolated an abnormal "metabolite" (a residual product after a substance is metabolized) in the blood of schizophrenics that produced schizophrenic symptoms when injected into animals and human volunteers. Heath called this substance taraxein, from the Greek *taraxis*, meaning confusion or a disordered mind.[41] A similar theory was proposed by two Canadians, Abram Hoffer and Humphry Osmond. Working in Saskatchewan, these two psychiatrists reported that when epinephrine was exposed to air a red pigment developed, which indicated that adrenochrome, an abnormal "metabolite," had developed. Hoffer and Osmond argued that adrenochrome (referred to as the "red spot") was capable of producing hallucinations and schizophrenic thought processes. Both Hoffer and Osmond tested adrenochrome on themselves and reported the effects:

> Ten minutes after taking it, Dr. Osmond noticed that the ceiling had changed color and that the lighting had become brighter. He closed his eyes and saw a brightly colored pattern of dots which gradually formed fish-like shapes. He felt he was at the bottom of the sea or in an aquarium with a shoal of brilliant fishes. At one moment he thought he was a sea anemone in this pool. . . . When he left the laboratory, he "found the corridors outside sinister and unfriendly." [Osmond reported] "I wondered what the cracks on the floor meant and why there were so many of them. Once we got out-of-doors the hospital buildings, which I know

well, seemed sharp and unfamiliar. As we drove through the streets the houses appeared to have some special meaning, but I couldn't tell what it was. In one window I saw a lamp burning, and I was astonished by its grace and brilliance. I drew my friends' attention to it but they were unimpressed."

The second time Dr. Osmond took adrenochrome he found he had no feelings for human beings. "As we drove back to Abe's [Hoffer's] house a pedestrian walked across the road in front of us. I thought we might run him down, and watched with detached curiosity. We did not knock him down. I began to wonder whether I was a person any more and to think that I might be a plant or a stone. . . . As my feeling for these inanimate objects increased, my feeling for and my interest in humans diminished." . . . The next day he [Osmond] attended a scientific meeting, and during it he wrote this note: "Dear Abe, this damn stuff is still working. The odd thing is that stress brings it on, after about fifteen minutes."[42]

Much significance was attributed to the fact that stress seemed to precipitate the abnormal perceptions, because stress was known to activate the secretion of epinephrine and norepinephrine, the presumed source of adrenochrome. Seymour Kety, the NIMH psychiatrist who headed the intramural research program at the institute, found the adrenochrome theory most interesting, and he gave a seminar on Hoffer and Osmond's work. Axelrod was in the audience and was stimulated by the presentation. Because he was now working at a mental health research institute, he felt obliged to do some research related to psychiatric disorders. He was well prepared from previous work to study how epinephrine was changed in the body. Kety, who was anxious to pursue Hoffer and Osmond's theory, obtained some radioactive (tritiated) labeled epinephrine and norepinephrine from the New England Nuclear Corporation for Axelrod to use in tracing the metabolic fate of these neurotransmitter's in the body and brain.[43]

Although adrenochrome was produced when epinephrine was exposed to air, Axelrod found no evidence that it could be produced in the body, and the adrenochrome theory and the taraxein theory of schizophrenia were eventually abandoned. In the process, however, Axelrod did learn an enormous amount about epinephrine and norepinephrine that eventually explained the action of the tricyclic antidepressant drugs. At the time, it was widely thought that the enzymatic degrading of norepinephrine by monoamine oxydase was the only way of terminating the action of that neurotransmitter. However, Axelrod and some colleagues had in 1961 published a paper in *Science* demonstrating another mechanism that worked in the peripheral nervous system. At a 1966 symposium held in

Washington, Axelrod, together with Jacques Glowinski and Leslie Iverson, noted that:

> It has been known for some time that many antidepressants drugs can act as inhibitors of norepinephrine [re]uptake at peripheral adrenergic synapses. . . . It has been suggested that similar mechanisms at central adrenergic synapses may explain the action of antidepressant drugs on the central nervous system [that is, the brain]. According to this hypothesis, norepinephrine and dopamine are considered to be neurotransmitters at central adrenergic synapses which have similar properties to peripheral adrenergic synapses. In the brain, the released catecholamines are inactivated similarly by a re-uptake into the presynaptic nerve terminals. Antidepressant drugs which interfere with this re-uptake mechanism may thus potentiate the actions of the released amines in the brain.[44]

Axelrod and his colleagues injected radioactive norepinephrine into the brain of rats, and afterward they determined how much of the injected norepinephrine had entered the cells. They then did the same thing after administering tricyclic antidepressants to the rats. They found that in the brain as well as in the peripheral nervous system, the tricyclic drugs blocked the reabsorption (reuptake) into the neurons. It was clear that enzymatic degrading by monoamine oxydase was not the only way that norepinephrine action was terminated, but rather it could also be accomplished by a reuptake process that removed the norepinephrine from the synapse. It thus became clear that both classes of antidepressants, the monoamine oxydase inhibitors and the tricyclic antidepressants, "potentiated" (enhanced) the action of amine neurotransmitters, one by inhibiting monoamine oxydase, the other by interfering with their reuptake. The reuptake mechanism is illustrated in Figure 3-1.

The Biogenic Amine Theory of Emotion Becomes Established

Three important review articles emanating from researchers at the influential National Institute of Mental Health played a major role in gaining wide acceptance for the biogenic theory of mood disorders. Two of these articles, both published in 1965, concluded that mood disorders, both depression and mania, were caused by abnormal functioning of brain biogenic amines, and the evidence and arguments presented were almost identical. William Bunney and John Davis, for example, reviewed the clinical evidence that drugs that elevate the biogenic amines "are clinically effective

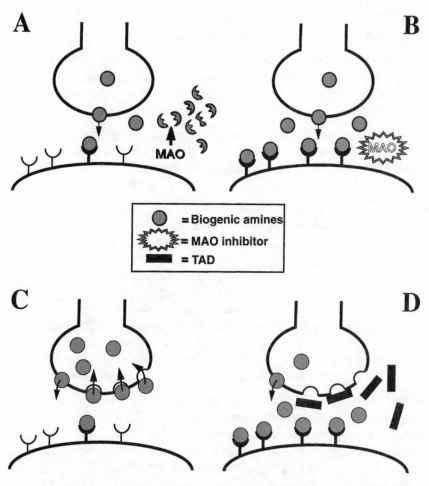

Figure 3-1 A comparison of the hypothesized action of the two main classes of anti-depressant drugs: monoamine oxydase inhibitors (MAO-I) and tricyclic antidepressants (TADs). A) It was believed that the action of the biogenic amines was terminated when the enzyme monoamine oxydase normally broke down (degraded or inactivated) these neuro-transmitters. B) MAO-I antidepressant drugs inhibit the action of the enzyme, which results in prolonging the action of the biogenic amines on postsynaptic receptors. C) Later, the research of Julius Axelrod and colleagues demonstrated that the main way biogenic amine activity is terminated is through a reuptake of the neurotransmitters into the presynaptic neuron that released them. D) The TADs prolong the action of the biogenic amines by blocking the reuptake of the neurotransmitter, leaving it in the synapse where it can con-tinue to act on postsynaptic receptors.

in the treatment of many depressives," while such drugs as reserpine "have been associated with severe depressive reactions in a significant number of hypertensive [high blood pressure] patients treated with these drugs."

Bunney and Davis did acknowledge that there were some important gaps in the evidence. For example, they wrote that:

> It has yet to be shown that an alteration in catecholamine metabolism occurs in the brain of depressed patients. . . . Although in this paper we have focused on NEP [norepinephrine] there are other neurohumors which may play a role in depressive reactions—serotonin and dopamine.[45]

The NIMH investigators became increasingly committed to establishing that the catecholamine norepinephrine was most critical for mood disturbances. Thus, in the second of the 1965 reviews, Joseph Schildkraut concluded:

> Those drugs which cause depletion and inactivation of norepinephrine centrally produce sedation or depression, while drugs which increase or potentiate norepinephrine are associated with behavioral stimulation or excitement and generally exert an antidepressant effect in man. From these findings . . . a number of investigators have formulated a hypothesis about the pathophysiology of the affective disorders. This hypothesis, which has been designated the "catecholamine hypothesis of affective disorders," proposes that some, if not all depressions are associated with an absolute or relative deficiency of catecholamines, particularly norepinephrine at functionally important adrenergic receptor sites in the brain. Elation conversely may be associated with an excess of such amines.[46]

Schildkraut acknowledged that it was troublesome for the theory that several drugs, such as amphetamine, that elevate catechol amine activity are not effective antidepressants, and as Bunney and Davis had noted, he admitted that it had not yet been established that manic or depressed patients have any abnormal catecholamine activity. Nevertheless, Schildkraut described several "escape hatches" that made it possible to discount studies that looked for, but did not find, abnormal amine levels in the brains of depressed or manic patients. First of all, excesses or deficiencies of norepinephrine might exist only at certain brain sites, and therefore, it might be missed when only total brain levels are measured. Schildkraut also noted that depression was not a single homogeneous disease entity, and it was possible that the catecholamine theory of mood disorders might be applicable only to certain subgroups of depressed patients. Furthermore, Schildkraut hypothesized that norepinephrine levels might be normal in depressed patients, but they might have a deficiency in the receptors that respond to this neurotransmitter.[47]

Two years later, in 1967, Schildkraut and Seymour Kety, the senior psychiatrist at NIMH, collaborated on an article entitled "Biogenic Amines and Emotion." The article was published as the lead article in the journal *Science*.[48] Schildkraut and Kety argued forcefully that it was norepinephrine rather than serotonin that regulated mood states. They maintained that pharmacological studies had shown that even though both norepinephrine and serotonin levels were decreased by reserpine, it was the norepinephrine decrease that was responsible for the depression produced by reserpine. Schildkraut and Kety used behavioral excitement in animals as an indication of mood, and they reported that when norepinephrine is elevated behavioral excitement occurs, but that in instances where serotonin is elevated alone "without an increase in norepinephrine, no behavioral excitement was observed." Schildkraut and Kety also claimed that the "brain reward system," as revealed by the self-stimulation studies in rats described above, was primarily responsive to manipulations of norepinephrine levels. They also claimed that both electro-convulsive shock therapy used to alleviate depression and lithium used to treat mania also had their greatest effect on norepinephrine levels.

The evidence and arguments presented by Schildkraut and Kety and the others proposing catecholamine theories appeared persuasive at the time, but, as will be discussed in the next chapter, it is much less convincing today.[49] In passing, however, it might be noted that while Schildkraut and Kety minimized the relevance of serotonin, Arvid Carlsson reached the opposite conclusion. Carlsson had observed that those tricyclic antidepressants which had their greatest effect in blocking norepinephrine reuptake, and therefore prolonged the activity of this neurotransmitter, tended to increase motor activity in animals, but not necessarily mood. In contrast, drugs that primarily inhibited serotonin reuptake seemed to elevate mood, but not activity. In clinical trials on patients, Carlsson found that the tricyclics that were most effective in blocking serotonin reuptake were most effective as antidepressants and that blocking norepinephrine reuptake did not add to the effectiveness of any of the drugs he tested.[50] The relative importance of serotonin and norepinephrine still has not been resolved, and the whole question of how antidepressant drugs work and what causes depression is no more clear today than it was in the 1960s. This whole issue will be discussed more fully and more critically in the following chapter.

Antipsychotic Drugs and Schizophrenia

Even though the controversy over the question of brain neurotransmitters had not been completely resolved in the mid-1950s, there were a number of neuropharmacologists who started speculating that neurotransmitters were somehow involved in mental disorders. While norepinephrine and serotonin were thought to be the neurotransmitters involved in depression, dopamine eventually assumed that role in schizophrenia. Before that, however, studies of the action of hallucinogenic plants had implicated serotonin in schizophrenia. In a 1954 article in *Science*, D. W. Woolley and E. Shaw, two investigators at the Rockefeller Institute for Medical Research, noted that LSD, harmaline, yohimbine, and other drugs obtained from hallucinogenic plants all block the action of serotonin on smooth muscles.[51] They went on to argue that the fact that serotonin has been found in the brain suggests that the mental changes caused by the drugs are the result of a serotonin deficiency that they induce in the brain. Woolley and Shaw concluded: "If this be true, then the naturally occurring mental disorders, for example, schizophrenia—which are mimicked by these drugs, may be pictured as being the result of a cerebral serotonin deficiency arising from a metabolic failure rather than from drug action." They then speculated that the naturally occurring mental disorders might be treated with serotonin.

Woolley and Shaw's 1954 article contained one of the first explicit statements that naturally occurring mental disorders might be caused by a biochemical abnormality, although the eminent British pharmacologist Sir John Gaddum (see p. 15) had speculated earlier that a serotonin deficiency might be the cause of mental illness after he demonstrated that LSD was capable of blocking some of the peripheral physiological effects of serotonin.[52]

Two years later, in April 1956, at a conference sponsored by the New York Academy of Science, serotonin was still afforded the dominant role in speculation about the cause of schizophrenia. The meeting, which was organized by the NIMH psychiatrist Seymour Kety, was entitled "Conference on the Pharmacology of Psychotomimetic & Psychotherapeutic Drugs."[53] The LSD-serotonin-schizophrenia connection was discussed by many of the participants. Even though Sir John Gaddum had provided the main evidence that LSD inhibited serotonin activity and he had earlier speculated that a serotonin deficiency might be the cause of schizophrenia, he pointed out that this could not be the sole explanation of that disorder. Gaddum noted that substances such as ergometrine and Dibenamine also block serotonin, but they do not produce psychotic states, and mescaline, which produces the same psychotic symptoms as LSD, does not block serotonin.[54]

A paper by Steve Brodie and Parkhurst Shore of NIH tried to salvage the "serotonin theory" by suggesting that norepinephrine may work in conjunction with serotonin to cause schizophrenia.[55] They noted that investigations of LSD and other psychotomimetics had raised the possibility that disturbed mental function might be due to a deficiency of brain serotonin activity, but there were a number of problems with this idea, as Gaddum had pointed out. Brodie and Shore noted that while both reserpine and chlorpromazine alleviated schizophrenia, only reserpine had a major influence on brain serotonin level, while chlorpromazine seemed to act predominately on norepinephrine. Despite this, surveys of psychiatrists in both the United States and France had indicated that chlorpromazine was more effective in treating schizophrenia than reserpine. Clearly, serotonin was not the whole story of schizophrenia.

Brodie and Shore proposed a compromise by suggesting that a critical balance between serotonin and norepinephrine was essential for normal mental states, and when the level of either neurotransmitter was substantially out of line, schizophrenia might develop. Arguing by analogy from the sympathetic and parasympathetic branches of the autonomic nervous system and from some peripheral effects of chlorpromazine and reserpine, Brodie and Shore proposed that both serotonin and norepinephrine activity could produce mental imbalance, but by different mechanisms—like pushing or pulling. Others developed similar theories involving norepinephrine and serotonin, but as more data became available the theories became increasing complicated and unsatisfactory and they were eventually replaced by a dopamine theory of schizophrenia.

The Dopamine Theory of Schizophrenia

The origin of the "dopamine theory" of schizophrenia was closely tied to the discovery of the role of that neurotransmitter in Parkinson's disease. It was well known that chlorpromazine, reserpine, and the other antipsychotic drugs used to treat schizophrenia often produced "extrapyramidal" impairments in movement similar to those seen in Parkinson's patients. In fact, H. J. Dasse, a prominent German psychiatrist, who agreed with others that "there is no antipsychotic effect without extrapyramidal side effects," developed a "handwriting test" to follow the effect over time of antipsychotic medication. Patients were asked to write the same line every day, the idea being that as the drug worked the handwriting would get smaller and smaller, as it tends to do with parkinsonism.[56]

There had been several reports from pathologists that the substantia nigra region in the brains of Parkinson's patients was abnormal.[57] These reports claimed that many of the characteristically black staining neurons, which had given the substantia nigra its name, were missing in the brains of Parkinson's patients. When Swedish histochemists demonstrated that a major dopamine pathway in the brain originated in the substantia nigra, it raised speculation that Parkinson's disease might be caused by a deficiency in dopamine, and the parkinsonlike symptoms produced by the antipsychotic drugs might result from a blocking of dopamine activity. Indeed, Arvid Carlsson and his coworkers in Sweden reported in 1957 that the parkinsonlike symptoms produced in experimental animals by reserpine could be blocked by administering dopa (a dopamine precursor), but not by a serotonin precursor.[58] These observations, however, were not pursued clinically until several years later, and it would be more than a decade before L-DOPA would be widely used to treat Parkinson's disease.

The speculation of the Swedish investigators that Parkinson's patients were suffering from a dopamine deficiency was confirmed in 1959 when the Viennese neuropharmacologist Oleh Hornykiewicz examined the brain of a patient who had died with Parkinson's disease. Hornykiewicz tested the brain with iodine, a substance that makes dopamine appear pink. Later, he recounted his excitement after he had examined the caudate nucleus and putamen (two brain areas in the striatum known to contain high levels of dopamine):

> Instead of the pink color given by the comparatively high amounts of dopamine in the control samples, the reaction vials containing the extracts of the Parkinson's disease striatum showed hardly a tinge of pink discoloration. The brain dopamine deficiency in Parkinson's disease, today needs no reference to the original observation—at that moment, however, I literally could see it with my own naked eye![59]

Later, it was demonstrated that the dopamine level in the brains of Parkinson's patients was only about 20 percent of normal, while serotonin and norepinephrine levels were either normal or close to normal. Not long after this, Hornykiewicz and the Austrian neurologist Walther Birkmayer began to treat Parkinson's patients with levodopa (L-DOPA), a precursor of dopamine capable of bypassing the blood brain barrier and entering the brain. While they observed some encouraging short-term benefits, which were published in 1961, it was found that the treatment caused nauseousness, vomiting, and other objectionable side effects. After several tests with equivocal results, George Cotzius and his colleagues at the Brookhaven National Laboratory reported in 1967 that when the dose level was gradually increased the side effects were much less severe and many (but not all) Parkinson's patients were helped by L-DOPA treatment.[60]

That a dopamine deficiency had been established to underlie Parkinson's disease and that antipsychotic drugs produced parkinsonlike symptoms suggested that these drugs might work by blocking dopamine activity, and schizophrenia might be caused by excessive dopamine activity. However, the search for evidence of abnormally high levels of dopamine in schizophrenics was not successful. It was possible, though, that schizophrenics did not have unusually high brain dopamine levels but might be hypersensitive to even normal dopamine levels. As the concept of "receptors" is critical to understanding the developments that followed, it is necessary to insert a small, but interesting, digression to explain how the concept of neurotransmitter "receptors" evolved.

Around the end of the nineteenth century, the British physiologist John Newport Langley was studying the capacity of different drugs to stimulate terminals of the autonomic nervous system. The autonomic nervous system refers to that part of the peripheral nervous system which stimulates visceral organs and glands. Among the drugs Langley experimented with were nicotine and muscarine. Nicotine, which had been isolated from tobacco leaves in 1828, had been chemically characterized around 1889, while the pharmacological properties of the alkaloid muscarine, obtained from the poisonous mushroom *Amanita muscaria*, had first been described in the 1860s. Langley discovered that these drugs stimulated some neurons that used the neurotransmitter acetylcholine, but at other acetylcholine sites they either had no effect or might produce an opposite effect, a "paralysis" caused by a blocking of all transmission across the synapse. It was clear to Langley that to understand what was going on, it was necessary to consider the interactions between the drug and the cell. There must be, Langley reasoned, different substances in cells that account for the different ways they respond to the same drug. Langley coined the term "receptive substances" to explain these drug-cell interactions.[61]

It was not very long before Langley's term "receptor substance" was shortened to just "receptor." It was also discovered that both muscarine and nicotine stimulated acetylcholine synapses, but there were differences. While the drug atropine blocked the action of muscarine at acetylcholine synapses, it did not block the effects of nicotine. From such experiments, it was concluded there must be at least two different types of acetylcholine receptors, a muscarinic and a nicotinic receptor. These important observations established for the first time that there were different receptor subtypes for a given neurotransmitter. The concept of receptor subtypes now plays a major role in current theorizing about the action of psychotherapeutic drugs, as will be discussed at a later point.

The concept of receptors was advanced enormously by Alfred Clark, a professor at the University of London and later at the University of Edinburgh.[62] During the 1920s, Clark had performed a series of quantitative studies on the responses of cells to different drug concentrations. He determined the threshold concentration of drugs, which is the dose just barely capable of evoking a weak response, and also the concentration that evoked the maximal response. Using a microinjection technique, Clark also found that many drugs had no effect when injected directly into a cell, but they did have an effect when the cell surface was immersed in a solution containing the drug. Clark concluded from these observations that many drugs act only on the surface, or membrane, of a cell. Furthermore, by calculating the size of different drug molecules and the area of the cell surface, Clark was able to determine that the maximum effect of a drug occurred long before the entire surface of a cell was covered by the drug. That was interpreted to mean that drugs did not act on the entire surface of the cell membrane, but only on some discrete units on the membrane. From such experiments Clark was able to draw many insightful conclusions about the properties of receptors, which he summarized in his seminal monograph published in 1933:

> Measurements of the quantities of drugs that suffice to produce an action on cells, prove that in the case of powerful drugs the amount fixed is only sufficient to cover a small fraction of the cell surface. . . .
>
> The simplest probable conception of drug action is that potent drugs occupy certain specific receptors on the cell surface, and that these specific receptors only comprise a small fraction of the total cell surface.[63]

Although the receptor was a hypothetical construct whose existence could only be inferred, Clark and others who followed him were able to use experimental results to infer a number of properties of drugs and receptors that proved to be amazingly prophetic. Clark inferred, for example, that some drugs were able to act at receptors as antagonists, blocking the action normally triggered by an agonistic drug. He also concluded that the number of receptors a cell possessed varied, and this was responsible for the effectiveness of a drug being different at different times. Clark was able to infer these changes from careful quantitative studies and an insightful analysis of the best way to interpret the data. Today, using radioactive drugs that bind to particular receptors and "scintillation counters" that can detect and quantify the amount of radioactivity, it is possible to estimate the number of receptors and the capacity of different drugs to bind to them.

One of the first specific suggestions that antipsychotic drugs might alleviate schizophrenia by blocking dopamine receptors was made in 1966 by J. M. Van Rossum, a professor of pharmacology at the University of Nijmegen in The Netherlands. As discussed above, it was known by this time that the movement disorder seen in Parkinson's patients was caused by a dopamine deficiency. Van Rossum had demonstrated earlier that the inverse was also true by showing that the increases in locomotor activity produced by such psychomotor stimulants as amphetamine and cocaine seemed to be caused by stimulating dopamine receptors. Van Rossum later found that antipsychotic drugs block the capacity of amphetamine to increase locomotion in rats and that such powerful antipsychotics as haloperidol are particularly potent in blocking amphetamine-induced locomotion. Since these antipsychotic drugs tested were found to be only weak antagonists of norepinephrine, Van Rossum concluded:

> The hypothesis that neuroleptic [antipsychotic] drugs may act by blocking dopamine receptors in the brain has been substantiated by preliminary experiments with a few selective and potent neuroleptic drugs. . . .
> When the hypothesis of dopamine blockade by neuroleptic agents can be further substantiated it may have fargoing consequences for the pathophysiology of schizophrenia. Overstimulation of dopamine receptors

could then be part of the etiology. Obviously such an over stimulation might be caused by overproduction of dopamine, production of substances with dopamine actions (methoxy derivatives), abnormal susceptibility of the receptors, etc.[64]

Van Rossum bolstered his argument by noting that antipsychotics block the blood pressure changes induced by dopamine and that the more clinically potent antipsychotics were more effective in blocking the blood pressure changes. Van Rossum argued that antipsychotics compete with dopamine in occupying dopamine receptors by noting that when amphetamine-induced locomotion is blocked by a neuroleptic drug, the blockade is overcome by increasing the dose of amphetamine. Although some of the results discussed by Van Rossum are subject to different interpretation, he concluded that taken together they support the "dopamine hypothesis," by which he meant that antipsychotics work by blocking dopamine receptors and that the pathophysiology of schizophrenia involved an "overstimulation" of dopamine receptors.

At about the same time, Arvid Carlsson was also studying the effects of antipsychotic drugs on dopamine activity, and his initial results, puzzling as they were, almost made him reject the "dopamine hypothesis" of schizophrenia. In the end, however, after solving the puzzle, Carlsson was able to increase our knowledge of the way the dopamine system (and probably other neurotransmitter systems as well) functions. Carlsson knew that when animals are given the dopamine precursor L-DOPA, brain dopamine levels increase and animals became more active. When an antipsychotic drug was given along with L-DOPA the animals did not become more active, which is what he expected would happen if the antipsychotic blocked the effects of dopamine. However, Carlsson was puzzled by the finding that the antipsychotics significantly increased the brain levels of the dopamine "metabolite" HVA (homovanillic acid is the main "metabolite," or breakdown product of dopamine). Trying to understand why this happened eventually led to a better understanding of how antipsychotic drugs work and how the dopamine system attempts to compensate for the action of these drugs. It occurred to Carlsson that it was possible to make sense of these paradoxical results, if the blocking of dopamine receptors activated a feedback signal that stimulated dopamine cells to fire more rapidly and to increase the amount of dopamine released at their terminals. This speculation has turned out to be true and it is now reasonably well understood, as explained in Figure 3-2.

Carlsson's work was a major contribution to our understanding of the dopamine system, but it was difficult to argue that it was the inhibition of dopamine that was critical for alleviating schizophrenia when all the antipsychotic drugs at the time also inhibited serotonin and norepineph-

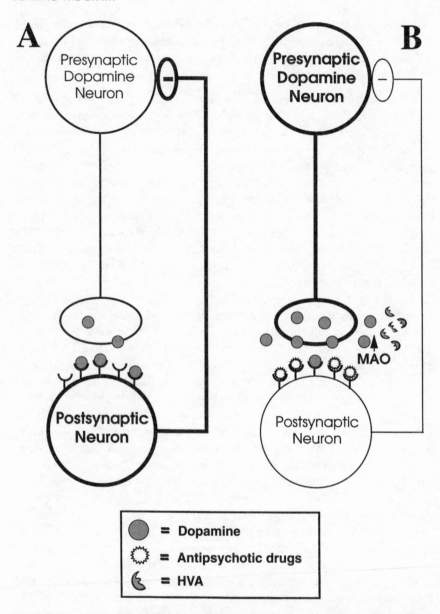

Figure 3-2 Arvid Carlsson's explanation of the effects of antipsychotic drugs on dopamine levels and on dopamine metabolites. A) When dopamine is normally released and activates the receptors across the synapse a "negative feedback" neural pathway inhibits the presynaptic neuron and less dopamine is released. B) When antipsychotic drugs block the dopamine receptors the "negative feedback" signal become weaker and more dopamine is released from the presynaptic neuron. Because the postsynaptic receptors are blocked by the antipsychotic drug, dopamine accumulates in the synapse where it is degraded by monoamine oxydase into its metabolite, homovanillic acid (HVA).

rine. How could it be shown that it was the blocking of dopamine, rather than the blocking of norepinephrine or serotonin activity, that determined a drug's effectiveness in alleviating schizophrenia? Philip Seeman and his colleagues at the University of Toronto attempted to answer this question by correlating the clinical potency of different antipsychotic drugs with their capacity to block dopamine activity. The potency of a drug refers to how small a dose is clinically effective. A potent drug requires only a low dose, while a less potent drug require a higher dose to be equally effective. There are many ways that a drug can inhibit the action of a neurotransmitter. A drug might, for example, block the synthesis of a neurotransmitter, or it might block the release of the transmitter from the presynaptic neuron, or it might block the receptors that the neurotransmitter acts on.

Seeman and his colleagues found that the drugs that were most potent clinically were also the most effective in inhibiting dopamine release. When these results were first published, it caused great excitement, as it appeared that Seeman had provided strong evidence that blocking dopamine release was what made antipsychotic drugs effective. Unfortunately, the excitement soon cooled when it was realized that the experiments had been done in vitro, in a dish, not on patients or even on animals, and that the doses required to inhibit the release of dopamine in a slice of brain tissue were several hundred times higher than what could be used clinically. The results did not seem to apply to realistic conditions, as Seeman eventually had to acknowledge: "To our dismay, all of these blocking actions occurred at concentrations much too high to be of clinical relevance."[65]

In 1975, both Seeman's group in Toronto and a group headed by Solomon Snyder at the Johns Hopkins Medical School in Baltimore took advantage of a newly developed technique for measuring the relative capacity of different drugs to bind to dopamine receptors and to block the receptors from being stimulated by dopamine. Both groups were able to report that with clinically relevant dose levels there was a high correlation between the potency of different antipsychotic drugs and their capacity to block dopamine receptors (Figure 3-3).[66]

As Snyder later wrote: "If blocking the action of dopamine relieves schizophrenic symptoms, then one could speculate that schizophrenic abnormalities are related to excess dopamine release or perhaps hypersensitive dopamine receptors."[67] Snyder recognized that "the actual schizophrenic abnormality might involve another system which, however, is neuronally linked to dopamine," and that it was not clear, therefore, whether dopamine is directly or indirectly involved. He concluded this neurotransmitter appears to play an important role in the etiology of schizophrenia.

During this same period, studies of the drug amphetamine, a psychomotor stimulant, also provided support for the idea that excessive

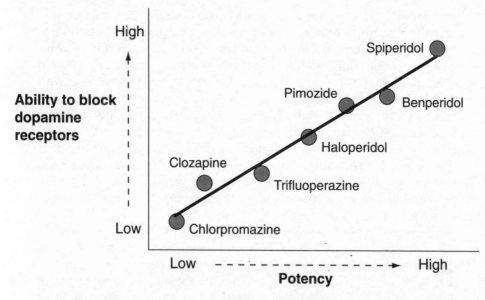

Figure 3-3 An illustration of the relationship claimed to exist between the capacity of antipsychotic drugs to block dopamine receptors and their potency in treating schizophrenia. As large individual differences exist in the effective dose of different antipsychotic drugs, the strength of the relationship may have been exaggerated by assigning a potency rating that makes the relationship appear particularly strong.

dopamine activity might be the cause of schizophrenia. During World War II, amphetamine was commonly used to maintain the alertness of pilots and other military personnel who had to be on duty continuously for long periods of time. Amphetamine increases the capacity for mental and physical work, but at high dose levels, the drug can produce euphoria (a psychological "high"), an exaggerated and unrealistic feeling of competence, and it may produce hallucinations and paranoid delusions that resemble those seen in schizophrenia.[68]

Shortly after World War II, amphetamine abuse became a serious drug problem in many countries. Following prolonged amphetamine use, people behaved so bizarrely they ended up in emergency wards, where they were commonly diagnosed as paranoid schizophrenics. When methamphetamine, a potent form of the drug, is used violent behavior often occurs. According to one study, in 1994, 45 percent of the people arrested for violent crimes tested positive for methamphetamine.

In the 1960s, there was great interest in finding out which effect of amphetamine was responsible for inducing schizophreniclike symptoms. It had been shown that amphetamine increases norepinephrine, dopamine, and serotonin activity, but it was not known which of these effects, if any, was responsible for the symptoms.[69] Because of obvious ethical concerns, only a few attempts to induce "amphetamine psychosis" experimentally were undertaken with human subjects, but extensive studies have been conducted on animals.[70] It was found that high doses of amphetamine produced extremely repetitive acts, called "stereotyped behavior," and this was widely used as an animal model of "amphetamine psychosis."[71]

Using drugs that blocked either norepinephrine, dopamine, or serotonin before administering amphetamine, it was determined that only the blocking of dopamine prevented amphetamine from evoking stereotyped behavior. Of course, animal stereotyped behavior was not schizophrenia, but humans who became paranoid under the influence of amphetamine often exhibited some type of stereotyped behavior. Human stereotyped behavior evoked by amphetamine was well known in the drug culture, and it even was given special names. For example, in Sweden stereotyped behavior was called "punding," and in the Haight-Ashbury district of San Francisco it was called "knick-knacking." Stereotyped behavior in humans is characterized by a repetitious examining, dismantling, rearranging, or cleaning of minutiae and sometimes scanning, probing, and prying behavior that could lead to paranoid thoughts.[72] Everett Ellinwood and Abraham Sudilovsky described a person experiencing paranoid delusions under the influence of amphetamine who said:

> I looked everywhere for clues, under the rugs, behind the pictures, and I took things apart. I read magazines looking at the periods with a magnifying glass, looking for codes. It would have helped me solve the mystery [of a boy friend's behavior].[73]

The results of the studies of amphetamine-induced stereotyped behavior provided further support for the belief that dopamine hyperactivity caused schizophrenia, because blocking dopamine activity alone seemed to prevent the behavior from occurring. Thus, it became increasingly accepted that excessive dopamine activity might be the cause of schizophrenia while blocking dopamine receptors seemed to be a common property of all antipsychotic drugs. Still, it was recognized that there was no direct evidence that schizophrenia was caused by excessive dopamine activity. Initially, this was only an inference drawn from the evidence that blocking dopamine seemed to be critical for alleviating this disorder. There have now been several claims that evidence of excessive dopamine activity has been found in the brains of schizophrenics, but as this evidence is controversial it is best discussed in the next chapter, where a more critical examination of the evidence and the inferences drawn from that evidence is provided.

Lithium and Mood Disorders

When John Cade discovered the lithium treatment of mania he had initially been looking for some toxic substance in the urine of mental patients that was the cause of their illness. As described in the previous chapter, lithium was used only inadvertently, simply as a convenient solvent for uric acid. Later, when Cade tested lithium on patients with different mental illnesses, he found that only the manic patients seemed to benefit from the treatment. He concluded that lithium was a calming drug, but he had no explanation of how it might work. When others demonstrated that not only manic patients but also patients suffering from some kinds of depression could benefit from lithium, many people were skeptical that one drug could both calm manics and elevate the mood of those who were depressed. It seemed that lithium somehow acted to normalize mood by preventing abnormal emotional swings in either direction, but no one knew how this might occur. Estimates of the effectiveness of lithium treatment vary widely and depending on the symptoms, but, on average, it is claimed that lithium prevents a relapse of manic-depressive disorder in about 60 percent of patients. However, it was found that placebo treatment was effective in about 20 percent of similar patients, which means that only about 40 percent of manic-depressive patients were actually helped by the lithium treatment.

The short answer to the question of how one drug could help patients with manic-depressive disorders, manic patients, and some who are only depressed, is that we do not know. The initial efforts to explain lithium's action concentrated on its effects on neurotransmitters. There have been claims that lithium decreases norepinephrine activity and increases serotonin activity, but these claims were not confirmed by others and the interpretation was complicated by the finding that the acute (short-term) effects on neurotransmitters may be opposite to the chronic (long-term) effects. Lithium can partially replace the sodium and calcium present in neurons and these electrolytes are known to modulate neuronal excitability and neurotransmitter release. Lithium also inhibits certain intracellular enzymes that are important for protein synthesis, and when it is administered early to immature fruit flies and frogs abnormal development often occurs. The unadulterated truth is that lithium has a huge number of effects, but no one really knows how any of these may relate to its therapeutic effectiveness.

Current theories have shifted the focus to the possibility that lithium might somehow affect the capacity of a neuron to respond to the activation of its receptors. The action that is being looked at takes place within the cell (rather than on the cell membrane) and involves what is called the "second messenger system."[74] In the parlance of neuroscientists, the "first messenger system" is the neurotransmitter (or hormone) that carries a "message" to a cell by acting on a receptor, generally located on the cell membrane. These receptors then pass the message along to a "second messenger" within the nerve cell and this starts a chain of chemical reactions that can modify the responsiveness of a neuron. Without getting too technical, since the hypothesis is highly speculative and far from proven, the idea is that lithium somehow interferes with the second messenger. If there is a shortage of the second messenger in all cells, then any neurotransmitter's effect would be dampened. Furthermore, if it is assumed (despite the lack of evidence) that both depression and mania are caused by the overactivity of a neurotransmitter system, although a different one for each condition, then dampening the capacity of all nerve cells to respond to neurotransmitters might prevent wild swings of mood in either direction. While not an illogical hypothesis, it remains only a highly speculative one.

A point that needs to be kept in mind is that unlike the case with depression and schizophrenia, where the treatment is usually assumed (although far from proven, as it will be argued in the next chapter) to be correcting a neurotransmitter excess or deficiency, no one thinks that any of the disorders that are helped by lithium treatment are actually caused by a lithium deficiency. There is no reason to assume that lithium is correcting the cause of any of the conditions it alleviates. Moreover, it has been shown that anticonvulsant drugs, such as carbamazepine (Tegretol) and valproate (Depakene), which have different neuropharmacological properties, can, in many instances, be just as effective as lithium in alleviating manic-depressive disorders.[75] There is no doubt that many patients suffering from mania, depression, or a manic-depressive disorder have been helped by lithium treatment or by one of the anticonvulsant drugs, but, as will be discussed, the proportion of patients that receive significant help from these drugs is considerably less than commonly asserted. Moreover, it should be recognized that no theory proposed to explain how any of these drugs work has been able to gather much support.

Anxiety, Anxiolytics, and Benzodiazepine Receptors

Although the benzodiazepine drugs proved to be much safer than either the barbiturates or meprobamate, all three classes of drugs had similar effects in alleviating anxiety, producing sedation, and causing muscles to relax. The possibility had to be considered that to a certain extent all of these drugs acted on the same neural structures (substrate). One way that pharmacologists determine whether drugs that have similar effects act on the same structures is to perform a "cross-tolerance" test. Drug tolerance refers to the tendency of a drug to lose effectiveness when it is repeatedly administered and a higher dose is required in order to produce the initial effect. A "cross-tolerance" test is performed by giving repeated doses of one drug until a tolerance has clearly developed and then administering a second drug at a dose that would normally be effective unless the tolerance to the first drug has transferred to the second drug. If a transfer occurs, it is assumed (although not really proven) that both drugs act on the same neural substrate, or at least on closely related structures.

In studies performed in the early 1960s, it turned out that not only was there a cross-tolerance between the barbiturates, meprobamate, and the benzodiazepines, but a cross-tolerance was also evident between alcohol and any of the above three classes of drugs. If a tolerance was developed to any one of these drugs, a tolerance also developed to all the others. This implied that all of the above drugs acted on the same physical structure or on closely interrelated structures that influenced each other. It had been thought for some time that alcohol and these other drugs must involve closely related structures, as alcohol consumed together with any of them could result in a dangerous potentiation, and a number of deaths were known to have occurred from suppression of respiration when people consumed alcohol together with either barbiturates, meprobamates, or one of the benzodiazepines.

The next step was to determine what action the barbiturates, meprobamate, and the benzodiazepines all had in common. It has turned out that what they had in common was that they all acted on the neurotransmitter gamma-aminobutyric acid (GABA), which has been shown to inhibit neuronal activity as the spontaneous activity of neurons exposed to GABA is decreased. Because GABA is estimated to be present at more than 25% of the synapses in the brain, it is believed to play a major inhibitory role. It was found that meprobamate, the barbiturates, and the benzodiazepines all enhance the inhibition produced by GABA neurons. Thus, these drugs seem to be all acting by potentiating (enhancing) the inhibitory action of the endogenous neurotransmitter GABA.

Since the benzodiazepines (such as Valium) are the drugs most commonly used for treating anxiety and muscle spasms, a concerted effort was made to find more precisely where in the brain these drugs act. Following the same technique used to locate other receptors, researchers affiliated with pharmaceutical companies in Switzerland and in Denmark succeeded in locating the receptor to which benzodiazepine drugs bind.[76] A radioactive preparation of a benzodiazepine drug such as Valium was mixed in different dishes, each containing brain tissue from a separate area. In this way, it was determined which brain area contained the receptors to which benzodiazepine drugs bind. In so-called "competitive binding studies," the relative capacity of different benzodiazepine drugs to bind to receptors was determined, and it was reported that the binding affinity correlated with the potency of different drugs to reduce anxiety.[77] Therefore, the benzodiazepine receptor was assumed to be the site through which the antianxiety effect of drugs was mediated.

It is now known that there are a number of drugs that do not bind directly to the benzodiazepine receptor, but can complement the action of the benzodiazepine receptor by potentiating the inhibitory action initiated at GABA receptors. This seems to be true for barbiturates, meprobamate, and alcohol, which have separate receptors, but these drugs all potentiate GABA-induced neuronal inhibition, although by different mechanisms. This has led to the belief that there exists a benzodiazepine-GABA receptor complex, a cluster of separate but highly interrelated receptors that enables benzodiazepines, meprobamate, alcohol, and barbiturates to potentiate each other's action by their similar capacity to potentiate the release of GABA from neurons.

It has been suggested that the benzodiazepine-GABA receptor complex may in some way be responsible for modulating fear and anxiety, which can be adaptive emotional states when they warn animals of danger. It is also adaptive to be able to reduce fear and anxiety when danger is no longer imminent. It was not unreasonable to speculate, therefore, that brain mechanisms capable of turning fear and anxiety on and off may have been "selected for" during the course of evolution. That the benzodiazepine receptor complex also inhibits muscle spasms has been viewed as consistent with the idea that fear and anxiety, within reasonable limits, are adaptive. Muscle spasms are an excessive response, but a more moderate tightening of muscles accompanying fear is adaptive as it puts an animal in a "response-ready mode," capable of making a "hair-trigger response" should it be necessary to "flee or fight." It makes sense to have an emotional state and preparation to make a possibly life-saving response tied together by a common mechanism.

It had to be considered highly unlikely that natural selection could have favored the evolution of receptors capable of responding to benzodiazepine drugs. However, receptors may have evolved to respond to some endogenous (natural) brain substance that is chemically similar to the benzodiazepine. Why else would there be specific benzodiazepine receptors in the brain? The search for an endogenous benzodiazepinelike neurotransmitter in the brain has led to a few possible candidates, but to date none seem to have all the properties necessary to convince most investigators that it normally acts to reduce anxiety. A group of substances called beta carbolines have been extracted from the brain, and when these are injected into humans they may evoke anxiety and sometimes a panic reaction. It is known that the beta carbolines act on the benzodiazepine receptor, but their action is opposite to that of Valium and the other benzodiazepine drugs. The beta carbolines are therefore called "inverse agonists" to denote that they do not simply block the action of the benzodiazepine agonists but produce opposite effects. Although there is considerable interest in the beta carbolines, most investigators are not yet convinced that these substances are responsible for evoking anxiety and panic reactions under physiological ("natural") conditions.

Moreover, it has been found that a panic attack can be triggered by a variety of substances such as sodium lactate, caffeine, and carbon dioxide, but they apparently do so only in people who have a panic disorder. These same substances do not produce panic in normal people. It has to be recognized that panic can be triggered by even environmental stimuli, such as an elevator or an airplane trip in people who have a relevant phobia.

It certainly has not been established that anxiety attacks and panic disorder are caused by some malfunctioning of the benzodiazepine-GABA receptor complex. Many substances that can trigger panic or anxiety do not seem to act on these brain receptors, and there are a number of drugs, such as buspirone, that sometimes alleviate anxiety but do not act on the benzodiazepine receptor complex.[78]

A Brief Look Ahead

As pharmacological knowledge increased, more and more problems arose for all of the biochemical theories of mental disorders. It was discovered that the brain has many more neurotransmitters than anyone suspected when the theories were first proposed. Drugs that were thought to act on only a few neurotransmitter systems are now known to initiate many different changes in the brain, and this has enormously complicated the problem of determining what is responsible for any therapeutic gain that is achieved. A number of the newer therapeutic drugs do not have the specific pharmacological action the early theories presumed was critical for improvement to occur. Much of the evidence and the arguments that seemed so compelling in the past have been weakened by what we have subsequently learned. We are currently in a position where it is clear that none of our theories is right, but we do not know what to replace them with. In the meantime, there are a number of groups that have their own reasons for promoting the theories and glossing over their serious deficiencies, rather than admitting that we really do no not know what causes mental disorders or why drugs are sometimes helpful.

Chapter 4

A CLOSER LOOK
AT THE EVIDENCE

"The devil is in the details."

W hen the first chemical theories of mental disorders were proposed only four or five neurotransmitters had been identified,
and some leading neurophysiologists still had not accepted
chemical transmission as the main way that neurons communicated with
each other in the brain. Chemical transmission is now universally accepted
and there may be more than one hundred different chemical substances
that function as either neurotransmitters or "neuromodulators." The latter also modify the activity of nerve cells, although their effect is not limited
to transmission across the synapse that divides two neurons. Large numbers of "neuromodulators"—information-conveying peptides, amino
acids, and hormones—are produced not only in the brain, but also in different organs in the body, from which they travel sometimes large dis-
tances to reach receptors in a localized region of the brain. Some of the
neurotransmitters bind to as many as fifteen receptor types, each of which
can presumably trigger a different cascading sequence of physiological changes. Add to this seemingly overwhelming complexity the fact
that the receptors are continually changing in number, sensitivity, and state
and it becomes clear why their ensuing effects may differ from moment to
moment.

Considering what we have learned about neuropharmacology, it is
indeed amazing how little the biochemical theories of mental disorders
have changed over the last half-century. The earliest theories of depression,
for example, were based on either serotonin or norepinephrine, or some
balance between them. This has not changed. Similarly, while the very earliest biochemical theory of schizophrenia also emphasized serotonin and to
a lesser extent norepinephrine, shortly after dopamine was recognized as a
separate neurotransmitter in the 1960s it assumed the central role in almost

all theoretical speculation about the etiology of this disorder. Judging from the latest antipsychotic drugs being marketed, dopamine is still thought to play the major role in schizophrenia. Is this conservatism the result of having been fortunate in getting the theories essentially right at the outset? No, but it reflects two facts: First, a theory that is wrong is considered preferable to admitting our ignorance. Second, the tendency of pharmaceutical companies to develop drugs that are similar to those being successfully marketed seemingly provides support for existing theories without ever really testing them.

The explanations of how psychotherapeutic drugs help to alleviate mental disorders rarely go beyond stating what chemical changes the drugs induce. The psychiatric literature rarely addresses how or why an excess or deficiency in serotonin or dopamine activity explains any particular mental disorder. There are few serious attempts to bridge the huge gap between neurochemistry and the psychological phenomena that must ultimately be explained. Unquestionably, our knowledge of how drugs interact with brain chemistry has increased enormously, but are we really any closer to understanding how psychiatric drugs alleviate mental disorders or what causes these disorders? I will argue that we have made little real progress in answering these questions, yet the chemical theories of mental disorders are widely promoted as though they are firmly established scientific facts.

During the past half-century we have seen more theoretical speculation about depression and schizophrenia than any other mental disorder. These two disorders will be the focus in evaluating the experimental and clinical evidence, while recognizing that similar criticisms apply to the theories about the origin of other mental disorders. Only the details may vary. We will explore two main lines of arguments claimed to have established the theory that neurotransmitter abnormalities are what causes mental disorders. The first is that the psychotherapeutic drugs that are most effective in alleviating a particular mental disorder tend to produce the same neurotransmitter changes in the brain. A closely related argument is derived from studies of the neurotransmitter changes induced by drugs that seem to cause mental disorders. The second line of argument is based on claims, not yet discussed, that biochemical abnormalities have been found in the brains of patients with specific mental disorders and that these are consistent with what would be predicted from what is known about the neuropharmacology of psychotherapeutic drugs. Through critical examination of the facts, it will be seen that in both instances the evidence does not support any of the biochemical theories of mental illness.

Antidepressant Drugs and Depression

Not long after the discovery of the first antidepressant drugs in the 1950s, theories based on the activity of the biogenic amine neurotransmitters began to emerge. By the early 1960s, it had become clear that the two major classes of antidepressants, the monoamine oxydase inhibitors that succeeded iproniazid, such as Marplan, Nardil, and Parnate, and the tricyclic antidepressants such as Tofranil and Janimine, enhanced the activity of norepinephrine and serotonin, although by different mechanisms. Various experimental paradigms were used to argue that the activity level of either serotonin or norepinephrine, or some balance between them, accounted for depression and explained the effectiveness of drug treatment. The claim that the drug reserpine often made humans depressed also played a major role in implicating serotonin and norepinephrine.

It had been observed that when reserpine was given to animals they became inactive and unresponsive. Reserpine had also been claimed to trigger a depressive episode in people. As depressed patients are generally inactive and unresponsive—unless they are in an agitated state—the inactivity of animals treated with reserpine was widely used as an experimental model of depression in humans. Neuropharmacological research had established that reserpine depletes the levels of all biogenic amines, including both norepinephrine (a catecholamine) and serotonin (an indole amine), but there was disagreement about which of these two neurotransmitters was most likely to be involved as a cause of depression. Arvid Carlsson, for example, found that a serotonin, but not a norepinephrine, precursor restored reserpine-treated animals to normal activity level, leading him to propose that reserpine was the amine neurotransmitter most critical to depression.[1] Joseph Schildkraut and Seymour Kety, on the other hand, reached the opposite conclusion based on observations that depleting norepinephrine, but not serotonin, tended to produce inactivity in animals. Others argued that a balance between serotonin and norepinephrine was critical. However, the evidence for all of these conclusions was weak, often flawed, and the many exceptions were usually glossed over in order to make a more convincing argument.

Contrary to the impression conveyed in a number of influential review articles, reserpine does not precipitate a clinical depression in most people. Yet at the time, it was commonly asserted as a well-established fact by those who argued that either a serotonin or a norepinephrine deficiency was the cause of depression. For example, in an influential article published in *Science*, Schildkraut and Kety stated that "such drug-induced depressions have been regarded by most observers as indistinguishable from naturally occurring depressive disorders.... In animals, reserpine produces sedation, a state which has been proposed by some investigators as a possible animal analog of depression in man."[2]

However, as Joseph Mendels and Alan Frazer of the Departments of Psychiatry and Pharmacology at the University of Pennsylvania made clear, a more careful reading of the relevant literature would have indicated that reserpine only rarely produces a true clinical depression. Despite high doses and many months of treatment with reserpine, only 6 percent of the patients developed symptoms even suggestive of depression. Moreover, an examination of these 6 percent of the patients led to the conclusion that all those who appeared to have had a genuine depression following reserpine treatment had a previous history of depression. Mendels and Frazer concluded that rather than reserpine causing depression it may reinstate a depression "in a relatively small number of susceptible persons."[3]

The belief that reserpine precipitated a depression was based on uncontrolled observations and essentially anecdotal reports. While such reports were accepted uncritically, a well-controlled prospective study that reached the opposite conclusion was virtually ignored. Bernstein and Kaufman had studied a group of fifty patients treated with reserpine and reported that there was no significant incidence of depression. In twelve patients, there developed a "pseudo depression" which seemed to be the result of "excessive tranquilization with diminished psychomotor activity." While these twelve patients seemed "tired" and lacked "push," they were not clinically depressed and none of them were "suicidal, self-deprecatory, crying, or blue."[4] There were even reports from a few studies that reserpine could have an antidepressant effect.[5] The idea that reserpine caused depression was undoubtedly accepted so uncritically because it fit so well with the prematurely accepted theory that this disorder was caused by diminished serotonin or norepinephrine activity.[6]

Mendels and Frazer also reviewed a number of studies in which patients were given drugs that blocked the synthesis of either norepinephrine or serotonin, and also dopamine.[7] Their summary of these articles should have delivered a crippling blow to any theory that assumed that either a serotonin or norepinephrine deficiency was the cause of depression, but actually it was ignored. Mendels and Frazer found that marked reductions of norepinephrine, serotonin, or dopamine did not actually produce depression in humans, even though it tended to produce animals that appeared depressed because they barely moved and sometimes remained huddled in a corner. Furthermore, as noted earlier by even some of those promoting the biogenic amine theory of depression, the fact that such drugs as amphetamine and cocaine, which increase serotonin and norepinephrine activity, do not alleviate depression was clearly contradictory to what the theory had to predict.

There are many other problems for any theory of depression that is based on assuming that a deficiency in the activity of serotonin or norepinephrine is the major cause of this disorder. The theory cannot explain why there are drugs that alleviate depression despite the fact that they have little or no effect on either norepinephrine or serotonin.[8] Another problem is that most antidepressants produce a number of different effects other than increasing norepinephrine and serotonin activity. Many of the tricyclic antidepressants, for example, have prominent effects on the neurotransmitter acetylcholine. Leopold Hofstatter, a Clinical Professor of Psychiatry at the University of Missouri School of Medicine, together with his colleague Makram Girgis, argue that the neurotransmitter acetylcholine must play a critical role in depression. They have pointed out that many antidepressants drugs decrease acetylcholine activity, and such drugs as physostigmine and some organophosphate insecticides that enhance acetylcholine activity can precipitate depressive episodes.[9] Hofstatter and Girgis have reviewed several lines of evidence that support the conclusion that the neurotransmitter acetylcholine plays a major role "in the etiology and the treatment of psychotic depression."[10] There are also recent reports that the effectiveness of antidepressants is correlated with their capacity to elevate dopamine receptors in the nucleus accumbens region of the brain.[11] The point is not that an acetylcholine or a dopamine theory of depression would be better than a norepinephrine- or a serotonin-based theory, but rather that all of the biochemical theories presented to explain depression involve a selective perception of the evidence, ignoring some findings and exaggerating and even distorting others.

A particularly troublesome fact for any of the biogenic theories of depression is that it takes a relatively long time before antidepressant drugs produce any elevation of mood. Antidepressant drugs produce their maximum elevation of serotonin and norepinephrine activity in only a day or two, but it may take several weeks before any improvement in mood occurs. During that time, a great many biochemical and other brain changes take place. Although the initial effect of antidepressant drugs may be mainly on biogenic amine activity, when drug treatment is continued for many weeks, many secondary, tertiary, and even more remote compensatory changes take place in the brain. Many of these changes do not involve biogenic amines. This introduces a serious problem in trying to understand what exactly has caused any therapeutic benefit that may have been achieved with antidepressant drugs. The number of different brain changes that can occur over a three-week period of drug treatment is huge, as every change produces a cascade of other changes until the complexities become unfathomable.

The Biogenic Amine Receptor Sensitivity Hypothesis

The "supersensitivity hypothesis" of depression can serve as an illustration of the many attempts to salvage the biogenic amine theory by revising and fine-tuning the basic idea. The "supersensitivity hypothesis" is an attempt to explain why it commonly takes several weeks before patients improve on antidepressants despite the fact that norepinephrine and serotonin levels reach their maximum in one or two days. According to this hypothesis, some critical biogenic amine receptors are "supersensitive" in depressed people. The sensitivity of receptors refers to the number of receptors on a nerve cell's outer membrane. With a large number of receptors present (a supersensitive receptor state), a cell will respond to low neurotransmitter levels. A supersensitive receptor state would tend to keep the biogenic amine neurotransmitter levels low because the cells would respond as though they were receiving too much stimulation and this would activate a "negative feedback circuit," reducing the levels of biogenic amines (see Figure 3-2, p. 86, for an explanation of this "negative feedback circuit"). There is some experimental evidence from animal studies that it takes several weeks of treatment before antidepressant drugs change receptors from a "supersensitive" to a "subsensitive" state. It is hoped that this might explain the long delay before antidepressants elevate mood. While exploring this hypothesis may produce some interesting neuropharmacological information, it does not help explain depression or how antidepressant drugs work. Unfortunately for the hypothesis, there are antidepressant drugs that do not change the sensitivity of the receptors believed to be critical. Nor does electroconvulsive shock therapy, which is often very effective in alleviating depression, change the sensitivity of the receptors most commonly considered to be critical. Moreover, there is no evidence that depressed people have any receptor "supersensitivity" or the low levels of biogenic amines that would be predicted if such a "supersensitivity" existed.

Although it is often stated with great confidence that depressed people have a serotonin or norepinephrine deficiency, the actual evidence contradicts these claims. It is not now possible to measure norepinephrine and serotonin in the brains of patients. Estimates of brain neurotransmitters can only be inferred from indirect evidence, which has a number of weaknesses. Several investigators have attempted to approximate this information by measuring biogenic amine breakdown products (metabolites) in the urine and cerebrospinal fluid. The assumption underlying this approach is that the level of biogenic amine metabolites in the urine and cerebrospinal fluid reflects the amount of the neurotransmitters being used. However, attempts to find abnormal metabolite levels of norepinephrine and serotonin in depressed patients have not been encouraging.[12]

Although some depressed patients do have low levels of either norepinephrine or serotonin metabolites or both, the majority do not. Estimates vary, but a reasonable average from several studies is that only about 25 percent of depressed patients have low levels of these metabolites. Some depressed patients actually have abnormally high levels of norepinephrine metabolites, while the levels of biogenic amine metabolites of the majority of depressed patients are well within the range of the normal population. Moreover, some patients with no history of depression also have low levels of these metabolites. In any case, there are serious problems with what is being measured, as less than one-half of the norepinephrine and serotonin metabolites found in the urine or cerebrospinal fluid comes from the brain. The other half come from various organs in the body.

There have also been some attempts to explain the etiology of depression based on the amount of the monoamine oxydase enzyme in the brain. It will be recalled that this enzyme degrades—that is, inactivates—biogenic amines and therefore abbreviates their action. High levels of monoamine oxydase in the brain might abbreviate the action of biogenic amine and produce an effect similar to a deficiency. Monoamine oxydase levels can be measured in blood platelets, and the levels obtained are claimed to reflect the amount of this enzyme in the brain. There have been claims from these "platelet studies" that depressed patients have abnormally high levels of monoamine oxydase and that the levels are normalized following effective antidepressant treatments. Here too, however, there have been failures to replicate the results, and once again, there are many depressed people who do not have high monoamine oxydase levels and some psychiatrically normal people who do.

It has become quite commonplace to explain variable results, whether they involve monoamine oxydase levels or some other biochemical measure, by proposing that they are applicable only to a particular subgroup of patients. Psychiatrists have at different times divided depressed patients into various subtypes based on either their symptoms, the way they respond to drug treatment, or the presumed cause of the depression. Thus, various clinical researchers have distinguished between "endogenous" depression, which was assumed to be caused by some internal biochemical problem, and "reactive" depression, whose cause is hypothesized to be some experience in the environment. There are other subcategories of depressions, such as "retarded" depression, in which the patient is inert and unresponsive, and "agitated" depression, in which the patients may anxiously pace up and down. Some depressed patients may lose their appetite for food and sex and suffer from insomnia, while others may eat and engage in sex compulsively or sleep excessively. There are also hybrid conditions, such as schizoaffective disorder, in which depression may be combined with some evidence of schizophreniclike delusional thought processes.

As meaningful as these distinctions may be in some instances, it has not been possible to demonstrate that any biochemical abnormality is associated with any of the subgroups of depression. Nor is it possible to predict which subgroup will respond to drug treatment. While it is certainly not illogical, for example, to hypothesize that patients with "endogenous" depression might be more likely to respond to drugs than patients with "reactive" depression, this does not seem to be the case. Moreover, there is no convincing evidence that links any biochemical measure to any particular type of depression.

The evidence is clear that none of the proposed biogenic amine theories of depression can possibly be correct. In the past the appearance of a convincing argument for one of these theories has resulted from selecting only the evidence that fits and ignoring that which does not. The various biogenic amine theories are often discussed in review articles and textbooks as though they were basically true, except for a few facts that have not yet been adequately explained. There are few rewards waiting for the person who claims that "the emperor is really nude" or who claims that we really do not know what causes depression or why an antidepressant sometimes helps to relieve this condition.

Prozac and Other Selective Serotonin Reuptake Inhibitors: The Science of Serenics

THE SELLING OF SEROTONIN

It is estimated that thirty million people worldwide have taken Prozac and many millions more have taken one of the other selective serotonin reuptake inhibitors (SSRIs). The enormous sales of these drugs partly reflect the theory that serotonin plays a critical role in the etiology of depression, but they also should be attributed to the growing number of people who believe that raising serotonin levels can have all kinds of positive mental and behavioral consequences. Increasing serotonin level is widely promoted as the way to achieve just about every personality trait that is desirable, including, but not limited to, self-confidence, creativity, emotional resilience, success, achievement, sociability, and high energy. This almost cultlike belief that high serotonin levels underlie happiness and serenity has led some skeptics to refer to this pursuit as the "science of serenics."

One could well ask if it is reasonable that serotonin, which is only one neurotransmitter out of more than one hundred chemical substances that modify brain activity, should be the major regulator of so many different attributes. What are all those other chemicals in the brain there for? It is a testimony to the strong need for simple solutions to complex problems that so many people are willing to accept these claims as established facts. The psychiatrist Peter Kramer's book *Listening to Prozac* has played a major role in conveying the idea that marvelous things happen to people when their serotonin levels are raised. The book is written in a seductive style, because Kramer appears to be neutral and objective. So, for example, while Kramer does not question any of the claims for what Prozac is believed to do, he raises ethical questions about whether it is right for a psychiatrist to change the personality of people who are not really mentally ill. However, most readers who are exposed to all the descriptions of people who have had their lives turned around by Prozac—people claimed to have been made happy, productive, and successful for the first time in their lives—are likely to request the pill and leave Peter Kramer to worry about the ethical questions.

Because Kramer's book is written in an anecdotal style, there is no way for a critical reader to assess whether the cases described are typical of the results generally produced by Prozac. Anecdotal reports in medicine often turn out to be unreliable and misleading. Several psychiatrists who have had considerable clinical experience with Prozac have pointed out that the wonderful changes described in Kramer's book are rare, but he manages to convey the impression that they are commonplace and representative of what happens to most people who take Prozac. Sherwin Nuland commented on this point in a review of Kramer's book:

> A reader of *Listening to Prozac* comes away with the impression that "the transformation powers of Prozac" are so commonly experienced by users that the very existence of the drug poses heretofore unthinkable ethical problems for our society. Is it right to use "cosmetic psychopharmacology" (a term coined by the author) to give each of us a buoyantly confident personality we never had before? What should the medical profession do to protect against possible misuse of this awe-inspiring pharmacological power?[13]

Objective studies of depressed patients treated with Prozac or any of the other SSRIs now on the market have found little difference in effectiveness between these drugs and such standard tricyclic antidepressants as Tofranil, Elavil, or Pamelor. The main advantage of the SSRIs is that for some, but not all, these drugs have fewer adverse side effects, and for that reason they are more likely not to discontinue taking the medication. Having fewer adverse side effects is certainly important, but it does not justify exaggerating what the SSRIs can do for the average person.

The public was first made aware of Prozac by articles in the popular media. The cover of an issue of *Newsweek* (26 March 1990), for example, pictured an enlarged Prozac pill with the heading: "A Breakthrough Drug for

Depression." The accompanying article presented no quantitative data comparing the effectiveness of Prozac with that of other antidepressants, but instead it reported anecdotal "testimonials" from Prozac believers. The cover of a later issue of *Newsweek* (7 February 1994) emphasized Prozac's alleged capacity to enhance personality: "Shy? Forgetful? Anxious? Fearful? Obsessed? How Science Will Let You Change Your Personality With a Pill."

In their book *The Serotonin Solution,* which is mostly about losing weight and "feeling great," Judith Wurtman and Susan Suffes attribute much more than binge eating to low serotonin levels: "Serotonin was one of the key neurotransmitters that seemed to malfunction in people who are stressed, anxious, depressed, tense, irritable, confused, angry, or mentally fatigued."[14] Even veterinarians are prescribing Prozac for dogs whose constant scratching or paw licking annoys their owners.

Low serotonin levels have been claimed to be responsible for almost every undesirable mental state and behavioral characteristic, such as depression, aggressiveness, suicide, stress, lack of self-confidence, failure, low impulse control, binge eating, and other forms of "substance abuse." This is true not merely of popular articles. Even the professional psychiatric literature conveys the impression that a low serotonin level is the cause of a host of undesirable traits, but here the language is more guarded and academic. Rather than stating that low serotonin causes depression, it is stated that "low serotonin is correlated with" whatever undesirable traits is being discussed in the article. However, the takeaway message for most readers is that most of the conditions described should be treated with medication that raises serotonin levels.

WHAT WE REALLY KNOW ABOUT SEROTONIN

The actual data relating serotonin metabolites to mood and behavior is much more variable and complex than the impression conveyed in the conclusions of many articles. In one study, for example, it was found that about one-half of a group of depressed patients had unusual cerebrospinal levels of the serotonin metabolite 5-HIAA. However, only one-half of those with abnormal levels—that is, one-quarter of the total population of depressed people—had low 5-HIAA levels. The remainder actually had levels that were higher than average. Moreover, one-half of the depressed patients had 5-HIAA levels well within the normal limits. While such results could well be considered to indicate that cerebrospinal levels of 5-HIAA are not a good predictor of depression, the authors preferred to hypothesize that the results suggest that there might be a subgroup of patients with affective disorders who suffer from a "serotonin depression."[15] In another study, it was found that 5-HIAA tended to be low in both manic and depressed patients, a result that certainly does not support the idea that low serotonin levels are associated with depression and a lack of confidence.[16]

An article entitled "5-HIAA in the Cerebrospinal Fluid: A Biochemical Suicide Predictor?" implied that serotonin levels may be a useful predictor of depression and suicide. The findings reported in the article were summarized as follows:

> Among the biological concomitants of depression, alterations in serotonin turnover has been in focus for several years. Evidence for the role of this neurotransmitter in depressive illness is derived, inter alia [among other things] from findings of low levels of serotonin in the brains from suicide victims and low levels of its metabolite, 5-hydroxyindoleacetic acid (5-HIAA) in the cerebrospinal fluid of depressed patients.[17]

There have been several reports that people who attempt suicide or who are violent tend to have low 5-HIAA levels. Aggressive monkeys are also reported to have low serotonin levels. However, despite the fact that the results may be statistically significant, the correlation is not high and there is considerable overlap in the level of serotonin metabolites obtained from "normal" comparison groups and from aggressive or suicidal populations. This has led several investigators to conclude that the low serotonin levels found in some aggressive animals and people and in some suicide victims may be secondary to the high level of stress commonly experienced by such individuals, rather than being the cause of their behavior. In studies of rhesus monkeys, for example, animals separated from their mothers and raised with peers tend to have lower levels of serotonin metabolites, higher incidence of aggressive behavior and, not surprisingly, lower levels of social competence as adults.[18] It could well be argued that separation from mothers is the cause and lower serotonin levels is an effect. The belief that low serotonin levels is the sole cause of depression and suicide is certainly not justified, as it has been shown that various life experiences can lower serotonin levels. There are good reasons to suspect that any relationship between behavior, personality, and serotonin activity is probably remote, indirect, and not causal.

Psychiatrists prescribe Prozac and the other selective serotonin reuptake inhibitors not only for depression, but also for obsessive-compulsive disorders, panic disorders, various food-related problems (including both anorexia and bulimia), premenstrual dysphoric syndrome (PMS), attention-deficit/hyperactivity disorder (ADHD), borderline personality disorder, drug and alcohol addiction, migraine headaches, social phobia, arthritis, autism, and behavioral and emotional problems in children, among many other conditions.[19] It is a paradox that a drug that is praised for the specificity of its pharmacological action should be prescribed as a treatment for such a variety of conditions. It certainly makes it difficult to justify the belief that the newer, more selectively acting drugs are correcting the unique biochemical abnormality that has caused each of the different mental disorders. It is sometimes claimed that there is a common etiology underlying all the different conditions that respond to the same drug. However, those who make this claim are not able to specify this underlying condition and to document its presence in an objective, noncircular manner, the claim has a hollow ring and it seems more defensive than convincing.

New Advances in Drug Development

Although the emphasis is now on developing drugs with greater and greater specificity, the specificity refers mainly to their pharmacological effects and not to their effects on behavior or mental and emotional states.[20] The first psychiatric drugs had relatively low pharmacological specificity, as they acted on many different neurotransmitters. Today, however, the pharmacological industry is capable of producing drugs that act on only one neurotransmitter system and potentially on only one receptor subtype of that system. All neurotransmitters are now known to act on several different receptors, each of which is presumed to have some different function, but actually little is known about the functional consequences of exciting or inhibiting any receptor subtype.[21] New discoveries reveal an ever-increasing number of receptors for each neurotransmitter system. In the case of serotonin, for example, fifteen different receptors ($5\text{-}HT_{1-15}$) have already been identified, but it would surprise no one if other serotonin receptors were discovered. Furthermore, each of the fifteen serotonin receptor subtypes can be further subdivided. Thus, in the case of the serotonin $5\text{-}HT_1$ receptor alone, at least four receptor subtypes ($5\text{-}HT_{1a}$, $5\text{-}HT_{1b}$, $5\text{-}HT_{1c}$, and $5\text{-}HT_{1d}$) have now been identified. When there is an indication that a new experimental drug binds more selectively to a particular serotonin receptor subtype there is a rush to try to find if any clinical trials will suggest that the new drug is either more effective or has fewer adverse side effects than drugs already on the market.

Developing drugs that bind selectively to one class of receptors used to be a very slow, tedious, and expensive process, and also one that was limited to the structures chemists could imagine and synthesize. Today, the whole process has become so automated that any promising compound—one obtained, for example, from a botanical specimen used in a folk remedy—can be run through equipment that can quickly determine if there is anything in that compound that binds to a particular receptor subtype.[22]

However, at present this search for compounds that can bind to specific receptor subtypes is usually driven by the same motivation as that of the mountain climber who climbs a mountain "because it is there." There is virtually no information about what behavior or psychological states are likely to be affected by stimulating or blocking a particular receptor subtype. Usually pharmaceutical companies become interested simply because a new receptor subtype has been discovered, not because anything even potentially useful is known about the properties of the receptor. Considering how often serendipity has played a role in the discovery of drugs, it would be foolhardy to rule out the possibility that something useful might come of this approach, but it should be recognized for what it is, basically "hunting in the dark with a shotgun."

The three major classes of antidepressant drugs currently available are the monoamine oxydase inhibitors (MAO-Is), the tricyclic antidepressants (TADs), and the selective serotonin reuptake inhibitors (SSRIs). The SSRIs are really a subclass of the tricyclics, except that they act more selectively on serotonin. Eli Lilly's drug fluoxetine, which was introduced in 1986 under the proprietary name Prozac, was the first and is the best-known of the SSRIs, but others are now marketed, such as Zoloft (Roerig, division of Pfizer), and Paxil (SmithKline Beecham). In the twelve-month period ending August 1997, more than 3.5 million prescriptions were written for the SSRIs—Lilly's sales of Prozac alone totaled over $1.8 billion, while Pfizer's sales of Zoloft were almost $1.2 billion.[23] The monoamine oxydase inhibitors require a number of dietary restrictions and more medical monitoring and they are less commonly used today.

New antidepressant SSRIs are being introduced with the claim that their action is more specific than that of those currently in use. One example is the drug nefazodone (marketed as Serzone), which is reported to act mainly on the serotonin 5-HT_2 receptor. Another new antidepressant is Flesinoxin, which is believed to elevate serotonin activity, but it does so by acting as a serotonin receptor "agonist" (a substance that acts to stimulate a receptor similar to the natural neurotransmitter), rather than by inhibiting reuptake as do the SSRIs.[24] In either case, serotonin activity is increased, either by blocking its reuptake and prolonging its action or by directly stimulating serotonin receptors. It is not clear why these two different actions should have a different effect, or whether, in fact, there is a difference. There are also some new antidepressants, such as venlafaxine (marketed as Effector), which are believed to selectively inhibit the reuptake of both norepinephrine and serotonin, indicating that interest in norepinephrine's role in depression has not been completely abandoned. A new antidepressant drug that received FDA approval in fall 1996 is mirtazapine (Remeron), manufactured by the Organon pharmaceutical company. Remeron also stimulates norepinephrine and some serotonin activity, but it accomplishes this by increasing the release of these neurotransmitters rather than by inhibiting reuptake or acting as an agonist. While Remeron stimulates some serotonin release, it also blocks two specific serotonin receptors (5-HT_2 and 5-HT_3) in the hope that its effectiveness may be increased while side effects are reduced.

Some new antidepressants are reported not to act on serotonin at all. For example, repoxetine (Edromax) has been approved in England as an antidepressant, and according to Pharmacia & Upjohn this drug is a "selective noradrenaline reuptake inhibitor." Noradrenaline is the name used in Great Britain for norepinephrine. Edromax is advertised to improve social functioning as well as being an antidepressant and, in general, it is claimed to have all the properties of the SSRIs without any action on serotonin mechanisms. Some new antidepressants block the reuptake of dopamine and norepinephrine, but not serotonin.[25]

In the absence of any real understanding of the cause of depression, the development of antidepressants is proceeding mainly by trial and error. Pharmaceutical companies develop drugs that act on a different combination of biogenic amine receptors in the hope that they will hit upon a combination that they can promote as having some advantage over drugs with which it must compete. The potential rewards are enormous, and it clearly must be worth the large investment and risk it takes to bring a drug to market. In 1997, there were about 125 antidepressants in various stages of development and clinical trials. The exploration, however, is extremely limited in scope, as almost all of these experimental drugs are designed to inhibit the reuptake of various combinations of the biogenic amines. The state of antidepressant drug development and our understanding of depression was recently summarized in an authoritative text:

> A major limitation of efforts to develop new mood-altering agents is the lack of a compelling rationale. The fundamental problem is the continued lack of a coherent pathophysiology, let alone etiology, of major depression and bipolar disorder, despite decades of important and useful contributions to the description of the syndromes. . . . To date, it has been very difficult to conceive of a mood-altering agent that does not affect central monoaminergic synaptic neurotransmission, particularly that mediated by either norepinephrine or serotonin. That impasse represents both a conceptual limitation to the imagination of preclinical scientists and a practical limit to industrial sponsors of new drug development.[26]

Almost all the antidepressant drugs currently being marketed or in various stages of development are based on the assumption that depression is caused by some deficiency in serotonin and norepinephrine activity, due to either low levels of secretion or some abnormality in receptor sensitivity. However, as we have noted, there is no convincing evidence that most depressed people have low levels of biogenic amine activity. Moreover, while antidepressants may produce a short-term increase in norepinephrine and serotonin activity, after several weeks of drug treatment and at the time when depression may first show signs of being alleviated, norepinephrine and serotonin activity are actually depressed because the compensatory mechanisms previously discussed (see Figure 3-2, p. 86) lead to a decrease in receptor sensitivity and, in some instances, also a decrease the amount of these neurotransmitters released into the synapse.

An Alternative Hypothesis to the Biogenic Amine Deficiency Theory of Depression

Despite the wide promotion of the biogenic amine deficiency theory of depression, most researchers working in the field recognize its inadequacy and are trying to come up with alternative theories. Ronald Duman, at Yale University, has proposed an alternative hypothesis about the cause of depression based on reports that the brains of some depressed people have lost nerve cells in the hippocampus, a structure located in the temporal lobe. The hippocampus is believed to participate in many functions, including memory and spatial abilities, but it has also been suggested that this brain structure plays a role in modulating emotional state. As there are reports that the high levels of adrenal hormones secreted during stress destroy hippocampal cells, Duman and his colleagues have speculated that depression could result from a stress-induced loss of hippocampal cells.[27] They believe that antidepressant drugs may work not because they correct a biogenic amine deficiency, but rather because they trigger the release of a nerve growth factor ("brain-derived neurotrophic factor") that stimulates a branching of hippocampal nerve cells that can compensate for its cell loss.

The hippocampus cell loss hypothesis of depression is interesting and worth pursuing, but, as Duman and his colleagues readily admit, the hypothesis could only apply to a relatively small subgroup of depressed people. This is because there is no evidence that most depressed people have lost hippocampal cells and depression is not always preceded by a high level of stress. In fact, it is not uncommon that the first episode of depression occurs at a time when everything seems to be going well. One aspect of the hippocampus hypothesis that is worth noting is that it broadens the search for a cause of depression. Rather than searching only for evidence of neurotransmitter abnormalities, this hypothesis looks at other biological variables and how they might be influenced by what is going on in a person's life.

In summary, while we have learned much about brain chemistry and the neuropharmacology of drug action, our theories have changed very little in the past fifty years. Our pharmacological knowledge and our technical skills are impressive, but most of the biochemical research on emotional states is concerned with at most three or four of the over one hundred neurotransmitters now estimated to be present in the brain. Moreover, the newest antidepressant drugs still act only on the same two or three neurotransmitters, although the receptor targets are more specific. Drug development is driven more by market considerations than by any clearer understanding of what causes depression or how drugs sometimes alleviate this condition. Although the often-repeated statement that antidepressants work by correcting the biochemical deficiency that is the cause of depression may be an effective promotional tack, it cannot be justified by the evidence.

Antipsychotic (Neuroleptic) Drugs and Schizophrenia

The earliest chemical theories of schizophrenia were focused on the neurotransmitter serotonin. This was because LSD and the other hallucinogens that produced mental and perceptual states that resembled schizophrenia blocked serotonin activity. It was hypothesized, therefore, that schizophrenia might be caused by a serotonin deficiency. However, the serotonin theory of schizophrenia was abandoned when it was realized that some hallucinogens did not block serotonin while some drugs that blocked serotonin activity did not produce hallucinations. Furthermore, in time it became clear that the "psychosis" produced by LSD and the other hallucinogens only superficially resembled schizophrenia, and once they had been alerted to the problem, psychiatrists could, in most instances, readily distinguish the real condition from the drug-induced states.[28]

The Argument for the "Dopamine Theory of Schizophrenia"

After dopamine was acknowledged to be a separate neurotransmitter, several lines of evidence suggested that it might play the critical role in schizophrenia's etiology and treatment. From the outset, it was observed that practically all of the available antipsychotic drugs used to treat schizophrenia produced motor symptoms that resembled those of parkinsonism. When it was discovered that Parkinson's patients were suffering from a dopamine deficiency, it was reasonable to hypothesize that antipsychotic drugs must be blocking dopamine activity. These observations led directly to the hypothesis that schizophrenics must suffer from excessive dopamine activity, which antipsychotic drugs correct.

The dopamine hypothesis evolved into a dopamine theory of schizophrenia when it was discovered that there was a strong relationship between the capacity of antipsychotic drugs to block dopamine receptors and their effectiveness (potency) in alleviating schizophrenia. Most antipsychotic drugs bind to dopamine receptors, but they do not trigger the normal physiological response that occurs when these receptors are activated by dopamine. Essentially, antipsychotic drugs are dopamine receptor antagonists—they block dopamine receptors and prevent dopamine (or dopamine agonistic drugs) from acting at these sites. This finding by Seeman and Lee and Snyder, together with their respective colleagues, seemed to be to be a major breakthrough, and it was published at approximately the same time in *Nature* and *Science,* the two most widely read scientific journals.[29] When it was later shown that a similar relationship did not hold for drugs that blocked either serotonin or norepinephrine receptors, the dopamine theory of schizophrenia was given a big boost.[30] Thus, although it was not possible to demonstrate any abnormally high levels of dopamine in schizophrenics, it appeared that this mental disorder might be caused by a hypersensitivity to dopamine. As Seeman later explained:

> Although the dopamine content is found to be normal in the schizo-phrenic brain, an elevation in receptor-density would stimulate a "hyper-dopamine-like" state. This is in contrast to drug-induced psychosis, as occurs in the hallucinations and delusions brought on by cocaine or high doses of L-DOPA. In these cases, the density of dopamine receptors is normal, but more dopamine is released, creating a hyper-dopamine and psychotic state.[31]

A more direct way of determining whether there were excessive numbers of dopamine receptors in the brains of schizophrenics was required. By 1978, a technique for estimating the number of receptors in different regions of the brains of deceased patients was available, and Seeman and Lee and their colleagues reported that they had found a high number of dopamine receptors in the brains of schizophrenics. They concluded that while earlier the evidence supporting the dopamine theory of schizophrenia had only been circumstantial, "We have now obtained direct evidence for some abnormalities in brain dopamine receptors in schizophrenia."[32]

Although Seeman and Lee's report of abnormally high numbers of dopamine receptors in the brains of schizophrenics seemed to provide strong support for the belief that these patients must be hypersensitive to dopamine, there were several reasons to have reservations about these initial findings. First of all, there were only twenty schizophrenic brains studied and there was an overlap in the dopamine receptor numbers obtained from the normal and from the schizophrenic brains. More critical, however, was the fact that most of the schizophrenic patients had been treated with antipsychotic drugs for some time before their death, and it is well known that the blocking of dopamine and other receptors produces a compensatory increase in receptor number (see Figure 4-1). It is more than

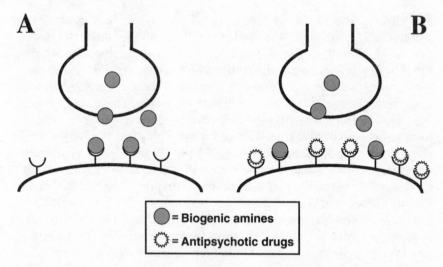

Figure 4-1 Blocking dopamine receptors with antipsychotic drugs leads to a compensatory increase in dopamine receptors. A) The number of receptors before administration of an antipsychotic drug. B) The blocking of the dopamine receptors by an antipsychotic drug produces a proliferation of these receptors. As the blocking of dopamine receptors also results in more dopamine being released (see Figure 3-2, page 86), it is difficult to know whether antipsychotic drugs result in a net increase or decrease in dopamine activity.

likely, therefore, that the higher receptor number found in some schizophrenic brains was a result of the treatment, rather than the cause of the disorder.

Seeman and Lee made an effort to obtain brains of schizophrenics who had not received any antipsychotic drug treatment, and they have reported that they have found an excessive number of dopamine receptors in the brains of schizophrenics never treated with drugs. Others, as will be described shortly, have not been able to replicate these findings. In the meantime, Seeman and Lee have refined their technique and have estimated the numbers of different dopamine receptor subtypes in the brains of schizophrenics. At least five different dopamine receptors have been identified. Using various radioactive drugs that bind somewhat selectively to one or another dopamine receptor types, Seeman and Lee claimed that the number of D_2 receptors was abnormally high in the brains of schizophrenics, even those not treated with drugs. They began to refer to the D_2 receptor as the "antipsychotic/dopamine receptor," implying that it was this receptor that was abnormal in schizophrenics and blocking these receptors accounted for the therapeutic effects of antipsychotic drugs.[33]

Thus, a number of lines of evidence seemingly confirmed the validity of the dopamine theory of schizophrenia. A more critical examination of the evidence, however, indicates that the theory is far from established.

A Critical Examination
of the Dopamine Theory

By picking and choosing the evidence to be included, a seemingly convincing argument can be made that schizophrenia is caused by some impairment of a brain dopamine system. However, a more critical examination of the total evidence available reveals that it is far from established that a dopamine impairment underlies schizophrenia. While it is often said that schizophrenics have been found to have an abnormally high number of dopamine receptors, the evidence for this statement is not at all compelling. Even in those studies that found more dopamine receptors in schizophrenics compared to normals, the difference was only on average and did not apply to many schizophrenics. Furthermore, most investigators have not been able to find any evidence of dopamine receptor abnormality in schizophrenics. A multinational research effort involving patients and researchers from Germany, the United Kingdom, and Austria concluded that any difference found in D_2 (or any other dopamine) receptors in the brains of schizophrenic is "entirely iatrogenic," meaning that any difference found was totally caused by prior treatment with antipsychotic drugs.[34] In another report, Arvid Carlsson, one of the foremost contributors to the field of psychopharmacology in general, and to our understanding of dopamine mechanisms in particular, concluded that there is:

> no good evidence for any perturbation of the dopamine function in schizophrenia. An increased density of dopamine D_2 receptors in the brains of schizophrenic patients analyzed postmortem has been reported, and one study with PET [Positron Emission Tomography] scan data showed the same thing, but the data from the Karolinska Institute by Farde and Sedvall show absolutely no difference at all.[35]

Other (PET) studies failed to find high numbers of any dopamine receptors in schizophrenics.[36] Thus there is far from any agreement that most schizophrenics have an excess of dopamine receptors other than that caused by antipsychotic drug treatment. Moreover, as will be discussed in the next chapter, it is not clear even in those schizophrenics who do seem to have high number of dopamine receptors, unrelated to drug treatment, whether the dopamine abnormality was the cause or the effect of the disorder.

Studies of dopamine receptors have become more complicated as a result of the discovery that there are more dopamine receptors than just the D_1 and D_2 types. For example, when Pierre Sokoloff and his colleagues in Paris reported in 1990 that they had identified the D_3 receptor, the interest in the report was so enormous that their paper was soon on the *Top Ten List of Biology's Hottest Papers* as tabulated by *Science Watch*.[37] Five different dopamine receptors (D_1–D_5) have now been identified, and each of these has a somewhat different anatomical distribution in the brain.

Antipsychotic drugs are claimed to bind mostly to the D_2 and D_3 receptors and much less so to the D_1, D_4, and D_5 receptors.[38] This might seem to implicate the D_2 and D_3 receptors as the active site for antipsychotic drugs, except that some of so-called "atypical antipsychotics" such as clozapine do not to bind to (or bind very little to) these receptors. (The "atypical antipsychotics" are drugs that do not produce the often irreversible and disfiguring motor symptoms known as "tardive dyskinesia.")[39] The "atypical antipsychotics" are at least as effective in treating schizophrenia as the more traditional antipsychotics that act primarily on D_2 and D_3 receptors. It has been shown that 30 percent of patients who did not respond to treatment with three different standard antipsychotic drugs responded to "atypical antipsychotics." A number of clinical investigators have argued that the nonresponding patients may represent a subgroup of schizophrenics who do not have the usual dopamine problem. However, this argument cannot be valid, as "atypical antipsychotics" are also effective with patients who respond to drugs that block dopamine D_2 receptors. Therefore, it is difficult to maintain that the antipsychotic drugs work because they correct the D_2 receptor abnormality that is the cause of schizophrenia when a diverse group of patients with this illness respond to "atypical antipsychotics" that do not act on this receptor. Furthermore, the fact that some "atypical antipsychotics" have their major effect on serotonin, not dopamine, receptors casts further doubt that any dopamine receptor is critically involved in the efficacy of antipsychotic drugs.

A recent report from Japan has described a decrease (not an increase) in dopamine D_1 receptors in the prefrontal cortex of schizophrenics, and its authors have speculated that this might underlie some cognitive impairment seen in this disorder.[40] Interesting as this finding may prove to be, it would seem to make it even more difficult to explain why blocking dopamine receptors should be helpful to schizophrenics. Perhaps some clarity will eventually emerge from all of these preliminary findings and speculation, but at present the evidence fails to implicate any dopamine receptor as either the cause of schizophrenia or the critical site where an antipsychotic must act in order to be effective.

Another major problem for the theory that schizophrenia is caused by excessive dopamine activity is that antipsychotic drugs, as is also true of the antidepressants, generally take several weeks before they exhibit any significant therapeutic effect.[41] This is true despite the fact that it has been demonstrated that the drugs block dopamine receptors in a matter of hours. After several weeks of drug treatment, there is a compensatory increase in the number of dopamine receptors and an increase in the firing rate of dopamine neurons. The increase in the number of receptors should increase the capacity of neurons to respond to dopamine, and when combined with an increase in firing rate of dopamine neurons and a consequent increase in the amount of dopamine released, dopamine activity might be expected to increase rather than decrease at the time that antipsychotic drugs first seem to be working—hardly a change that should correct excessive dopamine activity.

There have been some attempts to resolve this paradox by resorting to explanations based on what is known about the anatomical distribution of many D_2 receptors. Many of the D_2 receptors, which have been hypothesized to be critically involved in schizophrenia, are "autoreceptors." An "autoreceptor," which is located on the body of dopamine releasing neurons, acts like a brake, slowing the firing rate of dopamine neurons and decreasing the amount of dopamine released. If these autoreceptors are blocked by a drug, it has the effect of removing a brake (or stepping on the gas pedal), and the neuron's firing rate is increased. As most antipsychotic drugs block D_2 autoreceptors, this should produce an increase in the firing rate of dopamine neurons and an increase in the amount of dopamine released into synapses. Once again, a paradox appears, as an increase in the firing rate of dopamine neurons would seem to be just the opposite of what a drug should do in order to alleviate a theorized dopamine hyperactivity.

In an attempt to resolve the paradox, it has been suggested that when neurons fire at an abnormally high rate for about a three-week period, their cell membranes "depolarize." Depolarization refers to a reduction in the voltage differential between the cell membrane and the cytoplasm within the neuron, a condition that blocks the ability of a neuron to fire and to release its transmitter. It has been reported in a recent study that the capacity of chronic administration of different antipsychotic drugs to produce depolarization block of dopamine neurons was related to their antipsychotic efficacy in humans. While the depolarization block phenomenon may prove useful for screening new antipsychotic drugs, its significance for the dopamine theory of schizophrenia is not at all clear. The principal researchers working on the depolarization effects of antipsychotic drugs believe that there is no reason to think that depolarization represents a return to the normal state of the dopamine system, and they conclude that there is probably nothing at all wrong with the dopamine system in schizophrenics.[42]

Is Schizophrenia One Disease?

It should not be surprising that the search for biological correlates of schizophrenia has consistently produced variable and difficult-to-replicate results. Schizophrenic patients are a very heterogeneous group and most if not all mental health professionals think that it is likely the diagnosis covers several separate disorders with different etiologies. The German psychiatrist Emil Kraepelin, who provided one of the first classifications of psychiatric disorders around the turn of the century, called schizophrenia *dementia praecox* because he considered these patients to have "demented" thought processes that first became evident during adolescence.[43] Kraepelin divided *dementia praecox* into four types: simple, hebrephenic, catatonic, and paranoiac.[44] Eugen Bleuler, who introduced the term schizophrenia around 1910, referred to "the Group of Schizophrenias."[45] In the 1970s, the label schizophrenia was used so broadly in the United States that it was estimated that it was three times as likely that a patient would be diagnosed as schizophrenic in that country as in Great Britain.[46] In recent years, the diagnosis of schizophrenia has been made more objective by listing explicit criteria in the *Diagnostic and Statistical Manual (DSM)* published by the American Psychiatric Association and in other widely used manuals such as the *International Classification of Diseases* (ICD) published by the World Health Organization. Now that more objective diagnostic criteria are used, the incidence of schizophrenia is estimated at between 1 and 2 percent of the population in most countries.

The topic of diagnostic labeling will be discussed more fully in the next chapter, but it is important to recognize that different types of schizophrenia are still recognized, and many people believe that different causes may be involved and different treatments called for. The distinctions that are most commonly made today are between *acute* and *chronic* schizophrenia and between *Type 1* and *Type 2* schizophrenia. Acute and chronic refer, of course, to the duration of the illness, but there are other criteria as well. The acute schizophrenic usually has made a relatively good adjustment up to the time that the symptoms first manifest themselves, and the onset of the disorder is often relatively abrupt, although there are probably some early (prodromal) signs that the illness is developing. The symptoms most commonly associated with acute schizophrenia are delusions and hallucinations. Chronic schizophrenics, on the other hand, usually have a long history of marginal adjustment at work (if they can hold a job), and they tend to be socially withdrawn. Chronic schizophrenics often live somewhat isolated lives, have poor personal hygiene, exhibit bizarre behavior, have little affect, and may show signs of disturbed speech and writing, using nonexistent "words" (neologisms) and incomprehensible syntax ("word salad"). As in most typologies, there is a substantial gray area and much overlap, so, for example, there are chronic schizophrenics who have delusional thoughts and hallucinations, and acute schizophrenics may progress into a chronic deteriorated pattern.

Type 1 and Type 2 schizophrenics are distinguished primarily by their predominant symptoms, which overlap to a great extent with the acute-chronic distinction. "Positive" symptoms, which predominate in Type 1 schizophrenia, refer primarily to hallucinations and delusions, symptoms not seen in normals. "Negative" symptoms, which predominate in Type 2 schizophrenia, refer to pathology characterized by the absence (or deficiency) of behavior present in normals. Thus, "negative" symptoms include a severe lack of social skill, lack of emotional responses, and a lack of communication skills.[47] In general, positive symptoms predominate in acute schizophrenia and negative symptoms are characteristic of chronic schizophrenia.[48]

It is widely believed that dopamine has a closer relationship to positive symptoms than to negative symptoms. Antipsychotic drugs, which block dopamine receptors, are likely to be more effective in reducing hallucinations and delusions than they are in alleviating negative symptoms. Drugs that increase dopamine activity, such as amphetamine, tend to worsen positive symptoms, but they have little effect, one way or the other, on negative symptoms. Chronic schizophrenics tend to be less helped by antipsychotic drugs.

There has been speculation that different dopamine receptors may be related to positive and negative symptoms, and pharmaceutical companies are hoping that they will be able to develop drugs that will bind to the right combination of dopamine receptors to alleviate both positive and negative symptoms, without producing the adverse motor effects characteristic of most of the antipsychotic drugs. It has been proposed that there is a dopamine hyperactivity only in Type 1 schizophrenics and that is why they respond best to the antipsychotic drugs that block dopamine receptors. However, this hypothesis is contradicted by several lines of evidence. For example, positive symptoms have been shown to respond to those "atypical antipsychotics," such as clozapine, which are not particularly effective in blocking dopamine activity. Moreover, patients do not nicely divide themselves into Type 1 and Type 2 schizophrenia. Many patients exhibit a mixture of positive and negative symptoms, and there are schizophrenic symptoms that do not easily fit into either the Type 1 or Type 2 category.[49]

Current Status of Antipsychotic Drugs

Our present confusion about what causes schizophrenia and how drugs sometime help is revealed by some of the latest drugs that have been marketed to treat this disorder. Eli Lilly recently started to market the antipsychotic olanzapine (proprietary name Zyprexa), which primarily blocks serotonin and dopamine receptors, but it also blocks some norepinephrine, acetylcholine, and histamine receptors. Olanzapine also binds weakly to some GABA and benzodiazepine receptors. In its package insert Lilly acknowledges that how olanzapine or any other antipsychotic works is unknown, but it provides some speculation that the antagonism of dopamine and serotonin may be important. Lilly also includes a warning of the possibility of adverse side effects such as tardive dyskinesia and the potentially life-threatening neuroleptic malignant syndrome (NMS).

Essentially the same statements about pharmacological action and possible adverse side effects are made about the new antipsychotic risperidone (Janssen Pharmaceutical's Risperdal) and about other new antipsychotic drugs. Much current antipsychotic drug development is influenced by the action of "atypical antipsychotic drugs," which tend not to produce the same adverse motor effects as do most antipsychotics, but some of them have their own problems.[50] New antipsychotic drug development is often guided by an attempt to duplicate the profile of activity of the "atypical antipsychotics," but by making small chemical changes, it is hoped that it will be possible to improve efficacy and decrease the incidence of adverse side effects. Many of the newer antipsychotics tend to block the D_2 dopamine receptor and the 5-HT_{2A} serotonin receptor and are called "$D_2/5\text{-HT}_2$ antagonists." All of this drug development is essentially a trial-and-error approach, as there is so little known about the functional significance of any receptor subtype.

All of the antipsychotics fail to help a significant number of schizophrenic patients. John Kane, a professor of psychiatry at the Albert Einstein College of Medicine, has studied the effectiveness of antipsychotic drugs and has concluded that only about 50 percent of schizophrenic patients show any improvement after four weeks of treatment with these drugs.[51] Moreover, if the nonresponders are continued at the same dose of medication, or if the dose is increased, or if they are switched to another antipsychotic drug, only 9 percent of these nonresponders show any improvement after an additional four weeks of treatment. Clearly, the drugs do not help a substantial number of people, and the honest answer is that we don't know why.

Those who respond to antipsychotic drug treatment are often caught in a "Catch 22" dilemma. If the drug treatment is stopped even after the patient's condition has been in remission for over a year, over three-quarters of them will relapse. However, if the drug treatment is maintained, the patients run a 25 to 40 percent risk of developing tardive dyskinesia.[52] Moreover, there are several reports that schizophrenics treated with antipsychotic drugs that block dopamine activity are more likely to relapse into chronicity than patients not given drugs. A World Health Organization (WHO) study reported that schizophrenics in developing countries where drugs tend to be less prescribed do not relapse as often after a remission.[53] As will be discussed in the next chapter, it has been demonstrated that repeated exposure to stress and such drugs as amphetamine, cocaine, and opiates, which stimulate dopamine activity, can produce long-lasting and perhaps permanent sensitization of dopamine circuits. This raises the possibility that prolonged treatment with antipsychotics may also produce permanent changes in the brain that might increase the possibility of a relapse.

Looking Beyond Simplistic Theories of Mental Illness

There is no agreement that schizophrenics have a dopamine abnormality other than that caused by neuroleptic drug treatment. Pharmaceutical companies, however, have been so wedded to the "dopamine theory of schizophrenia" that the possibility that other systems may be involved has been neglected. For example, the drug ketamine, which is used widely as an anesthetic, blocks the neurotransmitter glutamate, and it is known that this drug can make normal people acutely psychotic and can worsen the symptoms in schizophrenia. Arvid Carlsson has recently reviewed other evidence that implicates glutamate in schizophrenia.[54] The importance of glutamate has also been emphasized by another group of clinical investigators, who concluded that "innovative approaches to the study of schizophrenia have provided *compelling evidence* suggesting a role for glutamate [an excitatory amino acid neurotransmitter] in schizophrenic illness" (emphasis added).[55] Another review chapter published in the same authoritative psychopharmacology text concluded: "It is clear that the role for 5-HT [serotonin] in the pathogenesis and treatment of schizophrenia is *compelling*" (emphasis added).[56]

It is safe to say that the compelling evidence for the involvement of glutamate and serotonin in schizophrenia does not exhaust the possibilities. Solomon Snyder has recently described some of the changes in our knowledge of brain chemistry since the 1960s:

> The history of neurotransmission is full of surprises. A reasonable person would assume that the brain could make do with few, perhaps only two, neurotransmitters—one excitatory and one inhibitory. For most of the 20th century this appeared to be the case, because between the 1920s (when acetylcholine was appreciated) and the 1960s only a handful of molecules were accepted as neurotransmitters, specifically biogenic amines and amino acids. Research on opiate receptors and enkephalins spurred interest into peptides, and, within a few years, up to 50 or more neuropeptides had been characterized. Though differing markedly in many properties, amines, amino acids, and peptides follow closely the conventional neurotransmitter dogma.[57]

Snyder went on to point out that while all the initially discovered neurotransmitters were stored in vesicles within neurons and located close to the synapse, more recently discovered substances have altered our thinking about communication between neurons. While neurotransmitters are believed to act only on adjacent neurons, many substances (such as nitric oxide) can influence the activity of neurons located a long distance away.

Despite the proliferation of known brain neurotransmitters and the complexities added by the different ways they exert their influence, biochemical theories of mental illness seemed to be rigidly tied to mechanisms that evolved when only a few neurotransmitters were known. Arvid Carlsson has commented on the discrepancy between our advances in neuropharmacology and the lack of any basic change in drug treatment:

> In view of the impressive developments in basic CNS [central nervous system] pharmacology during the last two decades, it is remarkable that the drugs used in psychiatry are essentially the same as those used in the 1950s. Why is this so? Certainly, the answer is not that these drugs are perfect and cannot be improved upon. Both the antipsychotic and the antidepressant drugs have troublesome side-effects, and they are far from ideal in terms of efficacy, rate of onset of action and so on.[58]

In 1997, Leslie Iverson, a professor of pharmacology at Oxford University, also commented on the lack of change over the years in the drug treatment of depression and schizophrenia:

> The monoamine era has not opened really new avenues for the discovery of medicines affecting the central nervous system. The basic mechanism underlying Prozac, inhibition of monoamine reuptake, is not different from that of the original tricyclic antidepressants imipramine and amitriptyline. Although more than 100 drugs have been introduced for the treatment of schizophrenia, they all resemble the original chlorpromazine in their mode of action.[59]

For some time, we have been defending and bolstering what should have been more widely acknowledged to be simplistic biogenic amine theories of depression as well as schizophrenia. (The biogenic amine neurotransmitters, it will be recalled, consist mainly of norepinephrine, serotonin, and dopamine.) David Healy, now in psychological medicine at the University of Wales, has observed that the so-called "psychopharmacological revolution" has actually been quite conservative in its resistance to new ideas.[60] In his book *The Structure of Scientific Revolutions,* Theodore Kuhn maintains that a scientific theory or "paradigm" tends to be accepted despite much contradictory data unless there is another theoretical paradigm to replace it. David Healy points out that the field has been so committed to the biogenic amine theory of depression that all kinds of "accessory" explanations are dug up in order to explain away contradictory data, rather than admitting that the theory is probably wrong. If, for example, an antidepressant drug does not act on the biogenic amine neurotransmitters, all kinds of strained biochemical processes are resorted to in order to demonstrate how the amines might actually be affected in some way. Or when the data on biogenic amine activity in a depressed population proves to be highly variable, this is explained away on the basis of the wrong patients being selected. Healy has given several examples of how the biogenic amine theory of depression has been sustained in the face of serious empirical challenges to its validity.

The psychiatrist Arthur Meltzer, an important contributor to the literature on the neuropharmacology of mental illness, recently spoke out about the catecholamine theory of depression and the dopamine theory of schizophrenia:

> They provided a structure and the hope that we were on the right track. It has turned out that the original versions of these hypotheses were seriously in error. They sought to explain too much. Its amazing how long the dopamine hypothesis was not seriously challenged given all that we know to be incompatible with it.
>
> I remember attempts in the 1980s to move beyond the catecholamine hypothesis into the endorphins and the opiates as well as an attempt to develop drugs related to GABA as antipsychotics. But the failure to find anything therapeutic brought the field back to dopamine. An early version of the serotonin hypothesis of schizophrenia, as explored in the 1950s and early 1960s, died because of the failure to validate any evidence for psychotomimetic indoleamines [serotonin] in urine and blood or postmortem specimens from schizophrenics and the absence of gross effects on the behavior of schizophrenics of enhancing and diminishing serotonergic activity.[61]

In a similar vein, Mogens Schou, the person who provided the critical experimental evidence demonstrating the effectiveness of lithium treatment, recently remarked:

> Another disappointment is that we still do not know the mechanism of action of lithium in affective illness. Many hypotheses exist, some of them ingenious and attractive, but none as yet proved correct. Moreover, in spite of what many believe, the same situation applies to antidepressants, anticonvulsants, and electroconvulsive treatment. As we do not know the pathophysiological basis of manic depressive illness, we do not know how treatments work; and as we do not know how treatments work, we cannot understand the pathophysiology of manic depressive illness. The locked box with the key inside appears to present an insoluble problem.[62]

The Limbic System, Emotions, and Mental Illness

By 1970, we had learned quite a bit about where in the brain the norepinephrine, serotonin, and dopamine circuits were located and how drugs affected the different neurotransmitter systems. Most of what was learned, however, concerned neuropharmacology and brain chemistry rather than any understanding of how changes in brain activity might produce various psychological phenomena. Relatively few people were (or even are today) thinking seriously about this problem beyond an occasional statement that this or that drug seems to act mostly on receptors located in a part of the brain (most commonly the limbic system or the hypothalamus, although sometimes the frontal lobes) suspected of having something to do with emotions. For example, because the nucleus accumbens is considered to be a brain structure located in the limbic system and because it also has dopamine receptors, it is constantly mentioned as playing a major role in the development of schizophrenia and in the action of antipsychotic drugs. But it is exceedingly rare to even find anyone speculating how dopamine activity in this brain structure might cause schizophrenia. Often the reasoning is no more sophisticated than arguing that the limbic system is involved in regulating the emotions, and mental disorders are considered emotional problems.

Actually, there are reasons to question whether the limbic system is solely responsible for regulating the emotions. Originally, this region of the brain was called the "grand lobe limbique" to connote those brain structures located immediately underneath and bordering the cerebral cortex. The French word *limbique* (derived from the Latin *limbus*) means border, threshold, or edge. When it was discovered that in animals and humans damage to some structures within this region could produce dramatic emotional changes, this anatomical region, together with the hypothalamus, began to be called the "limbic system," and its function was theorized to be the regulation of emotional responses and later also the memory of experience that evoked emotional responses. The limbic system was also called the "visceral brain" because stimulation of or damage to this region produced changes in the viscera (glands and smooth muscles like those in the gut). Thus, the limbic system was thought to be responsible for regulating both the gut and "gut feelings," that is, the emotions.

Most of the structures included in the limbic system were also considered to be part of the rhinencephalon or "smell brain" because the olfactory bulbs were connected to them. As the sense of smell signals that opportunities and dangers are in their vicinity, animals respond to these signals by becoming emotionally aroused. This connection with the sense of smell tended to support the idea that the limbic system evolved to regulate emotions even in humans, who do not depend to the same extent on the sense of smell. Thus, the limbic system began to be characterized as an evolutionary "primitive" part of the brain that humans shared with their animal ancestors. Moreover, it was claimed that this region functioned without much regulation from the more recently evolved cerebral cortex. It was thought that this might explain the separation between the "thinking brain" and the "emotional brain" and why the emotions were often unconscious and not controllable by conscious thought. All of these ideas seem to provide a biological and evolutionary basis for much speculation about the origin of mental disorders.

It is understandable that the concept of the limbic system assumed such a central position in the thinking of all biologically oriented psychiatrists. However, much that was written about the limbic system has turned out to be either oversimplified or untrue. For example, the limbic system and the cerebral cortex are more interconnected than originally thought, so that the idea that this "system" is unregulated by higher brain centers is not supported by modern anatomical information. Also, not all limbic system structures produce emotional changes when damaged or stimulated, and several major limbic structures are now known to play important roles in cognition. The hippocampus, for example, plays a major role in memory, particularly conscious (so-called "declarative") memories. Furthermore, some of the popular evolutionary ideas that the behavior of such animals as reptiles was completely dominated by emotional responses because they possesses a limbic system, but lack a mammalian-style neocortex, have turned out to be misleading in several respects. It is now known, for example, that the limbic structure in reptiles is organized differently than that in mammals, and it is able to carry on many functions, such as receiving and integrating sensory information, thought to belong exclusively to the more recently evolved cerebral cortex.

There are now a number of neuroscientists who have rejected the idea, so embraced by psychiatry, of an evolutionary "primitive" limbic system, divorced from any cognitive control and devoted exclusively to governing emotions. Even the idea of a limbic "system" has been rejected, as ultimately every part of the nervous system is connected, and what is called a system or a circuit is really an abstraction based on a theory about function. It is now recognized among many neuroscientists that the relation of limbic system activity to emotions has been overstated. Emotional responses are not divorced from cognitive processes, many other parts of the brain are involved in emotional expression, and limbic structures participate in many functions besides modulating emotional expression.[63] Yet most of the biochemical theories proposed to explain the action of psychotherapeutic drugs do not go beyond merely mentioning that a drug acts on receptors in some limbic structure without any further thought given to how that fact might be related to any specific mental aberration or therapeutic effect.

Biochemical theories of mental disorders are at present floundering, although only a few are willing to admit it. The initial biochemical theories are clearly inadequate to explain either drug action or the etiology of mental illness, but it is not known what can replace them. Not only is it highly speculative to patch up the theories by suggesting mechanisms that might explain why most drugs takes several weeks to have any effect, but it is difficult to understand how the drugs might produce changes in mental status. There is now evidence that many more neurotransmitters than previously suspected may be involved in the mediation of the effects of drug treatment, but we have little idea how (or if) they are also involved in the etiology of depression, schizophrenia, and the other mental disorders. While it might be assumed that all the additional knowledge of brain chemistry would make it easier to understand how psychotherapeutic drugs work and what causes mental disorders, in actuality it has just multiplied the number of interacting variables that must be considered and makes it that much more difficult to understand the cascading changes produced even by drugs that initially have a highly specific site of action. Moreover, most of our current speculation about possible biological factors in the development of various mental illnesses has been limited to searching for neurotransmitter abnormalities. Even within this arena the search has been limited to exploring a very few of the now large number of neurotransmitters, neuromodulators, and hormones known to influence neural activity and mental states.

Up to this point, the discussion of the biochemical theory of mental disorders has focused on an examination of the reliability of the empirical evidence. There are, however, a number of broader issues concerning how the empirical evidence should be interpreted even if there were complete agreement about the facts. These issues are addressed in the next chapter.

Chapter 5

THE INTERPRETATION
OF THE EVIDENCE

C ontrary to what is often claimed, no biochemical, anatomical, or functional signs have been found that reliably distinguish the brains of mental patients. While several investigators have reported that there is something different about the brains of schizophrenics, for example, other investigators have not been able to verify these findings. Even in the studies reporting positive results, many schizophrenics do not have the reputed brain "abnormality," while some of the people in the normal "control" group do, even though they have no history of any psychiatric disorder. The evidence of brain abnormalities in other mental disorders is even more tenuous than it is with schizophrenia. Furthermore, as explained in the preceding chapter, the indirect evidence of a biochemical disorder based on the belief that the most effective drugs for each major class of mental disorder produce the same biochemical changes is much less convincing than usually claimed.

It certainly cannot be ruled out that at some time in the future a strong and reliable relationship may be found between a biological marker and some mental disorder. Even if such a relationship is found, however, there will remain serious questions about what meaning should be attributed to it. This chapter will discuss some of the questions that must be considered in interpreting even the most reliable biological correlate of a mental disorder.

The Confusion of Cause and Effect

Most people know that a correlation, no matter how strong, does not prove causation, but it is easy to forget this fact. Of course, no one would suggest that the carrying of umbrellas causes rainfall, although umbrella carrying is highly associated with rain. Yet, if some biological marker in the brain is found to correlate with a mental disorder, it is easy to fall into the trap of believing the marker is the cause of the disorder. This may be, at least partly, because the brain is known to play a central role in all psychological experiences, but logically this relationship is not different from the example of the umbrella and rain. A person's mental state and experience can modify the brain just as surely as the other way around. When there is a correlation between two events, we should not assume that we always know which way causation flows. What is "cause" and what is "effect" can easily be confused. In fact, two events can be highly correlated without their being any causal relationship between them. In most countries, for example, people whose first name ends with a vowel are on average shorter than those whose names end in a consonant. However, as a little thought on the matter should make apparent, there is no need to assume that a causal relationship exists between final vowels and consonants and height.[1]

There is no reason to assume that any biochemical, anatomical, or functional difference found in the brains of mental patients is the cause of the disorder. It is well established that the drugs used to treat a mental disorder, for example, may induce long-lasting biochemical and even structural changes, which in the past were claimed to be the cause of the disorder, but may actually be an effect of the treatment. Drugs that block receptors or increase the amount of a neurotransmitter in the synapse initiate many compensatory changes in the number of receptors and in the firing rate of certain neurons. Drugs taken repeatedly tend to produce either sensitization or tolerance, so that the response produced by the same drug dose either increases or decreases. Long-lasting and even permanent physical changes in the brain underlie sensitization and tolerance to drugs. Recently, Terry Robinson and Bryan Kolb, two biopsychologists, have reported that more than a month after the completion of a series of amphetamine injections that produced a sensitization to this drug, some brain structures had undergone significant anatomical changes.[2] It is now difficult to find mental patients who have not had a history of drug treatment, and as a result many of the brain abnormalities found in these patients are probably iatrogenic, that is, produced by the treatment rather than being the cause of the disorder. There have been a few reports of abnormal receptor numbers in the brains of schizophrenics who never received any drug treatment, but as indicated in the last chapter, these findings have been difficult to replicate. Moreover, even in the studies reporting such abnormalities, it is only a trend that does not apply to all schizophrenics.

Experience Can Modify Brain Anatomy

While some of the physical changes found in the brains of mental patients may be the result of drug treatment, this is not the only possibility to be considered in interpreting these reports. Various experiences can also cause structural and functional changes in the brain. It has been shown in numerous experiments, for example, that exposure to stressful situations can produce long-lasting brain changes. Animals that are stressed repeatedly have an elevated response to an injection of amphetamine, even when the drug is administered several months later.[3] There is also evidence that stress can produce long-lasting changes in the same class of dopamine neurons on which antipsychotic drugs act. Even when dopamine neurons are removed from the brains of stressed animals and placed in a dish, amphetamine will cause excessive amounts of dopamine to be released.[4] These results indicate that stress can produce enduring physical changes in dopamine neurons that make them hypersensitive not only to drugs such as amphetamine, but also to subsequent exposure to stress. It has been suggested that this long-lasting sensitization of certain neurons may be the cause of "posttraumatic stress disorders (PTSD)." The effects of stress may not be restricted to sensitizing dopamine neurons. It is known that stress triggers secretion of certain adrenal gland hormones, and recently it has been found in animals that an excessive amount of these hormones can destroy neurons in the hippocampus, a brain area important for memory.[5] The enormous capacity of humans to recall past stressful events may greatly expand the possibilities for experiencing stress over and over again, and many patients suffering from mental disorders appear to be in a state of almost continuous stress.[6]

Furthermore, the effect of stress is not the only factor to be considered in evaluating reports of abnormalities found in the brains of mental patients. The anatomy of the brain is much more plastic than is usually acknowledged by investigators anxious to claim that they have found the cause of a mental disorder in some functional or structural differences in the brains of patients. There is now a huge amount of experimental evidence demonstrating that different types of experience can modify brain anatomy in the adult animal as well as in young animals.[7] Early studies demonstrated that neurons in the brains of rats raised in enriched environments are significantly more branched and presumably more capable of making connections than are comparable neurons of rats raised in impoverished environments. Subsequent studies have shown that various kinds of experiences, such as repeated training on a specific task, can also modify the structure of neurons in the brain areas involved in the those activities. Plasticity must be a basic property of neurons, as it is essential for learning and memory even in invertebrates. Eric Kandel of Columbia University, for example, has demonstrated that during the acquisition of conditioned reflexes, the neurons of aplysia (a marine snail) undergo structural changes that later facilitate the transmission across specific synapses.[8] Genes are responsible for establishing the scaffolding or fundamental organization of the brain, but a large amount of the neuronal growth that leads to the establishment of connections has been shown to be influenced (if not guided) by experience. There is no way that the one hundred thousand genes in the human genome could determine the precise configuration of the estimated 10 trillion synaptic connections in the human brain.

Evidence that experience can modify brain structure has also been reported in humans. It has been reported, for example, that the amount of branching of neuronal dendrites in the language area (Wernicke's area) of human brains is, on average, proportional to the amount of education. Thus, it was found that people who had a university education tend to have more branching in the language area than do people with only a high school education, and they in turn tend to have more branching than do people who did not go to high school. These results could not be explained by any differences in age or sex between the groups. While the authors recognize that differences in brain structures may have influenced people to seek different levels of education, they believe that it is much more likely that the different experiences associated with different levels of education had modified the brain.[9]

Also supporting the conclusion that behavior can modify brain anatomy is a recent report by Marc Breedlove, a psychologist at the University of California at Berkeley. Breedlove reported finding changes in the size of a central nervous system structure in rats given an opportunity to engage in frequent sexual behavior, and he concluded that the findings demonstrate the possibility "that differences in sexual behavior cause, rather than are caused by, differences in brain structure."[10] If activity below the waist can change the structure of the nervous system, there is no reason to believe that activity above the neck cannot have the same effect.

The now overwhelming evidence that experience can alter neuronal structure and function should make it clear that it is dangerous to assume that any distinctive anatomical or physiological characteristic found in the brains of people with mental disorders was the cause of that disorder. Mental patients may be so withdrawn into their own world that they are deprived of external stimulation, or they may engage repeatedly in some compulsive act, or they may be completely inactive, or they may continually pace back and forth in an agitated state, or they may eat or sleep excessively or very little, or they may be fixated on some obsessive thought. Any of these thought and behavior patterns, if sustained, might conceivably produce a physical change in the brain. It cannot be assumed, therefore, that every "biological marker" found in patients with a particular mental disorder is the cause of that disorder. Biochemical and other biological changes in the brain may well have been caused by a patient's mental and behavioral state.

Experience and Changes in Brain Function

In addition to physical changes in the brain, functional abnormalities have been reported in patients with particular mental disorders. New brain-imaging techniques have allowed researchers to detect unusual patterns of brain activity in regions where there may be no detectable structural or biochemical abnormality. However, abnormal functioning or pathophysiology can be the consequence of a mental disorder rather than its cause. In the zeal to report a possible cause of a mental disorder, it is often forgotten that brain activity is modifiable by all kinds of experiences. In some cases brain function can be modified consciously. In biofeedback experiments subjects have demonstrated that they are capable of modifying the electrical activity of their own brains, usually by imagining certain experiences.

A recent series of positron emission tomography (PET) studies bears directly on the issue of distinguishing between the effect and the cause of a mental disorder. PET is a brain-imaging instrument that makes it possible to study regional changes in brain activity while a subject is engaged in certain tasks or having certain experiences. In one experiment, patients suffering from obsessive-compulsive disorder were studied. Such patients are unable to free themselves from some disturbing thought, such as the fear that everything they touch is contaminated with germs. They may wash their hands compulsively, or they may not be able to stop sobbing over the loss of a parent who died fifteen years earlier. Several investigators have reported that obsessive-compulsive patients tend to exhibit abnormally high levels of activity in several brain regions, including the orbitofrontal cortex, the corpus striatum, and a region of the thalamus. It has been hypothesized that abnormal activity in a brain circuit involving these structures may cause obsessive-compulsive disorder. Investigators at UCLA's Brain Research Institute reported that following either behavior modification therapy or cognitive psychotherapy to reduce obsessive thoughts, the abnormal brain activity was reduced.[11] The reverse was also demonstrated, in a study in which the obsessive-compulsive symptoms were exacerbated by confronting patients with situations that intensified their obsessional concerns.[12] So, for example, a person with an obsession about contamination from germs was handed a filthy glove. Not surprisingly, the characteristic brain activity pattern was intensified. Thus, there was a good correlation between the intensity of the obsessive thoughts and the abnormal brain activity. But how should this relationship be interpreted?

The argument that the heightened brain activity in a particular brain circuit is the cause of the obsessive-compulsive disorder might appear to be persuasive because the abnormal brain pattern is present in many patients with obsessive-compulsive disorder and because it tends to disappear when the patients improve and is intensified when the symptoms become more severe. The flaw in the logic becomes obvious if once again we use the somewhat simplistic analogy of umbrellas as the cause of rainfall. Here too, we would find more umbrellas open when the rain is heavy, less when there is only a light drizzle, and none when the sun is shining. However, when the evidence involves an association between brain function and a mental disorder, the argument that a cause has been found seems convincing even though the logic is no less flawed. When one of the variables of a correlation involves the brain, it is much harder to resist the temptation of elevating its status to that of a cause.

It is possible that the characteristic brain activity pattern may not have initially caused the obsessive-compulsive disorder, but it may play a role in perpetuating or intensifying the disorder. Although it certainly has not been shown to be true, if it turned out that a certain state was playing a role in intensifying or sustaining some abnormal mood state or obsessive ideation, then it is possible that altering that brain state could provide some symptom relief. Several examples can serve to illustrate this possibility. As everyone has experienced, many emotional states are associated with a number of bodily changes, such as an increase in heart rate, changes in respiration, and other visceral changes not experienced consciously, such as increased adrenaline secretion and dilation of blood vessels to skeletal muscles. The correlation between the experience of emotion and these bodily changes is so strong that in the 1890s, William James and Carl Lange independently proposed that the experience of an emotion was nothing more than the awareness of the visceral changes that characterize each emotion. The theory was proven wrong, as people with their spinal cord transected, so that their brains cannot receive information about the state of their body, are still capable of experiencing emotions.

Even though visceral bodily changes are no longer considered the cause of emotional states, they do play a role in intensifying emotional experience. In experiments performed in the 1950s, Stanley Schachter produced many of the visceral changes associated with emotional states by injecting epinephrine (adrenaline) into subjects. It was found that the bodily changes produced by the injections did not determine the nature of the emotion experienced, but when the environment was manipulated so that the subjects were made to feel angry or happy, the appropriate emotional experience was intensified by an epinephrine injection.[13] Similarly, when a person is anxious and fearful, his or her muscles are usually tense. Even though it is not muscle tension that caused the anxious state, getting the muscles to relax with so-called "progressive relaxation" techniques often helps to reduce the intensity of the anxiety and fear. While it has not been proven that any of the suggested biological correlates of mental disorders have caused the disorders, it is possible that some of them may play a role in intensifying the disorder. However, this has yet to be demonstrated.

The Dexamethasone Suppression Test: An Illustrative Case

In the 1980s, it was almost impossible to pick up a psychiatric journal that did not contain several articles about the Dexamethasone Suppression Test (DST) for depression. Dexamethasone is a synthetic hormone, which has some, but not all, of the effects of the adrenal cortical hormone, cortisol. Cortisol not only has effects on the body, but also acts on the brain, and receptors for this hormone have been located in the hypothalamus (situated just above the pituitary gland) and other brain areas. The hypothalamus plays an important role in regulating pituitary gland secretions, including the adrenal cortical stimulating hormone (ACTH), which, in turn, stimulates the adrenal cortex to release cortisol. The brain senses high levels of cortisol and signals the pituitary gland to decrease its release of ACTH, which results in a reduction in cortisol secretion. In this respect, dexamethasone acts like cortisol in that it acts on the same brain receptors that produce a depression in the amount of cortisol secreted by the adrenal gland.

Because there were several reports that some depressed people had high cortisol levels, it was thought worth exploring whether depressed patients responded differently to an injection of dexamethasone. It was found that following an injection of dexamethasone, the serum (blood) cortisol levels of normal people is suppressed for about twenty-four hours, depending on the dose, while the cortisol levels of depressed patients were suppressed for a significantly shorter period. This failure of dexamethasone to evoke normal levels of suppression soon became a widely accepted tool for diagnosing different types of depression. It was claimed, for example, that the Dexamethasone Suppression Test distinguished endogenous depression, hypothesized to be caused by a biochemical or other biological factor, from "reactive" depression thought to be triggered by life experiences. Since it was the hypothalamus and some brain areas in the limbic system that responded to circulating cortisol levels and in turn controlled pituitary gland activity, the DST was believed to be revealing a functional abnormality either in the hypothalamus or in the limbic system of patients with endogenous depression.[14] The DST stimulated enormous research interest, and by the mid-1980s it had become the most extensively investigated "biological marker" of depression.

Despite all the excitement and the number of DST articles in the psychiatric journals, it was not clear whether the abnormal cortisol response to dexamethasone was pointing to the cause of depression or reflecting the behavioral and emotional state of depression. It was claimed that the abnormal cortisol suppression pattern would often vanish during treatment with antidepressants or electroconvulsive shock, even before there was any behavioral or emotional evidence that the patient had improved. These reports, however, proved difficult to replicate, and the possibility that cause and effect were being confused remained.[15]

A study published in the widely read medical journal *Lancet* strongly suggests the DST was not detecting a brain abnormality that caused depression, but rather it appears to reflect an effect caused by the loss of appetite and the consequent decrease in food consumption that characterizes most depressed patients.[16] The investigators placed subjects who had no history of depression on a diet that restricted their caloric intake to between one thousand and twelve hundred calories per day. The caloric restriction did not produce any evidence of depression or any change in the mood of the subjects. Yet when they were given the DST, a significant number of the subjects had a dexamethasone response pattern identical to that which was claimed to be a sign of depression. Although decreased food intake alone may not explain all the DST results obtained from depressed people, the results did suggest that the cortisol response need not necessarily indicate the pathophysiology responsible for depression. Rather, the test results may reflect some behavioral change that characterizes the depressive state. If the DST was not likely to tells us anything about the cause of depression, there was little need for it, as the presence of depression can normally be detected much more readily without a cumbersome laboratory test. By 1997, interest in the Dexamethasone Suppression Test had almost completely disappeared and only rarely are any articles on the subject published in current psychiatric journals.

On Treatments, Causes, and Diagnoses

In psychiatry, the cause of an illness is often inferred from the effectiveness of a treatment. Drawing conclusions about the nature of an illness and even making a diagnosis based on the effectiveness of treatment has been called *ex juvantibus* reasoning (Latin: from that which produces health).[17] Thus, if the diagnosis of a mental patient is not clear because there are symptoms of both depression and schizophrenia, the diagnosis and the etiology may be based on whether the patient responds to an antidepressant or an antipsychotic drug, or whether both types of drugs are required. It is easy to be drawn into *ex juvantibus* reasoning, but it can also be very misleading. There are many examples in medicine where the connection between the cause of an illness and a treatment is extremely remote and even nonexistent.

Studies of the drugs used to treat attention deficit/hyperactivity disorder (ADHD) illustrates how misleading it can be to draw conclusions about the cause of a disorder from a treatment just because it may be effective in ameliorating symptoms. Children diagnosed with ADHD are generally hyperactive, highly distractible, inattentive, and often disruptive in a classroom and elsewhere. The diagnosis of ADHD in many instances can be difficult, as children may manifest one or all of this behavior for many reasons and to varying degrees. According to Howard Morris of the National Attention Deficit Disorder Association, many physicians use the drug Ritalin as a diagnostic tool, assuming the attitude that if Ritalin works "then you've got it and if it doesn't, then you don't."[18]

Children with ADHD are assumed to have a biochemical abnormality because Ritalin, an amphetaminelike drug that is a psychomotor stimulant, produces a "paradoxical" slowing of activity and increases attention span in these children. A study by Judith Rapoport and her colleagues at the National Institute of Mental Health, however, demonstrated that the response of ADHD children to amphetamine is not paradoxical at all. These investigators administered Ritalin to children of professionals in the biomedical and mental health community and found that the drug also decreased activity and increased attention span in these normal children. Rapoport concluded that there may be some minimal brain damage (MBD) in a subset of children with ADHD, but the assumption that they have a biochemical abnormality has no foundation in hard evidence.[19] While there are circumstances when *ex juvantibus* reasoning can provide a clue to an underlying cause of a disease, a diagnosis should be linked to some understanding of the underlying disease process rather than being an inference made from the effect of a drug, whose action—at least with respect to the etiology of the disease—may be poorly understood.[20]

There are many reasons for regarding the connections between the effectiveness of a treatment and the etiology of a disease as exceedingly tenuous. Medical history is replete with examples of treatments that helped to alleviate illnesses, but did so without having any direct relationship to the cause of the illness. For example, diuretic drugs were used with some success to alleviate symptoms of congestive heart failure. The diuretics helped by causing the kidney to excrete more fluids and thereby relieve some of the work load on the heart, but there is nothing wrong with the kidneys in patients with congestive heart failure. Manic-depressive patients are often helped by lithium treatment, but there is no evidence that they suffer from a lithium deficiency any more than people with headaches are suffering from an aspirin deficiency.

The Relation of the Origin of a Disease to the Most Effective Treatment

It is a mistake to assume that because a disorder has a biological cause a biological treatment will be most effective. A condition may have a biological origin, but may be best treated by a psychological approach, and the converse is equally true. For example, most investigators who have studied autism believe that this condition is caused by some brain defect, although there is no agreement on the nature of the impairment or the precise brain structures involved. However, even if a brain impairment were found to be the cause of autism, it might not be possible to correct this condition, and the best treatment available might remain psychosocial and behavioral.

There are a number of examples of the dangers of *ex juvantibus* reasoning in psychiatry.[21] For example, because depression may be alleviated by drugs that elevate the activity of serotonin or norepinephrine or both it has been assumed that depression is caused by low levels of activity in those neurotransmitter systems. So committed is much of psychiatry to this *ex juvantibus* reasoning that when a drug that has little effect on either of these neurotransmitters proves to be an effective antidepressant, it is called an "atypical antidepressant." Rather than leading to questioning the biogenic amine theory of depression, such results are classified as atypical. Similarly, if patients appear to be depressed in many ways, but do not experience insomnia or a decreased interest in food and sex and may actually eat, sleep, and engage in sex excessively, they are often diagnosed as having an "atypical depression." It is a paradox, however, that patients with "atypical" depression, who may eat and sleep excessively, show no less improvement with antidepressant drugs that elevate serotonin and norepinephrine than do the patients with "typical" depression. The term "atypical" in both instances implies that the drugs or the patients are exceptions to the basic theory, which is rarely questioned. It is the same type of reasoning implied by the phrase that "they are exceptions that prove the rule," which, in reality, is never the case.

In other instances of *ex juvantibus* reasoning, when anxious patients respond to an antipsychotic rather than an antianxiety drug, they may be rediagnosed as schizophrenic. Or when a depressed patient with many of the classical symptoms of depression, including a feeling of worthlessness, suicidal thoughts, and a loss of appetite, doesn't respond to antidepressant treatment, but does show an abatement of symptoms when treated with antipsychotics, the diagnosis may be changed to a schizoaffective disorder. While a patient who is considered to have a schizoaffective condition may show some signs of a schizophrenic thought disorder along with the signs of depression, what may determine the diagnosis is that the patient improves with antipsychotic drug treatment. Many depressed patients also exhibit some loosening of their thought processes, but if they respond to antidepressants alone they are likely to be diagnosed as depressed rather than schizoaffective.

The experience of the Canadian psychologist Norman Endler provides an interesting way of illustrating the pitfalls of *ex juvantibus* reasoning. Endler, a highly productive researcher and clinician, wrote a book describing his own serious bout of depression.[22] At the time that he became depressed, Endler was in his mid-forties, a professor at York University, chairman of the largest department of psychology in Canada, and a consultant to Toronto's Clarke Institute of Psychiatry and to the Department of Psychiatry at the Toronto East General Hospital. In the midst of a busy schedule, teaching, doing research, consulting, and giving talks at international congresses, Endler began to feel anxious and unsure of himself. Within a week or so he could no longer concentrate or carry on any of his normal activities. In his own words, he was "anxious, uncertain, irritable, sad, upset, lacked confidence, cried, felt dejected, blue, shaky, and listless, could not eat, lost [his] sex drive, and was lethargic and sluggish, among other things." He was experiencing a crippling depression. Endler went to several psychiatrists but was not helped until he received the prescription that finally worked. After about twenty days of treatment, Endler returned to his former self. Again in his own words, "I had gone from an emotional cripple to feeling well. . . . I taught my first class; I also played my first game of tennis in more than three months and won. That night my sex drive returned." The treatment that seemed to work was not drugs. Neither monoamine oxydase inhibitors nor tricyclic antidepressants had helped and, moreover, Endler had problems with some of the side effects of the drugs. What actually helped Endler was electroconvulsive treatment (ECT). Was this an "atypical depression" simply because antidepressant drugs were not effective? This experience was presented not to illustrate that ECT is better than drugs, but to make the point that we often do not know why treatments work, and it is always risky to draw conclusions about etiology based on what works.[23] There has been much speculation, but no one knows why ECT so often is successful in relieving depression. Those who are wedded to a biogenic amine deficiency theory of depression have argued that ECT works because it elevates activity in those neurotransmitter systems. However, ECT produces a number of other physiological changes in the brain besides increasing biogenic amine activity, and in this instance, as in many others, we do not know why ECT should help when antidepressant drugs have not provided any meaningful help.

The truth is that it is really not known how drugs alleviate the symptoms of mental disorders, and it should not be assumed that they do so by correcting an endogenous chemical deficiency or excess. Anyone who has seen schizophrenics treated with antipsychotic drugs, for example, knows that they usually show signs of being sedated—often shuffling around the wards and responding slowly both physically and mentally. After several weeks of antipsychotic drug treatment, schizophrenics may seem less disturbed by their delusional thoughts or the voices, but on questioning they usually indicate that the delusional thoughts and the voices are still there. It is clear from their behavior, however, that the thoughts and voices are no longer commanding the same attention or evoking the intense emotional response they did when drug treatment began. The patients have gradually become indifferent to thoughts and voices, and when the treatment is successful they gradually fade into the background until they are no longer intrusive or even experienced and the patient may be able to resume a more normal life. Sedation may be important in this process, but it is clearly not sufficient, as sedatives are not effective antipsychotics. There is no chemical switch that suddenly turns off psychotic thoughts and hallucinations. During the period of gradual improvement many physiological and psychological changes take place, and it is not known what is responsible for any improvement that occurs.

And Vice Versa

Just as it is often misleading to draw conclusions about the cause of an illness from a treatment that may alleviate the symptoms of the illness, the converse is also true. It is equally dangerous to draw conclusions about the cause of an illness from a drug or from some other biological intervention that produces the symptoms of the illness. I described in Chapter 4 how the belief that the drug reserpine produced depression had convinced a great number of people that a deficiency in the biogenic amine neurotransmitters was the cause of depression. Actually, it turned out that reserpine only precipitated a depressive episode in people prone to depression. This experience with reserpine reminded me of a controversy I was involved in that concerned the claim that stimulating the brain through implanted electrodes was a reliable way of detecting the brain area that was triggering violent outbursts in patients prone to such behavior.[24] A careful review of the clinical literature and the evidence obtained from animal experiments revealed that aggressive behavior is triggered by brain stimulation at many sites that evoke emotional states such as fear, anxiety, and pain, but it did so only in subjects that were aggressive or subject to violent outbursts. In humans who tend to have violent outbursts, even a hard pinch on the arm is likely to evoke a violent response. It was clear that the capacity to evoke a violent response by brain stimulation was not a reliable way to determine the cause of the behavior when it occurred spontaneously.

Similarly, the fact that the drug Yohimbine often evokes panic attacks and "flashbacks" in Vietnam veterans suffering from "posttraumatic stress syndrome" does not indicate what brain chemical systems are normally involved in triggering the symptoms of this disorder. Yohimbine does not produce marked changes in mood states of normal subjects.[25] Likewise, intravenous infusions of sodium lactate often evoke panic attacks in patients subject to these attacks, but it does not have this effect in normal control subjects.[26] In other instances, the symptoms evoked by a drug only superficially resemble a mental disorder, as in the case of LSD-induced hallucinations, which, for a time, were mistakenly considered to indicate that a serotonin deficiency might be the cause of schizophrenia. It is now recognized that the hallucinations and other mental states produced by LSD differ from schizophrenia. For many reasons, therefore, the sometimes dramatic precipitation by a drug of what appears to be a mental disorder should not be accepted uncritically as evidence of what normally causes the disorder.

Scientific Explanations and Reductionism

The enormous advances in molecular biology over the last two decades have led to predictions that genetics will before long be able to explain almost everything important about a person, from intelligence and personality to probability of developing a specific physical or mental disorder. While some dismiss these predictions as "molecular euphoria," others are convinced that the only way that science advances is by reductionism. Reductionism refers to explanations of a phenomenon based on the properties of the constituent elements that compose it. Thus a reductionistic explanation of water would be based on the properties of hydrogen and oxygen. Molar explanations, on the other hand, are based on the properties of the whole, with the assumption that the "whole is more than (or different from) the sum of its parts." The study of behavior that seeks explanations based on the properties of the whole organism is a molar approach, while physiological explanation based on the properties of various organs in the body is a molecular approach. However, molar and molecular are commonly used in a relative sense. Physiological explanations are more molar than chemical ones, while explanations based on atomic physics are more molecular than chemical explanations. Thus, biochemical theories of mental disorders are more molecular and reductionistic than any theory based on the experiences of the whole person.

While reductionism often provides insight into underlying mechanisms that may prove helpful in understanding some properties of more molar phenomena, it is an error to assume that the "bottom-up" approach is the only way, or even always the best way, for science to proceed. In pursuing the biochemical approach to mental disorders an enormous amount has been learned about neurochemistry and drug action, but it is questionable how much has been learned about mental illness. We do not really know if a biochemical imbalance is the cause of any mental disorder, and we do not know how even the hypothesized biochemical imbalances could produce the emotional, cognitive, and behavioral symptoms that characterize any mental disorder. There remains a huge gap between the levels of these phenomena that has not been bridged.

It is a mistake to assume that causality can only be studied fruitfully from the bottom up—that is, by using molecular phenomena to explain molar phenomena. It is an error to assume that biochemical and other physiological phenomena can explain mental events, but the converse is never true. How should we think about such commonly reported experiences as salivating when thinking about biting into a juicy sour pickle or the genital and hormonal changes that result from a sexual fantasy?

Moreover, social interactions can initiate physiological changes that would not otherwise have taken place in isolation. In many birds, such as the ring dove, the female does not normally lay eggs when alone. It is only when a female dove is courted by a male that she undergoes the hormonal, physiological, and anatomical changes that result in egg-laying. Causality, in this case, must include psychosocial phenomena, and any study that relied exclusively on the physiology of female doves in isolation would miss much of what is essential for understanding egg-laying in this species. Those who would deny the importance of psychosocial phenomena as having a causal role in producing physiological changes must try to explain how a religious Jew (or Moslem) who is unaware that he is eating pork can get violently sick hours later after being told that he had inadvertently eaten the forbidden meat. Or how can we explain the documented cases of "voodoo death" studied by Walter Cannon, the eminent Harvard physiologist, and later by Curt Richter, the Johns Hopkins psychobiologist? In countries that practice voodoo, a perfectly healthy person may become emaciated and die after being told that a curse has been put on him. Not too long ago the medical and scientific community ridiculed the idea that stress could affect resistance to infections and the growth of tumors. It is now, however, widely accepted that there is persuasive experimental evidence that this does occur. How stress-induced hormones can suppress the immune system is now actively being studied by investigators working in a field whose very name, "psychoendocrineneuroimmunology," expresses the need to bridge phenomena at different levels.

Other examples illustrate the value of a "top-down" strategy in science. There are well-documented cases of children whose growth is stunted despite consuming an adequate diet, sometimes even despite their having a voracious appetite. In an actual case, a boy who was 5 years, 7 months in age weighed only 20 pounds (the weight of an average 9-month-old) and had a skeletal maturation of a 2-year-old. He could barely stand and could not walk. In another documented case, a girl who was over 14 years old weighed only 48 pounds (the weight of an average 7-year-old) and had the bone maturation of a 10-year-old and the general appearance of a 7-year-old.[27] Such children are said to be suffering from a condition called "psychosocial dwarfism," and it is claimed that their stunted growth is often the result of a stressful home environment and a dysfunctional family. Typically, these children do not respond to hormonal treatment, but when they are removed from their homes and placed in a supportive environment, they often experience a marked growth spurt, while such children left with their dysfunctional families rarely (only one out of thirty-five in one study) catch up to the normal size and weight for their age. If children are returned to their dysfunctional families, they often stop growing once again. It is an error to assume that every disorder exists solely within the gene-coded biochemistry of a patient, as many are social in origin. A physician has to treat the patient, but if every problem is "medicalized" to the point that only physiological causes are looked for, much that is critical may be missed. There is no way of understanding the phenomenon of "psychosocial dwarfism" unless the psychological and social environment is considered. There are those who believe that it is not possible to fully understand the development of any disease without considering psychosocial influences, but this especially true of mental disorders.

Explaining how physical events are related to mental events ultimately requires confronting the age-old conundrum, the "mind-body" problem. None of the recent spate of books attempting to explain the emergence of consciousness or the relation of mind to body is really an advance over what has been said for hundreds of years. Some writers dismiss mind and consciousness as simply epiphenomena that cannot influence physiological events and serve only to distract us from studying what is observable, namely, the brain and behavior. Many books seem to offer metaphors rather than understanding. It is not particularly helpful to be told that "the mind is to brain as time is to clock," or to be offered computer analogies, such as "mind is the software while the brain is the hardware." Our understanding is not advanced by these metaphors of the month.

It is probably impossible today to find any scientist who believes that a mind can exist without a brain like some free-floating, disembodied soul. This does not mean, however, that the mind can be understood by studying the properties of any of the molecular components of the brain. A reduc-

tionist approach that studies only the properties of organs, neurotransmitters, cells, or atoms cannot understand consciousness and thought.
Mental activity emerges from the integrated action of more than 20 billion brain cells (some of which are influenced by as many as ten thousand
synaptic connections). Moreover, it is impossible to understand consciousness and thought without considering the psychosocial context that not
only shapes the content of thought, but also the physical structure of the
brain. Mental activity (normal or disordered) simply does not exist at a
molecular level. *We must use methodologies that are appropriate to the level
at which a phenomenon exists.*

The point is illustrated by the story of the aliens who land on earth some
time in the future at a time when there is no longer any life on this planet.
When a library filled with books is discovered, the aliens, who do not know
what these objects are, give them to their scientists to study. The anatomists
report that "the specimens are a roughly rectangular block of fibrous material, covered ventrally and dorsally with two coarse, fibrous, encapsulated lam-
inae approximately three millimeters thick. Between these, lie several
hundred white lamellae, all fastened at one end and mobile at the other. On
closer inspection, these are found to contain a large number of black surface
markings arranged in linear groupings in a highly complex manner."[28]
Meanwhile, the alien chemists blend some books into a homogenate and
centrifuge out the black contaminants. The chemists report that the objects
have a cellulose structure with a molecular configuration as illustrated in an
accompanying diagram. As usually told, the story is longer, including many
other equally inappropriate analyses supplied by different scientific disciplines. The point of the story is not, however, the same as that of the "blind
men and the elephant," in which each man grasps a different part of the
truth. What the story really illustrates is that there is an appropriate level at
which to study a phenomenon, and a reductionist approach may miss the
whole point, or at least, the most important point. It is not my contention
here that reductionist approaches cannot provide insight into mechanisms
that are necessary for a more complete understanding of more molar phenomena. However, the knowledge of molecular principles must be used judi-
ciously to supplement the complexities and richness of more molar
phenomena, not as a substitute for them.

Most recent claims that a gene (or a couple of genes) has been discovered that causes alcoholism, manic-depressive disorder, schizophrenia,
homosexuality, and a host of other disorders and personality traits have
proven illusory, as others have either failed to replicate the findings or, at
best, the findings turned out to apply to only to a small subset of the people who possess the trait under study. A more fundamental criticism of
those claims is that genes do not produce behavioral or mental states.
Genes carry the instructions and template for producing and assembling

amino acids and proteins into anatomical structures. Behavior and mental traits, however, are the product of an interaction between anatomical structure and experience—remembered experiences from the past, present experiences, and anticipation of future experiences. Even where there is compelling evidence that some behavioral or mental trait is influenced by genetic factors it is almost always a predisposition, not a certainty. When one identical twin has schizophrenia or juvenile (Type 1) diabetes, the probability that the other twin will have that disorder is less than 50 percent—this despite the fact that identical twins possess identical genes.

"Anatomy is not destiny," and, moreover, genes are not even the sole determinant of anatomy. The expression of genes can be turned on and off by physiological concomitants of life experiences. Marian Diamond's book *Enriching Heredity: The Impact of the Environment on the Anatomy of the Brain* provides descriptions of many studies demonstrating that the anatomy of the brains of animals is influenced by life experiences.[29] Identical twins do not have identical brains, as Daniel Weinberger and his colleagues showed when they reported that there are significant differences even in the gross structure of the brains of identical twins.[30] The experiential factors that interact with the genetic endowment to shape the structure of the brain can occur before as well as after birth. There is evidence, for example, that male animals still in the uterus will later show both behavioral and neuroanatomical effects of maternal stress. It is believed that when pregnant animals are stressed, brain endorphins are released, and this suppresses testosterone. As a result of insufficient testosterone, a brain area known to differ in adult males and females may fail to undergo the masculine differentiation that normally occurs during fetal development. Later in life, the males born from stressed mothers tend to show inadequate male sexual behavior, and under some conditions, they may display female sexual patterns.[31]

There is no question that experiences (both prenatal and postnatal) shape brain anatomy and function and have a major impact on behavior and thought. It is unrealistic to believe that the cause of any behavior or mental disorder will ever be explained by concentrating only on the activity of a few neurotransmitters.

Neurotransmitters Are Not All of Biology

It is commonly assumed that anyone who criticizes the chemical theories of mental disorders must be against all biological explanations of behavior. Of course, this need not be the case and it certainly is not the view of this neuroscientist. To point out the weaknesses in the evidence used to support the theory that mental disorders are caused by biochemical imbalances, and even to argue that some of the logic employed is flawed, is not antibiological. Biochemistry is not all there is to biology. There are, for example, several theories about the causes of mental disorders that emphasize structural or functional brain anomalies, rather than biochemical factors. While it is sometimes argued that any brain anomaly must have biochemical consequences, this really begs the question about what is a cause and what is an effect. It may be no more justifiable to consider a biochemical anomaly the cause of a mental disorder than it is to consider tense muscles the cause of anxiety.

During the second half of the nineteenth century and continuing through the first half of this century, there were a great number of claims that the brain anomaly that causes schizophrenia had been found. Typical of these claims was that of the pathologist Alois Alzheimer, most remembered today for describing the dementia that bears his name. Alzheimer believed that he had found the cause of schizophrenia to be an abnormality in the frontal cortex of the brain.[32] This report could not be confirmed, but in fairness it must be noted that the techniques available to Alzheimer and others at the time were crude by today's standards, and the studies could only be done on autopsy material, commonly from older chronic patients. So many of the early reports of anomalies found in the brains of mental patients could not be confirmed by others that this period has been called "the era of brain mythology." In many instances the anomalies were later shown to have been caused by long-term institutionalization or by the way the brains had been preserved, rather than being the cause of schizophrenia. Because so many neuropathologists spent their lives searching for the brain anomaly that caused schizophrenia, it has been said that "schizophrenia was the graveyard of neuropathologists."[33]

By 1940, the enthusiasm for searching for brain abnormalities in mental patients had waned, as it had become widely accepted that the cause of mental disorders was to be found in the life experiences of those afflicted. Around 1960, however, the prevailing wind began to shift back to searching for biological causes. The shift back to biological explanations was the result of several factors, among them the availability of better-controlled epidemiological studies demonstrating a possible genetic cause of some mental disorders, the increasing acceptance that drugs could alleviate some mental disorders, and the growing suspicion that psychotherapy was not living up to its promise.

There are many current theories about what causes mental disorders that emphasize other biological factors besides neurotransmitters. Among the many factors proposed to cause mental disorders are a loss of brain cells, defective "biological rhythms," abnormal hemispheric lateralization, prenatal errors in brain development, birth trauma, incompatible immune systems between the fetus and the mother, exposure to maternal influenza, slow-acting viruses, and various genetic factors.[34] With the development of brain-scanning techniques, structural and functional anomalies have been reported to have been found in the prefrontal cortex, the basal ganglia, the hippocampus, the thalamus, the cerebellum, and other brain structures in different populations of mental patients, but especially in the brains of schizophrenics.[35] Daniel Weinberger and his colleagues at the National Institute of Mental Health (NIMH) have reported both functional and structural anomalies in schizophrenics. They have claimed, for example, that the dorsolateral region of the prefrontal cortex in schizophrenics is not normally activated when they are performing certain cognitive tasks that require frontal lobe participation.[36] Patricia Goldman-Rakic of Yale University has suggested that schizophrenics may have a deficit in the dorsolateral part of the prefrontal cortex that impairs the short-term memory needed to guide behavior and thought processes in a rational way.[37] There are also several reports that schizophrenics tend to have some anatomical abnormalities in the temporal lobes of the brain.[38] Nancy Andreasen and her colleagues in the Department of Psychiatry at the University of Iowa reported finding that the thalamus in schizophrenic brains tends to be smaller than normal. They suggest that because of its many connections to other brain areas, a thalamic abnormality might explain all of the symptoms of schizophrenia on the basis of a single factor—an explanation they regard as preferable to the "unparsimonious and conceptually unsatisfying" piecemeal approach of looking for a different brain structure to explain each symptom.[39] There are also several reports of brain anomalies found in depressed patients, and the reports that patients with obsessive-compulsive disorder exhibit hyperactivity in the prefrontal cortex, basal ganglia, and thalamus have been discussed earlier in this chapter.[40]

There is some supporting data to back up each of these biological theories, and in our present state of ignorance about the causes of mental disorders, there is no alternative but to cast a wide net in our research efforts. However, it is troubling that there are so few replications of any of the brain findings reported to date and so many different brain abnormalities have been proposed to be the cause of the same mental disorder, while the same structures have been reported to be involved in different disorders. With respect to schizophrenia, Nancy Andreasen has suggested, despite her claims for a central role of thalamic abnormality in schizophrenia, that all of the research concurs "that it must involve distributed circuits rather than a single specific 'localization,' and all suggest a key role for interrelationships among the prefrontal cortex, other interconnected cortical regions, particularly the thalamus and stiatum"[41] The idea that there may be a distributed circuit that is malfunctioning rather than a single specific localization is not unreasonable, but it may also be a convenient way to place the best "spin" on the many different brain anomalies reported to have been found in people with the same disorder. It is also not clear to what extent the increasing number of reports that the prefrontal cortex, the striatum, and the thalamus are structurally or functionally abnormal in different mental disorders indicates a common underlying impairment in all these disorders, as often claimed, or whether it is simply reflecting the current interest in these particular structures. One is reminded of the old saw, "Tell me what questions you are asking and I will tell you what you will find." Furthermore, in evaluating these various reports of brain abnormalities it has to be kept in mind that these are only trends based on averaged data, and none of the claims applies to all patients with the same mental disorder. Last, it is not clear, as already discussed, whether any reported brain pathophysiology is the cause or the effect of a mental disorder.

Despite the fact that the evidence and arguments claimed to support the various chemical theories of mental disorders are far from compelling, these theories have by far more supporters than any of the other biological theories. Many of the reasons for this are discussed in the next chapter, but one reason is that many people believe that drug research holds the greatest promise for an effective and easy-to-administer treatment. In contrast, even if a structural brain abnormality were convincingly demonstrated to be the cause of some mental disorder, it is not clear what could be done to correct this condition at this time.

These critical remarks are not meant to disparage speculation, which I am well aware often provides the motivation to undertake research, but rather to portray the weakness in all of the current biological explanations of the causes of mental disorders. Criticism of the claims that various deficiencies or excesses of neurotransmitter activity is the cause of mental illness is not antibiological, antiscientific, or propsychotherapy, but the result of an objective evaluation of the evidence and the arguments claimed to support the theory.

It's Not All Genetics

Consider the evidence that schizophrenia and depression, particularly manic-depressive disorder, tends to run in families. This by itself is not evidence of a genetic cause, as poverty also runs in families. However, modern epidemiological studies are now much more sophisticated than they were earlier. The strongest evidence supporting an inherited factor in mental disorders comes from studies comparing fraternal and identical twins and from data obtained from studies of adopted children.[42] Briefly, studies have shown that in the case of schizophrenia, if one of a pair of identical twins has been diagnosed as schizophrenic, the likelihood of the other twin being schizophrenic is between 35 and 50 percent, depending on the study cited.[43] In the case of same-sex fraternal twins, who do not have any more genes in common than do nontwin siblings, the agreement ("concordance rate") is much lower, somewhere between 7 and 14 percent. As identical and fraternal twins share the same family environment, although identical twins may be treated more similarly, this is generally accepted as strong evidence of a genetic factor in schizophrenia. Studies of adopted children who become schizophrenic also provide evidence of a genetic role. It has been shown that there is a greater incidence of schizophrenia in the biological parents of adopted children who develop schizophrenia than there is in the foster parents. Similar results have been obtained from studies of manic-depressive disorder.

To date, no reports of discovering the gene responsible for manic-depressive disorders or schizophrenia have replicated. In most instances, some kind of epidemiological artifact has invalidated such claims.[44] Nevertheless, most knowledgeable people who have examined the data are convinced that there is evidence that genetic factors play some role in the etiology of many mental disorders. It is certainly reasonable to assume that individuals may inherit a predisposition to develop a particular mental disorder. The term "diathesis," which was originally borrowed from pathology, implies that there is a constitutional predisposition or tendency toward developing a particular disease, but a predisposition is only realized under certain conditions.

Drug Specificity and the Search for the Magic Bullet

Pharmaceutical companies often suggest a specificity that is not supported by the evidence. As a marketing strategy, drugs that are identical or very similar chemically are given different names, and the marketing is aimed at different patient populations. Wellbutrin and Zyban, for example, are identical drugs, but the former is marketed as an antidepressant, while the latter is advertised as an aid to quitting smoking. Similar benzodiazepine drugs are used therapeutically for anxiety, for muscle spasms, and as an anticonvulsant. The specificity is in the packaging, not in the pharmacology. When clomipramine (Anafranil) was first developed, the Ciba-Geigy Company already had two other tricyclic antidepressants on the market, so a decision was made to market the drug as a specific treatment for obsessive-compulsive disorder, although the evidence that it was any more effective than other tricyclics for that purpose was questionable.[45] In the 1980s, when Upjohn was about to market its new benzodiazepine drug, Alprazolam, hearings in the U.S. Congress had aroused concern about the overuse of Valium and the other benzodiazepine drugs marketed to treat anxiety. Upjohn executives were uncertain how to market the drug, when the 1980 edition of the *Diagnostic and Statistical Manual (DSM III)* conveniently listed "panic disorder" as a new diagnostic category. It was decided to market Alprazolam as a specific panic disorder treatment, and by the mid-1980s, this marketing strategy had proved so successful that panic disorder started to be called the "Upjohn illness." David Healy, a professor at the University of Wales, has argued that the pharmaceutical industry often finds it useful to sell a mental illness as a way to sell a psychotherapeutic drug.

> It is clearly a mistake to think that mental illnesses are something that have an established reality and that the role of a drug company is to find the key that fits a predetermined lock, or the bullet that will hit a desired target. While there are clearly psychological disorders that drug treatments can modify, we are at present in a state where drug companies cannot only seek to find the key to the lock but can dictate a great deal of the shape of the lock to which a key must fit. The situation is rather similar in some respects to that described by J. K. Galbraith in *The New Industrial State,* in which it was proposed that the market place far from being shaped by the laws of supply and demand is constructed by large corporations, whatever the branch of industry involved.[46]

The lack of specificity of the drugs used to treat mental illness is also illustrated by the unpredictability of their effects in any instance. Prescribing drugs is basically a trial-and-error process in which the physician begins with his favorite drug for that particular illness and frequently moves down a list of alternative drugs trying to increase effectiveness and minimizing adverse side effects. In a recent description of his own battle with depression, Andrew Solomon recounts his experience with drugs. After listening to his complaints and asking specific questions, a psychiatrist assured him that his symptoms were "very classic indeed" and told him not to worry, as "we'll soon have you well." The initial prescription was for Xanax (an antianxiety drug) and Zoloft (an SSRI often given for depression). Solomon was told that the Zoloft would take some time, but the Xanax would alleviate his anxiety immediately. Solomon often woke up in a panic, which Xanax would relieve, but only if he took enough so that he "collapsed into thick, confusing, dream-heavy sleep." Since then, Solomon has been on Zoloft, Xanax, Paxil, Navane, Valium, BuSpar, and Wellbutrin.

Compared to others, Solomon writes, "this is a relatively short list," and he continues, in describing his experiences:

> Side effects arrive with the first pill and sometimes fade away with time. The real effects, at best, fade in with time. We cannot predict which medications will work for whom. Zoloft made me feel as though I'd had fifty-five cups of coffee. Paxil gave me diarrhea, but fortunately Xanax, though it made me exhausted, was also constipating. Paxil seemed better than Zoloft, and I soon adjusted to its making me feel as though I'd had *eleven* cups of coffee—which was definitely better than feeling as though I couldn't brush my own teeth.... The side effects for which antidepressants are known (tension, irascibility, sexlessness, headaches, indigestion) are easily confused with the complaints for which they are taken....[47]

So much for the claims of specificity and "magic bullets."

Politics and Fashion in Diagnosing Mental Disorders

At an early stage, most diseases are called a "syndrome" to designate a recurring cluster of similar signs and symptoms that are detrimental to health. With sufficient knowledge about the cause, the syndrome is elevated to a disease. While medical students may learn that the causes of a disease may be infectious, traumatic, neoplastic, toxic, autoimmune, and so on, in the case of mental disorders the situation is much more tenuous and disputable. How can a cause be found when there is so much disagreement about what constitutes a specific mental disease and where the range of proposed contributing causes is so large? We do not know if the diagnostic label used for any mental disorder represents a single disease entity or, as widely suspected, a label that includes heterogeneous disorders with many different causes. Moreover, the diagnostic labels themselves seem to have been more influenced by politics and fashion than by either science or objective criteria. The search for the cause of a mental disorder is a "Catch- 22" situation, much like trying to unlock a box when the key is inside.

There are so many different signs and syndromes among patients given the same diagnostic label that is questionable whether we are dealing with a disease or a syndrome, and the issue is commonly avoided by calling it a "disorder." Moreover, the changes in what is considered a mental disorder more often reflect theoretical biases and political action than scientific knowledge. In his book *A History of Psychiatry,* Edward Shorter has contrasted the problem of diagnosis in psychiatry with that in the rest of medicine:

> Just imagine a group of respirologists having heated battles over the cause of pneumonia, splitting into separate societies and founding their own journals over the issue. Not so in psychiatry, where genetics apart, the causes of few conditions are known. What is the cause of something like erotomania, the delusional belief that someone else is in love with you? Nobody knows. Psychiatric illness has tended therefore to be classified on the basis of symptoms rather than causes, which is where the rest of medicine was in the nineteenth century. Grouping the various symptoms into larger disease categories can thus be somewhat arbitrary: Is erotomania part of schizophrenia, part of a delusional disorder, or a separate illness? And the groupings themselves have been historically highly controversial, with entire schools of psychiatry rising and falling over the issue of how to classify "hysteria." These considerations suggest that in classification it is very easy for psychiatry to lose its way.[48]

To achieve some perspective on the politics of mental disorders, it is necessary to go back a little more than a half-century. In the 1930s, around the time psychiatry became a board-certified medical specialty, the profession began to mobilize itself against any and all competition in treating mental disorders. Those not trained in psychiatry were perceived as intruders. The intruders included physicians from other medical specialties, especially neurology, but also the growing numbers of nonmedical therapists who had begun to treat mental illness. At first psychiatry clearly dominated in this turf warfare, but by the 1950s, clinical psychologists, psychiatric social workers, and various counselors were starting to be licensed in most states, and when this happened they were in a better position to lobby more effectively for legislation that would strengthen their competitive position. Nonmedical mental health professionals tended to view any effort to medicalize mental disorders as an attempt to exclude them. Those opposed to medicalization resent such terms as patients, mental illness, and treatment and refer instead to clients, psychological distress or mental disorders, and therapy or counseling.

Anyone following this rivalry between the various professional groups treating mental disorders knows that there rarely has been a year when the national meetings of the respective organizations did not devote one or more sessions to a discussion of this problem. Typical of the program sessions held at the annual American Psychological Association meetings are those with such titles as "Qualms About Balms: Exploring the Limits of Biological Treatments for Psychological Distress," while recent psychiatric conventions held sessions with such titles as "The Problem of the Non-Medical Psychotherapists." Furthermore, it is obvious that economic considerations have played as important a role in shaping the position of various groups as has any theoretical difference. Those who would deny the importance of economic influence need to explain the substantial effort and money expended by the American Psychological Association, the American Psychiatric Association, and similar professional organizations in lobbying for or against proposed legislation that would affect the pocketbooks of its members. The disputes over Medicare reimbursement is only one of many such controversies. When, for example, the American Psychological Association was successful in getting the term "psychological care" substituted for "psychiatric care" and in getting the guidelines to stipulate that clinical psychologists should be reimbursed at the same level as psychiatrists, the American Psychiatric Association mustered a strong opposition that led to a reversal of the decision.

The views of the leading protagonists are not easy to classify, as many agree on some points and differ on others. Perhaps the major distinction that can be made is whether mental disorders should be considered "diseases" to be understood within a "medical model." Of course, to really resolve this controversy it would be necessary to know what was the cause of the different mental disorders. If, for example, it could be convincingly demonstrated that a specific mental disorder is caused by an inherited malfunctioning of some part of the brain, there would be little justification for objecting to calling that condition a medical disease. On the other hand, there are good reasons for objecting if it could be proven that mental disorders are caused by a particular pattern of experiences—what are usually called "psychosocial variables"—such as lack of nurturance and affection during some critical period of development, exposure to stress and trauma, growing up in a dysfunctional family, being abused, treated as a commodity in a highly competitive, capitalistic society, and an infinite number of other experiences that might adversely affect the developing psyche. Biological and psychosocial factors are so interrelated in mental disorders that they cannot be separated. It is unrealistic, therefore, to take an extreme position on either side of the debate. Moreover, most people recognize that biological and psychosocial factors may have a greater or lesser role in different mental disorders, so there is no logical reason that the same position has to be taken in regard to all such conditions. It is because we really do not know the cause of any mental disorder that the debate can be so heated.

The way mental disorders are conceptualized is certainly not always determined by professional identification, and there are a few psychiatrists who have opposed the medicalization of mental disorders, none more vigorously than Thomas Szasz. The titles of Szasz's books leave no room for uncertainty about his position. Following the publication of *The Myth of Mental Illness* in 1961, there were other books with much the same theme, although each with a different emphasis, such as *Law, Liberty, and Psychiatry: An Inquiry into the Social Uses of Mental Health Practices* (1963), *Psy-*

chiatric Justice (1965), and later *The Manufacture of Madness* and *Psychiatric Slavery.*[49] As these titles convey, Szasz has relentlessly hammered away
on the theme that mental "illnesses" or "diseases" (terms he uses synonyms)
are "myths" that have been perpetuated because they are useful for controlling those who are different, unwanted, or simply inconvenient.[50]

Szasz argues that the designation "disease" is only justified when the
cause can be related to a demonstrable anatomical lesion, infection, or some
other physiological defect. As there is no such evidence for any mental disorder, Szasz argues that the concept of "mental illness" is "fake or metaphorical illness" and psychiatry, therefore, is a "fake or metaphorical medicine,"
which confuses "disease with deviance, illness with immorality, cure with
control, treatment with torture."[51] Not only does Szasz attack biological
treatments, but in his *The Myth of Psychotherapy,* he also dismisses "talking
therapies" and has, therefore, alienated the majority of his fellow psychiatrists, some of whom have asked rhetorically: "What kind of a psychiatrist
is this?" Yet Szasz does raise an issue that has to be addressed. If a person's
behavior or thinking is maladaptive, is this sufficient grounds to say that he
or she has a disease? Are people who eat too much, gamble too much, smoke
too much, worry too much, think about sex too much all suffering from a
disease? Where do we draw the line and what criteria do we use to do so?

My own view is that there is merit in Szasz's point that the disease label
has been overextended, but his criticism of the "mental disease" label seems
to throw out the baby with the bathwater, and it does not make allowance
for the fact that knowledge in medicine, as in everything else, is always
evolving. Szasz maintains that if there is no clear evidence of patho-
anatomy, or a pathogenic organism, or pathophysiology, it is misleading
to speak of a "disease."[52] This could be considered just a definitional matter,
distinguishing "syndromes" from "diseases," but when Szasz uses such
phrases as the "myth of mental illness" he seems to be trying to persuade
his audience that the whole field is a "fake" and that there are no real health
problems out there, just "manufactured diseases" used for ulterior purposes. Moreover, Szasz fails to acknowledge that at some period in history
the cause of every "legitimate" disease was unknown, and they all were at
one time "syndromes" or "disorders" characterized by common signs and
symptoms. There will always be "idiopathic" conditions where the cause is
unknown, but using labels to designate conditions that appear similar can
facilitate research and the finding of a cause. Moreover, the designation of
syndrome or a disorder can be useful for organizing information about
probable prognosis and response to different treatments.

One cogent reason for objecting to the premature use of the disease
label is that it can lead to overlooking important psychosocial factors that
contribute to the etiology of mental disorders. The heart of this controversy

is whether the causes are thought to be mainly biological or psychosocial. This issue has consistently divided psychiatrists and other mental health professionals, with one side or the other gaining predominance for a period until the pendulum swung back again. The history of "general paresis" illustrates this division, and it has often been used by those biological psychiatrists who believe all mental disorders will eventually be proven to be physical diseases. During the early part of this century, a large number of patients in mental asylums were diagnosed as having general paresis. The people afflicted with general paresis underwent a progressive mental deterioration, exhibiting many classical signs and symptoms of psychosis, and because in the later stages of the condition a motor paralysis developed, it was often called "general paralysis of the insane."

By the early 1900s, there was a suspicion that general paresis and neurosyphilis were the same disease, but there was still much debate, and several prominent psychiatrists remained convinced that it was a "functional" disorder caused by moral turpitude and sexual excesses. Thomas Smith Clouston, master of the Edinburgh asylum, believed that a lifestyle could cause general paresis:

> Sexual excess, especially if indulged in at or after middle life and alcoholic intemperance, especially if impure or bad drinks are used . . . I cannot agree that syphilis is the sole cause always, because I have had many cases in which the existence of personal syphilis was excluded by every sort of reliable evidence. Mental shocks and strains of all sorts will of themselves cause the disease.[53]

Clouston, however, went on to note that he had observed that a certain temperament predisposed one to general paresis: "ambition and energy, sociability and a large capacity for enjoyment, a firm belief in oneself, and a preference for handsome women."

Clouston straddled the fence between functional and biological causes of general paresis, as he concluded that the predisposition to behave in certain ways was definitely inherited, citing a case of general paresis in twin brothers.

The issue was not completely resolved until 1910, when J. W. Moore sent slides of the brains of patients who had died from either "paralysis of the insane" or syphilis to Hideyo Noguchi, a bacteriologist at the Rockefeller Institute of Medical Research in New York. Noguchi concluded that the same spirochete was the cause in both sets of cases, thus ending the "syphilis–general paralysis" controversy.[54] This history is cited frequently by biological psychiatrists, who use it as an illustration of what they believe will be the fate of all psychiatric disorders after the biological cause is discovered.[55]

There are several striking instances of disorders that psychiatrists believed to result from life experiences that are now recognized to have a biological cause. This does not mean, however, that every mental disorder will have a biological cause. I don't believe so, yet it is often assumed to be a proven fact by some of the more enthusiastic advocates of biological psychiatry. For example, the neuroscientist Candace Pert has asserted: "People who act crazy are acting that way because they have too much or too little of some chemicals in their brains."[56] Not only is it assumed that biological causes underlie all mental disorders, but it is argued that biological explanations underlie the effectiveness of even nonbiological treatments. Thus, Paul Mohl, director of psychotherapy services at the University of Texas, San Antonio, has argued:

> Psychotherapy is a biological treatment that acts through biological mechanisms on biologic problems. . . . Medication, dream interpretations, and empathy become simply different ways to alter different neurotransmitters. . . . Modern developments in basic neuroscience are uncovering the underlying medical nature of psychotherapy.[57]

This statement does not simply imply that every mental change must be accompanied by a physical change. That would be trite. Mohl is clearly suggesting that neurotransmitter problems are the cause of mental disorders and that "basic neuroscience" has started to demonstrate that when psychotherapy is effective it is because it is correcting the neurotransmitter problem. This statement goes so far beyond any supporting evidence that even many who disagree with Szasz's extreme position on a number of issues might understand his comment that "one can only marvel at such monumental medical megalomania."[58] There probably are a number of biological, but not necessarily biochemical, factors that predispose individuals toward different mental disorders, but this does not justify neglecting psychosocial factors that also contribute to the etiology. We should not, for example, assume only a biological cause for anorexia nervosa and neglect the fact that this disorder occurs most commonly among women from those classes which place a value on thinness or who are involved in competitive sports such as gymnastics that consider all fat a handicap.

Besides neglecting the importance of psychosocial factors in understanding the etiology of mental disorders, at least one other reason has been given for objecting to the overextension of the disease model and the medicalization of all human problems. A number of observers have argued that diagnostic labels are used as a social weapon to justify isolating or silencing people who are perceived as being disruptive to society. There is some truth in these assertions, although they have been overstated in an attempt to deny any reality to the concept of mental diseases. In 1851, for example, Dr. Samuel Cartwright, a prominent Louisiana physician who practiced in the New Orleans area, headed a committee to study "the diseases and physical peculiarities of the Negro race." Cartwright's report was published as the lead article in the *New Orleans Medical and Surgical Journal.* Commenting on the "behavioral abnormality" of the runaway slave, Cartwright attributed this behavior to a "disease of the mind" that he called "drapetomania" (from the Greek *drapetes,* which conveyed the idea of absconding or running away), and he suggested a method of "curing them" of this disease.[59]

In more recent times, there is good evidence that psychiatry in the Soviet Union was used to incarcerate dissenters to the political system. There have been a number of documented cases of people who had no mental disorders, but opposed the Soviet regime, being forcibly committed to Moscow's Serbsky Institute for Forensic Psychiatry and to other psychiatric institutions. These people were held in psychiatric institutions for years and were subdued with "major tranquilizers" (antipsychotics) and by different forms of debilitating physical "treatments." Schizophrenia was broadened to include "sluggish schizophrenia" and "shiftlike schizophrenia" so that anyone who did not conform and was perceived as a threat to the system could be said to have "reformist delusions," a "poor adaptation to the social environment," and other such arbitrarily defined criteria of schizophrenia.[60]

Bruce Ennis, a civil rights lawyer in the United States, has described how psychiatric labels have been used to deprive people of due process and their civil liberties, although this was rarely done for political purposes:

> The most important function of mental hospitals is to provide custodial welfare. They used to be called insane asylums, but before that they were called, more accurately, poorhouses. Almost all mental patients are poor, or black, or both, and most of them are old.
>
> Less than 5 percent of these patients are dangerous to themselves or to others. Indeed, the incarceration of mental patients cannot be justified by their threat to the community at large. Studies have shown that they are less dangerous than the "average" citizen. They are put away not because they are, in fact, dangerous, but because they are useless, unproductive, "odd," or "different."[61]

Ennis may have overstated the coercive role of psychiatric institutions, as Ken Kesey did in *One Flew Over the Cuckoo's Nest,* but there is little doubt that in the not-too-distant past people were locked away as "prisoners" in psychiatric institutions for the convenience of others.[62] Psychiatric labels make it easier to commit people to institutions because they lend credence to the claim that it was for their own good. The views of the psychiatrist Peter Breggin are quite similar to those of Thomas Szasz in the United States and Michel Foucault in France in that they also have argued that psychiatric institutions and drug treatment are used to incarcerate and subdue people who are unwanted and inconvenient, rather than for treating people with illnesses:

> The modern use of the various major psychiatric drugs cannot be thoroughly understood without placing these drugs in the historical context of the state mental hospital. The state mental hospital began in response to the industrial revolution as an urban solution to the presence of large numbers of dispossessed, indigent, chronically ill, and socially ostracized individuals. Throughout the western world these giant lockups developed for the primary purpose of handling this influx of a poverty class into the cities. To this day poverty is the most common denominator of individuals locked up in state hospitals. Over a 300 year period a variety of oppressive technologies were developed for the purpose of subduing this incarcerated population. The major tranquilizers are merely the most recent and by far the most effective method for rendering these individuals docile.[63]

The vast majority of psychiatrists would certainly not agree that the "major tranquilizers" are used primarily to make malcontents docile, and many are convinced that these drugs alleviate schizophrenia through their action on specific biochemical systems in the brain. Nevertheless, it has to be recognized that until relatively recently there were no objective criteria for classifying and diagnosing mental disorders, so there was ample opportunity for subjective views of what constitutes mental illness to have a substantial influence. Throughout the nineteenth century, mental disorders were at best loosely classified, and there were no generally accepted criteria. For the most part, lists of mental disorders were grouped by what was assumed to be their cause, such as alcohol, sexual excesses, worry, mental strain, financial difficulties, and gynecological disorders.

The person who had the greatest influence on the classification of mental disorders during the early part of this century was the German psychiatrist Emil Kraepelin, whose *Textbook of Psychiatry* underwent eight editions between 1883 and 1915. The early editions of the textbook followed the existing trend of listing many different types of mental disorders based on presumed causes. Thus, Kraepelin listed such disorders as "masturbatory insanity" and "wedding night psychosis." However, Kraepelin kept data cards on his patients and over time he accumulated information on the outcome of the various disorders. This information was used in later editions of his textbook, in which Kraepelin lumped together many of what were originally conceived of as separate disorders. Thus, Kraepelin originally distinguished more than six kinds of mood disorders, but he finally decided that they were all different expressions of manic-depressive psychoses. Similarly, he came to believe that dementia praecox (schizophrenia) could be manifested as hebephrenia, catatonia, or paranoia, but he believed there was a common core that justified classifying it as a single disease. Kraepelin's classification has been described as "descriptive psychiatry" because he offered few ideas about the cause of any mental disorders. His classifications were based mainly on prognosis. He described dementia praecox, for example, as a progressive, deteriorating disorder that offered little hope for recovery regardless of the particular form it took, but he reported that remissions were common in manic-depressive psychoses.[64]

Despite the authoritative position of Kraepelin's textbook, psychiatry resisted any system for classifying mental disorders. Some psychiatrists argued that the indications for different diagnostic categories overlapped so much that it was difficult to accept that they were separate diseases, while others maintained that no meaningful classification system was possible until it was known what had caused the diseases. Despite Kraepelin's enormous influence, most psychiatrists did not limit themselves to his terminology. In the 1950s and 1960s, a time when psychoanalytic theory dominated much of American psychiatry, there was relatively little interest in classifying mental disorders, as what was believed most critical was not a label, but uncovering the repressed conflicts that were at the root of all mental problems.

The impetus to create a standardized psychiatric description and classification in the United States actually came from outside psychiatry. The first official attempt to collate information about mental disease was the inclusion of the category "idiocy/insanity" in the 1840 census. By 1880, the census included seven categories of mental illness: mania, melancholia, monomania, paresis, dementia, dipsomania, and epilepsy. Because of the need for more practical statistical information at the turn of the century, the Bureau of the Census conducted surveys of the institutionalized insane, first in 1904 and again in 1908. The data collected emphasized ethnic and race differences, but nosological distinctions were given little thought. Recognizing the inadequacy of the data, the Bureau of the Census asked the American Medico-Psychological Association, which later became the American Psychiatric Association, to appoint a Committee on Nomenclature and Disease to develop a classification schema that was acceptable to the profession. Working together with the National Committee for Mental Hygiene, the Committee on Nomenclature finally completed the *Statistical Manual for the Use of Institutions for the Insane* in 1918. The *Statistical Manual* listed twenty-two diagnostic categories, the vast majority of which reflected the strong somatic bias of the period. Among the categories listed were traumatic psychoses, senile psychoses, cerebral psychoses with syphilis, alcohol psychoses, toxic psychosis, psychoses with pellagra, epileptic psychoses, and psychoses with mental deficiency. This emphasis was not surprising as the overwhelming majority of psychiatrists at the time were employed in insane asylums and one of the main goals of the *Manual* was to assist such institutions in keeping records.

Not everyone agreed that a classification scheme was a progressive move. The "Statistical Manual" was opposed by some of the more prominent members of the profession. Adolf Meyer, who insisted on the importance of integrating life experiences with biological data, thought that any one-word diagnosis could never capture the relevant facts about an individual.[65] Samuel T. Orton criticized the *Statistical Manual,* describing it as illogical and inconsistent in that the diagnostic categories were based sometimes on etiology, sometimes on pathology, and at other times on clinical observations.[66] Despite the opposition, the *Statistical Manual* underwent ten editions between 1918 and 1942. The tenth edition continued to emphasize biology, but unlike the earlier editions it was not restricted to so-called "psychotic" conditions, and it included diagnostic labels for many psychoneurotic and behavioral disorders, such as hysteria, compulsive states, and adult and child maladjustments.

A broader classification of mental disorders had been developed by the United States Army and later modified by the Veterans Administration. The list included a number of personality and acute disorders that could be treated on an outpatient basis. The World Health Organization incorporated much of the Veterans Administration nomenclature in the *International Classification of Diseases (ICD),* which included, for the first time, in the sixth edition (*ICD-*6) a section on mental disorders. In the meantime, several coalescing factors were responsible for the changes that took place between the last edition of the *Statistical Manual* and the first edition of the *Diagnostic and Statistical Manual (DSM).*[67] These factors included the enormous increase in the number of psychiatrists after the Second World War, particularly among those in private practice rather than in public institutions; the growing influence of psychodynamic concepts, which provided an impetus to include many psychoneurotic and adjustment problems; and the acceptance of the idea, partly based on wartime experience and psychoanalytic theory, that many mental disorders were caused by stress and other life experiences.

After much discussion, debate, and revision, *DSM*-I was officially released by the American Psychiatric Association in 1952. Mental disorders were divided into two major groupings. The first group consisted of mental disorders caused by physical factors such as infection, drugs, trauma, circulatory problems, and neoplasms; the second grouping consisted of disorders in which biological factors were not considered the primary cause. This second grouping was subdivided into psychotic and psychoneurotic divisions. The psychotic group consisted mainly of manic-depressive and schizophrenic disorders, while the psychoneurotic group was a large and heterogeneous list including anxiety and phobias, conversion hysterias, obsessive-compulsive disorders, depression, and a separate listing of many "personality disorders" such as alcoholism and emotional instability. Of the twenty-one members of the APA Committee on Nomenclature and Statistics at least ten belonged to psychoanalytic organizations, and as a result a number of psychodynamic concepts were included in DSM-I.[68] Psychoanalytic theory tended to blur the distinction between psychoses and neuroses, as the same early childhood experiences were thought to underlie all mental disorders. Actually, despite all the effort expended, there was not much interest in classification. Robert Spitzer, the Columbia University psychiatrist who later became the major architect of the DSM-III, described the attitude of most psychiatrists: "The academic psychiatrists interested in presenting their work on descriptive diagnosis would be scheduled for the final day in the late afternoon. No one would attend. Psychiatrists simply were not interested in the issue of diagnosis."[69]

DSM-II and the World Health Organization's ICD-8 were both published in 1968, but it wasn't long before these manuals were widely criticized. The criteria were found to be ambiguous, and several studies made it embarrassingly clear that diagnostic labels were often being used arbitrarily. The criteria for diagnosing schizophrenia, for example, varied between institutions and between countries. In general, patients were diagnosed as schizophrenic much more commonly in the United States that in most of Europe. Even as late as the 1970s, psychiatrists in the United States used the schizophrenia label much more frequently than their British colleagues. In one study published in 1971, psychiatrists from the two countries viewed a tape of a patient being interviewed. About 69 percent of American psychiatrists diagnosed the patient as schizophrenic, whereas only 2 percent of the British psychiatrists did so.[70] It was often difficult comparing data from different institutions because it was not clear whether the same kinds of patients were being discussed. Moreover, the availability of different drugs for treating depression, schizophrenia, and anxiety made it increasingly important to arrive at the correct diagnosis. The American Psychiatric Association formed a task force composed of a large group of mental health professionals to work on DSM-III, and this manual and ICD-9 both became available in 1974. Despite the effort spent field-testing these manuals, they too were still found wanting.

A revision of DSM-III called DSM-III-R was published in 1983. The manual had by this time quadrupled in size, listing two hundred separate disorders clustered into sixteen categories. Instead of vague descriptions, a special effort was made in DSM-III-R to provide objective criteria for assigning diagnostic labels in the hope that psychiatrists using the manual anywhere could at least agree on what to call a particular disorder and perhaps would also agree on the diagnosis for the same patient. The revision helped, but patients often did not fit any of the descriptions, and their idiosyncratic combinations of symptoms still made it difficult to chose the right label in too many instances. In 1984, the American Psychiatric Association task force started its work on a new manual, proceeding in close cooperation with those working on the *ICD*. The *DSM*-IV and the *ICD*-10 manuals were both published in 1994.

All of the diagnostic and statistical manuals have been atheoretical and basically descriptive in nature. The authors were frank to admit that the causes of mental disorders, except for those involving obvious brain damage, were not known. In a sense, the diagnostic manuals were following the precedent established by Kraepelin in being completely descriptive in nature, but where Kraepelin worked alone and tended to clump different symptoms together under a few diagnostic categories, the large group of specialized consultants working on the later *DSM* editions split different symptoms into distinct disorders, which often simply reflected the specialized interests of the consultants, rather than any compelling scientific rationale.

There is, of course, no shortage of different ideas about the etiology of specific mental disorders, but those responsible for the most recent version of the *Diagnostic and Statistical Manual* avoided opening up a "hornets' nest" of criticism that would surely have followed if statements about etiology were included. Phobias, for example, could be explained within a framework of learning theory, with its experimental data on the conditioning of fear reactions, or it could explained within a psychodynamic framework, with the feared object having some symbolic connection to an early sexual trauma, or it might be explained on the basis of some biochemically induced predisposition. The explicit purpose of the manuals, therefore, was limited to trying to get all mental health professionals to agree on terminology so that a patient diagnosed as schizophrenic in one part of the country would receive the same label anywhere else. The Preface to *DSM*-IV is explicit in stating this purpose: "The purpose of DSM-IV is to provide clear descriptions of diagnostic categories in order to enable clinicians and investigators to diagnose, communicate about, study, and treat people with various mental disorders" (p. xxvii). It is also clear that the authors of *DSM*-IV, as was true of the authors of *DSM*-III and *DSM*-III-R, recognized that the same criteria could not be used in describing different mental disorders:

> The concept of mental disorder, like many other concepts in medicine and science, lacks a consistent operational definition that covers all situations. All medical conditions are defined on various levels of abstraction—for example, structural pathology (e.g., ulcerative colitis), symptom presentation (e.g., migraine), deviance from a physiological norm (e.g., hypertension), and etiology (e.g., pneumococcal pneumonia). Mental disorders have also been defined by a variety of concepts (e.g., distress, dyscontrol, disadvantage, disability, inflexibility, irrationality, syndromal pattern, etiology, and statistical deviation). Each is a useful indicator for a mental disorder, but none is equivalent to the concept, and different situations call for different definitions.

The authors of *DSM*-IV attempted to avoid controversy between different mental health professionals by avoiding the term "disease," and they fudged the issue of whether the etiology of mental disorders has mainly a physical or functional origin:

> The term *mental disorder* unfortunately implies a distinction between "mental" disorders and "physical" disorders that is a reductionistic anachronism of mind/body dualism. A compelling literature documents that there is much "physical" in "mental" disorders and much "mental" in "physical" disorders. The problem raised by the term "mental" disorders has been much clearer than its solution, and, unfortunately, the term persists in the DSM-IV because we have not found an appropriate substitute. (p. xxi)

There are, for example, "mood disorders," "schizophrenic and other psychotic disorders," "anxiety disorders," "personality disorders," and "substance abuse disorders." The authors of *DSM*-IV even seem to equivocate about whether the diagnostic categories are real entities when stating that it is not implied that there are schizophrenics, only that there are people who manifest the symptoms listed as criteria for using the diagnosis "schizophrenic disorder." Recognizing that there will inevitably be people who have symptoms that do not fit any of the designated categories, the authors even specified criteria for indicating diagnostic uncertainty.

Despite the substitution of "disorder" for "disease," the *DSM* is still criticized for implicitly following the "medical model" of mental disorders in its emphasis on diagnosis and on the individual as an isolated unit divorced from a social context.

DSM-IV exerts an enormous influence. Therapists must use it to obtain reimbursement from insurance companies, and its terminology is used in courts, social agencies, prisons, schools, and elsewhere. *DSM*-IV has been criticized for its proliferation of mental disorders and the variety of behavioral traits that are listed as mental disorders. Thus in a *New York Times* op-ed article, "Is Bad Writing a Mental Disorder?" Stuart Kirk and Herb Kutchins, both professors of social work in California, argued:

> Since there are no biological tests for the vast majority of mental disorders, the psychiatric association has tremendous leeway in what it chooses to classify or not classify as illness. Unfortunately, there are few actions or traits that the association does not consider to be possible symptoms of some disorder.
>
> Insomnia, worrying, restlessness, getting drunk, seeking approval, reacting to criticism, feeling sad and bearing grudges are all considered possible signs of a psychiatric illness. Where the association draws the line between mental illness and well-being arbitrarily determines how much "mental illness" there will be in the population.

The association is so eager to create and label disorders that it has revised the manual three times in 15 years and has expanded it from 106 mental disorders in the first edition to more than 300 in the new one. . . .

These disorders and the criteria that describe them include the tragic, the strange and the ridiculous. . . .

Consider code 315.2 which the manual says is marked by the poor use of grammar, or punctuation, sloppy paragraph organization, awful spelling and bad handwriting. . . .

Is it any wonder that a survey this year by the University of Michigan, based on the manual, found that half of all Americans suffered from psychiatric disorders.[71]

If they are taken out of context, it is easy to ridicule such categories as "Disorder of Written Expression," or Code 315.1, "Mathematic Disorder." The manual, however, makes it clear that these categories should only be applied when there is clear evidence that the behavior has deteriorated from a previous level, as it must:

Fall substantially below those expected given the individual's chronological age, measured intelligence, and age-appropriate education. (Criterion A) The disturbance in written expression significantly interferes with academic achievement or with activities of daily living that require writing skills. (Criterion B) If a sensory deficit is present, the difficulties in writing skills are in excess of those usually associated with it. (Criterion C)

Certainly if a person's performance in some important area has deteriorated, it is a serious problem and listing it as a "disorder" might seem to be a problem only to those engaged in a "turf war" with psychiatrists. There clearly are some mental health professionals who seem to object to the *DSM*-IV mainly because it is a document written primarily by psychiatrists and published by the American Psychiatric Association. There is a valid point to be made, however, that has nothing to do with jurisdictional disputes. Simply listing a seemingly endless number of behavioral deficits and maladaptive behaviors as distinct "disorders," without any knowledge of etiology may be a meaningless exercise. Alfred North Whitehead called this "the fallacy of misplaced concreteness," which others have related to psychiatric diagnoses:

Nowhere is this more true than with mental, intellectual, or behavioral disorders. Contemporary psychiatry is going through a paroxysm of line drawing. It is attempting to divide all human behavior into discrete categories of "illness" decided by a consensus. . . . The schizophrenic label provides the best example of an arbitrary and fluid designation wreaking havoc in its effort to assume the authority of a "disease." Schizophrenia is a German invention (it could not have been called a discovery).[72]

Although those who directed the *DSM*-IV project claim that "there has been a stronger emphasis on research data than with previous revisions," scientific considerations do not play a significant role in the manual. Instead, the psychiatric tradition and sociopolitical considerations seem to have played the major roles in shaping this document. Dr. Allen Frances, who directed the *DSM*-IV project, stated that "we didn't want to disrupt clinical practice by eliminating diagnoses in wide use."[73] Very different symptoms are included under the rubric of "schizophrenia" mainly because they have always been grouped together, rather than because of any new scientific evidence that they share a common etiology. In fact, schizophrenia seems to be a "catch-all" disorder for any serious thought disorder, as long as a number of specific factors such as age, brain damage, toxins, generalized dementia, or an overriding mood disorder can be ruled out. Even if a patient has delusional thoughts, but also has signs of a major depression, the manual states that a diagnosis of schizophrenia should not be used. Why this should be so is not explained, and most psychiatrists would probably treat such a patient with a combination of antidepressants and antischizophrenic medication.

Earlier editions of the *DSM* discouraged using the label schizophrenia if the first signs of the disorder occurred late in life, but in *DSM*-IV it is acceptable to do so. No scientific advance was behind this change either. Among people diagnosed as schizophrenic there are some who have had a long history of marginal social adjustment, while others seem to have made an excellent adjustment until their first psychotic episode. Some schizophrenics have both hallucinations and delusions, while others have only delusions, which may also be seen in cases of major depression. Some schizophrenics undergo progressive deterioration, while others improve—some of these in response to drugs, but others may improve without medication. Some schizophrenics have either functional or anatomical brain abnormalities—of different types—while no such abnormalities can be found in other schizophrenics Some schizophrenics have impaired performance on certain cognitive or behavioral tasks, but not all schizophrenics do, while the performance of patients with a different diagnoses may be impaired on these same tasks. How many different mental disorders with different etiologies, prognoses, and deficits are subsumed under the label schizophrenia is not all clear and the *DSM*-IV does not help in this regard.

Not very long ago, it was common to distinguish endogenous depression from reactive depression. It was assumed that the former was caused by a biochemical imbalance and that this type of depression responded to antidepressant drug treatment. A reactive depression was described as being precipitated by some tragic experience and, therefore, less likely to respond to antidepressant drug treatment. It is now widely accepted that antidepressant drugs are equally effective in relieving depression regardless of its etiology. Should we now use *ex juvantibus* reasoning and assume that because the two types of depression respond equally to the same treatment, they are really one disease? The manual offers little that is helpful with such questions. It is easy to form the impression that the manual was written by some committee responsible for tabulating mental disorders.

It is not difficult to point to instances in which political rather than scientific considerations have been the major impetus for changes made between the different editions of the *DSM*. For example, members of the gay community and the feminist movement—both mental health professionals and lay persons—have had a major influence in removing or altering the criteria for such diagnostic categories as "homosexuality," "masochistic and self-defeating personality disorder," and the "premenstrual (or periluteal) dysphoric disorder" in the later editions of the *DSM*. *DSM*-II listed homosexuality along with other "sexual deviances," including fetishism, pedophilia, transvestitism, exhibitionism, voyeurism, sadism, and masochism. The American Psychiatric Association decided in the 1970s that homosexuality should not be considered a mental disorder unless a patient explicitly wanted to change sexual orientation and desired to experience heterosexual arousal. This was explicitly stated in *DSM*-III, published in 1980. The 1994, *DSM*-IV does not even use the word "homosexuality," but the section that treats "sexual identity disorders" makes it clear that a "strong and persistent cross-gender identification" should be considered a disorder only when there is "evidence of clinically significant distress or impairment in social, occupational, or other important areas of functioning" (*DSM*-IV, pp. 532–33). Feminists campaigned successfully to have the category "self-defeating personality disorder" deleted, while Vietnam veterans influenced the addition of the "post-traumatic stress disorder."

DSM-IV is not an exciting document. It is purely descriptive and presents no new scientific insights or any theories about what causes the many mental disorders it lists. Moreover, *DSM*-IV offers little to defend the position that the categories listed as distinct entities may not actually be "catch-all" heterogeneous labels that embrace disorders that have different etiologies. Considering the present state of our understanding of mental disorders, there may not have been any alternative. Those responsible for the manual wanted to create a document that would be widely adopted and would increase the agreement in the way diagnostic labels were used. To have included anything about the etiologies of the different mental disorders would surely have generated considerable controversy and even more criticism. Understandably, the authors of *DSM*-IV were limited by the lack of available knowledge about the etiology of mental disorders. While an agreement on the criteria for using diagnostic labels will make it easier to compare results obtained by different investigators, until we have more confidence that these labels reflect homogeneous entities our search for the causes of mental disorders and explanations of why different treatments help will be seriously limited.

Considering all the limitations discussed in the preceding chapters, why are the chemical theories of mental disorders so widely accepted? The next two chapters will discuss this question.

Chapter 6

HOW THE PHARMACEUTICAL INDUSTRY PROMOTES DRUGS AND CHEMICAL THEORIES OF MENTAL ILLNESS

I f psychotherapeutic drugs did not help anyone they would not be prescribed in such large numbers and there would not be any chemical theories of mental disorders. However, the percentage of patients who are helped by psychotherapeutic drugs is much lower than commonly claimed, and many patients experience some fairly serious adverse side effects from drug treatment. Moreover, the evidence claimed to support the various chemical theories of mental illness is not strong, and there is much evidence that contradicts the prevailing view. I have examined the arguments for these theories with an open mind and have tried to tell a coherent and convincing story when lecturing to graduate students, but there is just too much data that indicate that the theories could not be right. Also, I have often found the logic employed to draw conclusions from the data flawed and unconvincing. As a result, I have been forced to conclude that these theories rest on a very shaky foundation and may well be wrong.

The truth is that we still do not know what causes any mental disorder or how drugs sometimes help patients get better. Yet, despite this, the theory that mental disorders arise from biochemical imbalance is widely accepted. I believe this is partly because relatively few people, including mental health professionals, have the time, inclination, or background to critically examine the evidence and partly because powerful special interest groups have influenced the way people think about drug treatment and mental disorders. In this and the following chapter, I discuss the dynamics and inner workings of these groups and how their enormous influence is exerted.

Pharmaceutical Companies: "There's Gold in Them Thar Pills"[1]

The pharmaceutical industry is huge. In the United States alone, there are more than one hundred companies involved in developing and marketing drugs. The market value of the drugs sold in the United States in 1997 has been estimated to be nearly $92 billion. The sales of psychotherapeutic drugs has conservatively been estimated to exceed $8 billion in the United States, while the worldwide sales of antidepressants alone were reported to be over $6 billion.[2] Considering how much money is involved, it is no surprise to find that economic factors play a powerful role in all stages of drug development, research, clinical trials, and marketing.

The pharmaceutical industry spends enormous sums to influence the opinions and behavior of both physicians, and the public and the effectiveness of their marketing strategies cannot be overestimated. Physicians are usually offended by the implication that they are influenced by promotional schemes and insist that they know the difference between scientific evidence and advertising. However, studies indicate that most physicians read little of the scientific literature—certainly not much outside their own field—they are not trained to evaluate research design and statistical data, and they are greatly influenced by drug promotion. Most drugs that physicians prescribe were not even mentioned during their medical school education. Obviously, their prescribing behavior must be subject to later influences. Studies have shown that much of this influence comes from drug promotion. One study found that 58 percent of family practitioners mentioned the company representative as the source of information for the last drug they prescribed, four times more than any other source mentioned.[3] This is well known by the pharmaceutical industry and certainly influences the amount of money it spends in promoting its drugs directly to physicians.

In a recent interview, the prominent psychopharmacologist Frank Ayd contrasted the pharmaceutical industry as he remembered it with the way it is today:

> The [pharmaceutical] industry has changed. When I first started, and you ask anybody, what it was like 35–40 years ago, you dealt with physicians. They ran the pharmaceutical industry. Today they aren't running the industry, they have some input but not a major input. Decisions are made by the business people, who think in terms of the bottom line and that's their prime interest, there's no question about that. Some companies are a little more aggressive than others and I think all colleges have to be very careful.

There have been some publications recently about, for example journal supplements and certain journals have been identified now as taking huge sums of money from the industry and publishing supplements. How peer reviewed these are is a big question and how much are they really used for promotion rather than scientific purposes is another concern. And if a company wants to get a speaker on a programme they can do it. You've seen this in England and it happens almost everywhere.[4]

The Selling of Thorazine

It is unlikely that there is a qualitative difference in the way pharmaceutical companies promoted their drugs thirty-five to forty years ago. There is just more money available for promotion today. The marketing of chlorpromazine (Thorazine) in the 1950s can serve to illustrate this point. Immediately after Smith Kline & French (SK&F) obtained the U.S. license to sell Thorazine, it began to plan its marketing strategy. It was 1954, a time when most psychiatrists in private practice were committed to psychotherapy and psychodynamic theory, and many of them viewed the claims made for drug treatment with considerable skepticism, if not antagonism. Jackson Smith, a Nebraska psychiatrist, expressed this skepticism at a conference held in Cambridge, England, in 1959:

> The treatment of the mentally ill has shown the following degrees of success; a Massachusetts hospital reports a discharge rate of 84 per cent, a Virginia hospital 91 per cent and in Columbus, Ohio a recovery rate of 100 per cent can hardly be exceeded. Unfortunately, these results do not reflect the influence of either the tranquilizers [referring to "major tranquilizers" or antipsychotics] or the energizers [antidepressants] since they were all published between 1833 and 1842.[5]

State legislators and hospital administrators, however, were much more receptive to economic arguments, such as the argument that the cost of maintaining outpatients on Thorazine would be much lower than the expense of long-term institutional care.[6] Recognizing this, Smith Kline & French undertook a well-orchestrated "marketing blitz" that has been described with remarkable frankness by those who planned the strategy:

> When SK&F marketed Thorazine, we found that we had a concept problem with office practice psychiatrists. They were generally separable into two groups, the electroshock people and the analysts and related psychotherapists, both with a great commitment to their years of experience and basic training philosophy, and some resistance to the use of drugs.

Then we began approaching mental hospitals, and found they were more interested in trying Thorazine.... SK&F personnel surveyed state and Veterans Administration hospitals and saw that there would be a need to educate supervisors, business managers, and staff people about the potential therapeutic value of Thorazine and the vast administrative savings it offered in reduced damage to plant and reduced inpatient population. We also saw that we would have to go to work with, and similarly educate, state legislators on the need for higher drug budgets for the state hospitals....

In 1954, the company's professional sales force, a part of the marketing division, numbered about 300 men.... We had to work with the whole system, from the legislature in a state through its entire public mental hospital system and civic groups. Thus we created a special task force of about 50 men, whose members worked intensively with state legislatures and with mental hospitals and their staff ... the task force sometimes had to use "drastic"procedures. In one state, for example, through the efforts of SK&F and other interested groups, a special legislative session took place at one of the state hospitals, with the governor's and the legislative leaders' blessings. The entire session was filmed by the "Today" show, and in that state it was the breakthrough that eventually committed the legislature to funding an intensive-treatment program for the state hospital system....

Among our other activities, we set up a speakers' training program to work with psychiatric administrators on effectively presenting their treatment program proposals. We helped them with their oral delivery, the organization of their data and other statistics, and so forth. This planning bureau was the start of SK&F's Community Relations Bureau ... we had to draw up economic figures on treatment costs, collated with various dose levels of Thorazine with comparative figures for custodial-care costs, etc.... including factors such as staff turnover, and less cost for such things as broken windows and damaged furniture....

... about 18 months after Thorazine had been used ... we began to get feedback static ... about released patients coming back to the hospitals in droves, and complaints that the return rate was undermining all the institutions' savings that Thorazine had helped to effect.... We found that one reason for the initially high return rate was [that] when patients went home, to their families and private physicians, they were put on a low maintenance dose of Thorazine.... SK&F's involvement with aftercare included a great deal of initial "pump priming," in which we funded or gave free drugs to several pilot aftercare projects....

We helped to organize the first VA [Veterans Administration] research conferences and helped their statisticians gather data to study the effects of the drugs on patients in VA hospitals.... Another of our activities concerned the bridging process between hospital psychiatrists and their patients and the private practitioners and community to whom the patient would return when he was discharged from the hospital. For example, we helped to organize and sponsor symposia such as those held by the American Psychiatric Association . . . and helped to inform private practitioners about their patents' needs through SK&F publications.[7]

This marketing campaign was highly successful, and Thorazine became a "cash cow" for SK&F almost immediately. Only eight months from the start of marketing, Thorazine had already been given to about 2 million patients, and in the fall of 1955, only six months later, the director of Saint Elizabeths Hospital, Winfred Overholser, estimated that 4 million patients in the United States had been treated with the drug.[8] The argument that the annual cost of maintaining outpatients on Thorazine was only $46 compared to $912 (in 1956 dollars) for institutional care was irresistible, and states began to allocate substantial amounts of money for the drug.

Drugs and Deinstitutionalization

It was not long after the introduction of chlorpromazine that a dramatic decline in the number of institutionalized psychiatric patients occurred in much of the world. It has been estimated that between 1955 and 1989 the number of hospitalized psychiatric patients in the United States decreased from 500,000 to approximately 150,000, despite an increase in the number of people diagnosed as having mental disorders. Pharmaceutical companies have frequently claimed that the drop in the number of institutionalized psychiatric patients was a direct result of the introduction of psychotherapeutic drugs. There is no doubt that chlorpromazine, and the other drugs that soon became available, did quiet agitated and difficult-to-manage patients, making it possible to discharge many of them, but this is not the whole explanation of deinstitutionalization.

There had been pressure to reduce the number of psychiatric patients in state hospitals in the United States and in other industrial countries at least a decade before the introduction of chlorpromazine in 1954. The staggering cost of housing and caring for the increasing numbers of institutionalized psychiatric patients had made it necessary to consider changes even before drugs became available. In 1943, there were one hundred thousand new admissions to mental institutions in the United States and only sixty-five thousand discharges. In 1946, approximately one-half of all hospital beds in the United States were occupied by psychiatric patients.[9]

Something had to be done to cut costs, and at the 1954 Governors' Conference on Mental Health, held in Michigan, there was general agreement that hospital stays for the mentally ill had to be shortened.

Cost was not the only consideration. During the 1940s, the horrendous conditions in many psychiatric institutions in the United States were described vividly in such widely read books as Mary Jane Ward's *The Snake Pit* (1946) and Albert Deutsch's *The Shame of the States* (1948).[10] Deutsch had toured the country's asylums with a photographer, and his book described the conditions he had seen as a national disgrace. In writing about the conditions at the Philadelphia State Hospital for Mental Disease in Byberry, Deutsch considered what he had seen as comparable to the pictures that usually illustrate Dante's *Inferno.* In one "incontinent male ward . . . three hundred nude men stood, squatted and sprawled in this bare room, amid shrieks, groans, and unearthly laughter." An article in *Life* magazine (6 May 1946) entitled "Bedlam 1946" used some of Deutsch's pictures and described the conditions in many state hospitals as having degenerated "into little more than concentration camps in the Belsen pattern." Mary Jane Ward's semiautobiographical book was made into a movie *(The Snake Pit)* starring Olivia de Havilland, who was pictured in the role on the cover of *Time* magazine (20 December 1948). The movie dramatized the fact that being locked up in most psychiatric institutions was likely to make patients worse, many of them deteriorating to the point where they were beyond help. There were also reports at the time that long-term institutionalization made patients completely dependent and totally unable to adjust to living on the outside. Moreover, studies were revealing that psychiatric institutions were also unhealthy in other ways. One report, for example, indicated that over 17 percent of the patients in New York State's mental hospitals had contracted tuberculosis and there was a 25 percent mortality rate among schizophrenic patients.[11] All these considerations were behind the widespread movement to deinstitutionalize psychiatric patients, and when drugs became available they acted mainly as a catalyst, especially at the most crowded institutions.

The claim that psychiatric drugs were solely responsible for the decline in the number of institutionalized patients has been critically examined in Ann Johnson's excellent book *Out of Bedlam: The Truth about Deinstitutionalization.*[12] Studies of the hospital patient population before and after the introduction of psychiatric drugs revealed that in hospitals that had a good therapeutic environment the introduction of drugs had little or no effect on discharge rate.[13] It was only in the worst hospitals, with low discharge rates, that the introduction of drugs had a marked influence on the number of patients discharged, but many of the patients discharged were still somewhat institutionalized in state-financed community arrangements.[14] Others ended up as homeless street people, and it is now obvious that this "discharge and be damned" philosophy was not always in the best interest of the patient. In other countries, the introduction of psychiatric drugs did not automatically result in discharging large numbers of patients unless there was such a movement already underway. There was no increase in the rate of discharging institutionalized psychiatric patients in Germany and Austria, for example, despite the use of large amounts of the new psychiatric drugs. Psychiatric drugs were definitely not the whole explanation for the decline in the number of hospitalized psychiatric patients as the pharmaceutical industry has always maintained.

The pharmaceutical industry has from the outset used large mental institutions to test new psychotherapeutic drugs, and it is often the results of these tests that provide the data for later promotional material. This was true when Jean Delay and Pierre Deniker tested chlorpromazine in France for the Rhône-Poulenc company or when the Geigy company obtained the help of Kuhn to test imipramine. There are many obvious advantages, most notably that there are large numbers of patients available whose living conditions are relatively homogeneous and also controllable. Other factors may also influence the outcome of these tests, even though these may not be the reason large institutions are selected. Large institutions tend to place a premium on those changes that decrease custodial care problems and have less opportunity to appraise how well a patient might function in the less-protected environment of the outside world.

Increasing Drug Sales

Once a drug is approved for marketing, the pharmaceutical industry employs different strategies to increase sales. One strategy is to suggest that a drug might be used preventively even where no clear medical problem exists. When the synthetic estrogen diethylstilbestrol (DES) became available, for example, it was initially marketed to prevent miscarriages. There was a pressing need for a treatment that would help women who had a history of miscarriages, and the drug was approved even though the evidence for its effectiveness and safety was not convincing. A number of pharmaceutical companies were soon marketing DES under different proprietary names. While the potential market among women who had a history of miscarriages was substantial, it was obvious that the market could be increased enormously if the drug was prescribed prophylactically for all pregnancies. As Figure 6-1 illustrates, pharmaceutical companies began to recommend that DES be used preventively even in the absence of any history of miscarriages. As stated in an advertisement that appeared in the *American Journal of Obstetrics and Gynecology* (June 1956), "desPLEX," one of the proprietary names for diethylstilbestrol, is **"recommended for ALL**

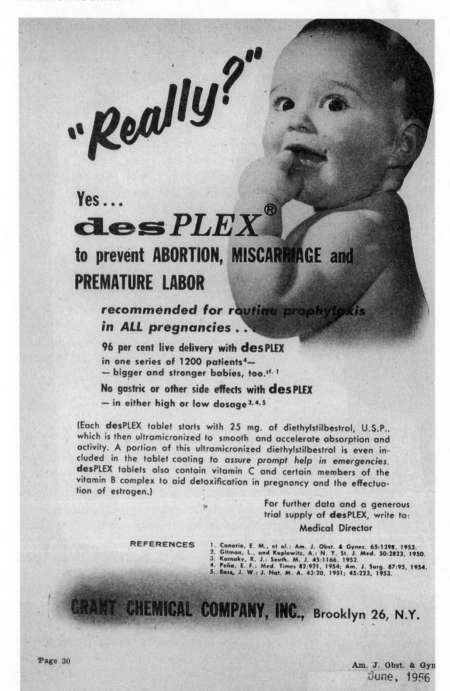

Figure 6-1 An ad promoting diethylstilbestrol addressed to obstetricians.

pregnancies." The drug was reported to make even normal pregnancies safer and better and it was claimed that "in one series of 1200 patients— bigger and stronger babies, too" resulted when DES was taken during the pregnancy.[15] It was not very long afterward that it was discovered that DES masculinized some female babies and also increased the incidence of sterility and cancer in children of both sexes.

There are many current instances in which companies have initiated aggressive marketing strategies to increase the sales of one of their drugs. For example, the Genentech company, using recombinant DNA techniques, was able to produce human growth hormone, which they named Protropin. The Food and Drug Administration (FDA) sanctioned its use for children who suffer from pituitary dwarfism. It is estimated that about seven thousand in the United States have this problem. Those who market drugs, however, are well aware that the FDA has little control over the way doctors prescribe a drug once it has been approved for any use. It was easily calculated that with about three million children born annually, about ninety thousand children fall below the third percentile for height. If Genentech could convince the parents of these ninety thousand children to get their physicians to prescribe Protropin, it would generate between $8 billion and $10 billion annually. Genentech began to employ a strategy to get shortness perceived as a disease. Genentech and also Eli Lilly, which markets a competing growth hormone, provided substantial funding to the Human Growth Foundation in Falls Church, Virginia, and the Magic Foundation in Oak Park, Illinois. Both of these foundations had been screening the height of children in schools, shopping malls, and state fairs. They began to send out letters to school officials and parents, which identified the children who had a height problem. The financial support of Genentech and Eli Lilly was not acknowledged in these letters.

Many of the parents notified that their children had a serious growth problem sought help from physicians. During this time, physicians, particularly pediatric endocrinologists, were receiving information about the availability of growth hormone and its effectiveness in dealing with a neglected medical problem. After the passage of only a few years, close to twenty-five thousand children were being treated with growth hormone. Recent surveys have found that in 1997 about thirty thousand children in the United States were being given growth hormone at an annual cost between ten thousand and fifty thousand dollars per child, depending on body weight. The treatment often involves painful intramuscular injections three times a week, and there is considerable uncertainty about the long-term effects of growth hormone given to children with no demonstrated hormone deficiency.

Although Genentech claimed that about 90 percent of the children receiving Protropin had a growth hormone deficiency, an NIH study concluded that the actual figure was closer to 50 percent. Another study found that the growth hormone did little for children who were short but did not have a growth hormone deficiency. With the help of growth hormone, these children may have reached their maximum height a little sooner, but they did not end up much taller. One Japanese study found that slow-growing boys who did not have a growth hormone deficiency actually ended up being nearly three inches shorter than a matched untreated group. A recent editorial in the *British Medical Journal* stated that "the treatment of short normal patients in the mistaken belief that the treatment could improve final height is a cruel illusion and an expensive mistake."[16] Even in children with a growth hormone deficiency, the results of treatment are often disappointing when children are followed longitudinally to determine their final height. A recent study in France, for example, followed over three thousand children, in some instances for as long as twenty years. The authors concluded that "the outcome of children of short stature who were treated with growth hormone has been less favorable than initially assumed."[17] A number of pediatric endocrinologists began to question whether spending large amounts of money for small cosmetic changes could be justified when hospitals, such as the Boston City Hospital, were running out of funds to immunize children. While Protropin is still selling well, such criticism eventually led to discontinuing the indiscriminate screening of children for shortness, and this has reduced much of the overuse of the drug.[18]

Prozac and the SSRIs: Good for Whatever Ails You

The selective serotonin reuptake inhibitors (SSRIs) provide another example of aggressive marketing. As noted earlier, the sales of this class of drugs are enormous. The annual sales of the SSRIs in 1996 exceeded $4.5 billion. The worldwide sales for Eli Lilly's Prozac were approximately $2.5 billion ($1.73 billion in the U.S.), while the sales for Pfizer's Zoloft exceeded $1 billion. The SSRIs were originally marketed as antidepressants, but these drugs have been used for a number of other conditions. Pharmaceutical companies have often spread the word both explicitly in promotional material and through suggestions by their detail (sales) personnel that the SSRIs can effectively treat many different conditions. For example, when Pfizer was still waiting for permission to market Zoloft to treat obsessive-compulsive disorder as well as depression, the FDA cited it for "jumping the gun" and marketing the drug not only for those disorders, but also for premenstrual depression, chronic low-grade depression, panic attacks, and posttraumatic stress syndrome. In addition, Pfizer implied in its promotional material that Zoloft was safe for treating depression in patients who had had heart attacks, despite the fact that the company's own clinical tests indicated that the drug might cause chest pains and could produce changes in blood pressure and an elevation of heart rate. The FDA sent a stern warning to Pfizer, demanding that it stop making unauthorized and misleading medical claims for Zoloft and ordering it to publish corrective ads in every journal in which the drug had been advertised and also to send corrective letters to physicians and institutions that had received Zoloft promotional material.[19]

The FDA specifically prohibits pharmaceutical salespeople from recommending a drug for applications that have not been approved. While some of the salespeople are careful to adhere to these prohibitions, others do not, and many physicians report that they have often been told "informally" that different drugs have been found useful in treating conditions that had not been approved by the FDA. The company sales staff has the dual mission of providing information about a drug and promoting the drug. These two missions—promotion and education—are likely to conflict, and when they do it will not often be the promotional role that gives way. Moreover, the written promotional material left in physicians' offices has also been found to mention unproved applications of a drug, even though this practice is specifically prohibited by FDA regulations.[20] The FDA does not have the funds or personnel to monitor these promotional practices adequately and the results are quite predictable. For example, although the SSRI antidepressants had not been approved for use with children, an article in *The New York Times* indicated that in 1996 there were six hundred thousand children under the age of eighteen who were given prescriptions for one of the three leading drugs of this class (Prozac, Paxil, and Zoloft). Over 203,000 prescriptions for Prozac alone were written for children between six and twelve years of age in 1996. This is an increase of 298 percent from 1995.[21]

The marketing of the diet pill dexfenfluramine (marketed in the United States as Redux and elsewhere as either Adifax or Isomeride) also illustrates the way pharmaceutical companies try to increase their sales, even when it may involve some risk for consumers. Dexfenfluramine was developed by a French pharmaceutical company, Laboratories Servier SA. The closely related drug Fenfluramine had been marketed by Servier as a diet pill a number of years earlier, and it had been licensed to A. H. Robins (now a subsidiary of American Home Products) for marketing in the United States under the name Pondimin. Dexfenfluramine had not yet been tested as a diet drug when Richard Wurtman, an MIT neuroscientist, determined in the 1980s that it also reduced appetite. Wurtman, together with MIT, obtained a "use pattern" claiming a "novel use" of the drug and founded the Interneuron company, which was granted the United States rights for the drug from Servier.[22]

Redux was approved by the FDA in April 1996. By the fall of the same year, newspapers were describing the growing concern over the casual use of what some people regarded as a potentially dangerous drug.[23] When the FDA approved Redux, it explicitly stated that the marketing of the drug should be restricted to "morbidly obese" patients. By November 1996, however, monthly sales of Redux were growing rapidly, and some physicians running diet clinics had used bikini-clad models in ads claiming that the "Redux Plan" could get you to lose those extra pounds before your holiday vacation. Although one American Home Products representative responded to criticism by stating that the marketing of Redux was "very low-key" and not geared to cosmetic weight loss, Fred Hassan, the executive vice-president of the company, was quoted as having said about the promotion of Redux that "we're putting a lot into it," adding that more than one thousand salespeople had been assigned to its marketing.[24]

Redux promotional material was not sent only to obesity specialists, but also to general practitioners, psychiatrists, cardiologists, internists, and gynecologists, many of whom were unfamiliar with the way the drug worked and its potentially dangerous interactions with other drugs. Many depressed people, for example, are obese and are being treated for their depression by SSRI drugs that enhance the action of serotonin. Redux also enhances serotonin, and there is a concern that the combined action of an SSRI and Redux might increase serotonin activity to the point that tremors, seizures, and even organ failures could occur. Physicians have commented that many of the company's salespeople seem to be unfamiliar with the potential side effects of Redux, and they have described it as safe for use over a lifetime, even though the clinical trials were for periods of less than a year. There is now strong evidence that Pondimin (fenfluramine) and Redux (dexfenfluramine) can produce a serious heart valve condition and also a condition known as pulmonary hypertension, a rare but dangerous and sometimes fatal disorder. Furthermore, it has recently been revealed that the pharmaceutical companies marketing these drugs had been informed of the heart valve problems among consumers of these diet pills as early as 1994, three years before a Mayo Clinic study led to these drugs being pulled from the U.S. market.[25] There is also compelling evidence that these same serious medical conditions occur following the fen-phen diet treatment. Fen-phen refers to the treatment involving a combination of fenfluramine and phentermine, a related drug.

Drugs and Patient Advocacy Groups

Another way that pharmaceutical companies increase the market for psychotherapeutic drugs is to support various patient advocacy groups that encourage people to seek help from such drugs. There are a large number of such groups, including the National Alliance of Mental Patients, The

National Alliance for the Mentally Ill, the National Depressive and Manic Depressive Association, the National Foundation for Depressive Illness, the National Mental Health Association, Neurotics Anonymous, OCD Foundation, Phobia Society of America, the Schizophrenia Association of America, and the Children and Adults with Attention Deficit Disorders. These patient advocacy groups have an influence that complements the promotional material of pharmaceutical companies.

Many patient advocate groups receive funding from the pharmaceutical industry, which enables the groups to increase newspaper and magazine advertising and the information they distribute by other means. Typically, patient advocacy material has a prodrug bias, encouraging people to seek medication often by exaggerating the effectiveness of drugs and the scientific foundation on which they rest. In 1995, the National Alliance for Research on Schizophrenia and Depression (NARSAD) placed an ad in newspapers nationwide (see Figure 6-2).[26] The ad was part of NARSAD's "Depression: A Flaw in Chemistry, not Character" campaign developed with an advertising agency. After describing depression as a physical disease requiring medication, just as diabetes requires insulin treatment, the ad makes the claim that research has shown that depression results from an insufficient level of serotonin in the frontal lobes of the brain. A "brain scan" depicting enlarged ventricles is included in the ad, with the statement that this condition has been "found in many severe cases of depression." While there are some reports of enlarged ventricles in a small group of chronic schizophrenics, this has not been found in depressed patients. Moreover, this finding has no logical connection to any biochemical deficiency, let alone to a specific deficiency of serotonin in the frontal lobes. The fact that the information in the ad is completely in error seems not to have troubled anyone. The ad promotes the message that now that we know that depression is caused by a biochemical anomaly, it can be "curable instead of just treatable."

Another pamphlet widely circulated by NARSAD entitled "Conquering Depression," funded by an educational grant from the Wyeth-Ayerst pharmaceutical company, mentions several possible causes of depression, but the emphasis is clearly on biochemical imbalances and drug treatment.

> Scientists believe that major depressive disorder is caused by an imbalance of neurotransmitters—natural chemicals that allow brain cells to communicate with one another.

And under the section heading "Are Antidepressant Medications Effective?":

> They most certainly are. Estimates are that eight or nine of every ten patients with depression can be helped by currently available antidepressant medications.

Depression.
A flaw in chemistry,
not character.

People with cancer aren't expected to heal themselves. People with diabetes can't will themselves out of needing insulin.

And yet you probably think, like millions of people do, that you or someone you know should be able to overcome another debilitating disease,

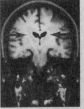

What causes depression? According to recent medical research, depression is caused when an insufficient level of the neurotransmitter serotonin is passed through the synapses in the frontal lobe of the brain. A condition, once triggered, that can last for months, years, or even lifetimes.

Above: Brain scan of a "normal" brain.

Below: Brain abnormality found in many severe cases of depression or manic-depression.

depression, through sheer will and fortitude. For untold decades, it has been thought that depression is the symptom of a weak character or underlying laziness. In reality, nothing could be further from the truth.

Recent medical research has taught us that depression is often biological, caused by a chemical imbalance in the brain. We've even found that depression has a genetic link.

An inherited disease? You probably think that sounds pretty hopeless. But when it comes to depression, it's actually good news. Because it reclassifies depression as a physical disease instead of a mental illness. A distinction that's the difference between it being curable instead of just treatable.

While these recent discoveries should help relieve the stigma associated with depression, a look at history also helps. It's a well documented fact that Abraham Lincoln was depressed for most of his adolescent and adult life. Sir Winston Churchill referred to his depression as "the black dog," starting after the failure of the 1915 Dardanelles Expedition and shadowing him his entire life. You see, depression doesn't discriminate. Anyone can get it. And today you can find books written about admitted sufferers Mike Wallace, Joan Rivers, and Dick Cavett just to name a few.

The reality is, there's never been a better time to be depressed. With new therapies, drug company and academic research, and ever increasing medical interest, help is available today that only 5 years ago didn't exist. Call 1-800-717-3111 if you or someone you know needs help. With this better understanding of depression, we hope you'll see the only shame would be not calling.

The date was January 1, 1863. It was the day of one of Abraham Lincoln's most eloquent speeches, the Emancipation Proclamation. He had succeeded in freeing millions of repressed, impoverished slaves. For anyone, the accomplishment of a lifetime. Still, Lincoln battled depression, the cloud that would follow him always.

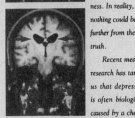

Here they are. The keys to happiness. A few of the thousands of synapses that have the power to make any given day one of the most joyous in your life or the most despairing. All based on whether these channels for neurotransmission can properly send certain signals to the brain.

©1995 by Scientific American Library from *Molecules And Mental Illness.* Permission of W.H. Freeman and Co.

Figure 6-2 An advertisement placed by the National Alliance for Research on Schizophrenia and Depression (NARSAD) that appeared in many major newspapers throughout the United States. Reprinted by permission from The Advertising Council.

An 80 to 90 percent estimate of effectiveness of antidepressant drugs is clearly an exaggerated figure, which can be contrasted with the faint praise given for "cognitive-behavioral therapy," for which there is considerable evidence of effectiveness:

> Some evidence indicates that cognitive-behavioral therapy can relieve the symptoms of less severe forms of depression.

Even that faint praise is further diluted by the statement that psychotherapy has been found to be "much more effective when used in combination with drugs." There is no mention of the now considerable evidence that some forms of brief psychotherapy can be as effective as, and in some instances more effective than, medication for depression.

In an article entitled "Turning Points in Twentieth-Century American Psychiatry," Melvin Sabshin commented on the important influence of patient advocate groups:

> The National Alliance for the Mentally Ill has grown rapidly in size and power; its passionate espousal of biological psychiatry will be of great interest to psychiatric historians in the next century. The families of the severely ill mental patients, rightly or wrongly, felt attacked by psychotherapeutic and sociotherapeutic concepts in psychiatry. To the extent that genetic, biological variables became preemptive etiologically, the familiar poignant struggle to deal with severely ill family members became more easily explainable [to others].[27]

While it is important to encourage people who need professional help to seek it out, that does not justify the distribution of biased information and even misinformation. The ads are sometimes carefully crafted to seem balanced, but they clearly leave readers with the message that it has been firmly established that biochemical imbalances cause depression and that drugs are now available to correct that condition. It is not surprising that the pharmaceutical industry finds it in its interest to support groups that are helping it get this message out.

The grants from the pharmaceutical industry to patient advocacy groups not only help to promote drugs, but also can provide a channel to counter adverse reports about drugs and to communicate a company's own "spin" on the issue. This is illustrated by recent reports about the drug Ritalin and attention deficit/hyperactivity disorder (ADHD). An article in *The New York Times* noted that the "Children and Adults with Attention Deficit Disorder (CHADD)" support group received a cash grant of nine hundred thousand dollars from the Ciba-Geigy Company, the manufacturer of Ritalin. This grant was reported to have made it possible for CHADD to grow "into a national powerhouse with 35,000 members and 650 chapters, and real clout in Washington, DC."[28] The organization has helped to make people aware that the drug Ritalin is available to treat ADHD.

However, according to a second article in *The New York Times,* there was concern that Ritalin was being prescribed too casually. In 1995, psychomotor stimulants (mostly Ritalin) were prescribed for approximately 2.5 million school-age children. This is between 3 and 5 percent of all school children.[29] The criteria for diagnosing ADHD are primarily based on evidence of inattention, hyperactivity, and impulsiveness, but there is a great amount of subjectivity in making a specific diagnosis in many instances. Some doctors were said to be relying entirely on the recommendation of teachers and parents for prescribing Ritalin. Furthermore, there is an abuse potential with Ritalin and there has been increasing concern that the drug is getting into the hands of children who take the drug for the psychological "high" (euphoria) it can produce. A Ciba representative was quoted in the same article as stating that the company was now distributing informational pamphlets to nurses and school officials requesting that they take steps to ensure that the drug does not fall into the hands of children for whom it was not prescribed. At the same time doctors and pharmacists were sent information informing them that Ritalin has proved useful not only in severe cases of ADHD, but also for moderate hyperactivity. It is apparent that while the "informational pamphlets" sent to nurses and school officials may be good for public relations, they will have virtually no effect in decreasing sales. However, the information sent to physicians may well increase the amount of Ritalin that is prescribed.

Anyone waiting in a doctor's office knows that there are usually many informational pamphlets left for patients to read and to take home. Most of these pamphlets are supplied to doctors by pharmaceutical companies, and the information typically contains a considerable amount of promotional emphasis. For example, Figure 6-3 is from a pad of "tearaway sheets" that Eli Lilly supplied to psychiatrists to hand out to their patients. These handouts are designed to convince the layperson that it is known that depression is caused by a deficiency of serotonin and that Eli Lilly's drug Prozac corrects this deficiency by blocking the reuptake of serotonin. The ad also includes the usual statement about depression being a physical illness "like diabetes or arthritis."

While pharmaceutical companies compete with one another, they also benefit from cooperative efforts that encourage people with mental disorders to seek out drug treatment. "America's Pharmaceutical Research Companies" is a consortium of some of the leading pharmaceutical companies that develop and market drugs for treating mental disorders. The consortium places ads in newspapers and magazines and distributes *Health Guide* booklets directly to the public. One such booklet, entitled "New Hope for

Figure 6-3 Eli Lilly sent pads of this Prozac promotional handout to psychiatrists to distribute to patients.

Depression and Other Mental Illnesses," was inserted into all copies of the September 1996 issues of *Time, Newsweek,* and the *Readers Digest.* The booklet opened with the story of Laura, who had her first episode of depression while in high school ten years earlier. Laura had gone several times to seek help from psychiatrists, but no medication was prescribed and she continued to have crippling depressive episodes. Finally, Laura was put on antidepressant medication, and she is now quoted as saying, "The medicine has changed my life. I've never felt better." A few representative passages from the booklet illustrate its overall thrust:

> What many people fail to realize, however, is that mental illnesses are medical illnesses just like diabetes, high blood pressure or heart disease. And like physical illnesses they can be treated effectively.

> For years, people suffering from mental disorders, along with their families, were blamed and stigmatized for the illness. It was thought to be the "fault" of the individual—due to a weakness in character, lack of self control, or an unhappy childhood. We now know this isn't the case.

> Today, scientists know that many people suffering from mental illnesses have imbalances in the way their brains metabolize certain chemicals called neurotransmitters. Too much or too little of these chemicals may result in depression, anxiety, or other emotional or physical disorders.
> This knowledge has allowed pharmaceutical company researchers to develop medicines that can alter the way in which the brain produces, stores, and releases neurotransmitter chemicals, thereby alleviating the symptoms of some mental illnesses.

These booklets were obviously written to encourage people to seek out drug treatment. A full-page ad paid for by the same consortium of pharmaceutical companies began with the statement that "A Chemical That Triggers Mental Illness Is Now Being Used to Stop It," and it continued with the assertion that:

> Scientists now know the causes of schizophrenia and psychosis are often rooted in powerful chemicals in the brain called neurotransmitters. One of these neurotransmitters is dopamine. Schizophrenia and psychosis can result when the brain has abnormal dopamine levels. Because of recent advances, drugs that are able to alter dopamine levels free many patients from the terrible effects of mental illness.[30]

Such statements are more than just exaggerations or putting the best "spin" on information. To state that because of recent advances "scientists now know" that schizophrenia is caused by "abnormal dopamine levels" is a clear distortion of the evidence.

Psychotherapeutic Drugs and Primary Care Physicians

The pharmaceutical industry employs many different strategies to increase the sales of its drugs, and some of these can be quite subtle. For example, it is known that primary care physicians write about 80 percent of the prescriptions for antidepressants, and they prescribe significantly more psychotherapeutic drugs, in general, than any other medical group, including psychiatrists. Primary care physicians care for about 70 percent of the people who have mental disorders, and according to the World Federation of Mental Health, depression and anxiety disorders alone account for between one-quarter and one-third of all visits to primary health care facilities.[31] No doubt influenced by these statistics, the Pfizer company supported the development of a questionnaire designed to make it easier for the busy general practitioner to diagnose mental disorders. The questionnaire is the PRIME-MD (a trademark of the Pfizer pharmaceutical company), which stands for Primary Care Evaluation of Mental Disorders. The PRIME-MD is claimed to makes it possible for family doctors to diagnose 90 percent of all psychiatric complaints in less than eight and one-half minutes.[32] It is a sign of the times that one primary care physician commented that even that short time might be too long:

> While the PRIME-MD is a worthy instrument, it is too time consuming for the busy internist. However, it or other instruments could be potentially administered by nurses or other members of the office staff, or it could be administered to participants via computer.[33]

And indeed, it has recently been reported that when the PRIME-MD is administered by computer, patients were more forthcoming in admitting symptoms suggesting alcohol abuse or an obsessive-compulsive disorder.[34]

The PRIME-MD is based on "yes" or "no" answers to twenty-five questions, such as "Do you feel your heart pounding?" is "your eating out of control?" and are you "feeling down, depressed, or hopeless?" One of the authors of an article describing the results of a field test of the PRIME-MD questionnaire stated that "you don't need psychiatric training" to diagnose and treat most psychiatric complaints.[35] Once a psychiatric diagnosis is arrived at, the only treatment that primary care physicians are generally equipped to undertake is drug treatment. A recent pilot study has shown that the use of the PRIME-MD increases the number of prescriptions primary care physicians write for antidepressant drugs.[36] It is not surprising that Pfizer supported the development and field testing of the questionnaire and distribution of copies of the questionnaire and a videotape demonstrating how it should be used. The Eli Lilly company has also been interested in making primary care physicians more aware of psychiatric illness. Lilly, which markets the drug Prozac, which is commonly prescribed by general practitioners, has recently provided support for a symposium (held 8 May 1997) on primary care physicians and psychiatric disorders.

The sponsoring of "consensus panels" is another way that the pharmaceutical industry may increase the use of drugs. One such "consensus panel," consisting of psychiatrists, family practitioners, and managed care experts, was held in Dallas, Texas, with the support of an "educational grant" from SmithKline Beecham Pharmaceuticals. The purpose of the meeting was to establish guidelines to assist primary care physicians in "tailoring the length of antidepressant therapy" to the needs of individual patients. A report of the meeting, which was chaired by John Rush, a professor of psychiatry at the University of Texas, emphasized that primary care physicians need to appreciate that antidepressant drug therapy can be prescribed along with treatment of other conditions and that there is strong evidence that untreated depression contributes to poor outcomes in such conditions as myocardial infarction and stroke.[37] In addition, the report included a flow chart advising general practitioners how long treatment on antidepressants should be continued. Thus, for example, the report recommended that if the patient is clearly getting better after four weeks of drug treatment, the drug should be continued for at least six months after what appears to be a complete remission. If there is a less than 25 percent reduction of symptoms after four weeks, the dose should be increased and the results reassessed after another four weeks. Even if there is no improvement at all after the initial four weeks of treatment, it is recommended that the drug dose be increased or another antidepressant be substituted. Whether this advice is fully supported by scientific evidence can be disputed, but there is no reason to doubt that the advice given—and circulated with support from SmithKline Beecham—maximizes the use of antidepressants before considering any nondrug treatment. Only a token nod is given to psychotherapy and counseling, which are described as "useful adjuncts for many patients on antidepressant medication," adding that a qualified psychotherapist "may help patients repair relationships damaged by depression and improve compliance with medication regimens."

Another "consensus statement" summarized a meeting hosted by the National Depressive and Manic-Depressive Association.[38] Psychiatrists, family doctors, patients and their families, and representatives of medical insurance companies were in attendance. The expenses of the participants were paid by the Bristol-Myers Squibb pharmaceutical company, which manufactures Serzone, an antidepressant drug. Representatives of other pharmaceutical companies also attended the meeting. The consensus statement, which received wide coverage in many newspapers, emphasized that depression is one of the most common and costly medical illnesses and that it is often undiagnosed and either untreated or undertreated. It was pointed out that primary care doctors commonly fail to recognize signs of depression, and even when they do, they often prescribe too low a dose of antidepressants and for too short a time. It was noted that 31 percent of the patients being treated for depression at one major medical center had received no antidepressants or too low a dose of these drugs during an eight-week period of inpatient care. The report was critical of those managed-care programs which discourage doctors from prescribing the newer antidepressants, because they are more expensive. To address these and the other problems noted, it was recommended that strategies be developed for expediting the identification, assessment, and treatment of depression, for enhancing the education of the public, and for reducing the stigma that keeps some people from seeking professional help.

While the psychiatrists who wrote the "consensus statement" described above would have no trouble defending their report on the underdiagnosis and treatment of depression, the statement also serves the interests of the pharmaceutical company that sponsored the meeting. It has been noted that many consensus conferences are sponsored by pharmaceutical companies, and the reports issued after these conferences are often not distinguishable from the promotional material distributed by these companies. Several observers have commented that the so-called "consensus conferences" have become another way for pharmaceutical companies to expand their promotional activities. Statements are often issued without reference to adequate data and with the careful selection of participants guaranteeing the conclusions that are reached. Yet most physicians treat the results of consensus meetings as educational rather than promotional material.[39]

Continuing Education for Psychiatrists

The influence of the pharmaceutical industry often combines its own self-interest with goals that are admirable and appear to be selfless. For example, the industry exerts a considerable influence over the field of psychiatry, while providing support for the education and training of psychiatrists. This is not a new trend, as a 1988 report by the Senate Labor and Human Resources Committee chaired by Senator Ted Kennedy indicated that eighteen pharmaceutical companies spent $86 million to fund symposia.[40] The pharmaceutical industry also provide substantial support for speakers at the Grand Rounds presentations where psychiatry staff and residents learn about new developments in their field. The Grand Rounds are an important part of the training of residents in all medical specialties. Bringing prominent speakers from around the country and from abroad can be quite expensive, and departments of psychiatry commonly apply to pharmaceutical companies for funds, usually including in their request a list of the speakers they plan to invite. While pharmaceutical companies certainly do not insist that the speakers they support tout their drugs, they are more likely to support speakers who emphasize drug treatment and are much less likely to support speakers who talk about the adverse side effects of drugs or who favor other treatment modalities, such as psychotherapy.

Pharmaceutical companies also help sponsor free-standing symposia, conferences, and continuing-education programs, a number of which are made particularly attractive by including recreational opportunities. There have been instances of pharmaceutical companies supporting meetings on cruise ships. Some weekend meetings have only about three hours of medical content, but they provide ample opportunity to bring new drugs to the attention of physicians. The extent of the support of postgraduate medical education by the pharmaceutical industry has led one observer, writing in *Lancet*, to comment:

> Doctors are becoming so accustomed to sponsored postgraduate medical education that it is difficult to attract them to meetings where they have to pay for their own registration and refreshments. Postgraduate education is thus tending to become the responsibility of the drug industry.[41]

The pharmaceutical industry also provides a substantial amount of money to support symposia held at the annual meetings of the American Psychiatric Association (APA). By the author's count, approximately 25 percent of all the symposia at the 1996 meeting of the APA listed support from pharmaceutical companies. Invited speakers often receive honoraria, and they regularly receive reimbursement of expenses. Virtually all the APA symposia discussing psychiatric drugs receive drug company support, while the symposia that were not supported dealt with psychotherapy, or such esoteric topics as "Psychiatry in Arab Countries," "Psychiatric Treatment of Orthodox Jews," and "Poets, Playwrights, and Psychiatrists"[42] The APA also receives other support from the pharmaceutical industry, including an average of $1.9 million annually for ads placed in their *Psychiatric News, American Journal of Psychiatry,* and *Psychiatric Services.* A significant percentage of the $450,000 the APA receives for rental of exhibit space at their meetings comes from the pharmaceutical industry. In 1994, the APA received just under $2 million from pharmaceutical companies to support educational activities at their meetings, and during the same year they received $469,900 for fellowship programs for residents, production of tape programs on the biosocial management of depression, and production of English/Spanish comic books on teenage depression.[43]

The APA has become sensitive about all the money it receives from the pharmaceutical industry and has made an effort to point out that it has established guidelines to ensure that their programs at meetings are not being influenced by the pharmaceutical industry. Various spokespersons for the APA have mentioned that they do not accept "prepackaged" symposia organized by the pharmaceutical industry and that they have their own screening mechanisms for selecting symposia topics. Essentially, the APA maintains that its speakers and symposia programs are selected only on merit and that contributions play no role. It is no doubt true that an effort is always made to select interesting topics and qualified speakers, but it is impossible to defend the statement that the pharmaceutical industry has no influence, when so much of the money is given for the support of certain topics and not for others.

Why Does Industry Sponsor Research?

Research in psychiatry is also shaped by funding from the pharmaceutical industry. According to government reports, the pharmaceutical industry is the largest funder of medical research in both the United States and Canada, and this is overwhelmingly true when it comes to research and clinical trials on psychiatric drugs.[44] American companies in general spend much more money on research than does the federal government. According to estimates made by the National Science Foundation, private companies will have spent $130.6 billion for research and development in 1997, and it is the pharmaceutical and electronic industries that spend the largest amount of money for this purpose. In contrast, the federal government spends $20.8 billion, only about 15 percent of what private companies spend for research and development.[45] The largest proportion of the money spent for research by private companies is for product development, while a smaller proportion over the last decade was spent for basic research, defined as research to elucidate fundamental principles without a specific product application in mind.

The pharmaceutical industry invests a large amount of money to sponsor biomedical research in universities and in their affiliated hospitals and medical school departments. It has been estimated that in 1994 the pharmaceutical industry funded more than six thousand projects and expended nearly $1.5 billion for academic research.[46] Some of this money is spent on grants to biochemists, pharmacologists, and others who are doing basic research on the ways drugs affect brain chemistry. These grants are mutually beneficial to researchers and to the companies—the companies benefiting if the researchers develop a technique or obtain some information useful to them in product development. The financial support offered by pharmaceutical companies can also shape the direction of the research, making it more useful to them. Sponsorship of university research has been estimated to produce returns to pharmaceutical companies in patents, new products, and sales equal to the returns from any other of their research investments. Moreover, more than half of the companies acknowledge that contact with university faculty helps to keep their own staff current on new ideas and techniques.[47] Many graduate students and young medical researchers get drawn into research areas that pharmaceutical companies support—because that is where funds are available to provide stipends for them—and once they have acquired the relevant knowledge and skills they often continue these interests throughout much of their careers in research. The funds that are invested in university and medical school research by pharmaceutical companies are crafted by enlightened self-interest.

Pharmaceutical companies spend large sums on clinical trials to test the effectiveness and safety of new drugs before marketing. To obtain FDA approval to market a drug, data from clinical trials must be submitted. Later, after approval has been obtained, the results of these clinical trials can be used in promotional material designed to persuade physicians to adopt the drug. Whether pharmaceutical companies bias the outcome of clinical trials by selecting "favorably disposed" clinicians can be disputed, but there is little doubt that these companies are unlikely to fund clinicians who are known to have been skeptical of claims of drug effectiveness in the past or have the reputation of being "overly sensitive" to the adverse side effects of drugs. Pharmaceutical companies pay for most clinical trials, as it is their drugs that are being tested, and they usually select the "principal investigators" who coordinate the trials, often conducted at different facilities.

There are many reasons clinical trials may not provide a completely adequate assessment of the efficacy and safety of a new drug. There may, for example, be long-term effects of a drug that would not appear in trials of shorter duration, and there may be individuals who respond adversely or not at all who are not included in the sample of people tested. Although some precautions can be taken to minimize the likelihood that unanticipated adverse reactions will occur, it is impossible to eliminate all risks. There are, however, other reasons why the reports of clinical trials may not reflect future experience with a drug. Pharmaceutical companies invest large sums to develop a drug, and they have much to lose or to gain from the outcome of clinical trials. Besides commonly selecting the physicians who conduct the clinical trials, company representatives often visit at various stages to find out about trends and to offer suggestions. At a conference discussing the conduct of clinical trials, forty-six representatives of the pharmaceutical industry were asked a series of questions concerning the appropriateness of sponsors' getting involved in the conduct of clinical trials. More than three-quarters of the company representatives did not agree that sponsors' bias should be minimized by excluding them from monitoring the data and more than 50 percent of them thought it acceptable for the sponsors to participate in the data collection and data analysis. The majority of the company representatives also rejected the idea that the data belong to the investigator.[48] It is understandable that pharmaceutical companies do not want to see their investment wasted because of poorly conducted clinical trials, but there are clear dangers when they are in a position to influence the way trials are conducted and the way the data is presented.

Studies of clinical trials have shown that those supported by pharmaceutical companies are more likely to report results favorable to a company's products. One review of more than one hundred controlled clinical trials published in five leading medical journals found that those funded by pharmaceutical companies were much more likely to conclude that the new drug had advantages over a traditional treatment than were studies funded by government agencies. While several different interpretations can be given of these findings, those conducting these studies of clinical trials believe that some of the investigators funded by the pharmaceutical industry "may fear discontinued funding if negative trials are submitted and published."[49] In addition to the fear of loss of funding, others who have studied the factors that might explain why clinical trials tend to favor a sponsor's products list found, among other factors, biases in experimental design, in the questions asked, in the variables measured, in the choice of dose, and in the selection of statistical tests. Also mentioned was an occasional incident of fraudulent reporting.[50]

Putting the Best Spin on the Data

Pharmaceutical companies almost always exaggerate the effectiveness of their drugs while tending to minimize their adverse side effects. This is not done by fabricating data, but by citing the studies that show the best results and by placing their own "spin" on the way the data are presented. When a company is marketing a new drug that it believes has a good chance of replacing one of its older drugs used for the same purpose, it may for the first time be completely candid about some of the weaknesses of the older drug. For example, in an article describing the new antipsychotic Zyprexa (olanzapine), the authors, who are Eli Lilly staff, wrote:

> Conventional antipsychotic agents show therapeutic limitations. This class of drugs, the by-product of dopamine D2 receptor screening efforts, is effective in suppressing positive symptoms in some schizophrenic

patients; however, nearly one-half of patients experience incomplete or no response. Other symptoms (e.g., negative or mood features) are marginally benefited or even exacerbated. Furthermore, neuroleptic-induced adverse events [such adverse side effects as tardive dyskinesia] contribute to rates of approaching 50%.[51]

It was not possible to find such a frank statement of the limitations of Eli Lilly's "conventional antipsychotic" drug before the availability of Zyprexa. Similar examples could be provided from the literature distributed by almost any pharmaceutical company.

Pharmaceutical companies give much thought to how psychiatrists will respond to promotional material, and they may pay psychiatrists to help them evaluate material that they plan to use. One psychiatrist has recently commented on this practice:

I recall being present at a drug company–sponsored marketing consultant dinner for which I and the other psychiatrists attending were paid $500 each (and given a free meal). The drug company was presenting video and brochure material for the marketing of a new product, and wanted consumer feedback from the psychiatrists.[52]

Although pharmaceutical companies invest heavily in studies that will help to get a drug approved by the FDA, they typically show little interest in postmarketing surveillance of already approved drugs, as follow-up studies are likely to uncover additional adverse side effects. In practice, most postmarketing detection of adverse effects of a drug comes from unsolicited reports from physicians who notify the manufacturer or a governmental agency that they have observed such effects. However, this is clearly an inadequate way to discover adverse effects of drugs, as it has been reported that less than a third of physicians have ever seen the FDA form for reporting adverse reactions. Many physicians do not know how to report this kind of information, and the FDA does not have the funding to evaluate the unsolicited reports that it does receive.[53]

Some Ways That Pharmaceutical Companies Influence Research

Pharmaceutical companies often approach physicians to try a newly approved drug, ostensibly for the purpose of helping them get additional information, but these "studies" serve several other useful purposes. The psychiatrists approached need not be experienced researchers as long as they have access to an appropriate patient population, and there is often no expectation that a publication will result. In general, physicians are quite willing to accept the "research" funds, as the extra work is usually not burdensome, and the grants sometimes include some travel expenses and money for hiring clerical and research assistants, who may have time to assist the physician in other ways. Physicians may also have an interest in determining whether the new drug is better than one they are using for the same purpose. If it turns out that better results were obtained with the new drug, the pharmaceutical company can refer to these results in its promotional material even though no publication ever results. Even if the new drug proves only to be equal to the standard drugs used, the company representative has an opportunity to talk to the physicians doing the study, putting the best spin on the results, informing them of better results obtained by others, and in many ways convincing them that it would be wise to switch to the new drugs. If, on the other hand, the study indicates that the new drug is less efficacious than the drugs currently in use, not very much is usually lost, as the study is unlikely to be published, especially since the pharmaceutical company, by virtue of having paid for the study, often retains control over any publication of results. I am aware of one instance in which a pharmaceutical company did stand to lose something, because the physician who conducted the study decided to remove the new drug from the hospitals formulary (list of approved drugs) because the results were inferior to those obtained from the standard drugs, and the new drug was also more expensive. A representative of the pharmaceutical company tried to prevent this action by threatening to contact hospital administrators, informing them that the physician's study was flawed and by claiming that the hospital would be legally vulnerable if it deprived patients of a drug that "was proven" to be superior. In this instance, the physician stood by his guns and claimed that he would publicize the whole incident if the pharmaceutical company carried out its threat.

A few examples can serve to illustrate how pharmaceutical companies influence the scientific literature. Seymour Fisher, a senior and highly productive psychologist, recently described an experience that he had in publishing the results of a study comparing the adverse reactions experienced by more than twenty-seven hundred patients treated with one of the two most popular SSRI antidepressants. Fisher found that patients reported more adverse reactions to sertraline (Zoloft) than to fluoxetine (Prozac), and he submitted a manuscript to the *Journal of Clinical Psychiatry* describing the results. All three outside reviewers agreed that the manuscript should be published, and the editor accepted the article for publication. However, the editor later informed Fisher that he had decided to write an accompanying editorial, entitled "What Will This Drug Do to Me, Doctor?" According to Fisher, the editorial implied that the results might be spurious, and that physicians need not take them seriously. None of the outside reviewers had expressed any need for such a caveat, and as editorial comments of this sort were rare in this particular journal Fisher suspected that Pfizer, which markets Zoloft through its Roerig Division, was attempting to discredit the article and to minimize any effect it might have on sales. It is important to appreciate that the *Journal of Clinical Psychiatry* is distributed without charge to all psychiatrists in this country and, as a result, it is substantially dependent on the revenue it receives from the pharmaceutical company advertising that appears in every issue.

Fisher informed the editor that he objected to the editorial, and after an exchange of letters, the editor wrote that he had "softened" his comments. However, the softer version still stated that it would be "premature to treat this report as gospel" and that additional testing was required to determine "the actual incidence of side effects of these two SSRIs." Dr. Fisher still found the editorial comments objectionable, and he insisted that if the editor's comments were to be published, he should be permitted to write a reply in the same issue of the journal. Dr. Fisher wrote a reply consisting of a brief statement supporting the reliability and validity of his study and some questions about whether external pressure from advertisers had anything to do with the decision to include the editorial comment. Not surprisingly, the editor was reluctant to publish Dr. Fisher's comment, and, according to Fisher, after several more exchanges the editor, who later admitted to Fisher that he had conferred with a representative of Pfizer, finally agreed to publish the article without his editorial. Dr. Fisher, who reports having had similar experiences with other pharmaceutical companies, concluded that the editor and Pfizer had decided that publication of disputing comments would only draw additional attention to the article. The article was finally published, but only after an unusually long delay, especially for an article that had received only favorable reviews.[54]

This is not by any means an isolated incident of a pharmaceutical company appearing to influence the publication of articles that could have a detrimental effect on sales. Pharmaceutical companies have at times exerted considerable pressure on researchers, journal editors, universities, and even governmental agencies in order to protect their financial interests. Several examples of this pressure are described in the notes at the back of the book.[55] A study of university-industry research centers found that 35 percent of the agreements signed between the pharmaceutical company and an investigator allowed the company to delete information from publications, 50 percent included provisions for delaying publications, and 30 percent allowed for both.[56] A recent survey of over two thousand faculty in the life sciences revealed that 20 percent of them had experienced delays of over six months in their articles scheduled for publications and a significant number of those who experienced delays indicated that it had been done "to slow dissemination of undesired results."[57]

Pharmaceutical companies often use critical comments from hand-picked reviewers to discredit information that they regard as harmful to their interests. The critical comments are made to appear to be a consensus from independent reviewers, but this is rarely the case. The company selects the reviewers, asks the questions, often supplies additional information, which may not be factually correct—or at least, not an unbiased presentation of the facts—while those whose work is being criticized usually have no opportunity to react to the process. An article on drugs and public health included a comment on this trend:

> A ... distressing development has been the attitude of some self-proclaimed pharmicoepidemiologists that their job is to attack competent studies as consultants to drug companies, who pay them handsomely and even award grants to their research unit as a form of reward. Often the sponsorship of these "disinterested" reviews is not clearly stated. The most pernicious of these articles are characterized by an unwillingness to focus on the totality of the evidence and a concentration on real and imagined flaws that could not possibly account for strong associations.[58]

Pharmaceutical companies are often in a position to influence governmental decisions, policies, and legislature. This should not surprise anyone aware of the large contributions of the pharmaceutical industry to political campaigns. Andrew Herxheimer, chairman of the International Society of Drug Bulletins, has described the pressure exerted by Minden Pharma, a subsidiary of the large German pharmaceutical company BASF AG.[59] The drug involved was Cordichin, used for the treating cardiac arrhythmias. The drug had been associated with several deaths, and this led the Federal Institute for Drugs and Medical Products (Bundesinstitut fur Arzneimittel und Medizinprodukte) to take steps to withdraw the license to market the drug and to publish a report explaining why these steps were being taken. When the report was scheduled to be published in the official journal of the German Medical Association (Deutsche Arzteblatt), Minden Pharma obtained an injunction against publishing it on the grounds that it was libelous. The company then successfully persuaded a German court to issue a judgment preventing professional and other media from circulating unfavorable assessments of a drug before a final decision has been made by the Federal Institute for Drugs and Medicine. It is to be noted that this decision conflicts with an earlier legal decision made after the 1970 thalidomide case: "The scientific uncertainty as to whether a drug causes an adverse effect or not must not be resolved at the patient's expense because the patient's rights to health ranks above the manufacturer's rights to market his product without hindrance."[60]

As noted earlier, the pharmaceutical industry's influence is often subtle and difficult to assess or even, sometimes, to detect. One of these ambiguous situations, concerning the drug dexfenfluramine (proprietary name Redux), occurred recently. Redux alters serotonin activity in the brain and is claimed to modify mood and suppress appetite. A report from the International Primary Pulmonary Hypertension Study Group was published in *The New England Journal of Medicine* (29 August 1996) claiming that the incidence of this lung disease was thirty times greater among those people who had taken Redux for more than three months than had occurred in a random sample of the population. As there was little information about the long-term effects of taking Redux, and the drug was being used for long-term treatment of obesity, the article concluded that careful surveillance was needed.

When the article appeared in *The New England Journal of Medicine,* an editorial published in the same issue argued that Redux might avoid many more deaths from complications of obesity than could be caused by any risk of increases in a rare (one case per five hundred thousand persons) lung disease. There apparently was a leak that the editorial was about to appear, because shortly before it was published, the stock of Interneuron, the company that controls the marketing of Redux, rose 13 percent in one day.[61] To the embarrassment of the editor of the journal, it was later discovered that the coauthors of the editorial, one affiliated with Harvard University's Medical School and the other with the University of Pennsylvania, had received money as consultants from Interneuron Pharmaceuticals and also from the companies that market the same drug in Europe, as Adifax and Isomeride. They had testified as paid consultants at the original FDA hearing on Redux. The arguments raised in the editorial were not unreasonable, and there is no way of knowing whether the authors' ties to pharmaceutical companies had influenced their opinions and their motivation to write the editorial. It is likely that the authors themselves do not know if that factor influenced them. It should be noted, however, that the editorial was not at all balanced. For instance, it did not refer to other risks, such as the heart-valve problems that were suspected of being caused by this drug. Nor was there any mention of the reports from Mark Molliver, a neuroscientist at Johns Hopkins University, that high doses of Redux produced brain damage in animals. Several other neuroscientists had also reported to the FDA that Redux produces neurotoxicity.[62] Although some of these claims are contested, they probably would have been mentioned in a more balanced review of the risks and benefits of this drug.

There is probably no one who testifies as an expert who would not be highly indignant at a suggestion that his or her ties to industry might influence their opinion, but it would be naive to think that it doesn't in a number of instances. A recent study of published papers on a class of drugs called "calcium channel blockers" goes a long way toward documenting the extent of that influence. Although relatively new, these drugs are widely prescribed to treat hypertension, angina, and some other cardiovascular problems, and their annual U.S. sales have been estimated to be about $4 billion. However, there have been several reports that have raised questions about the safety of "calcium channel blockers," and a controversy has ensued over whether, considering the risk, these drugs should be preferred over the so-called "beta blocker" drugs, considering the risk. A team of physicians in Toronto examined seventy research papers and classified them as "supportive," "neutral," or "opposed" to the "calcium channel blockers." They then determined whether the authors of the research papers had received any money from the companies that market these drugs. The results showed that 96 percent of the authors who supported the "calcium channel blockers" received money from the companies that sell these drugs, while only 37 percent of those whose reports were "opposed" to these drug had any financial ties to these companies. Although the financial ties varied, as some authors received honoraria, others were paid consultants and 79 percent had received funding for their research from the companies that market "calcium channel blockers." The article noted that the ties to the pharmaceutical industry are commonly not disclosed. It was found, for example, that while the majority of the authors of the seventy papers studied had ties to either the pharmaceutical companies that sell "calcium channel blockers" or competing drugs, in only two instances out of the seventy were those ties acknowledged in the articles.[63]

There is now considerable evidence of serious complications from some of the drugs marketed for losing weight.[64] A recent study out of the Mayo Clinic reported a number of major heart valve abnormalities among people on the diet treatment known as fen-phen. The fen-phen treatment involves two separate drugs, fenfluramine (Pondimin) and phentermine. Both drugs were approved by the FDA for separate use, but following reports of greater success in suppressing appetite when they were used together, fen-phen treatment was adopted enthusiastically without any additional scrutiny. Over 18 million prescription were written for fen-phen in 1996. There were major shock waves following the reports on all the national news service that twenty four patients, who had no previous heart problems, had developed a serious heart valve condition while taking fen-phen, and that others had developed pulmonary hypertension. Some of the people had been taking fen-phen for as little as one month before the symptoms developed. The particular type of valvular heart disease that developed is normally quite rare in people with a mean age of only forty-three years.[65] Reports now indicate that these same serious heart problems can occur after treatment with either fenfluramine (Pondimin) or dexfenfluramine (Redux) when administered alone. Early reports from five different surveys indicate that heart valve problems may be detected in as many as 30 percent of people who took these drugs, alone or in combination, although not all of them had symptoms. It is typical of the first response of pharmaceutical companies to reports of adverse effects of one of their products that the Wyeth-Ayerst Laboratories, the manufacturer of fenfluramine (Pondimin) and the distributors of Interneuron's Redux, quickly issued a statement, following the first Mayo Clinic report, that "the data are limited and therefore inconclusive" and that it needs to be kept in mind that obesity itself "is associated with serious health disorders."[66]

Fen-phen has not only been used to suppress appetite. One physician running a fen-phen clinic has claimed that these two drugs have successfully treated not only obesity, but also drug, sexual, and alcohol addictions as well as asthma, hives, lupus, depression, chronic fatigue syndrome, obsessive-compulsive disorders, nail-biting, and much more. Furthermore, it was claimed that *"promising results"* have also been reported in patients with AIDS or Persian Gulf Syndrome, and in Vietnam veterans suffering from posttraumatic stress disorder. Evidence of adverse effects of drugs is often slow in reaching the physicians and patients who have to make choices about therapeutic alternatives. In an excellent review of this problem, Dr. Andrew Herxheimer, the chairman of the International Society of Drug Bulletins, lists the following three major reasons why drug information may not get to the people who need it: First, there is no mechanism for the systematic collection, analysis, and distribution of postmarketing information about adverse reactions to drugs; second, pharmaceutical companies have not always been sufficiently forthcoming in disclosing information on adverse side effects; and third, it is the practice of some pharmaceutical companies to discredit and to suppress information that casts doubt on the safety or efficacy of their drugs.[67]

It is not only information about adverse effects of drugs and other treatments that does not freely circulate, but even information that might facilitate health-related research may not become freely available because pharmaceutical companies often insist on withholding information until they have established their proprietary rights. This has become a common problem in recent years, as an increasing number of academic researchers have ties to the pharmaceutical industry and are restricted by the terms of their contracts from releasing information without prior approval. Steven Rosenberg, of the National Cancer Institute, has recently described several personal experiences he has had in this regard and has concluded that:

> The support of medical research by biotechnology and pharmaceutical companies has introduced new pressures in the communication of scientific information. Scientists are pulled in opposite directions by the desire to share research information and the need to protect the investors who have supported the research.[68]

Concern has also been expressed about the accuracy of the information conveyed in the advertising that appears in medical journals. As long ago as 1951, the pharmaceutical industry was reported to be spending about $352 million annually on advertising in U.S. medical journals, but today, the figure is in the many billions. It is estimated that more than $12.3 billion is spent by the industry in promoting drugs in the United states alone and over five thousand dollars is spent annually to influence the prescribing habits of every physician. This investment gets a good return, as a study commissioned by five large pharmaceutical companies showed that ads in medical journals increase the number of new prescriptions written by physicians.[69]

David Kessler, who was at the time the commissioner of the Food and Drug Administration, commented on the results of the agency's study of the accuracy of the information conveyed by pharmaceutical ads in medical journals: "A disturbingly high proportion of these advertisements contained misleading information and appeared to violate existing Food and Drug Administration (FDA) regulations governing the accuracy and balance of prescription drug advertising."[70] Kessler has also described how statistics from clinical trials are commonly mishandled, leading to unwarranted and misleading claims.[71] If, for example, a company would like to be able to claim that its new drug is as good as the leading drug in the field, all it has to do is to make certain that the sample size is small. Because of biological variability, it is usually not possible to obtain a statistically significant difference between two drugs, even if they really do differ in their efficacy, without a large database. Furthermore, it is misleading to claim that a lack of statistical difference, which could be explained on the basis of insensitive measures as well as too small a sample, proves that there is no difference between different drugs. Statisticians frequently find it necessary to point out that it is not possible to prove the "null hypothesis," which is their way of saying that statistics cannot prove that no difference exists between two variables, only whether a difference that was obtained was likely to have happened by chance.

Kessler referred to another misleading use of statistics as "data dredging," which is a term used to refer to the practice of trying to capitalize on chance occurrences. If, for example, a great many different measures of symptoms are made after patients take a drug, it is likely that a few of these measures will have improved just by chance. If the number of items assessed is large enough, one should expect that a few of these will show "statistically significant differences" between a drug and a placebo. That is why it is not unusual for five heads in a row to occur once or twice if a coin is flipped many hundreds of times. It is misleading to take advantage of statistically spurious events to claim significant effects for a drug, but it is commonly done in trying to maximize the appearance of effectiveness of a drug in promotional material.

In a study designed to evaluate the accuracy of pharmaceutical company advertising, each of 109 full-page ads that had appeared in ten leading medical journals was sent to three evaluators (two physicians experienced in peer review of articles and knowledgeable in the relevant clinical area and one academic clinical pharmacist).[72] The evaluators found that: 40 percent of the ads did not appropriately balance information on efficacy and adverse side effects; 32 percent of the "headlines" appearing at the top of the ads were misleading about efficacy; and 57 percent of the ads were judged to have little educational value. In general, the evaluators concluded that 62 percent of the ads should not have been published, or major revisions should have been insisted on before publication. The authors of the study also made an extensive effort, through library research, letters, and telephone calls, to track down the "references" cited in the ads, but they could not locate many of them, as apparently they were either unpublished articles or confidential and unavailable "in-house" reports.

As often happens, a spokesman for a pharmaceutical industry consortium tried to discredit this study demonstrating that drug ads are often misleading. In a letter published in the same medical journal, the spokesman claimed that the study was flawed and should be discounted.[73] The industry spokesman, however, made no mention of the fact that essentially the same results were obtained in several other studies. In another study, for example, all of the promotional material left by pharmaceutical company sales personnel for physicians at three different sites was analyzed, and much of it was found to be "misleading, unbalanced, and to contain unsupported statements." Some of the material was designed to look like educational material, but only the drugs marketed by the company distributing the material were mentioned. Even though the material was intended for physicians, it often contained advertising phrases rather than complete sentences. A flyer describing an antibiotic, for example, was headed in bold type by the slogan: "Floxin—The Scourge of Microbial Villains."[74]

When physicians see advertising or receive information from the pharmaceutical industry, they are usually aware that it is probably promotional material, but this is not always the case. There are an increasing number of supplements to professional journals that are printed in the same style as the journal, but the articles often are not "peer reviewed." Some of these supplemental issues of journals are supported by pharmaceutical companies, and the articles in those issues commonly report favorable results of a clinical trial of one of the company's products. Physicians also receive huge amounts of mail in which the involvement of a pharmaceutical company is not at all apparent. For example, many psychiatrists received information about antidepressants that was circulated by the PCS Health Systems, one of the largest groups providing information to health care managers, pharmacies, and physicians. According to the president and chief executive of the PCS, the information it provides is designed to "have a positive impact on helping improve patient care and lower health care costs." The PCS information dated October 1996 compared the aggregate health service expenditures of three leading antidepressants, the selective serotonin reuptake inhibitors Prozac, Zoloft, and Paxil. The graph and the text indicated that the expenditures for "patients receiving Paxil was $285 greater compared to patients receiving Prozac" while the costs for "patients receiving Zoloft was $316 greater compared to patients receiving Prozac." The Eli Lilly company manufactures and markets Prozac, but few psychiatrists who received this material had any idea that PCS Health Systems is totally owned by Eli Lilly.

The pharmaceutical industry and clinical research are so completely intertwined that it is frequently difficult to find experts who are not in some way tied to the industry. This is illustrated by an incidental finding of the study described above in which experts evaluated pharmaceutical company ads in medical journals.[75] Originally the authors of the study wanted to exclude any evaluator who had accepted money from the pharmaceutical industry in excess of three hundred dollars during the previous two months. This exclusion criterion had to be dropped, as three-quarters of the physicians contacted had recently received money from pharmaceutical companies. A recent study of close to eight hundred articles that appeared in fourteen leading biomedical journals, including *Science, Nature, Lancet, The New England Journal of Medicine,* and the *Proceedings of the National Academy of Medicine,* indicates the degree of commingling of industry and biological research.[76] It was found that about 34 percent of the primary authors had financial interests in the work they published in academic journals. The study defined "financial interest" as: the author being an inventor of a patent or a patent application closely related to the published work; serving on a scientific advisory board of a company doing work related to the topic of the publication; or serving as an officer or being a major shareholder of a company with commercial interests related to the research. Actually, the criteria used underestimated the importance of the financial interests of the "experts," as the authors did not consider consultancies, personal financial holdings, or receiving honoraria as an indication of a "financial interest."

A Potential Brain Drain?

Over the last decade or so, an increasing number of the most productive and creative scientists in the biomedical field have either created or been affiliated in some way with biotechnology companies. Most of these "biotech" companies are started with "venture capital" investment money, but they soon have a "cash flow" problem, as they usually have no products and no dependable source of income. At this point, many of the companies are bankrolled by some large pharmaceutical company that is willing to invest in the ideas and the potential products. Pharmaceutical companies are usually also needed to conduct the expensive multisite clinical trials and for marketing and sales of any drugs that may result. While such a marriage of interests is undoubtedly useful in many instances, there are other aspects of these arrangements that have raised some major concerns. In most instances, these creative scientists, including a number of Nobel Laureates, hold academic positions, and the secrecy that almost always accompanies any activity in which many millions (sometimes billions) of dollars may be involved has definitely curtailed the free exchange of information that once characterized science in academic settings.

There is also concern that because so much is at stake, the focus of creative scientists is being shifted away from fundamental biological questions to pursuing marketable products. If the products are truly helpful, this certainly can be a major contribution to public welfare, but there are many reasons to be concerned about this trend. The fate of a small company may depend on convincing the FDA that a drug that it has "bet the bankroll on" is safe and effective. Moreover, there are pressures to take "shortcuts," as there can be huge financial consequences of being the first to gain FDA approval for a new class of drugs. Scientists who have accepted large amounts of stock in a company rather than the salary they might otherwise command can become multimillionaires almost overnight if FDA approval is secured. Many of the more prominent clinical investigators hired as consultants also have a substantial investment in the success of the company, and they can sometimes exert an influence on what drugs are approved and for what purposes. Security analysts of investment firms have been known to congregate in the halls outside the room where an FDA committee is conducting hearings on a new drug, and stock prices may skyrocket or bottom out depending on the outcome of these hearings. The pressures are enormous, and in many ways the commingling of science and business is changing biomedical research, often to the detriment of objectivity in evaluating scientific evidence. Linda Marsa has described this process in her fascinating book *Prescription for Profits.*[77]

The emphasis here on the many ways that the pharmaceutical industry influences the sale of psychotherapeutic drugs and the acceptance of the "biochemical theories of mental disorders" is not meant to deny that the industry has made many contributions to public health. That is another story, however, and one that the industry itself promotes very effectively.[78] There is no doubt that the pharmaceutical industry views its influence through a different prism than the one used here, and it would have no trouble explaining its actions by stressing the importance of making physicians and the public aware of effective drugs that are available and by countering misinformation that might prevent people from getting the help they need. Although it may not shock anyone to read that the pharmaceutical industry is not different from any other major industry in devising ways to advance and protect its own interest, many are not aware of the enormous influence that the industry has in shaping our views of mental disorders and the effectiveness of psychotherapeutic drugs.

Chapter 7

OTHER SPECIAL
INTEREST GROUPS

A lthough the pharmaceutical industry has the resources and is in a position to have the greatest influence in promoting drug treatment and the chemical theories of mental illness, other groups play an important role as well.

Psychiatry and the Chemical Theories of Mental Illness

Even a casual examination of the history of psychiatry makes it clear that many factors besides scientific progress have influenced the way psychiatrists have perceived mental disorders and how they currently regard drug treatment of these disorders. During the last century, most psychiatrists, or "alienists" as they were commonly called, worked in insane asylums located in rural areas. It was not only the physical separation, however, that isolated the "alienists" from the rest of medicine. The superintendents of these insane asylums did not want to be absorbed into the traditional medical societies, as they considered themselves in a privileged position compared to most physicians. The superintendents, for example, usually had a guaranteed salary and benefits including a house and meals. Up to 1884, the superintendents had their own professional organization, called The Association of Medical Superintendents of American Institutions for the Insane (AMSAII), and on several occasions they rejected overtures to affiliate with the American Medical Association.

On the other hand, many physicians were highly critical of those who treated the mentally ill and did not consider them to be a part of medicine. Neurologists, in particular were highly critical of the psychiatrists working in the asylums. In 1878, Edward Spitzka, a twenty-five-year-old neurologist, gave a speech entitled "The Study of Insanity Considered as a Branch of Neurology and the Relations of the General Medical Body to

This Branch." He attacked the institutions and the superintendents, stating that after he read their reports he had concluded:

> That certain superintendents are experts in gardening and farming (although the farm account frequently comes out on the wrong side of the ledger), tin roofing (although the roof and cupola is usually leaky), drain-pipe laying (although the grounds are often moist and unhealthy), engineering (although the wards are either too hot or too cold), history (although their facts are incorrect and their inferences beyond all measure so); in short, experts at everything except the diagnosis, pathology and treatment of insanity.[1]

Seven years later, after Spitzka was elected president of the American Neurological Association, he spearheaded neurology's attack on institutional psychiatry. At the first meeting of the American Neurological Association in 1875, a vote to bar the superintendents from membership was passed without opposition, and the neurologists began publishing the *Journal of Nervous and Mental Disease* in competition with the *American Journal of Insanity,* which represented the superintendents. The antagonism between the two groups was so strong that it exploded into a public debate with vitriolic exchanges taking place in *The New York Times,* which wrote several editorials about the dispute. In one editorial the *Times* suggested that the neurologists had exaggerated their scientific knowledge with all their "elegant talk about the wonderful properties of nerve cells."

In 1894, AMSAII celebrated its fiftieth anniversary and on that occasion changed its name to the American Medico-Psychological Association. The members invited S. Weir Mitchell, the leading neurologist of the day, to give the keynote address at their anniversary meeting. This represented an attempt at a rapprochement, but Weir Mitchell did not hesitate to criticize them. He asserted that since the days of Benjamin Rush, psychiatrists had isolated themselves and:

> You have never come back into line. It is easy to see how this came about. You soon began to live apart, and you still do so. Your hospitals are not our hospitals; your ways are not our ways. You live out of range of critical shot; you are not preceded and followed in your ward by clever rivals, or watched by able residents fresh with the learning of the schools.[2]

Although much of this criticism was justified, there is little doubt that it was fueled by the competition between neurologists and psychiatrists for control of the treatment of the mentally ill.

Even though few psychiatrists were employed in academic settings in the United States, a strong biological bias dominated all of psychiatry throughout most of its early history. The only psychiatrist to receive the

Nobel Prize (awarded in 1927) was Julius Wagner-Jauregg, the Austrian psychiatrist who introduced the malaria fever treatment for "general paralysis of the insane."[3] From the 1920s through the 1950s, there seemed to be few limits to the somatic treatments psychiatrists were willing to explore. In the state psychiatric hospital in Trenton, New Jersey, teeth were extracted, tonsils removed, and large intestines were even sectioned in an attempt to remove the "focal infections" that were hypothesized to travel to the brain where they were the cause of mental disorders. In many institutions, schizophrenics were treated with a regimen of carbon dioxide breathing, and there was some exploration of the effects of increasing oxygen by placing mental patients in hyperbolic chambers. Mental patients in one North Carolina hospital were injected with horse serum to increase their leukocytes and give them a "fresh regenerative impulse." The "exhausted nervous systems" of depressed patients were treated with sleep therapy, a prolonged narcosis induced by barbiturates and opium derivatives. Within a five-year period in the 1930s, insulin coma, metrazol shock, electroconvulsive therapy, and prefrontal lobotomy were all introduced, and during much of the 1940s and 1950s they were widely prescribed by psychiatrists throughout the world.[4]

While psychiatrists were certainly not all of the same mind, most of them believed that a biological factor, either an inherited physical defect or some infectious agent or toxic substance, would eventually be found to have caused most mental illnesses. When "general paralysis of the insane" was discovered to be caused by neurosyphilis, and the malaria fever treatment was found to be effective in arresting the progress of this disease, it was often cited as an illustration of what would eventually be the fate of all so-called "psychiatric diseases."

In 1921, the American Medico-Psychological Association became the American Psychiatric Association (APA), but even as late as 1930, almost three-quarters of the APA membership worked in state mental hospitals. Neurologists, being the authorities on the nervous system, had routinely treated the "nervous disorders" of noninstitutionalized patients. During the discussion leading up to the establishment of a separate certifying board for psychiatrists, the American Neurological Association tried to preempt the issue by establishing a neurology board to certify "neuropsychiatrists." Psychiatry did, however, become a separate certified specialty in the mid-1930s, and gradually departments of psychiatry were established in hospitals and medical schools.

There were clear signs as early as 1930 that "lay therapists" were in competition with psychiatrists. In his presidential address to the American Psychiatric Association in 1932, William Russell noted with considerable alarm that "psychologists without any medical and psychiatric training and social workers who have been instructed in psychoanalysis are attempting to treat psychiatric conditions in private practice." He also was clearly disturbed when he learned that a psychological clinic had been established in a psychology department of a major university and that the National Research Council, with Carnegie Foundation money, was supporting a psychologist to study "the present status of mental disorders." Russell attempted to denigrate psychology by declaring that the discipline "grew out of philosophy and metaphysics," whereas psychiatry was rooted in medicine. James May repeated much the same theme and concerns the following year in his own presidential address to the American Psychiatric Association. Among the dangerous trends noted by May was the large number of psychologists attempting to become "lay analysts" and the growing practice by psychology departments of offering courses in "abnormal psychology," a subject he asserted was "psychiatry pure and simple, and does not belong within the domain of psychology."[5]

The psychologist Carl Rogers's book *Client-Centered Therapy* was published in 1951, and shortly afterward psychiatrists became engaged in a vigorous campaign to get him replaced as the head of the Rochester Guidance Center on the grounds that a psychologist should not be in charge of a mental health agency. Later, at the University of Chicago, a succession of Psychiatry Department chairmen tried to close down the Counseling Center he headed by claiming that psychologists were practicing medicine (namely, psychotherapy) without a license.[6] Of course, economic considerations were never raised as an issue and the arguments aired in public were always based on the need for medical knowledge to protect patients and to assure proper treatment. For a number of years, even admission to psychoanalytic training institutes was restricted to physicians, despite the fact that Freud had written that medical knowledge was not necessary to practice psychoanalysis. After 1960, however, the monopoly could no longer be maintained, and nonmedical therapists were gradually admitted to psychoanalytic institutes for training as "lay analysts."

From approximately 1945 to 1965, biological explanations within psychiatry receded into the background as the influence of psychoanalytic ideas grew and the origin of mental disorders was sought in childhood psychosexual experiences. Before the 1940s, when most psychiatrists spoke about mental disorders, they had in mind institutionalized patients suffering from psychotic conditions: either dementia praecox (schizophrenia) or serious mood disorders such as mania and major depression. Psychoanalytic theory, however, blurred the distinction between the psychoses and the neuroses, as all mental disorders were thought to have similar origins. As a result, many less severe emotional and behavioral problems began to be considered conditions that could be improved with therapy.

With the rise of Nazism, a number of leading European psychoanalysts emigrated to the United States. There was a particularly receptive climate for psychoanalytic theory in the United States, and starting shortly after the end of the World War II, this theory began to force biological psychiatry into the background. Moreover, many people suspected that biological psychiatry was tainted by being associated with European fascism and racist ideology, and any emphasis on constitutional and immutable factors was suspect. Psychoanalysis, on the other hand, stressed early experiences in the family, and this seemed more optimistic, subject to change, and certainly more in line with the postwar mood.

Although biological psychiatry receded into the background during the period of psychoanalytic dominance, it definitely did not disappear. Psychoanalytic concepts dominated much of the theoretical speculation within psychiatry, and psychoanalytic themes were enthusiastically adopted in the arts and the popular media. However, biological psychiatry was still heavily represented in the treatment of patients, especially, but not exclusively, institutionalized patients. Through much of the 1950s, insulin coma, electroshock, and lobotomy were still used to treat many patients. By 1960, drug treatment had moved to the forefront of biological psychiatry.

During the 1950s, explanations of how the various physical treatments worked were often a strange and strained marriage of psychoanalytic concepts and some rather primitive ideas of how the brain functioned. Nowhere was this more evident than in the experimental treatments used by D. Ewen Cameron, a man little remembered today, but in the 1950s one of the most prominent psychiatrists in the world. Cameron was elected president of the American Psychiatric Association, the American Psychopathological Association, the Society of Biological Psychiatry, the Quebec Psychiatric Association, and the Canadian Psychiatric Association, and he was the chief architect and first president of the World Psychiatric Association. One psychiatrist remarked at the time that more societies would have to be created to honor Cameron.

D. Ewen Cameron was born in 1901 in Scotland, where he received his medical school education and training in psychiatry at Glasgow University. Afterward he worked briefly in Zurich under Jakob Klaesi, the main proponent of sleep therapy. Cameron emigrated to the United States, and at Johns Hopkins University he came under the influence of Adolf Meyer, then regarded as the "Dean of American Psychiatry." Cameron then went on to head psychiatry at the Albany Medical College in New York, becoming a naturalized U.S. citizen in 1942, but the following year he left Albany to become chairman of McGill's Psychiatry Department and director of the Allan Memorial Institute, a new psychiatric facility administered by McGill and the Royal Victoria Hospital. Cameron held these positions in Montreal from 1943 until 1964.

Cameron was an empire builder and fiercely ambitious, and while at the Allan Memorial Institute he seemed to be willing to try anything in order to make a major breakthrough in the treatment of mental disorders. He was primarily interested in developing techniques to cancel out troublesome memories and to replace them with healthy thoughts. Cameron explored different physical methods that he felt might "erase" the disturbing thoughts or repressed conflicts of patients and replace these with ideas that he judged would be therapeutically beneficial. Cameron called the erasing process "depatterning," and the process of implanting healthier thoughts, he called "psychic driving" or "reprogramming." The methods Cameron employed kept changing in an unrestrained and unsystematic "trial-and-error" pattern, but basically "depatterning" consisted of using extreme physical methods to erase memories and to put the patients in a state where they were not able to resist "psychic driving" and "reprogramming."

In the beginning, Cameron used insulin-induced coma during "depatterning," but in most instances a regimen of "intensive electroshock therapy" was administered during a drug-induced sleep state. Cameron described "depatterning" as an "extensive breakup of the existing patterns of behavior, both normal and pathologic, by means of an intensive electroshock therapy usually carried out in association with prolonged sleep."[7] The drug-induced sleep state was sometimes maintained as long as sixty days, except for brief waking periods for bowel movements and eating. Sometimes Cameron tried administering electroshock while the patient was under the influence of LSD or chlorpromazine. Following the intensive electroshock, the patients were confused and amnesic, but Cameron did not like calling it "regressive electroshock therapy," the term used by other psychiatrists who at the time were also administering many electroshock sessions every day, because "There is no evidence of the use of childhood types of verbal behavior [or infantile forms of motor activity] such as were reported by Gesell and Piaget and there is no evidence of a return to childhood physiological functioning."[8] Cameron described the successful "depatterning" as achieving a "differential amnesia," a state he characterized as follows:

> The third stage of depatterning is reached when the patient loses all recollection of the fact that he formerly possessed a space time image which served to explain the events of the day to him. With this loss, all anxiety disappears. In the third stage, his conceptual span is limited to a few minutes and to entirely concrete events. He volunteers a few statements on questioning. He says that he is sleepy or that he feels fine. He cannot conceptualize where he is, nor does he recognize those who treat him. There is also an extremely interesting constriction of the range of recollections

and anticipations. . . . His remarks are entirely uninfluenced by previous recollections—nor are they governed in any way by his forward anticipations. He lives in the immediate present. All schizophrenic symptoms have disappeared.[9]

Following "depatterning," the patient was ready for "psychic driving." Messages were played over and over again from a continuous loop tape delivery system. Cameron was influenced by the research that was being claimed at the time to have demonstrated a potential for substantial learning during sleep. The messages were delivered while the patient was in a drug-induced sleep state. He was able to acquire a state-of-the-art tape recorder that allowed him to deliver different messages repeatedly and simultaneously to eight patients, each in his or her own cubicle. The messages were derived from earlier psychotherapeutic sessions and were called "dynamic implants," a term implying that they had psychodynamic (psychoanalytic) significance for the patient, such as statements involving some experience of the patient with his or her mother. The messages were varied over time, some emphasizing a patient's negative traits, others suggesting alternative ways of behaving and relating to others, some designed to desensitize patients to fearful situations, and so on. None of this really worked, and it may have done harm to some patients. In retrospect, the theory (if it should be called that) was founded on the most superficial elements of psychoanalysis, brain physiology, and learning theory.

Donald Hebb, the noted psychologist, who was familiar with Cameron's therapeutic program, remarked that the fatal flaw was that "he wasn't so much driven by wanting to know—he was driven with wanting to be important—to make that breakthrough. It made him a bad scientist. He was criminally stupid."[10] However, Hebb's remark was made at a much later time. During the 1950s, Cameron was highly respected among biological psychiatrists, as the many honors he received clearly indicates. Moreover, Hebb at the time was exploring some related questions, although in a more academic setting. During the 1950s, when the Korean War was on, there was interest in investigating "brainwashing," as the Chinese and North Koreans were suspected of using some new techniques on prisoners of war. Hebb and his associates received funding from the Canadian Defense Department to study how people's ideas could be influenced while they were maintained in a condition of extreme sensory deprivation. Student volunteers were paid handsomely to undergo severe sensory deprivation, during which time they wore cuffs to prevent them from experiencing touch, plastic masks that prevented any pattern vision, and foam surrounding their heads, that blocked sound. At various interval, messages were delivered to the subjects. None of the student volunteers could stand the extreme deprivation for more than a week, but during this time their capacity to think deteriorated and some of them began to hallucinate and to accept ideas they normally would have rejected.

Although Cameron died in 1967 and his work was forgotten, it was later brought into the public limelight in an unexpected way.[11] I happen to be quite familiar with this part of the story as a result of being asked to be an expert witness on some pending litigation involving Cameron's activities at the Allan Memorial Institute. In 1977, *The New York Times* had printed an article describing a number of CIA-supported programs investigating behavior control techniques, and Cameron was mentioned as one of the recipients of the agency's funds. What had happened was that the CIA was also interested in the possibility that the Chinese and North Koreans were using brainwashing techniques when a psychologist working at the agency in 1956 noticed an article by Cameron published in the *American Journal of Psychiatry*. The article's description of "depatterning" and "psychic driving" using tape-recorded messages seemed very much like brainwashing. It was decided to facilitate Cameron's work by funneling funds to him through a "front" organization called the Society for the Investigation of Human Ecology. Between 1957 and 1960, Cameron received $54,467 from the agency, most of which was used to purchase a sophisticated tape recorder and to hire an assistant to run it.

The *New York Times* article received a great amount of attention and soon led a group of eight former patients of Cameron to join in a lawsuit against the CIA. The attorneys for the plaintiffs alleged that their clients had all been involved as guinea pigs in a brainwashing project. As all of the patients involved were Canadian—one being the wife of a former member of Parliament—the lawsuit had international ramifications. Actually, Cameron's experimental program was well under way before he received any CIA funds, and as far as could be determined, he was totally unaware of the true source of the U.S. money he received. Furthermore, such were the times that all of the physical techniques used by Cameron—LSD and other drugs, sleep therapy, and repeated shock treatment—were used by many prominent psychiatrists in Europe and in the Western Hemisphere. There were even a number of international psychiatry congresses held to exchange experiences with these techniques. Probably for that reason, the claimants were willing to settle without a trial for the amount of money offered by a CIA anxious to avoid any further adverse publicity.

After 1950, the number and diversity of people treating the mentally ill increased manyfold and with that increase, so did the competition. The number of psychiatrists increased about threefold between 1950 and 1970, and the membership of the American Psychiatric Association increased from 5,856 to 18,407.[12] The numbers of nonmedical people treating the mentally ill also increased enormously. At the end of the Second World

War, the Veterans Administration had financed a large training program for clinical psychologists, and by 1960s, the movement to license psychologists was well under way.[13] Today all states have established academic and experiential criteria for the licensing of clinical psychologists and other mental health professionals. In addition to the large number of clinical psychologists, it has been estimated that by 1990 there were about eighty thousand clinical social workers in the United States.

Licensing gave nonmedical therapists legal stature and political clout, both of which had the effect of increasing their acceptance by patients and by third-party medical insurers. The American Psychiatric Association has consistently fought against this growing competition by lobbying on federal and state levels and using its political influence with legislatures and private medical insurers to exclude psychologists and other mental health professionals from participating in HMOs, Blue Cross, Medicare, and other third-party medical insurers. This "war" continues today, with battles seemingly won alternately by the two sides of the dispute.

As approximately 30 percent of the population in the United States is estimated to have a mental disorder or an addiction problem in any given year, it might be thought that with these numbers there should be no concern about competition within the different mental health professions. However, only about one-quarter of the people estimated to be suffering from a mental disorder seek professional help, and most of those who seek help do not go to psychiatrists. A recent survey of over four thousand people who had sought professional help for a mental disorder found that only 20 percent had seen a psychiatrist, whereas 37 percent went to psychologists, and 14 percent to social workers, and the remaining 27 percent sought help from marriage counselors, support groups, or their family physicians.[14] Nonmedical therapists are usually more available, and they customarily charge significantly less than psychiatrists for their services.[15]

Psychiatrists are better trained to detect any physical condition that might underlie a mental disorder, but if such a condition is suspected, patients are usually referred to the appropriate medical specialist. The only treatments that psychiatrists can provide for mental disorders that nonmedical therapists cannot are drugs and ECT. While it can certainly be argued whether this fact colors the way psychiatrists assess the effectiveness and safety of drug treatment, there is little doubt that since the 1960s, psychiatry has increasingly emphasized biochemical factors as the cause of mental disorders. Moreover, while psychiatrists certainly do not all have the same perspective on these issues, there is an increasing tendency among them to deprecate the effectiveness of psychotherapy, in contrast to drug treatment.

The book *Understanding Depression: A Complete Guide to Its Diagnosis and Treatment,* by Donald Klein and Paul Wender, professors of psychiatry at Columbia and Utah, illustrates this bias favoring drug treatment over all alternatives.[16] Klein and Wender assert that there is convincing evidence that in most instances depression has a biological rather than a psychological cause. They advise being wary of diagnosis by nonmedical therapists and bearing in mind that "only physicians can prescribe antidepressant medication"—a treatment that in most instances is "effective, moderately fast and inexpensive." Elsewhere, Klein was quoted as stating his belief that "[psycho]therapy will probably be excluded from treatment in the long run."[17] Klein and Wender argue that if patients are treated with psychotherapy and the depression turns out to have a biological cause this "may waste considerable time and money," and they propose that drugs should always be tried first and psychotherapy should be the last resort if drug treatment fails. Even if a specific instance of depression should have a psychological cause, Klein and Wender argue, this can be determined "cheaply and fairly rapidly." However, the effectiveness of drug treatment cannot be determined as rapidly as Klein and Wender imply, as it may take many months to determine if medication will be effective, and when it is not, the usual practice is to increase the dose and try again or to switch to other drugs, each of which can take several months to evaluate. Much of the literature written by biological psychiatrists is designed to convince readers that there is no question that drugs have been proven to be more effective than all forms of psychotherapeutic treatment of mental disorders. However, the actual evidence for belief is much less convincing.

Effectiveness of Different Treatments of Mental Disorders

There are now a considerable number of studies that have compared the effectiveness of drugs with that of the briefer forms of psychotherapy such as cognitive or interpersonal therapy and also, in some instances, with behavior therapies. It would be a tedious and probably futile exercise to review all this literature, because the number of studies and the different methodologies involved make it unlikely that any conclusion reached would persuade anyone not already convinced. It might be helpful, however, to highlight some of the more commonly obtained results of these studies.

Most of the studies comparing the effectiveness of different treatments have looked at depression, but there are also a few studies that have compared treatments for obsessive-compulsive disorders, anxiety and panic disorders, specific phobias, and various substance abuse disorders, including bulimia. In the 1950s, there were several psychotherapists, such as Harry Stack Sullivan, Frieda Fromm-Reichmann, and John Rosen, who claimed that they were successful in treating schizophrenia, but most mental health professionals today do not believe that psychotherapy by itself can effectively treat this disorder. There are, however, several reports that some forms of psychotherapy (for example, helping schizophrenics cope with stress-related emotions) may be quite effective when combined with drug treatment.[18] Even those few therapists who believe that psychotherapy can help schizophrenics acknowledge that because the treatment is so time-consuming and labor-intensive, it is not a practical alternative in most instances. Nonmedical therapists commonly refer schizophrenic patients to psychiatrists for drug treatment, not because they are necessarily convinced that drugs will be effective, but because, as one psychotherapist phrased it, "It's not possible to do psychotherapy with someone who is continually disrupted by voices coming out of the toilet bowl."

Although there is not much experimental evidence available, psychotherapists generally believe that even with schizophrenia a more complete and lasting recovery results if psychotherapy is combined with drug treatment. Most studies indicate that, at best, drug treatment provides significant help in only about 50 percent of schizophrenic patients, and it is less effective in cases in which negative symptoms (primarily impoverished speech and affect) predominate. Moreover, antipsychotic drugs are notorious for producing adverse side effects in addition to tardive dyskinesia, which has received the most attention. Patients on antipsychotic medication often complain about feeling like a "zombie," "weird," "dull," "fuzzy," and "lacking will power and spontaneity." These adverse side effects are a major reason many patients refuse to take the prescribed medications, and psychiatrists have recognized these common complaints by describing them with such terms as "pharmacological depression" and "neuroleptic dysphoria."[19]

Most psychotherapists also agree that psychotherapy alone is rarely effective in treating bipolar depression (manic-depressive disorder), while lithium and other mood-stabilizing drugs are often quite effective. However, at least 30 percent to 40 percent of manic-depressives are not helped sufficiently by lithium or by any of the other mood stabilizers, such as valproate and carbamazepine, and there are reports that therapy and counseling, particularly if it includes family members, will increase the probability of a good and a lasting recovery.[20] In any case, manic-depressive disorder and schizophrenia together probably constitute only about 2 percent of all mental disorders.

There are many difficulties in evaluating the effectiveness of psychotherapy, as it is not easy to standardize the treatment, psychotherapists vary in skill, and their effectiveness varies with different types of patients.

Moreover, the criteria for assessing effectiveness will influence the results. Some treatments may produce quicker results and look better if there is only a short follow-up period, but they might not look so good with longer follow-up periods if they reveal a high incidence of relapse. Furthermore, although carefully controlled studies may seem desirable, it has been argued that the results might not apply to more realistic conditions. In carefully controlled clinical investigations subjects are generally selected on the basis of having one clear-cut syndrome, in the hope that this will reduce variability and make comparisons easier. However, because most patients seeking help have multiple problems and mixed syndromes, the conclusions drawn from the controlled studies may not have broad applicability.[21]

Despite the many difficulties inherent in comparing the effectiveness of different treatments, some conclusions seem to be justifiable. There are now a large number of studies that have shown that the briefer forms of psychotherapy, such as cognitive and interpersonal therapies, are as effective as drug treatment for depression. When behavior therapies are also included in the comparisons, the nondrug treatments seem to be as effective as drug treatment for obsessive-compulsive disorders and substance abuse disorders (both of which are often difficult to treat with any method), anxiety, panic disorder, and phobias, as well as depression. Taken together, these conditions constitute the vast majority of mental disorders. The results, of course, vary, with some studies finding no difference between treatments, while others conclude that either the drug treatment or the nondrug treatment is the most effective.

Some studies have found that psychotherapy produces more lasting improvement with lower relapse rates than drug treatment, but other studies do not replicate this finding. Other studies report that longer lasting psychotherapy produces more improvement than the briefer psychotherapy (called the "dose response effect" in psychotherapy), while most studies have found the briefer cognitive therapies to be equally or even more effective. A recent study comparing medication and different types of psychotherapy in the treatment of bulimia nervosa ("neurotic binge eating"), for example, found that cognitive-behavioral therapy was more effective in alleviating symptoms than either medication or the other forms of psychotherapy tested. When medication was combined with cognitive-behavioral therapy the results were somewhat better, but the authors concluded that "the modest gains of adding medication to psychotherapy must be weighed against the risk of adverse side effects and the costs of medication and monitoring."[22] While some studies report that psychotherapy is not as effective as drug treatment for the more severe cases of depression, other studies find them equally effective even for major depression. Of course, there is nothing mutually exclusive about drug treatment and psychotherapy, and an argument could be made for combining the best features of both treatments. There is a tendency, however, among those heavily committed to drug treatment to reduce the time spent engaged in any form of psychotherapy, and as will be discussed below, there is pressure from medical insurers to favor drug treatment over psychotherapy.

All of the studies comparing treatments for mental disorders can be criticized. Studies that have found psychotherapy less effective are often discounted by charging that only inexperienced psychotherapists were used, while studies finding drug treatment inferior are criticized on the ground that the wrong drug dose was used or the latest drugs were not included in the study. Those who criticize the effectiveness of drugs are likely to emphasize the adverse side effects of medication or the fact that there is a potential danger in maintaining people continuously on drugs in order to prevent a relapse. Those who are critical of psychotherapy often describe the adverse consequences, including suicide, that they attribute to inappropriate or ineffective psychotherapy.

Consumer Reports recently surveyed the reaction of more than four thousand subscribers to their magazine who had received various treatments for mental disorders. Although not a controlled study, the *Consumer Reports* study is the largest survey of the effectiveness of psychotherapy as judged by "consumer" satisfaction.[23] While only a few people surveyed received only drug treatment without any psychotherapy at all, those who received drug treatment combined with psychotherapy reported no greater improvement than those who received only psychotherapy. Moreover, close to 90 percent of the people who received only psychotherapy reported that they were helped. It might be argued that the subscribers to *Consumer Reports* are not a representative sample, or that what patients express about the success of different treatments may not be the best way to evaluate effectiveness, but the survey should give pause to those who assert categorically that only drugs are effective in treating mental disorders.

Individuals vary in their response to different treatment modalities as much as they vary in their response to different drugs, but on average the evidence indicates that for patients suffering from the most common mental disorders, nondrug treatment is at least as effective as drug treatment. However, in many different ways the effectiveness of drug treatment is often exaggerated, while the success of psychotherapy is minimized and often ridiculed. Certainly, there is no justification for the often-repeated statement that psychotherapy is helpful only to the extent that it is successful in persuading patients to take their drugs. It was previously mentioned that some of the patient advocate groups have recently placed ads, with support from the pharmaceutical industry, claiming that 90 percent of depressed patients are helped by drugs. The average figure from drug studies is actually closer to 65 percent, and this too is inflated, as approximately 25 percent of depressed people improve when given a placebo rather than a real drug. The one conclusion that can be made with utmost confidence is that the way studies of the effectiveness of different treatments are conducted and the way the results are perceived, evaluated, accepted, or rejected reflects the turf war between psychiatrists, who can administer drugs, and psychologists and social workers, who cannot.

It is not easy to evaluate the relative effectiveness of different ways of treating mental disorders or to evaluate the results of a clinical trial of a new psychotherapeutic drug. While the effectiveness of most medical treatments can be assessed by measuring changes in some objective biological measure or in survival rates, the assessment of changes in a patient's mental and behavioral status is much more difficult. The assessment of the changes in the severity of a patient's mental disorder can be very time-consuming, and therefore too expensive and not practical. It is obvious that to get psychiatrists to cooperate in a study assessing the mental status of patients before and at various stages during and after drug treatment, a procedure that does not require much time is necessary. To meet that demand, there are today a great number of tests for assessing the severity of psychiatric symptoms and the effectiveness of different treatments. For example, for depression there is the Revised Hamilton Rating Scale for Depression, the Beck Depression Inventory, and the Raskin Severity of Depression Scale; for anxiety there is the Hamilton Anxiety Scale; for obsessive-compulsive disorder there is the Yale-Brown Obsessive Compulsive Scale (Y-BOCS) and the NIMH Global OC test; and for schizophrenia there is the Brief Psychiatric Rating Scale. There are a great many more such scales. Most are patented and a substantial amount of money is involved in the sale of instructional material and scoring blanks. What these assessment tools all have in common is that they can be administered quickly, in many instances in less than fifteen minutes, and they lend themselves to a single quantitative score that can be presented as evidence of the effectiveness of any treatment (most often a new drug) in ameliorating psychiatric symptoms. However, as illustrated below, the interpretation of the results of these brief tests is not always clear.

Literally two days after the FDA approved the new antipsychotic drug Zyprexa (Eli Lilly's proprietary name for olanzapine), this author received a glossy brochure describing the results of a clinical trial with this drug. I received the brochure and a visit from a member of Eli Lilly's sales force in response to my telephone call requesting information about the drug. Huge numbers of the same brochure were mailed directly to psychiatrists and other physicians. The brochure touted the effectiveness of this new drug in treating schizophrenic patients. The evidence for this was the reduction in symptom severity as indicated by changes in scores on the Brief Psychiatric Rating Scale (BPRS). The BPRS requires raters to evaluate the severity (on a one-to-seven scale) of eighteen schizophrenic symptoms, subdivided into positive, negative, and general symptoms, such as hallucinations, blunted affect, and disorientation. The brochure indicated that after both one and six weeks of treatment with Zyprexa, the positive, the negative, and the overall symptom picture had improved.

The results of the Zyprexa trials as presented in Eli Lilly's brochure were depicted on a series of bar graphs that were designed to make the improvement appear huge. However, it was really not possible to evaluate this conclusion from the way the data were presented. For example, to support the claim that Zyprexa significantly reduced the positive and negative schizophrenic symptoms, a bar graph displayed a "mean improvement score" of 2.82 on the BPRS. In other words, the symptom severity of the average patient in the clinical trial was reduced by 2.82 points. But what does that mean? The score the patients had before the treatment or even after the treatment was not given. The only figure provided was how much they improved. Improved from what and to what? For example, the subtest used to evaluate positive and negative symptoms separately each consisted of seven symptom items with possible scores ranging from one (no symptoms) to seven (most impaired). Thus, theoretically, a person's total score could vary between seven and forty nine. Since these are patients with presumably severe symptoms, the scores achieved were certainly much closer to forty nine than to seven. Although the improvement was made to appear dramatic on the graphs in the promotional brochure, it is not possible to know whether the improvement is sufficient for a patient to hold a job or get along with people, whether their judgment can be trusted, whether they are mentally alert, whether they have any motivation, and in general, whether they can function independently in the real world. In evaluating the relative effectiveness of drugs and other ways of treating mental disorders, it must be kept in mind that pharmaceutical companies spend a lot of time designing ways to present the results of clinical trials to make their products look as good as possible, and their presentations should never be taken as objective evidence presented by a disinterested scientist.

Health Maintenance Organizations (HMOs) and Medical Insurers

The relative effectiveness of drug and nondrug therapy is not the only criterion used in selecting the treatment modality to be used. Cost is certainly a consideration. In an attempt to limit the expense of treating mental disorders, health maintenance organizations and medical insurers have become particularly wary of psychotherapy, because of the fear that it is likely to be prolonged and expensive. Administrators of managed care programs have been known to argue that psychotherapy, particularly long-term psychotherapy, is "enhancement not treatment." They claim that rather than being a legitimate medical expense, it is more like "searching for greater meaning in one's life," "self-actualizing," or "continuing education." Because 20 percent of the psychotherapists in the United States practice in the Greater New York area, psychotherapy has been ridiculed by referring to it as the "New York treatment" for the "Woody Allen syndrome."

In any case, there has in recent years been an attempt on the part of healthcare providers to limit the number of psychotherapy sessions. Moreover, the amount of money allotted to reimburse psychotherapists for each session is, in some instances, only one-half of their customary charge. Many health plans pay 80 percent of the average fee of physicians who dispense antidepressants, but only 50 percent of a psychotherapist's normal fee. In some instances, managed-care employees have been instructed to recommend using drug treatment and to discourage hospitalizing mental patients. The net effect of all these reimbursement policies of managed-care companies is to increase the use of drug treatment.

Psychologists: If You Can't Beat Them, Join Them

The pressure to limit the number of psychotherapy and counseling sessions that medical insurers will cover is causing considerable concern among nonmedical mental health professionals. Despite the fact that clinical psychologists have often written about the overuse of drugs and the exaggeration of their effectiveness and safety, there has been a strong movement based in the American Psychological Association (APA) and its state affiliates to gain permission for psychologists to write prescriptions for psychotherapeutic drugs. After considerable discussion, the council of the APA voted overwhelmingly in favor of legislation that would grant prescription privileges to clinical psychologists who had completed a postgraduate training program in psychopharmacology. The council cited Senator Inouye's concern that large numbers of people were not getting the psychotherapeutic drugs they need. The senator also noted favorably a pilot program in the U.S. Army that permitted psychologists with special training to prescribe drugs. The APA has been supporting the efforts of psychologists in Georgia, Illinois, Iowa, Louisiana, Nebraska, and Oklahoma in developing educational programs in psychopharmacology and in their legislative initiatives to obtain prescription privileges for those who completed the program. Early in 1997, the Illinois School of Professional Psychology enrolled the first clinical psychologists in an educational program specifically designed to prepare them to prescribe drugs.[24]

It should come as no surprise that the other APA, the American Psychiatric Association, is vehemently opposed to any legislation that would enable psychologists to prescribe psychotherapeutic drugs. A bill supported in California by psychologists never made it out of committee after the California Psychiatric Association and other medical groups testified that "to give psychologists, mental health professionals with typically no training in the biological and health sciences, the authority to prescribe is to abrogate your responsibility to protect the interests of all citizens, particularly those with mental illnesses."[25] It is not within the scope of this book to evaluate all the arguments for and against granting limited permission to nonmedical mental health professionals to prescribe psychotherapeutic drugs. It is obvious, however, that all the altruistic arguments raised on both sides of this issue cannot possibly conceal the basic conflict of interest.

Patients Would Rather Have a Physical Than a Mental Disorder

It has already been mentioned in several different contexts that most patients with mental disorders and their families prefer to believe that the problem is physical rather than psychological. Although the difference may only be semantic, as there is presumably a physical correlate of all mental states, most people believe that the distinction is real, and for that reason alone it has important practical consequences. Among the more important reasons for this preference is the fact that a psychological diagnosis often carries a stigma, as many still believe that a psychological problem implies that the person is weak and has not tried hard enough to overcome the problem. This is similar to accusing an alcoholic of a lack of will power or a moral weakness. Family members often feel that a psychological diagnosis reflects on them, and other people may think that if they had behaved differently the problem would never have developed. Moreover, if the problem is described as biochemical it is easier to believe that it can be corrected by drugs. There are many people who would rather not reveal personal things to anyone, including a psychotherapist, and they would not have to do this if their problem was physical.

There is much evidence that people who have suffered from mental disorders and their families often are among the strongest advocates of the "biochemical theory of mental illness." This, of course, is especially true if they improved while receiving drug treatment, even though it may be difficult to determine how much of the improvement should be attributed to the drugs. Several examples from the popular media serve to illustrate the way patients become advocates for the "biochemical theory." On the popular Oprah Winfrey television program, one of the guest "experts" questioned whether the enthusiasm for the drug Prozac was actually justified by objective evidence. Apparently, the audience was filled with people who had personal experience with the drug.[26] The guest "expert" was immediately shouted down by members of the audience, and several of them asserted with absolute certainty that Prozac had saved their lives by correcting the chemical imbalance responsible for their mental problems. Of course, none of these people had any independent way of knowing whether they had a biochemical imbalance. They were almost surely repeating what they had read or what their psychiatrist had told them, despite the fact the psychiatrist had no way of knowing if they really had a biochemical imbalance. A woman writing to the *Dear Abby* syndicated newspaper column explained that she had been against drugs until her psychiatrist explained that just as "a diabetic lacks insulin to process sugar, some people lack sufficient chemicals to permit their brains to function properly."[27]

Many more examples could be provided to illustrate that the quality of empirical evidence alone does not account for the enthusiastic acceptance of the biochemical theories of mental disorders by so many different groups. Most people have little first hand exposure to the empirical evidence about drug efficacy and safety. They are forced to depend on information that is really promotional material, or, at the very least, is information that is filtered and shaped by various interests groups. There is compelling evidence that, in diverse ways, economic factors play major roles in determining the data that is collected, how it is evaluated, and whether it is widely circulated, suppressed, or discredited. What physicians and the public are reading about drugs and what causes mental disorders is by no means a neutral reflection of all the information that is available.

Chapter 8

REPRISE, CONCLUSIONS, AND REFLECTIONS

It is not possible for me to summarize in these concluding remarks all the evidence and arguments that led me to reject the existing chemical theories of mental illness. That was done throughout the book. I can, however, review some of the main arguments by critically examining several statements about psychotherapeutic drugs and mental disorders that are repeated so often they are thought to be axiomatic and incontestable. One such statement is that *psychotherapeutic drugs treat mental disorders in the same way that insulin treats diabetes.* What is implied by this statement is that psychotherapeutic drugs, like insulin, correct known chemical deficiencies (or excesses, in other instances). This analogy is repeated over and over again not only in promotional material from pharmaceutical companies and in articles published in professional journals, but, judging from reports from patients, every day in the offices of psychiatrists and other physicians. One psychiatrist, who no longer accepts this dogma, recalls what she learned during her psychiatric residency:

> As a psychiatric resident, I found these terms helpful when talking with patients and their families. Taking the lead of various mentors, I would explain that mental illness is caused by a chemical imbalance in the brain. Mental illness resembles diabetes, which involves a chemical imbalance in the body, I would explain. The patient's psychiatric disorder is chronic, I would say, and requires medication every day for the rest of the person's life. I would then assure the patient that if he took the medication, he would probably live a more normal life.[1]

Most people accept the analogy between psychotherapeutic drugs and insulin uncritically, being persuaded by what seems to be a completely valid and sensible argument. Moreover, the analogy with insulin treatment suggests that it might be necessary to take psychotherapeutic drugs for life, or at least for a long time, just as diabetics and people suffering from other hormonal deficiencies have to take medication for life. Despite its seeming reasonableness, I do not believe that the analogy between insulin and psychotherapeutic drugs can be justified.

When insulin is prescribed for a diabetic it is only after a reliable test has measured the extent of the patient's glucose metabolism problem, from which, in most instances, an insulin deficiency can be inferred. The dose of insulin that is prescribed can be based on a reasonably good estimate of the magnitude of the deficiency. Moreover, we also have a good understanding of how insulin regulates glucose metabolism and how a deficiency of that hormone can produce diabetic symptoms. In sharp contrast, a psychiatrist performs no laboratory test to determine if a mental patient has any chemical deficiency or excess. Instead, the implication that the drug prescribed is correcting an abnormal biochemical condition is, at best, an inference made in part from weak and unreliable group trends reported in the experimental literature, but based mainly on the simple belief that the drug will help. Moreover, while we have a good understanding of how insulin alleviates the symptoms of diabetes, we do not know how psychotherapeutic drugs alleviate the symptoms of mental disorders or why they often fail to do so. Of course, many will insist that there is abundant indirect evidence that indicates that patients with a particular mental disorder do have a specific biochemical abnormality, even if there are no convenient laboratory tests available to confirm it in a given patient. I am convinced that they overstate their case.

There is no shortage of claims, for example, that schizophrenia is caused by a hyperactive dopamine system and that depressed patients have low serotonin levels, but these claims do not stand up to a critical examination. The "dopamine theory of schizophrenia" has been held on to tenaciously in the face of considerable contradictory data because of the hunger for an explanation, however inadequate it might be. When it was found that schizophrenics do not have high levels of dopamine activity, it was then hypothesized that they might have an excess of dopamine receptors, making them hypersensitive to normal dopamine levels. However, it has never been proved that schizophrenics have high numbers of dopamine receptors, although there are a few claims that high levels of a particular type of dopamine receptor have been found in a localized brain region of some schizophrenics. However, other equally competent investigators have not been able to confirm these claims.

Even in those studies demonstrating that on average schizophrenics have high numbers of a particular dopamine receptor subtype, many schizophrenics do not show this trend, while some normal subjects do, despite not having any history of mental disorder. Moreover, it is now known that receptor numbers can be an effect of either drug treatment or a mental or emotional state common to some schizophrenics, rather than, as is often assumed, the cause of the disorder. What is a cause and what is an effect of a mental disorder has often been confused.

There are still other difficulties with the "dopamine theory of schizo-phrenia." There are, for example, antipsychotic drugs that do not block the dopamine receptors that a few investigators have hypothesized are respon-sible for schizophrenia. The fact that it usually takes several weeks before any therapeutic effect is seen following the beginning of drug treatment has made it extremely difficult to know what is actually responsible for any improvement seen. A number of investigators are now suggesting that other neurotransmitters and other brain conditions must be involved in the etiology and treatment of schizophrenia. There does not really seem to be much left to the dopamine hypothesis of schizophrenia, as Arvid Carls-son, one of the foremost contributors to our knowledge of dopamine neu-ropharmacology, has recently commented:

> The dopamine hypothesis rests almost entirely on indirect, pharmaco-logical evidence and not even this evidence is unambiguous. For example, treatment with antidopaminergic agents is often only partially success-ful in schizophrenia and is frequently attained only at the expense of troublesome side effects. Moreover, the symptomatology of schizophre-nia is mimicked not only by dopaminergic agents but also by drugs that act on other neurotransmitter systems.[2]

Even psychiatrists committed to the idea that schizophrenia is a brain dis-ease have had to admit that recent studies of people with that disorder have failed to provide unequivocal evidence of dopamine hyperactivity in the brains of patients with this disorder.[3]

The evidence that depression is caused by a biochemical abnormality is even weaker than it is for schizophrenia. Shortly after the discovery of the first few antidepressants, it was hypothesized that patients suffering from depression must be deficient in serotonin or norepinephrine, or both, because the drugs increased the activity of these two neurotransmitter sys-tems. This hypothesis became more firmly entrenched because of the claims that the drug reserpine, which lowers serotonin and norepinephrine levels, can cause depression. However, carefully controlled studies subse-quently revealed that reserpine and other drugs that decrease serotonin and norepinephrine rarely produce depression, except, occasionally, in people who are prone to developing depression. Furthermore, there is no con-vincing evidence that depressed people have a serotonin or norepinephrine deficiency.

These considerations and other evidence and arguments discussed throughout the book have led me to conclude that there is really little solid evidence for either the serotonin/norepinephrine deficiency theory of depression or the dopamine theory of schizophrenia. Yet in all kinds of promotional literature they are touted as though they have been firmly established.

I have become convinced after examining the evidence and following the twists and turns in the various arguments supporting the different versions of the chemical theories of mental disorders that all of the impressive knowledge of neuropharmacology has not really brought us closer to understanding the origin of mental disorders or even to any real understanding of how drugs may help to alleviate these conditions. People with mental disorders may be encouraged when they are told that the prescribed drugs will do for them just what insulin does for a diabetic, but the analogy is certainly not justified. What is much clearer, however, is that there are a number of groups that benefit from promoting the analogy.

Another statement that needs to be examined more closely is that *mental disorders are physical diseases*. What is really implied by this statement is that mental disorders are *caused* by some identified physical (physiological) condition. There may well be biological factors that predispose some individuals toward developing mental disorders, but a predisposition is not a cause. How and whether a predisposition is expressed depends on many nonbiological factors, especially on life experiences and on input from the environment in many different ways. The statement that mental disorders are physical diseases ignores the relevance of psychosocial factors and implies by this omission that such factors are of little importance.

Some of my colleagues have defended the statement that mental disorders are physical diseases by claiming that the statement implies only that all mental states—those that are healthy as well as those that characterize a mental disorder—do not exist in a vacuum, but must emerge from some physical substrate. However, there is more than a little sophistry in this argument. It is surely unnecessary to make such a benign point over and over again, as few people today believe that a mental event can exist without a brain event. The reason pharmaceutical ads for antidepressants and antipsychotics assert that these disorders are physical diseases is that it serves as an easy and natural segue to promoting the chemical theories of mental disorders and drug treatment.

Perhaps the strongest evidence of the importance of biological factors in mental disorders comes from genetic studies. Data obtained by comparing identical and fraternal twins and comparing adopted children with their biological and foster parents suggest that genetic factors may influence personality, temperament, emotionality, and behavior and also predispose some individuals toward developing a mental disorder. However, while genetic factors may predispose people to develop in certain ways, they certainly do not dictate personality, mental traits, or behavior. For example, if one identical twin has schizophrenia or a manic-depressive disorder—the two disorders thought to have the strongest genetic contribution—the probability is less than 50 percent that the second twin will have the same disorder, despite the fact that most identical twins have very similar experiences.[4] While there are some physical factors that are not genetic, such as exposure to toxins, infections, and injury that may be a factor in the development of a mental disorder, social and psychological factors undoubtedly play a major role in determining whether and how any predisposition will be expressed. We even know that gross features of the brains of identical twins differ, and a number of studies have shown that life experiences can modify brain anatomy. Some of the differences in brain anatomy between identical twins may well result from different life experiences. The statement that mental disorders are physical diseases implies a lot more than can be justified.

The idea that mental disorders are physical diseases has been widely promoted and accepted for several reasons. It is known that people suffering from mental disorders and especially their families generally prefer a diagnosis of a "physical disease" because it does not convey the stigma and blame commonly associated with "psychological problems." Also, a "physical disease" often suggests a more optimistic prognosis and a briefer, less expensive course of treatment. However, while patients may be relieved to be told that they have a "physical disease," they may adopt a passive role in their own recovery, becoming completely dependent on a physical treatment to remedy their condition. It is clear that "physical disease" is often a code word for a chemical excess or deficiency and a justification for drug treatment. It is known that mental patients are often more amenable to drug treatment when they are told that they have a physical disease. Furthermore, as discussed earlier at some length, influential groups such as the pharmaceutical industry, psychiatrists, HMOs, and other medical insurers are likely to be favorably disposed to any theory that emphasizes chemical causes and drug treatment. Most of those who promote the chemical theories of mental disorders genuinely believe that the evidence supporting the theory is convincing, but theories that support one's interest always seem to make the most sense.

Another statement frequently made, especially during recent years, is that *psychotherapeutic drugs are becoming increasingly specific.* This is true, but misleading. New techniques have made it possible to develop drugs that will bind to only one neurotransmitter receptor subtype. These new, highly specific drugs are promoted as "smart missiles" capable of seeking out and eliminating the different chemical causes underlying each mental disorder. While this argument may sound eminently reasonable to many, there are good reasons for being highly skeptical about such claims.

In the first place, it is necessary to distinguish between several different meanings of "specificity." A drug may truly have "pharmacological specificity," in that it acts primarily on one receptor target (or a very few), but this will not necessarily give it "functional specificity." Even though a drug may bind primarily to one receptor type, there is no reason to believe that the effect of stimulating or blocking the activity of this receptor will be confined to any one mental symptom. On the contrary, there is every reason to believe that all receptors have an influence on many different mental activities and emotional states. Moreover, mental disorders are not simple homogeneous entities. They involve impairment of language, perception, memory, motivation, emotions, and much more. The belief that the complex cognitive and emotional states that underlie any mental disorder are regulated by a single neurotransmitter receptor subtype is probably no more valid than the idea held earlier by phrenologists who believed that complex mental attributes could be localized in one specific part of the brain. Moreover, as with any complex, highly integrated system, changing one component will have effects that inevitably cascade through the entire system. The concept of a specific target refers only to an initial and momentary effect of a drug. Pharmacological specificity refers only to the "first domino" in a series of brain reactions triggered by a drug. Regardless of its pharmacological specificity, it is unrealistic to think that the ultimate effect of any drug will be similarly limited.

I have described the dangerous side effects produced by the diet pills Pondimin and Redux as well as by the so-called fen-phen treatment. These drug treatments were hypothesized to work by increasing brain serotonin. However, unanticipated adverse side effects can occur even when a drug target is relatively specific. Serotonin is not limited to the brain, and it certainly is not involved only in regulating appetite, although some promotional material conveys that impression. Serotonin is located in many parts of the body as well as the brain, and serious heart-valve and lung conditions result from the drugs' increasing serotonin in those organs.

It is easy to get the impression from the many uncritical books on the wonders of the "psychopharmacology revolution" that increasing serotonin will only enhance personality, making people more self-confident and cheerful, while decreasing any undesirable behavioral traits. Commonly overlooked is the fact that serotonin was originally named for its capacity to constrict blood vessels. There is much that is illusory and misleading about the claims of increased specificity for the newer psychiatric drugs, and it is not yet clear whether these drugs will produce less adverse side effects than their predecessors or just different ones.

Actually the pharmaceutical industry has a very complex and somewhat ambivalent attitude toward the issue of specificity. On the one hand, the companies promote their new ability to design drugs with much more pharmaceutical specificity, making it appear that these drugs will be capable of seeking out and correcting the unique condition that underlies each mental disorder, providing the one key that can fit a predetermined lock. The problem is that there are good reasons for doubting that there is a specific condition that is common to all patients suffering from the same mental disorder. Considering the heterogeneity of patients diagnosed with the same label, many, if not most, clinical investigators believe that it is likely that different etiologies are involved. Sometimes pharmaceutical companies' ads will give the impression that their drug has some unique properties that equip it to treat a specific condition even though the drug does not differ significantly from other drugs being marketed. Alprazolan, a benzodiazepine drug, for example, was promoted as a specific treatment for "panic disorder" because it became available around the time that psychiatrists began to use this term as a separate diagnostic category and because of the concern at the time that such benzodiazepine drugs as Valium were being overprescribed for every one of life's stresses.

Arguing against the claim of drug specificity is the tendency of pharmaceutical companies to encourage the broadening of applications of every drug that they market. Thus, Prozac and the other SSRIs, for example, were initially introduced as antidepressants, but they are now used to treat so many different conditions that it brings into question the whole idea of a specific chemical abnormality underlying each mental disorder. Sometimes a pharmaceutical company will sell the exact same pill under different names for different purposes. Thus the antidepressant Wellbutrin (buproprion hydrochloride) is marketed as Zyban, a pill to help break the smoking habit. There is no convincing evidence, however, that the smoking habit and depression (or most of the other disorders treated by a single drug) have a common etiology.

It is more than a little ironic that despite all the claims being made for drugs with specific pharmacological action, a number of the latest drugs introduced, such as the new antipsychotic olanzapine (Zyprexa), act on many different neurotransmitter systems, and their wide spectrum of pharmacological activity is promoted as a way of increasing effectiveness.

The drugs marketed to treat the same mental disorder tend to have very similar sites of action. Thus, for example, most of the latest antidepressant drugs are designed to act primarily on serotonin or on serotonin and norepinephrine, while most antipsychotics act primarily on the dopamine system. This is often promoted as evidence that the chemical abnormalities underlying these disorders have been identified. However, that is not the only possible explanation. A major factor accounting for the similarities in the action of drugs that are marketed as treatments of the same disorder is the high cost of bringing a new drug to market. This cost tends to make pharmaceutical companies "risk aversive" and generally quite conservative in their development of new drugs. It has been estimated that it takes between ten and twelve years to develop, test, and market a new drug, and the cost is between $150 million and $250 million. Therefore, most new drugs are only small modifications of drugs already being marketed successfully. Unless there is a major advance in our knowledge of what causes the different mental disorders, or a serendipitous discovery of a different class of drugs that is effective in treating a particular mental disorder, most new drugs will continue to be essentially "copycat" or "me too" drugs, which do not differ significantly from the drugs that preceded them.

All of these considerations and other evidence and arguments presented throughout this book led me to conclude that the theory that mental disorders are caused by specific biochemical imbalances was much weaker than claimed. I began to think more about who was promoting the theory and the many different ways that this is done. It would be disingenuous to pretend that I was unaware when I started this project that certain groups benefited from the chemical theories of mental disorders and reliance on drug treatment, but when I started to dig more deeply into this topic I became aware of the enormity of the influence of these groups and the many different ways that influence is exerted.

For psychiatrists, medical insurance companies, and especially the pharmaceutical industry the benefit derived from promoting drug treatment and chemical theories of mental disorders is primarily economic. Of course, the argument is never framed in that way. Starting around 1930, psychiatrists became increasingly aware of growing competition from nonmedical therapists, mainly psychologists, psychiatric social workers, and counselors of various stripes. Over the years, psychiatrists have been attracted to physical treatments, over and above any therapeutic value these treatments may have had. In the first place, physical treatments give psychiatrists a treatment modality that was not available to the nonmedical competition. Insulin coma, metrazol shock, prefrontal lobotomy, and electroconvulsive treatment have all been useful in this way. Moreover, physical therapies and the theories on which they have been based have helped to make psychiatry more acceptable to the rest of the medical profession, which historically has been skeptical of the scientific basis of the "talking therapies." Psychotherapeutic drugs, like the other physical therapies before it, have served the interests of the psychiatric profession. Of course, psychiatrists are not all of one mind, but in various ways the profession as a whole tends to promote drugs by exaggerating what is known about the chemical basis of mental disorders and the effectiveness of drugs, and often by discrediting alternative treatment modalities. While traditionally nonmedical therapists such as clinical psychologists have been opposed to physical therapies, lately their attitude toward drugs and the chemical theories of mental disorders has become ambivalent, and many are currently trying to obtain prescription privileges through aggressive lobbying of state legislators. Quite predictably, psychiatrists have moved to protect their turf and have actively lobbied against granting prescription privileges to nonmedical therapists.

Medical insurers are obviously concerned with cost, and they particularly want to discourage treatments that may involve many contact hours and considerable expense. By adjusting payment schedules, medical insurers are playing a major role in shifting treatment toward drugs and away from psychotherapy. The argument advanced for drug treatment and biochemical explanations of mental disorders is always based on claims that the evidence demonstrates the correctness of the chemical theories and the effectiveness and safety of drugs. It is not that a reasonable-sounding argument cannot be presented, but rather that the argument is not based on an objective evaluation of all the evidence. Numerous studies have made it clear that a person's interest and biases influence the way evidence is selected and evaluated and how persuasive various arguments will seem to him or her. Logical fallacies in an argument are frequently overlooked when one agrees with the conclusions, and when the conclusions do not conform to one's biases, logical fallacies are often "detected" even when they do not exist.

The influence of the pharmaceutical industry is by far the greatest, not only because of the enormous resources at its disposal, but also because of the diverse ways that influence is exerted. In the United States alone, pharmaceutical companies spend about $12.3 billion a year on advertising and other types of promotion, which is about 22.5 percent of the $54.7 billion estimated to be the total sales of U.S. pharmaceuticals.[5] The pharmaceutical industry spends huge amounts of money to influence the prescribing habits of physicians. This influence is exerted through massive advertising in professional journals and through direct contact with physicians by the industry's sales force. Studies have shown that the advertisements placed by pharmaceutical companies in professional journals or distributed directly to physicians are often exaggerated and misleading. While physicians typically resent any suggestion that they cannot recognize the difference between scientific evidence and promotional material, it has been shown repeatedly that their prescription preferences are heavily influenced by promotional material from pharmaceutical companies.

Pharmaceutical companies distribute large amounts of educational material (literature, films, slides) free of charge to medical schools, and they also contribute money to support speaker programs that help in the training of residents and in keeping the attending physicians informed about new trends. Numerous symposia and workshops are sponsored by pharmaceutical companies. Some of the motivation of the pharmaceutical companies that underwrite these expenses is to establish "goodwill." The "educational" material can be informative and helpful. Rarely is it so heavyhanded as to promote a specific product, but the contents almost always includes a point of view designed to ultimately increase sales of drugs that the company markets. So, for example, the psychiatric material will stress the evidence that suggests that depression has a chemical origin and can be treated successfully with antidepressant drugs. This message will help a company that markets antidepressant drugs even though a specific drug may never be mentioned.

Furthermore, there have been a number of incidents in which pharmaceutical companies have exerted pressure to suppress, delay, discredit, or modify information that they judge will be detrimental to the sales of one of their products. The ads placed by pharmaceutical companies provide a substantial source of support for many medical journals, and while it is certainly not true of all, editors are often reluctant to offend their advertisers. In some cases, the impact of a study critical of a drug's efficacy or safety is diminished by including a comment written by "experts," who on several occasions have turned out to be consultants to the company marketing the drug. Surveys have revealed how difficult it is to find an "expert" in a specific medical area who is not tethered by some financial interest to either a pharmaceutical company or one of the smaller "biotech" companies that are developing drugs in that same area. When a study reveals that a particular drug appears to cause some previously unsuspected adverse effects, even before there is time for any additional investigation of the problem, the company involved is likely to issue a statement designed to discredit the study by claiming it is flawed and inconclusive and should not be taken seriously.

Pharmaceutical companies also sponsor most clinical trials of new drugs, and they employ "trial monitors," medical doctors and Ph.D.s in psychopharmacology and other specialties, who design the experiments, choose the clinical investigators involved in collecting the data, fund the collection of the data, check on how the study is coming along, suggest changes in midstream, and often assume the major responsibility for summarizing and publishing the results. As the saying goes: "If you pay the piper, you can call the tune." The importance of the clinical trials cannot be overestimated, as they provide the data for judging the efficacy and safety of a new drug that the FDA uses in approving a drug for marketing. Once a drug is approved, physicians can exercise their own judgment in prescribing it for other purposes, and pharmaceutical companies may use their sales force and other promotional avenues to encourage physicians to use a drug for purposes other than those for which it was approved.

I have described how pharmaceutical companies are increasing sales of psychotherapeutic drugs by encouraging primary care physicians to use screening devices that will enable them to more readily detect patients who may have a mental disorder. It has been estimated that over 30 million Americans have had a depressive or anxiety disorder, and primary care physicians are known to prescribe more antidepressant and antianxiety drugs that any other group of physicians, including psychiatrists. There is a huge potential here that has only been partially tapped, and pharmaceutical companies have not only supported the development of brief questionnaires that patients can complete while waiting in the doctor's office, but they are actively involved in promoting the use of these materials. Preliminary data indicate that this is exactly what happens when primary care physicians use these screening devices.

Not all of the pharmaceutical industry's promotional schemes are directed toward physicians. Many are aimed directly at patients, the ultimate consumers of drugs. The amount of money spent promoting prescription drugs directly to patients has been increasing by leaps and bounds over the past several years. There are increasing numbers of patients asking physicians to prescribe a drug they read about in an ad in the popular media, and pharmaceutical companies are aware of studies that indicate that as many as 90 percent of physicians are likely to comply with such requests.[6] This trend is likely to accelerate as the FDA, responding to pressure from congressmen, recently (as of 8 August 1997) made it legal for pharmaceutical companies to advertise their prescription drugs over radio and television, and several pharmaceutical companies almost immediately announced the beginning of large television advertising campaigns for their prescription drugs.

The pharmaceutical industry has for a number of years used patient support groups to get its message to consumers. There are now large numbers of support groups for patients (and their families) who suffer from every conceivable psychiatric disorder. Thus, for example, there are support groups for patients with schizophrenia, depression, obsessive-compulsive disorder, substance abuse problems, attentional deficit disorders, and much more. Most of these support groups receive substantial financial support from the pharmaceutical industry, and this has enabled them to increase their membership, to afford large newspaper ads, and to distribute all kinds of informational brochures, much of which helps to promote the basic premises of the chemical theories of mental disorders. I have described how, not infrequently, the information circulated by patient support groups is exaggerated and misleading, but almost always the message is exactly what the pharmaceutical companies want the public to receive.

Undoubtedly, there will be readers who will consider this account of the activities of the pharmaceutical industry unbalanced and exaggerated. I have already had conversations with friends and colleagues who have expressed this point of view. In responding, I have pointed out that all the statements made in these concluding remarks are well-documented with specific examples in the body of the book. I am convinced that the pharmaceutical industry spends enormous amounts of money to increase its sales and profits by influencing physicians and the public in ways that sometimes bend the truth and that are often not in the best interests of science or the public.

There is no doubt that the pharmaceutical industry has made important contributions to public health and to research. Drug companies support numerous symposia and other forums that provide opportunities for clinicians and basic scientists to exchange information with their colleagues and to learn about new developments. Many neuroscientists (and I include myself among them) have received help from pharmaceutical companies in various ways. Experimental drugs used in research are often provided without charge, and technical advice and assistance is often given. I have stayed at a "guest house" in London maintained by a pharmaceutical company, and this made it possible for me to do research at the Wellcome Foundation's History of Medicine and Science Museum, which is supported by the Glaxo Wellcome pharmaceutical company. Innumerable basic neuroscientists and clinical investigators have received the funding from the pharmaceutical industry that was necessary to undertake research projects. Faculty responsible for the education of graduate students in the life sciences or for training psychiatric residents or other mental health professionals regularly receive support from the pharmaceutical industry that makes it possible to invite speakers, and the industry provides all kinds of helpful literature and films without charge.

While researchers, educators, and clinicians know that the pharmaceutical industry is in the business of selling drugs, they appreciate any help they receive, and most believe that a healthy, symbiotic relationship exists between them and the industry. They would certainly resent any suggestion that the support they receive (and might continue to receive) influences their judgment on any matter. Nevertheless, in the opinion of many who have investigated this issue, there is a substantial influence, although it is often subtle. Those with the largest grants have the most contact with company personnel and are most exposed to the arguments, evidence, and point of view that support that company's position on any disputed issue. In my experience, those who have been the recipients of the largest benefits from the industry tend to be most adamant in denying the possibility of any influence. These are often the same people called on for opinions that influence public policy about drugs and the pharmaceutical industry. The influence of the pharmaceutical industry is so pervasive that it often goes unrecognized.

All companies prefer "doing good while doing well," but they must do well to stay in business. The profit motive is not a secondary concern for pharmaceutical companies any more than it is for any company. A recent ad soliciting investment funds placed by a major pharmaceutical company announced that its "objective remains to increase its earnings per share by 20% in 1997 and 1998."[7] When I am told that pharmaceutical companies behave differently from other companies because they are concerned with public health, I am reminded of a number of incidents, such as a major U.S. pharmaceutical company agreeing to pay a $325 million fine when it was charged with fraud for billing the government for lab tests never ordered and in some instances never performed.[8]

The stakes are enormous and the resources that pharmaceutical companies can invest to advance and protect their interests is commensurate. The annual sales of a single drug can total several billion dollars. With such sums involved, pharmaceutical companies are constantly exploring ways to increase their sales and to protect them when they are threatened by competition or negative reports. Like any other large corporation, pharmaceutical companies give much thought to ways to promote their products and to protect their interests. We should not really be surprised, for example, to learn that the person in charge of marketing drugs for Merck was formerly promoting soft drinks and food for PepsiCo.[9] The line between giving the best "spin" to a product and "bending" the truth is often fuzzy. It is unrealistic to believe that companies that market so-called "ethical" (prescription) drugs will be either more or less ethical than any other large company when it comes to marketing.

The influence of the pharmaceutical industry has grown stronger because its enormous resources are being concentrated in fewer hands as a result of the many recent mergers. Among the more notable mergers has been that of the Upjohn Company of Michigan with Pharmacia A.B. of Sweden to form Pharmacia & Upjohn. This company more recently merged with Amersham International, a British health and technology concern, creating Amersham Pharmacia Biotech. Also, Glaxo Holdings has merged with Wellcome to form Glaxo Wellcome, and Ciba-Geigy, which was an earlier merger between Ciba and Geigy, has joined with Sandoz to form Novartis A.G., now the world's largest drug company. In 1995, the Swiss pharmaceutical giant Roche Holding Ltd. (the parent of Hoffman–La Roche, Inc.) purchased the Syntex Corporation of California, and in 1997 they purchased Boehringer Mannheim, a German company. Even as I write this, there is talk in the financial community of other huge mergers of drug companies.

Another recent trend, involving a type of merger that will concentrate power even further, is the takeover by pharmaceutical companies of clinics that prescribe drugs. Recently, the British pharmaceutical company Zeneca took over the management of eleven cancer clinics, some located at major American hospitals. The possibility that one company may control both the manufacture and prescribing of a drug has raised justifiable concern. Although a comparable takeover of psychiatric clinics by a pharmaceutical company has not yet occurred, the existence of chains of proprietary psychiatric clinics may increase the possibility of that occurring. The dangers are apparent, as Arthur Caplan, a bioethicist at the University of Pennsylvania, has noted:

> I think we will see more deals like this in the future and the real question is what sorts of checks and balances ought to be in place. Having your doctor, your clinic, your pharmacy and your testing lab all owned by the same person is not the optimal structure for health care.[10]

The chemical theories of mental disorders are particularly seductive because they suggest that a relatively simple explanation and solution exist for a problem that has been regarded as complex and often stubbornly resistant to treatment. We are living in an age that has little tolerance for uncertainty and ambiguity. Proposals that might have been rejected at an earlier time as unrealistic are now accepted with great credulity. Those who write popular books are well aware of the public's voracious appetite for ideas and tools for self-improvement, whether they come in the form of a gadget for achieving "washboard abs" or pills that makes it easy to lose weight or to achieve a better personality. Over the last decade, there has been a spate of popularly written books that have not only exaggerated the capacity of drugs to cure mental disorders, but also frequently claim that there are now new drugs available that can produce "cosmetic" personality changes by adjusting the balance between a few critical neurotransmitters.

A book written by Ronald Kotulak, a Pulitzer Prize–winning science writer and past president of the National Association of Science Writers, is typical of many who claim that personality and behavior can be understood by the perturbations of one or two neurotransmitters.[11] Kotulak's "revolutionary discoveries of how the mind works" rest on the claim that much of personality and many behavioral traits are determined by the balance between serotonin and norepinephrine. Kotulak maintains that when norepinephrine levels are high it produces "impulsive hot-blooded" acts of violence, while low norepinephrine levels produce "premeditated cold blooded acts of violence" and thrill seeking. A high serotonin level, on the other hand, is said to increase shyness, obsessive-compulsive disorders, a lack of self-confidence, and "unduly dampened aggression," while low serotonin is claimed to create a tendency toward depression, suicide, alcoholism, explosive rage, sexual deviance, and impulsive aggression.

The claim that all these different behavioral propensities can be explained by the levels of two neurotransmitters, while neglecting all other variables, both biological and psychosocial, is totally unjustified. The only evidence for such claims is some "weak" trends based on group averages of a relatively small sample of individuals. There is such a morass of experimental and clinical literature of questionable reliability and validity that it is possible to find studies that can support any theory that someone dreams up and wants to promote. Furthermore, there is a built-in bias in the professional literature, because studies that do not confirm trends previously reported only rarely get published, while in the popular media even "weak" trends may be described as though they represent a "revolutionary discovery." The claims that complex mental and personality traits can be explained by the balance between a couple of neurotransmitters is no more valid than the Hippocratic theory that claimed many of these same traits are determined by the balance between the four basic humors: blood, phlegm, black bile, and choler (yellow bile). Yet, many of these recent claims are widely accepted as true, and the books that promote them are adding to the growing conviction that personality and mental health are completely determined by the levels of a few neurotransmitters that can be adjusted by drugs.

For the reasons just given and for all the additional reasons discussed throughout this book, I now believe that not only has it not been established that chemical imbalances are the major cause of mental disorders, but the theory from which these ideas emanate may well be wrong. The theory has been so widely accepted because a number of groups, each with its own agenda, have promoted this idea, not infrequently by exaggerating and distorting what is known about mental disorders and the effectiveness and safety of the drugs used to treat them.

There are so many diverse interests involved in supporting the various chemical theories of mental disorders that I anticipate the thesis of this book will be criticized on many different grounds. I welcome that and hope that the criticisms are offered in a constructive fashion, as there has hardly been any questioning of the basic assumptions underlying these chemical theories. By questioning basic assumptions, I do not mean a discussion about whether it is this or that receptor subtype that is the cause of schizophrenia or depression. Rather, I hope this book can help to start a dialogue about whether any chemical imbalance has really been shown to be the cause of mental disorders and whether we really know how drugs sometimes help to alleviate these disorders.

Many points might be raised about the evidence and arguments presented throughout this book. It is not possible to anticipate and answer them all, and besides, it could be considered an exercise in "shadowboxing," much easier than getting into the ring with a real opponent. It may help, however, to respond briefly to a couple of general criticisms that I am certain will be made.

There will probably be some critics who agree that the evidence in the past was not convincing, but will argue that this book has not seriously considered the most recent experimental work and theories, which provide much stronger support for the chemical theories. My response would have to be that a serious effort was made to include a consideration of what was judged to be the more important of the recent theories, and this did not change the basic conclusions. I certainly do not want to prejudge any future developments, but I believe that an honest effort was made to consider the most important of the latest revisions of the chemical theories of mental illness, and none of these convinced me to change my basic conclusion.

There are also likely to be critics who will accuse me of being irresponsible in discouraging people suffering from mental disorders from seeking the drugs they badly need to help them. I have stated several times that I am convinced that some people have received significant help from psychotherapeutic drugs, and I certainly would not discourage anyone from trying them. It is possible that a few readers, who are reluctant to take "mind-altering" drugs, may become as a result of reading this book more critical of the claim that the medication prescribed for them acts as insulin does in treating diabetes. I think, however, that such an effect, if there is any at all, will be minimal. When patients trust their physicians it is usually sufficient that they be told that a number of people with conditions like theirs improve on the medication, and it is, therefore, worth trying. A theoretical explanation of how a treatment is supposed to work is rarely necessary, and if a patient insists on one, it should not be assumed that he or she will be turned off by the statement that "we really do not know." A patient may actually gain respect for a physician who is secure enough to admit to not knowing.

A more challenging criticism of the book is whether it really matters whether the chemical theories of mental disorders are right or wrong. It has been argued that what really matters is whether psychotherapeutic drugs work and not whether the theory is correct. This is what is implied by the old saw, "Read all these crackpot theories, if you must. In facts and figures only put your trust." Theories come and go, but what is important is the effectiveness and safety of a treatment. Many examples can be given that seem to support this argument. Aspirin's capacity to alleviate pain, fever, and inflammation, for example, was not altered by the fact that for much of the time it has been used, the theories proposed to explain its action were either inadequate or completely wrong. As one critic said sarcastically: "It does not matter how well it works in practice, what's important is that it doesn't work in theory." Certainly, results should not be discredited because there is no adequate theory to explain them. Nevertheless, I am convinced that it is a mistake to trivialize theory, as it can have enormous practical consequences. Practice and theory are not independent of each other, and this is particularly true with respect to drug treatment and the chemical theories of mental disorders, as I will attempt to illustrate in the remaining pages of this chapter.

To accept the chemical theories of mental disorders without reservations is to believe that these disorders are caused by chemical imbalances and that drugs are effective because they correct the underlying chemical origin of such disorders. Accepting this strong version of the theory has significant implications for the way patients are treated, for the mental health professions, and for the research that is undertaken. While I did not write this book to give advice to anyone or to any group, I believe that there is a responsibility to discuss some of the practical implications of its conclusions.

I agree that the validity of the chemical theories of mental disorders should not be the basis for accepting or rejecting drug therapy. Having agreed on that point, it is necessary to add that the effectiveness of psychotherapeutic drugs is considerably less than commonly asserted. Drug effectiveness is consistently exaggerated, often by presenting anecdotes of people who seem to have been "miraculously" cured after they started taking a drug. Some of these stories are undoubtedly true, even though they may not be representative, but without experimental controls we never know what is really responsible for any improvement. Medical history is filled with examples of how easy it is to be misled when generalizations are made from a few anecdotal reports. We do know from numerous studies that a significant number of people with mental disorders improve with no drug treatment at all. In a recent well-balanced book on antidepressant drugs, for example, it was noted that:

> Seventy percent of all people taking antidepressants report an improvement, meaning that there is at least a 50 percent reduction in their symptoms. This is in comparison with 40 percent of people taking a placebo.[12]

This means that only 30 percent of the improvement is attributable to the action of the drugs and even some of that was only a partial improvement. Even with many more drugs now available, there are still substantial numbers of patients who are not helped by any of them. Not only do the figures cited usually exaggerate the percentage of people likely to improve on drug treatment, but all the improvement that occurs is credited to the drugs.

It is claimed that patients tolerate the newer drugs better because they produce fewer side effects. Still, every drug has some undesirable side effects, and we will not know what side effects the newer drugs will have until they have been in use for a sufficient period of time. Relapse is also a problem. For some mental conditions, as many as 50 percent of the patients who improve with drug treatment have a recurrence of their condition within a year. It is commonly recommended that patients be maintained on drugs for eight months or more. The possibility of serious and permanent side effects from prolonged treatment cannot be discounted. To frame the issue more realistically, *it is not a question of a perfect solution that lacks an adequate explanation, but rather a case of a far-from-perfect solution that is being pushed too vigorously because of a heavily promoted theory that has been accepted uncritically.*

If therapists are persuaded that chemical imbalances are the only factor that has to be considered in treating mental disorders, they will neglect other factors that may play an equal or even more important role. Increasingly, the advice given to psychiatrists is to try drug treatment first, and if that proves ineffective after a sufficient trial period, the drug dose should be increased. If improvement is still not evident, the advice is to try a different drug of the same class. A case the author was quite familiar with might help to illustrate the point.

A highly productive and creative research biochemist, who was a colleague and collaborator of the author, began to develop classic manic-depressive symptoms. He had periods of great energy and productivity, requiring less and less sleep, but gradually his behavior became increasingly inappropriate, unrealistic, and eventually quite bizarre. This cycle was repeated a number of times and was regularly followed by a period of dysphoria in which his mood turned ugly. At this point he was usually verbally and physically aggressive, and his driving behavior was clearly a danger to himself and to others. Almost overnight, he would "crash" into a deep depression and become almost totally immobilized with suicidal thoughts. Lithium and the other mood-stabilizing drugs were tried at different dose levels, but at best they provided only minimal help, and the manic-depressive cycles recurred repeatedly with little or no abatement in the intensity of the emotional swings. He was hospitalized several times and was treated almost exclusively with mood-stabilizing drugs, but without significant abatement of his condition.

At long last, a psychiatrist began to pay attention to the coincidence of the manic-depressive episodes, long hours working in the laboratory, and the inevitable successes and failures that all research activity involves. There was probably an underlying predisposition, although it had not expressed itself in the six previous years that we were close colleagues. Judging from when these manic episodes started, there clearly seemed to be some environmental events that may have triggered, or least exacerbated, the emotional swings. After discussing the problem with the psychiatrist, my colleague agreed that he would try to rearrange his life to limit his research activities and to shift to doing the more predictable and steady work of supervising biochemical tests in a medical laboratory. A low dose of lithium was also recommended and prescribed, even though this dose had been completely ineffective when tried earlier. Of course, this too is an anecdote, and it does not prove any causal relationships, but over the following five years, with the changes in his life combined with lithium treatment, my colleague's mood seemed to have finally been stabilized.

The case involved a patient who was probably helped by both drugs and psychotherapy in combination. There are patients who are helped by psychotherapy or counseling without drugs, and other patients who are helped by drugs alone. Kay Jamison, who in her book *An Unquiet Mind* describes how lithium helped stabilize her mood swings, has also commented that she would probably be dead if it were not for psychotherapy.[13] The problem that has to be faced is that psychiatrists are increasingly being pressured to rely more and more on drugs and to spend less time trying to look for those psychological factors, interpersonal relationships, and environmental contingencies that often play a major role in the development and exacerbation of mental disorders.

Admittedly, it is often not as easy to find a practical and effective way to help a patient to restructure their lives as it was in the above case. It is often necessary to try to help a patient change a much more intractable pattern of living and some very persistent thought patterns. It is unfortunate, however, that many of those promoting the advantages of drugs find it necessary to deprecate the effectiveness of all psychotherapy and counseling. This is usually done by contrasting drug treatment with a caricature of psychoanalytic therapy in which a number of sessions a week are continued for years, seemingly without any end in sight or any demonstrable benefit. Psychotherapy is described as a way of life, commonly ridiculed by referring to it as "New York" treatment for the "Woody Allen" syndrome. What seems to be purposely overlooked is that most psychotherapy today bears no resemblance to this parody.

If anxiety, phobias, panic disorders, depression, mania, obsessions, compulsions, substance abuse, and other mental disorders are seen only as a reflection of abnormal brain chemistry, then psychic content and life experiences are likely to be regarded as irrelevant. It is highly likely, in my view, that in the past there was too much emphasis on ferreting out the early roots of intrapsychic conflict and the hidden meaning of symptoms, but today most psychotherapy is concerned less with the past and more with exploring ways of establishing healthier mental attitudes and lifestyles for persons with particular predispositions. There is convincing evidence that many of the briefer forms of psychotherapy and counseling may, for some conditions, be as effective as, if not more effective and more lasting than, drug treatment. There is also evidence that psychotherapy or behavior therapy sometimes increases the effectiveness of drug treatment. However, psychiatric residents are being offered less and less training in any form of psychotherapy and are spending an increasing amount of time learning about drugs and neuropharmacology. The number of medical students wanting to become psychiatrists has decreased, and expressions of dissatisfaction with the profession are increasing. As one psychiatric resident expressed it: "I did not select this specialty to dispense drugs like a pharmacist," but increasingly that is the way psychiatrists have been forced to function, and that is the way their patients perceive them.

In many settings, the treatment of those with mental disorders is increasingly influenced, if not dictated, by health maintenance organizations, a number of which are large for-profit corporations. HMOs exert pressure to rely more and more on drugs and to limit the amount of contact with patients. In many settings, there is not sufficient time allotted to learn very much about the lives of patients. We may not have quite reached the point where the treatment is being dictated by the results of "time and motion" studies, but it often seems that we are not far from that point. As one distinguished psychiatrist recently commented:

> What's really transforming the situation is the way mental health care is being structured by huge insurance companies and managed care—who pay physicians only to do pharmacology. They fund 10/15 minutes with a patient once a month for a review of drug treatment. They will not pay adequately for psychotherapy. That will be funded only by someone being willing [or able] to pay for it out of his or her pocket. That aspect of a psychiatrist's professional life will diminish greatly. The American medical student is turning away from psychiatry because of poor reimbursement and because they don't want to do just pharmacotherapy.[14]

Leon Eisenberg, professor of social medicine at the Harvard Medical School, commented that "managed care and psychotropic drugs are a satanic mix."[15] However, that is only part of the problem. Increasingly, the practice of psychiatry is being controlled by two powerful market forces. On one side, HMOs are exerting pressure to rely mostly on drugs, and on the other side, much of the information about drugs is provided by the pharmaceutical industry.

In a speech delivered in 1986, Morton Reiser, a psychiatrist affiliated with the Yale University School of Medicine, expressed his concern over the little interest many resident psychiatrists seem to have in getting to know their patients:

> I talked with some of the residents and found that their approach and mind set in the interviews was astoundingly unpsychological. Once they had done the DSM-III "inventory" and had identified target symptoms for psychopharmacology, the diagnostic workup and meaningful communication stopped. Worse than that, to my mind, so did the residents' curiosity about the patient as a person—even to the point where often there was no answer to such basic questions as why the patient came for treatment at this time and what seemed to be worrying him or her. Most of these residents could and would have learned more about a stranger who was sitting next to them for an hour on an airplane trip than they had learned in these formal psychiatric interviews.[16]

In 1983, Lewis Thomas commented on this same problem as it applied to all of medicine:

The longest and most personal conversations held with hospital patients when they come to the hospital are discussions of finances, and insurance, engaged in by personnel trained in accountancy.[17]

There is every reason to believe that the problem has become more acute in recent years.

When I started this project I planned to describe the changes that have taken place in the way people think about mental disorders and how best to treat them, and the factors that were responsible for bringing about these changes. Along the way, I became convinced that it was also important to evaluate the evidence and arguments that support the now-prevailing theory that mental disorders are caused by chemical errors that are corrected by drugs. I have concluded that this theory, which is guiding much of clinical practice and our research efforts, is not supported by the evidence and may well be wrong. Yet for reasons that have little to do with science, the theory is being pursued relentlessly on a path filled with many dangers. It is like a ship without any navigational guidance being driven forward by a powerful motor through a sea with many uncharted reefs.

Notes

1. Introduction

1. See statement by Bertram Brown, former director of the National Institute of Mental Health (*American J. Psychiatry,* 1976, 133, 489–95, especially p. 492).

2. Altshuler, K. Z., Whatever happened to intensive psychotherapy? *Am. J. Psychiatry,* 1990, 428–30.

3. Gunderson, J. G., Drugs and psychosocial treatment of schizophrenia revisited, *Journal of Continuing Education in Psychiatry,* 1977, December, 25–40.

4. Norden, Michael J., *Beyond Prozac* (New York: Regan Books [Harper Collins], 1995).

5. Kotulak, R., *Inside the Brain: Revolutionary Discoveries of How the Mind Works.* (Kansas City, Mo.: Andrews & McMeel, 1996).

6. Snyder, S. H., Brain peptides as neurotransmitters, *Science,* 1980, 209, 976–83.

7. Vaughan, S. C., *The Talking Cure: The Science Behind Psychotherapy* (New York: Grosset/Putnam, 1997).

2. Discoveries of Psychotherapeutic Drugs

1. Sneader, W. *Drug discovery: The Evolution of Modern Medicines* (Chichester: Wiley, 1985).

2. There are Sumerian tablets estimated to have been inscribed about 4,000 years before the birth of Christ that refer to a "joy plant" thought to be the opium poppy. Some stone sculptures of "magic mushrooms" *(Psilocybe mexicana)* found in El Salvador, Guatemala, and Mexico are older than 500 B.C. Priests that came with Cortés to Mexico recorded the hallucinations experienced by natives who consumed a preparation from the peyote cactus. In some instances, hallucinogens were used to induce religious-mystical experiences, as in the "sacred mushroom" ceremonies of some Mexican Indian cultures. Both psilocybin, the active ingredient in the Mexican mushrooms, and mescaline, the active ingredient in the peyote cactus, can produce perceptual distortions and mental states resembling psychosis.

3. Evidence has been discovered that Neolithic farmers in what is now Iran were making wine from grapes over seven thousand years ago (estimated age from 5400 to 5000 B.C.). The technique was quite sophistocated, indicating a much ear-

lier origin of wine making, as resin (obtained from evergreen trees) was used to inhibit growth of the bacteria that turns wine to vinegar. This practice is similar to that used in making Greek retsina wine.

4. Throughout history, there are passing references to the idea that psychotropic drugs influenced emotions and mental states by modifying normal brain mechanisms, but such speculation was not pursued. One of the earlier statements was made by the French psychiatrist Moreau de Tours, who, after learning about hashish in Egypt, formed a "hashish club" in Paris, which included among its notable members Honoré de Balzac and Alexandre Dumas. Moreau speculated that hashish evoked the emotion of "joy" because it induced a brain state similar to that underlying the natural emotion. Moreau (de Tours), J. J., Du Hachisch et de l'aliénation mentale, in *Du Hachisch et de l'Aliénation Mentale,* ed. Moreau, J. J. (Librairie de Fortin, Paris: Masson et Cie, 1845).

5. Laehr, H., *Über Irrsein und Irrenanstalten* (Halle: Pfeffer, 1852). Quoted in Shorter, E. *The History of Psychiatry* (New York: Wiley, 1997), p. 262.

6. Thudichum, J. W. L., *A Treatise on the Chemical Constitution of the Brain* (London: Balliere, Tindell & Cox, 1884). Thudichum had far-ranging interests and was clearly ahead of his time. Among his diverse scientific and medical contributions were studies of the pathology of urine, the origin and treatment of gallstones, fractures of the humerus, sewage purification, the mange, the physiology of the Turkish bath, and books on wine, cookery, and the chemistry of the brain, among others. His book on the chemistry of the brain was remarkable for its time, but it emphasized an analysis of fatty tissue. Considering the little that was known about neurophysiology and humoral transmission between nerve cells, it would have been impossible for Thudichum to have provided the foundation for understanding how drugs acted on the brain. For more background on Thudichum see Drabkin, David L., *Thudichum, Chemist of the Brain* (Philadelphia: University of Pennsylvania Press, 1958).

7. Kraepelin, E., *Ueber die Beeinflussung einfacher psychischer Vorgänge durch einige Arzneimittel* (Jena: Verlag von Gustaf Fischer, 1892), p. 227.

8. Freud, S., Letter to Maria Bonaparte, 15 January 1930, in *The Life and Work of Sigmund Freud,* vol. 3, ed. Jones, E. (New York: Basic Books, 1957), p. 480.

9. Fiamberti, A. M., L'Acétylcholine dans la physio-pathogénèse et dans la thérapie de la schizophrénie, *Premier Congrès Mondial de Psychiatrie Paris,* 1950, 4, 16–22; Fiamberti, A. M., Sul meccanismo d'azione terapeutica della 'burrasca vascolare' provocate con derivati della colina, *Giornale di psichiatria e di neuropatologia,* 1969, 67, 270–80.

10. De Boor, W., *Pharmakopsychologie und Psychopathologie* (Berlin: Springer, 1956).

11. Sullivan, H. S., The modified psychoanalytic treatment of schizophrenia. *Am. J. Psychiatry,* 1931, 519–40 (see p. 533).

12. See Gaddum, J. H., in *Ciba Foundation Symposium on Hypertension: Humoral and Neurogenic Factors* (Boston: Little Brown, 1954), pp. 75–77, and Woolley, D. W., and Shaw, E., *Science,* 1954, 119, 587–88.

13. St. Anthony is considered the patron saint of those suffering from the gangrenous form of ergotism. The last large epidemic of ergotism occurred in southern Russia in 1926–27.

14. Ergot causes a vigorous and prolonged contraction of the uterus, which precipitates childbirth and inhibits bleeding after delivery.

15. Hofmann was never certain how he was exposed to the drug, but he speculated that he might have gotten a small amount of the crystal on a finger, and it was absorbed through the skin.

16. Hofmann, A., *LSD: My Problem Child: Reflections on Sacred Drugs* (Los Angeles: J.P. Tarcher, 1983), pp. 17–18. Although Albert Hofmann did not do so when the effects of LSD were first reported in the 1940s, later he speculated that certain mental disorders that were thought to be purely psychic in origin might turn out to have a biochemical cause.

17. Huxley, A., *The Doors of Perception* (London: Chatto & Windus, 1954); Huxley, A., *Heaven and Hell* (London: Chatto & Windus, 1956).

18. Berquist, L., "The Curious Story Behind the New Cary Grant," *Look*, 1 September 1959, pp. 57–59; Joe Hyams, "What Psychiatry Has Done for Cary Grant," *New York Herald Tribune*, 20 April 1959, p. 16. An authoritative account of the experimentation with LSD has been written by Steven Novak (LSD before Leary, Sidney Cohen's critique of 1950s psychedelic drug research, *ISIS*, 1997, 88, 87–110).

19. See, for example, Dunlap, J. *Exploring Inner Space* (New York: Harcourt Brace & World, 1961), and Newland, C. A. *My Self and I: The Intimate and Completely Frank Record of One Woman's Courageous Experiment with Psychiatry's Newest Drug, LSD 25* (New York: Signet, 1963).

20. The First European Symposium on LSD in Psychotherapy was held at the University of Göttingen in Octorber 1960. In March 1966, a symposium entitled "The Use of Psychotomimetic Agents as Treatments in Psychiatry" was held in Washington, D.C.: Brill, H., Cole, J., Deniker, P., Hippius, H., and Bradley, P., eds., *Proceeding of the Fifth International Congress of the Collegium Internationale Neuro-Psycho-Pharmacologicum* (Amsterdam: Excerpta Medica Foundation, 1967), pp. 391–449.

21. Cohen, S., and Eisner, E., *J. Nerv. and Ment. Dis.*, 1958, 127, 6.

22. Maslow, A., *Religions, Values, and Peak Experiences* (Columbus: Ohio State University Press, 1964), p. 27 (quotation from p. 76).

23. Lilly, J. C., Dolphin-human relation and LSD 25, in Abramson, H. A., ed., *The Use of LSD in Psychotherapy and Alcoholism* (New York: Bobbs-Merrill, 1967), pp. 47–52.

24. Hofmann, A., op. cit., p. 209.

25. Twarog, B. M., Serotonin: History of a discovery, *Comparative Biochemistry and Physiology*, 1988, 91C, 21–24.; Twarog, B. M., and Page, I. H., Serotonin content of some mammalian tissues and urine and a method for its determination, *Am. J. Physiology*, 1953, 175, 157–161. Betty Twarog has written that her original paper on serotonin was submitted in 1952, but was not published until 1954

because the editor had rejected it as unimportant, and when after a long delay she finally learned of the decision, she had to resubmit the article to another journal.

26. An account of the early history of "sleep therapy" is given in Shorter, E. A., *History of Psychiatry* (New York: John Wiley, 1997), pp. 200–207.

27. Slater, E., Psychiatry in the 'thirties,' *Contemporary Review*, 1975, 226, 70–75, (quotation from p. 74).

28. Meduna emigrated to the United States in 1939 and became a staff psychiatrist at Loyola University in Chicago. When he came to the United States he changed his name to Ladislas Joseph Meduna (Meduna, L., Autobiography of L. J. Meduna [Part 1] and [Part 2] *Convulsive Therapy*, 1985, 1 [No. 1], 45–57 and [No. 2] 121–35).

29. The Manfred Sakel Institute in New York was supported by the Gimbel Foundation.

30. For a more complete discussion of the history of insulin treatment see Valenstein, E. S., *Great and Desperate Cures* (New York: Basic Books, 1986), pp. 46–48.; Shorter, E., *A History of Psychiatry* (New York: John Wiley, 1997), pp. 208–13.

31. Smith Ely Jelliffe was an influential and prominent psychoanalyst. He had been Karl Menninger's teacher, had written a successful psychiatry text with his friend William Alanson White, and served as an expert witness in the "murder case of the century"—the shooting of the architect Stanford White—and also in the highly publicized Leopold and Loeb case.

32. Jelliffe, S. E., Discussion of hypoglycemic treatment of schizophrenia at Rockland State Hospital, *J. Nerv. & Ment. Dis.*, 1938, 87, 500.

33. Casamajor, L., Notes for an intimate history of neurology and psychiatry in America, *J. Nerv. & Mental Diseases*, 1943, 98, 600–608 (quotation from p. 607).

34. Ross, C. A., Errors of logic in biological psychiatry, in Ross, C. A., and Pam, A., eds., *Pseudoscience in Biological Psychiatry. Blaming the Body* (New York: Wiley, 1995), pp. 85–128 (quotation from p. 86).

35. Of course, the reality is much more complicated, as in each of these categories there may be several classes of drugs, distinguishable by their chemical structures and their presumed physiological actions. A further complication to any classification of psychiatric drugs is that they are most effective in alleviating symptoms, rather than diagnostic categories, so that in practice it is not uncommon for both antidepressant and antischizophrenic medication to be prescribed if, for example, a patient has schizophrenialike delusions combined with a depressed mood.

36. The study was directed by John Vernon Kinross-Wright of Baylor University in Houston and quoted in Swazey, J. P., *Chlorpromazine in Psychiatry* (Cambridge: MIT Press, 1974).

37. The Ciba company had a few medicinal drugs on the market at the end of the last century, but Geigy did not market its first drug until 1938. See Reidl, R. A., A brief history of the pharmaceutical industry in Basel, in Liebenau, J., Higby, G. J., and Stroud, E. C., *Pill Peddlers. Essays on the History of the Pharmaceutical Industry* (Madison, Wisc.: Amer. Inst. of the History of Pharmacy, 1990), pp. 49–72. There is an excellent account of the events leading up to the discovery of chlorpromazine in Swazey, J. P., *Chlorpromazine in Psychiatry* (Cambridge: MIT Press, 1974).

38. Sir Henry Dale and others found that histamine produced an increase in the capillary permeability, with the result that fluid leaked into tissues. This effect, combined with histamine's causing blood vessels to dilate, resulted in a dramatic decline in blood pressure and, sometimes, resulted in cardiac arrest. Dale recognized that these effects were similar to those seen in anaphylactic shock and other allergic reactions. It was discovered that histamine is present naturally in all mammals and that it is released as a defense against foreign protein that gets into the body. However, when this otherwise adaptive response is excessive, it may cause an allergic reactions and even a life-threatening anaphylactic shock.

39. Deniker, P., Discovery of the clinical use of neuroleptics, in Parnham, M. J., and Bruinvels, J., eds., *Discoveries in Pharmacology, Vol I Psycho- and Neuro-Pharmacology* (Amsterdam: Elsevier, 1983), pp. 163–80.

40. This was at the time when Hans Selye made his classic studies of the "general adaptation syndrome" (the term he used to refer to a neuroendocrine response pattern that was a common reaction to all stress).

41. Laborit was looking for a combination of drugs that would stabilize the vegetative (autonomic) nervous system. What he eventually used was actually several "cocktails," as he ended up administering procaine and synthetic antihistamines before surgery; procaine, curare, the ganglionic blocking drug TEA, atropine, and synthetic antihistamines during surgery; and procaine, TEA, atropine, and synthetic antihistamines after surgery; and for 24 to 48 hours postsurgery, more atropine and histamines were administered.

42. Swazey, J., op. cit., pp. 62–77, has an extensive discussion of the many properties of phenothiazines thought useful for combating surgical shock.

43. Quoted as a "personal interview" of Laborit by Swazey, J., op. cit., p. 79.

44. Quoted by Swazey, J., op. cit., pp. 78 and 79.

45. Caldwell, A. E., *Origins of Psychopharmacology from CPZ to LSD* (Springfield, Ill.: Charles Thomas, 1970), pp. 25–26.

46. Traditionally, the nervous system is divided into "central" and "peripheral" components. The central nervous system (or CNS) refers to the part of the nervous system in bone (skull or spinal cord) and therefore includes the brain and spinal cord. The peripheral nervous system (or PNS) refers to the nerves that innervate the skeletal muscles, the glands, and the visceral organs.

47. Several of these central nervous system effects were being pursued because of the possibility that they might have medical applications. It was thought that some compounds might be useful as antiparkinsonian agents, as anticonvulsants for epileptic patients, and because of a reported action on cerebral amino acids, it was even thought possible that one of the compounds might be useful in treating psychiatric disorders. In fact, as early as 1950, the Rhône-Poulenc company had conducted some clinical trials of promethazine on agitated patients and found they were much calmer when on the drug.

48. RP stands for Rhône-Poulenc. Experimental drugs are routinely numbered by pharmaceutical companies and only named when they are to be marketed.

49. Swazey, J., op. cit., pp. 123–24.

50. See Swazey, J., op. cit., pp. 114–16, for a more complete description of these early reports on chlorpromazine trials in psychiatry and relevant references.

51. Winter and Flataker (*J. Pharmacol. Exp. Ther.*, 1951, 101, 156–62), for example, reported in 1951 that chlorpromazine made rats indifferent to a bell that had been associated with a shock, and they speculated that the central action of the drug might help eliminate the conditioned fear thought to underlie some mental illness. See Swazey, J., op. cit., pp. 114–16, for a more complete description of early reports of the psychiatric effects of chlorpromazine.

52. Laborit, H., Huguenard, P., and Alluaume, R., Un nouveau stabilisateur végétatif (le 4560 RP), *Presse Méd.*, 1952, 60, 206–208.

53. Quoted in Swazey, J., op. cit., p. 105.

54. Laborit commented: "The product [chlorpromazine] does not cause any loss of consciousness, no alteration of the psychic state, but merely a certain tendency to sleep and especially "disinterest" on the part of the patient in his environment. The facts suggest certain indications of the product in psychiatry, whereby its potentiating action can be used as a sleep agent with a positive reduction of the use of barbiturates" (quoted by Swazey, J., op. cit., p. 105).

55. Hamon, J., Paraire, J., and Velluz, J., Remarques sur l'action du 4560 RP sur l'agitation maniaque, *Ann. Méd. Psychol.*, 1952, 110, 331–35.

56. The historian Judith Swazey commented that Laborit's role in chlorpromazine's development has at various times been "ignored, debated, minimized, and overstated." She concludes that considering the many contemporary investigations of the behavioral effects of phenothiazines, the discovery of chlorpromazine's application to psychiatry would probably have been made without him (Swazey, J., op. cit., pp. 87–88).

57. Delay, J., Deniker, P., and Harl, J. M., Utilization en thérapeutique psychiatrique d'une phénothiazine d'action centrale élective (4560 R.P.), *Ann. Méd-Psychol. (Paris)*, 1952, 110, 112–17.

58. Delay, J., Deniker, P., and Harl, J. M., Traitement des états d'excitation et d'agitation par une méthode médicamenteuse dérivée de l'hibernothérapie. *Ann. Méd. Psychol.*, 1952, 110, 262–67. For other Delay and Deniker references to 1952 publications on chlorpromazine see Deniker, P., Discovery of the clinical use of neuroleptics, in Parnham, M. J., and Bruinvels, J., eds., *Discoveries in Pharmacology, Vol. I: Psycho- and Neuro-Pharmacology* (Amsterdam: Elsevier, 1983), pp. 163–80.

59. The Greek "lepto" means fine or delicate. The extrapyramidal system in the brain is assumed to play a major role in making movements smooth. Disorders of the extrapyramidal system can produce spastic movements or tremors. Parkinson's disease is considered an extrapyramidal disorder. In the World Health Organization's *Lexicon of Psychiatric and Mental Health Terms* the term "neuroleptic" is defined as follows: "A term applied by Jean Delay and Pierre Deniker to the drugs, phenothiazines, reserpine, alkaloids, butyrophenomes whose supposedly specifically antipsychotic action is associated with the induction of a neurological syndrome of the extrapyramidal type. The value of the term is dubious and its use is to be deprecated." For a similar view, see also Collard, J., The main clinical classification of neuroleptics, *Acta Psychiat. Belg.* 1974, 74, 462–69.

60. The results summarized in this paragraph were described in several Delay and Deniker papers published in 1952, parts of which were translated and reproduced by Swazey, J., op. cit., pp. 136–37. Deniker's description of his presentation at a meeting was from a personal interview conducted by Swazey, J., op. cit., p. 137.

61. The countries were France, England, Switzerland, Algeria, Argentina, Senegal, Belgium, Italy, and The Netherlands.

62. See Swazey, J., op. cit., pp. 96–106, for a description of the different clinical trials, and Chapter 5 for the contributions of others, besides Delay and Deniker, who had reported results of early tests of chlorpromazine on psychiatric patients.

63. Freeman, W., Prefrontal lobotomy: Final report of 500 Freeman and Watts patients followed for 10 to 20 years, *Southern Medical Journal*, 1958, 51, 739–45.

64. Stockton State Hospital case 56332, 2 March 1955, continuous notes, 27. Reported in Braslow, J., *Mental Ills and Bodily Cures, Psychiatric Treatment in the First Half of the Twentieth Century* (Berkeley: University of California Press, 1997), p. 169.

65. There were many prior meetings to discuss the use of insulin and metrazol in psychiatry, but these are generally not considered psychopharmacological drugs. Swiss psychiatrists may have initially been interested in chlorpromazine as an adjunct to sleep therapy, which had been widely used in that country (Largactil-Symposion in der psychiatrischen Universitätsklinik Basel am 28 November 1953–1954, *Schweiz. Arch. Neurol. Psychiat.*, 73 [1 and 2]: 288–369). In England, Joel Elkes and C. Elkes reported in December 1953 that chlorpromazine made "overactive chronic psychotic patients" quieter, more amenable to suggestions, and more capable of carrying out simple ward tasks. However, they qualified the usefulness of chlorpromazine by noting that "ingrained psychotic thought disorder seemed to be unchanged," and even though three psychotic patients were considered to have improved sufficiently to try a "parole," no patient was judged suitable for discharge (Elkes, J., and Elkes, C., Effects of chlorpromazine on the behavior of chronically overactive psychotic patients, *Brit. Med. J.*, 1954, 2, 560–65).

66. A young German, Dr. Ruth Koeppe-Kajander, interning at the Oshawa (Ontario) General Hospital gave chlorpromazine to twenty-five psychiatric patients and reported at a meeting in November 1953 that the drug "calmed restless, excited patients without sedating them to the level where they could not function." Koeppe-Kajander never published her findings. See Griffin, J., An historic oversight, *Canadian Psychiatric Assoc. Bulletin*, 1994, 26, 5.

67. Personal interview, quoted by Swazey, J., op. cit., p. 156.

68. The expressionless, "wooden" faces are characteristic of patients with Parkinson's disease.

69. Lehmann, H. E., and Hanrahan, G. E., Chlorpromazine, new inhibiting agent for psychomotor excitement and manic states, *AMA Arch. Neurol. Psychiat.*, 1954, 71, 227–37.

70. Heinz Lehmann's comments are from a personal interview conducted by Swazey, J., op. cit., pp. 156–58. It should be noted that today electroshock treatment is not considered effective for schizophrenia, and controlled studies of insulin coma treatment found its effectiveness to be much less than was commonly reported earlier.

71. Deniker, P., Discovery of the clinical use of neuroleptics, in Parnham, M. J., and Bruinvels, J., eds., *Discoveries in Pharmacology, vol. 1: Psycho- and Neuro-Pharmacology* (Elsevier Science Publishers, 1983), pp. 163–80. A bibliography of Delay and Deniker articles on chlorpromazine up to 1961 can be found in Delay, J., and Deniker, P., *Méthodes Chimiothérapiques en Psychiatrie*, vol. I, (Paris: Masson, 1961).

72. Steck, H., Le syndrome extra-pyramidal et diencéphalique au cours des traitements au Largactil et au Serpasil, *Ann. Méd. Psychol.*, 1954, 112, 737–43.

73. Memos are cited by Swazey, J., op. cit., pp. 176–78.

74. Quoted in Swazey, J., op. cit., p. 181.

75. Quoted in Swazey, J., op. cit., p. 188.

76. Winkelman, N. W., Jr., Chlorpromazine in the treatment of neuropsychiatric disorders, *J.A.M.A.*, 1954, 155, 18–21.

77. It was not possible from Courvoisier's description to know whether the rats given chlorpromazine were unable to learn how to avoid the shock, whether they had learned the avoidance response but were too indifferent to the warning signal to bother responding, or whether the motor impairment produced by the drug simply made it impossible for them to climb the rope in order to avoid the shock. Courvoisier, S., Fournel, J., Ducrot, R., Kolsky, M., and Koetschet, P., Propriétés pharmacodynamiques du chlorhydrate de chloro-3-(diméthylamino-3'propyl)-10 phénothiazine (4560 R.P.), *Arch. Int. Pharmacodyn.*, 1953, 92, 305–61.

78. Winkelman, op. cit., p. 21.

79. Kinross-Wright, V., Chlorpromazine—a major advance in psychiatric treatment, *Postgrad. Med.*, 1954, 16, 297–99. Winkelman continued to use Thorazine, and by the early spring of 1956, he reported his experience with 1,090 patients who were treated with this drug (Winkelman, N. W., Jr., An appraisal of chlorpromazine. General principles for administration of chlorpromazine based on experience with 1,090 patients, *Am. J. Psychiat.*, 1957, 113, 961–71). The results had been presented earlier at the American Psychiatric Association meeting in Chicago, April 30–May 4, 1956. Another early clinical trial with chlorpromazine was conducted at McLean Hospital in Massachusetts. See Bower, W. H., Chlorpromazine in psychiatric illness, *The New England Journal of Medicine*, 1954, 251, 689–92.

80. *Time*, 7 March 1955, p. 56.

81. By this time there were at least six other phenothiazines (Trilafon, Dartal, Compazine, Vesprin, Sparine, and Pacatal) besides Thorazine available in the United States.

82. There had been a proliferation of phenothiazines, as pharmaceutical companies were anxious to get a share of the chlorpromazine market. One researcher and head of a pharmaceutical company wrote that by 1967 "10 to 15 thousand drugs with effects similar to those of CPZ have been synthesized. Some are up to 10,000 times as potent. In our own labs we have made about 3,000 such drugs, although only a few have reached the clinic" (Janssen, P. A., Questions and comments of antipsychotic agents sessions; Invited comments, in *Psychopharmacology, A Review of Progress: 1957–1967. The Proceedings of the Sixth Annual Meeting of the American College of Neuropharmacology, San Juan, Puerto Rico, December*

12–15, 1967, Efron, D. H., Cole, J. O., Levine, J., and Wittenborn, J. R., eds., pp. 1177–81 (quotation from p. 1177). Public Health Service Publ. 1836 (Washington, D.C.: U.S. Government Printing Office).

83. Ayd, Jr., F. J., A comparative study of phenothiazine tranquilizers, in Masserman, J. H., ed., *Biological Psychiatry,* Vol. 1 (New York: Grune and Stratton, 1959), pp. 311–15.

84. The NIMH study of the effectiveness of phenothiazines was published in the March 1964 issue of the *Archives of General Psychiatry.*

85. Margolis, L. H., Pharmacotherapy in psychiatry: A review, *Annals of the New York Academy of Sciences,* 1956, pp. 698–718.

86. Cole, J. O., and Gerard, R. W., eds., *Psychopharmacology, Problems in Evaluation* (Washington, D.C.: National Academy of Sciences–National Research Council, Publ. 583, 1959), p. v.

87. Neural signals generated by external stimuli are relayed through the thalamus to the neocortex, the brain region believed to be essential for consciousness.

88. Jefferson, Sir Jeffrey, The reticular formation and clinical neurology, in Jasper, H., Proctor, L., Knighton, R., Noshay, W., and Costello, R., eds., *Reticular Formation of the Brain* (Boston: Little, Brown, 1958), p. 729.

89. Redlich, F. C., and Freedman, D. X., *The Theory and Practice of Psychiatry* (New York: Basic Books, 1966), p. 307.

90. Janssen, P. A. J., The butyrophenone story, in Ayd, F. J., ed., *Haloperidol Update: 1958–1980* (Baltimore, Md.: Ayd Medical Communications, 1980).

91. For a review of amphetamine-induced psychosis and stereotyped behavior see Cooper, S., and Dourish, C., An introduction to the concept of stereotypy and a historical perspective on the role of brain dopamine, in Cooper, S., and Dourish, C., eds., *Neurobiology of Stereotyped Behaviour* (Oxford: Clarendon Press, 1990), pp. 1–24.

92. An interesting history of how these compounds were discovered to combat the tubercular bacillus can be found in Fox, H. H., The chemical attack on tuberculosis, *N.Y. Acad. Sciences,* 1953, 15, 234–42.

93. Bloch, R. G. et al., *Ann. Int. Med.,* 1954, 40, 881.

94. Cited in Pratt, R. T. C., Clinical effects of amine oxidase inhibitors, in Vane, J. R., ed., *Adrenergic Mechanisms* (Boston: Little, Brown, 1960), pp. 446–53.

95. Kline, N. S., *From Sad to Glad: Kline on Depression* (New York: Putnam, 1974), p. 122.

96. Nathan Kline was also at various times during his career Clinical Professor at Columbia University College of Physicians and Surgeons; Founding Fellow of the Royal College of Psychiatrists; President of the American College of Neuropharmacology; and a member of the Expert Advisory Committee on Mental Health of the World Health Organization.

97. Loomer, H. P., Saunders, J. C., and Kline, N. S., Iproniazid, an amine oxydase inhibitor, as an example of a psychic energizer, *Congress Rec.,* 1957, 1382–90; Loomer, H. P., Saunders, J. C., and Kline, N. S. A clinical and pharmacodynamic evaluation of iproniazid as a psychic energizer, *Psychiat. Res. Report No. 8, Am. Psychiatric Assoc.,* 1958, 129–41.

98. Kline, N. S., *From Sad to Glad: Kline on Depression* (New York: Putnam, 1974), p. 123.

99. Some of this early history is summarized in Sandler, M., Monoamine oxidase inhibitors in depression: history and mythology, *J. of Psychopharmacology* (Oxford: Oxford Univ. Press, 1990), pp. 4, 136–39.

100. Kuhn, R., The imipramine story, in Ayd, F. J., Jr., and Blackwell B., eds., *Discoveries in Biological Psychiatry* (Philadelphia: Lippincott, 1970), pp. 205–17 (quotation from p. 211).

101. Kuhn, R., The treatment of depressive states with G22355 (imipramine hydrochloride), *Am. J. Psychiat.* 1958, 115, 459–464. (quotation from pp. 459–60).

102. Ibid., p. 460.

103. Quoted in Strobusch, A. D., and Jefferson, A. W., The checkered history of lithium in medicine, *Pharmacy in Medicine,* 1980, 22, 72–76. There were many other legal judgments concerning lithium (see Johnson, F. N., *The History of Lithium Therapy* [London: Macmillan, 1984], p. 148, footnote 137).

104. Aurelianus, C., *On Acute Diseases and Chronic Diseases,* Drabkin, I. E., ed. and transl. (Chicago: Chicago University Press, 1950), p. 522.

105. This little-known history has been recounted in Amdisen, A., Lithium treatment of mania and depression over one hundred years, in Corsini, G. U., ed., *Current Trends in Lithium and Rubidium Therapy* (Lancaster: MIT Press, 1984), pp. 11–26.

106. Hammond, W. A., *A Treatise on Diseases of the Nervous System* (New York: D. Appleton, 1871), pp. 380–81. I am indebted to Samuel Gershon for bringing this historical note to my attention. See also Yeragani, V. K., and Gershon, S., Hammond and lithium: Historical update, *Biological Psychiatry,* 1986, 21, 1101–1102.

107. Waldron, A. M., Lithium intoxication, *JAMA,* 1949, 139, 733.

108. Hamlon, L. W., Romaine, M. III, Gilroy, F.J., and Deitrick, J. E., Lithium chloride as a substitute for sodium chloride in the diet. Observations on its toxicity, *JAMA,* 1949, 139, 688–92.

109. John Cade was not the first person to search for a biochemical basis of mania by injecting experimental animals with fluids obtained from mental patients. Perry Baird, at the time a successful Boston dermatologist who suffered from a manic-depressive disorder, injected blood from a manic patient into adrenalectomized animals. He took his lead from a report (not confirmed) that manic patients have enlarged adrenal glands. He reported that adrenalectomized animals survived three times longer than controls if they received injections of blood drawn from manic patients. Baird, P.C., Biochemical component of manic-depressive psychosis. *J. Nerv. and Ment. Dis.,* 1944, 99, 359–366. See also Baird, P. C. and Baird, M. S., Echoes from a dungeon cell: A doctor's view of his incarceration, *Psychiatric Service,* 1996, 47, 581–82.

110. Cade, J. F. J., *Mending the Mind: A Short History of Twentieth Century Psychiatry* (Melbourne: Sun Books, 1979), pp. 70–71.

111. Kline, N., Lithium: The history of its use in psychiatry, *Modern Problems of Pharmacopsychiatry,* vol. 3 (Basel: S. Karger, 1969).

112. Schou, M., Phases in the development of lithium treatment in psychiatry, in Samson, F., and Adelman, G., eds., *The Neuroscience: Paths of Discovery II* (Boston: Birkhäuser, 1992), pp. 149–66 (quotation from p. 150).

113. Cade, J., Lithium salts in the treatment of psychotic excitement, *Med. J. Australia,* 1949, 36, 349–52.

114. Ibid., p. 350.

115. Ibid., 36, 349–352.

116. Cade, J., The story of lithium, in Ayd, F. J., Jr., and Blackwell, B., eds., *Discoveries in Biological Psychiatry* (Philadelphia: Lippincott, 1970), pp. 218–29; quotation from p. 219). See also Cade, J., *Mending the Mind* (Melbourne: Sun Books, 1979), and Obituary in *Med. J. Australia,* 2 May 1981, p. 489. One of the first histories of lithium was Kline, N. S., Lithium: The history of its use in psychiatry, *Modern Problems in Pharmacopsychiatry,* 1969, 3, 75–92.

117. Johnson, F. N., *The History of Lithium Therapy* (London: Macmillan, 1984), pp. 40–41.

118. Gershon, S., and Yuwiler, A., Lithium ion: A specific psychopharmacological approach to the treatment of mania, *J. Neuropsychiatry* 1960, 1, 229–41.

119. Ashburner, J. V., Correspondence—A case of chronic mania treated with lithium citrate and terminating fatally, *Med. J. Australia,* 1950, 37, 386; Roberts, E. L., A case of chronic mania treated with lithium citrate and terminating fatally, *Med. J. Australia,* 1950, 37, 261–62.

120. Wickler, A., *The Relation of Psychiatry to Pharmacology* (Baltimore: Williams and Wilkins, 1957).

121. Goodman, L. S., and Gilman, A., *The Pharmacological Basis of Therapeutics,* 2d ed. (New York: Macmillan, 1958), p. 817.

122. Talbott, J., Use of lithium salts as a substitute for sodium chloride, *Archives of Internal Medicine,* 1950, 85, 1–10. For more details concerning the work of others who contributed to the methodology for monitoring serum levels of lithium see Johnson, F. N., *The History of Lithium Therapy* (London: Macmillan, 1984), pp. 55–57.

123. They were published in 1963.

124. Gershon, W., and Yuwiler, A., Lithium ion: A specific psychopharmacological approach to the treatment of mania, *J. of Neuropsychiatry,* 1960, 1, 229–41.

125. Blackwell, B., and Shepherd, M., Prophylactic lithium: Another therapeutic myth? An examination of evidence to date, *Lancet,* 1968, i, 968–71; Blackwell, B., Lithium: Prophylactic or panacea? *Lancet,* 1969, i, 52–59; Blackwell, B., Prophylactic lithium: Science or science fiction? *American Heart Journal,* 1972, 83, 139–41.

126. On Lewis and Shepherd see Wilkinson, G., ed., *Talking About Psychiatry,* (London: Gaskell, 1993), p. 167.

127. FDA, Lithium carbonate, *FDA Current Drug Information,* April 1970.

128. Fieve, R., *Mood Swing: The Third Revolution* (New York: William Morrow, 1975).

129. Ibid., p. 41.

130. Ibid., p. 29.

131. Ibid., p. 23.

132. Gershon, S., and Shopsin, B., Introduction, in Gershon, S., and Shopsin, B., eds., *Lithium: Its Role in Psychiatric Research and Treatment* (New York: Plenum Press, 1973), pp. 1–3; Fieve, R. R., Overview of therapeutic and prophylactic trials with lithium in psychiatric patients, in Gershon, S., and Shopsin, B., eds., *Lithium: Its Role in Psychiatric Research and Treatment* (New York: Plenum Press, 1973), pp. 317–50 (see p. 319).

133. Amdisen, A., Lithium treatment of mania and depression over one hundred years, in Corsini, G. U., ed., *Current Trends in Lithium and Rubidium Therapy* (Lancaster: MIT Press, 1984), pp. 11–26; Johnson, F. N., *The History of Lithium Therapy* (London: Macmillan, 1984).

134. Personal communication of J. Mendels cited in Johnson, F. N., *The History of Lithium Therapy* (London: Macmillan, 1984), p. 117.

135. Jamison, K., *An Unquiet Mind* (New York: Knopf, 1995).

136. In pharmacology, the term "hypnotic" refers to a general category of drugs that depress the nervous system and induce sleep or drowsiness.

137. Berger, F. M., and Bradley, W., The pharmacological properties of α, β–ihydroxy-γ- (2–methylphenoxy)-propane (Myanesin), *Br. J. Pharmacol.*, 1946, 1, 265–72; Berger, F. M., Anxiety and the discovery of the tranquilizers, in Ayd, F. J., and B., Blackwell, eds., *Discoveries in Biological Psychiatry* (Philadelphia: Lippincott, 1970), pp. 115–29.

138. The antianxiety drugs have sometimes been referred to as "minor tranquilizers," in contrast to the phenothiazines and reserpine, which have been called "major tranquilizers."

139. The rights to market Miltown were held by Carter Products, which licensed Wyeth Pharmaceutical to market the drug under the trade name of Equanil.

140. Barbiturates suppress breathing, and the lethal dose is only a few times greater than the dose required to induce sleep. For a number of years, barbiturates were the drug most commonly used to commit suicide.

141. Geller, I., and Seifter, J., The effects of meprobamate, barbiturates, d-amphetamine and promazine on experimentally induced conflict in the rat, *Pharmacologia (Berlin)*, 1960, 1, 482–92; Geller, I., Backman, E., and Seifter, J., Effects of reserpine and morphine on behavior suppressed by punishment, *Life Sciences*, 1963, 4, 226–31.

142. Woods, J. H., Katz, J. L., and Winger, G., Benzodiazepines: Use, abuse, and consequences, *Pharmacological Reviews*, 1992, 44, 151–347.

143. The Rolling Stones's song "Mother's Little Helper" was written by Mick Jagger and Keith Richards.

3. Theories of Drug Action and Biochemical Causes of Mental Disorder

1. Abood, L., A chemical approach to the problem of mental disease, In D. Jackson, ed., *The Etiology of Schizophrenia* (New York: Basic Books, 1960), pp. 99–119.

2. Lewandowsky, M., *Arch. Anat. Physiol. Lpz. (Physiol. Abt.)*, 1899, 360. Also, see confirmation by Langley, J. N., *J. Physiol.*, 1901, 27, 234.

3. Elliott, T. R., *J. Physiol.*, 1904, 31, Proc. XX.

4. Dale, H., Opening address, in Vane, J. R., ed., *Adrenergic Mechanisms* (Boston: Little, Brown, 1961), p. 4.

5. Fulton, J. F., *Physiology of the Nervous System*, 2d ed., revised (New York: Oxford University Press, 1943), pp. 79–80.

6. Fulton, J. F., *Physiology of the Nervous System*, 3d ed., revised (New York: Oxford University Press), 1949, see pp. 66 and 73. John Eccles, who later received the Nobel Prize for his work in neuronal physiology, maintained until at least the mid-1950s that communication between neurons was electrical, not chemical. See Eccles, J. C., *Facing Reality. Philosophical Adventures by a Brain Scientist* (New York: Springer-Verlag, 1970), pp. 104–106.

7. Morgan, C., and Stellar, E., *Physiological Psychology*, 2d ed., (New York: McGraw-Hill, 1950), quotations from p. 98.

8. Ranson, S. W., revised by Clark, S. L., *The Anatomy of the Nervous System, Its Development and Function* (Phildelphia: W. B. Saunders, 1953), see p. 101.

9. Grundfest, H., General problems of drug action on bioelectric phenomena, *Annals of the New York Academy of Sciences*, 1957, 537–91.

10. An early debate on electrical versus chemical transmission that took place between John Eccles and Henry Dale is described by Sir Bernard Katz in Squires, L., *The History of Neuroscience in Autobiography*, vol. 1 (Washington, D.C.: Society of Neuroscience, 1996), p. 373.

11. Interview of Pierre Pichot in Healy, D., *The Psychopharmacologists* (London: Chapman & Hall, 1996), quotation from p. 1.

12. Falck, B., Hillarp, N. A., Thieme, G., and Torp, A. J., Fluorescence of catecholamines and related compounds condensed with formaldehyde, *Histochem. Cytochem.*, 1962, 10, 348–54; Anden, N. E., Carlsson, A., Dalström, A., Fuxe, F., Hillarp, N. A., and Larsson, K., Demonstration and mapping out of nigro-neostriatal dopamine neurons, *Life Sciences*, 1964, 3, 523–30; Dalström, A., and Fuxe, K., A method for the demonstration of monoamine containing nerve fibers in the central nervous system, *Acta Physiol. Scand.*, 1964, 60, 293–95. Even as late as 1964 an article by one of the leading members of the "Swedish group" was entitled "Evidence for the existence of monoamine neurons in the central nervous system," indicating that some uncertainty about the role of these neurotransmitters still persisted. See Fuxe, K., Evidence for the existence of monoamine neurons in the central nervous system: IV, Distribution of monoamine nerve terminals in the central nervous system, *Acta Physiol. Scand.*, 1965, 64, Suppl. 247, 36–85.

13. Carlsson, A., Early psychopharmacology and the rise of modern brain research, *J. of Psychopharmacology*, 1990, 4, 120–26 (quotation from p. 122).

14. Hess, W. R., *Diencephalon: Autonomic and Extrapyramidal Functions* (New York: Grune & Stratton, 1954).

15. For reviews of the early studies of the behavior that could be elicited by hypothalamic stimulation, see Valenstein, E. S., *Brain Control* (New York: Wiley-Interscience, 1973), pp. 13–63.

16. Olds, J., and Milner, P., Positive reinforcement produced by electrical stimulation of septal area and other regions of rat brain, *J. Comp. Physiol. Psychol.*, 1954, 419–27.

17. See, for example, Olds, J., Self-stimulation of the brain, *Science*, 1958, 127, 315–24; Valenstein, E. S., and Beer, B., Continuous opportunity for reinforcing brain stimulation. *Journal of Experimental Analysis of Behavior*, 1964, 7, 183–84.

18. Andersson, B., The effect of injection of hypertonic NaCl-solutions into different parts of the hyperthalamus of goats, *Acta Physiol. Scand.*, 1953, 28, 188–201.

19. Fisher, A., Maternal and sexual behavior induced by intracranial chemical stimulation, *Science*, 1956, 124, 228–29.

20. Delgado, J. M. R., Cerebral structures involved in transmission and elaboration of noxious stimulation, *J. Neurophysiol.*, 1955, 18, 261–75; MacLean, P. D., Chemical and electrical stimulation of hippocampus in unrestrained animals: II, Behavioral findings, *Arch. Neurol. Psychiat.*, 1957, 78, 128–42. Carbachol was frequently used in the early chemical stimulation studies because its action had a longer duration than that of acetycholine.

21. Maclean, P. D., op. cit.

22. Neal Miller, who was Sebastian Grossman's faculty mentor, has reported that he had also started to think about stimulation with neurotransmitters as a result of a visit to Julius Axelrod's laboratory at the National Institute of Mental Health. Miller, N., Behavior to the brain to health, in Samson, F., and Adelman, G., eds., *The Neurosciences: Paths of Discovery II* (Boston: Birkhaüser, 1992, pp. 283–305 (see p. 295).

23. Grossman, S. P., Eating or drinking elicited by direct adrenergic or cholinergic stimulation of hypothalamus, *Science*, 1960, 132, 301–302.

24. Grossman, S. P., Direct adrenergic and cholinergic stimulation of hypothalamus, *Amer. J. Physiology*, 1962, 202, 872–82.

25. Miller, N. E., Chemical coding of behavior in the brain, *Science*, 1965, 148, 328–38 (first quotation taken from p. 330, second quotation from pp. 337–38).

26. Stein, L., Psychopharmacological substrates of mental depression, in Garattini, S., et al., eds., *Antidepressant Drugs* (Amsterdam: Excerpta Medica Foundation, 1967), 130–40 (quotation from p. 130). The quotation came from an address Larry Stein presented at the First International Symposium on Antidepressant Drugs held in Milan in April 1996, but similar ideas were expressed as early as 1962.

27. A number of studies (see review in Wise, R. A., and Rompre, P.-P., Brain dopamine and reward, in *Annual Rev. Psychol.*, 1989, 40, 191–225) have demonstrated a reasonably close (but not perfect) anatomical correspondence between self-stimulation sites and catecholamine distribution in the brain. Stein (see references above) emphasized norepinephrine as critical for reward and pleasure, while Roy Wise has argued that it was dopamine that was critical. Others have criticized both hypotheses as premature, confounded with motor effects, and in other ways failing to distinguish between performance and reward in self-stimulation experiments. See discussion of dopamine and pleasure in Robinson, T. E., and Berridge, K. C., The neural basis of drug craving: An incentive-sensitization theory of addiction, *Brain Research Reviews*, 1993, 18, 247–91.; Berridge, K. C., Food reward: Brain

substrates of wanting and liking, *Neuroscience & Behav. Reviews,* 1995, 20, 1–25. On speculation about the relation of biochemistry and the self-stimulation phenomenon to mood, motivation, memory, and various psychiatric disorders, see Stein, L., Psychopharmacological substrate of mental depression, in Garattini, S., and Dukes, N. M. G., eds., *Antidepressant Drugs* (Amsterdam: Excerpta Medica Foundation, 1967), pp. 130–40.; Stein, L., Wise, D., and Berger, B., in McGaugh, ed., *The Chemistry of Mood, Motivation, and Memory* (New York: Plenum, 1972), pp. 81–103; Wise, D. C., and Stein, L., Evidence of a central noradrenergic deficiency in schizophrenia, in Domino, E. F., and Davis, J. M., eds. and publishers, *Neurotransmitter Balance and Regulatory Behavior* (Ann Arbor, Mich.: 1975), pp. 99–123.

28. Swedish pharmacologist Arvid Carlsson has described the experiments that led up to his proposing that dopamine was a neurotransmitter in its own right, not just a precursor of epinephrine (adrenaline) and norepinephrine (noradrenaline). In 1958, Carlsson and Waldeck developed a technique for the identification and quantification of dopamine and this made it possible to demonstrate that dopamine's location in the brain was not identical to that of norepinephrine and epineprine. It seemed reasonable to conclude that dopamine must have a function in addition to its role as a precursor. Carlsson, A., Antipsychotic agents: Elucidation of their mode of action, In Parnham, M. J., and Bruinvels, J., eds., *Discoveries in Pharmacology, Volume I: Psycho- and Neuro-Pharmacology* (Elsevier Science, 1983), pp. 197–206. One of the earliest statements indicating that dopamine was probably a separate neurotransmitter appeared in 1960 in Carlsson, A., Lindquist, M., and Magnusson, T., On the biochemistry and possible function of dopamine and noradrenaline in brain, in Vane, J. R., ed., *Adrenergic Mechanisms* (Boston: Little, Brown, 1960), pp. 432–43. One of the earliest statements suggesting a central role of dopamine in schizophrenia appeared in a 1967 publication. See Van Rossum, M., The significance of dopamine receptor blockade for the action of neuroleptic drugs, in Brill, H., et al., *Proceedings of the Fifth Collegium Internationale Neuropharmacologicum* (Amsterdam: Excerpta Medica Foundation, 1967), pp. 321–29.

29. Zeller, E. A., Barsky, J., Fouts, J. R., Kirchheimer, W. F., and Van Orden, L. S., Influence of isonicotinic acid hydrazide (INH) and 1-isonicotinyl-2-isopropyl hydrazide (IIH) on bacterial and mammalian enzymes, *Experientia,* 1952, 8, 349–50 (quotation from p. 350).

30. Sen, G., and Bose, K. C., *Rauwolfia serpentina,* a new Indian drug for insanity and high blood pressure, *Ind. Med. Journal,* 1931, 2, 194–201; Roy, P. K., Effects of *Rauwolfia serpentina* on manic patients, *Ind. J. Neurology & Psychiat.,* 1950, 2, 350–55. The name *Rauwolfia* was taken from Leonard Rauwolf of Augsburg, Germany, who identified the plant in 1582.

31. Kline, N. S., Use of *Rauwolfia serpentina Benth* in neuropsychiatric conditions, *Annals of NY Acad. of Sciences,* 1954, 59, 107–32.

32. This incident is described by Nathan Kline in his book *From Sad to Glad: Kline on Depression* (New York: Putnam, 1974), pp. 74–79.

33. Moynihan, D. P., Congress builds a coffin, *The New York Review of Books,* 11 January 1996, vol. XLIII, no. 1, p. 35. This incident was also reported in the *Congressional Record,* 12 December 1995.

34. Shore, P. A., Silver, S. L., and Brodie, B. B., *Science,* 1954, 122, 284–85.

35. Carlsson, A., and Hillarp, N.-A., *Kgl. Fysiogr. Sällsk. Förhandl.,* 1956, 26, no. 8.

36. Reserpine causes the amine neurotransmitters to leak out from protected storage in the synaptic vesicles of the neurons. After being released, some of the neurotransmitter first stimulates other neurons, but most of it is broken down (inactivated) by the enzyme monoamine oxydase. Therefore, after the relatively brief "excitatory" period, reserpine produces a depletion of the amine neurotransmitters and immobility. Because the antidepressant drug iproniazid interferes with the monoamine oxydase enzyme, the combination of this drug with reserpine brings about the release of amine neurotransmitters, but they are not inactivated because the enzyme has been depleted. The result is the prolongation of the "excitatory" period.

37. See, for example, Brady, J. V., A comparative approach to the evaluation of drug effects upon affective behavior, *Annals NY Acad. of Sci.,* 1956, 64, 632–43.

38. Everett, G. M., and Toman, J. E. P., Mode of action of Rauwolfia alkaloids and motor activity, in Masserman, J. H., ed., *Biological Psychiatry,* Vol. I, 1959, pp. 75–81 (quotation from p. 80).

39. Jacobsen, E., The theoretical basis of the chemotherapy of depression, in Davies, E. B., ed., *Depression: Proceedings of the Symposium Held at Cambridge, 22 to 26 September, 1959* (New York: Cambridge University Press, 1964), pp. 208–14 (quotation from pp. 212–13.)

40. Axelrod, J. An unexpected life in research, in *Annual Review of Pharmacology and Toxicology* (Palo Alto, Calif.: Annual Reviews, Inc.), pp. 1–24.

41. Heath, R. G., Martens, S., Leach, B. E., Cohen, M. & Angel, C., *Am. J. Psychiatry,* 1957, 114, 14.

42. Some of the history of the adrenochrome theory is included in a popular book by Hoffer, A., and Osmond, H., *How to Live with Schizophrenia* (Secaucus, N.J.: Citadel Press, 1979, quotation from pp. 57–58). More scientific details are given in Hoffer, A., *Niacin Therapy and Psychiatry* (Springfield, Ill.: Charles Thomas, 1952).

43. Axelrod, J., An unexpected life in research, in *Annual Review of Pharmacology and Toxicology* (Palo Alto, Calif.: Annual Reviews, Inc.), pp. 1–24.

44. Iverson, L. I., Axelrod, J., and Glowinski, J., The effect of antidepressant drugs on the uptake and metabolism of catecholamines in the brain, in Brill, H., Cole, J., Deniker, P., Hippius, P., and Bradley, P., *Neuro-Psycho-Pharmacology, Proceedings of the Fifth International Congress of the Collegium Internationale Neuro-Psycho-Pharmacologicum* (Amsterdam: Excerpta Medica Foundation, 1967), 362–66 (quotation from pp. 362–64); Axelrod, J., Whitby, L., and Hertting, G., *Science,* 1961, 133, 383. This highly productive period of neuropharmacological research at NIH has been called the "Camelot of Neuropharmacology" and it has been described in an excellent popular book by Robert Kanigel, *Apprentice to Genius: The Making of a Scientific Dynasty* (New York: Macmillan, 1986).

45. Bunney, W. E., Jr., and Davis, J. M., Norepinephrine in depressive reactions: A review, *Arch. Gen. Psychiat,* 1965, 13, 483–94 (quotations from pp. 491–92).

46. Schildkraut, J. J., The catecholamine hypothesis of affective disorders: A review of the supporting evidence, *Am. J. Psychiat.,* 1965, 122, 509–22 (quotation

from 509). See also Prange, A. J., Jr., The pharmacology and biochemistry of depression, *Dis. Nerv. Syst.*, 1964, 25, 217–21.

47. Other mechanisms Schildkraut mentioned that could account for low levels of norepinephrine activity, despite normal levels of the neurotransmitter, included a decrease (or increase in the case of mania) in norepinephrine biosynthesis rate, impairment of the capacity to store epinephrine, increased extracellular release that would lead to excessive degradation by monoamine oxydase, and a decrease in the number of the sensitivity of norepinephrine receptors.

48. Schildkraut, J., and Kety S. S., Biogenic amines and emotion, *Science*, 1967, 156, 21–30 (quotation from p. 25).

49. For example, it is no longer believed that norepinephrine is critical to the "brain reward system" or to lithium effectiveness in treating bipolar mood disorders.

50. Carlsson, A., Rationale and design of a selective inhibitor of 5-HT reuptake, *British Journal of Clinical Practice: A Symposium*, 1982, 19, 19–22.

51. Woolley, D. W., and Shaw, E., A biochemical and pharmacological suggestion about certain mental disorders, *Science*, 1954, 119, 587–88.

52. It has been reported Woolley and Shaw corresponded with Gaddum about which of them had been the first to propose a relationship between brain serotonin and mental illness. The evidence suggests that the idea occurred to them independently. See comment by Arvid Carlsson in Healy, D., *The Psychopharmacologists* (London: Chapman & Hall, 1966), pp. 52–53.

53. The conference was published in the *Annals of the New York Academy of Sciences*, 14 March 1957, vol. 66, pp. 417–840. The term "psychotomimetic" was proposed by Ralph Gerard to designate substances such as LSD that produced hallucinations and other mind-altering states that occur in the psychoses. Walter Loewe had suggested the term "phrenotropic," because of its broader implication, but it was never widely used. The term "ataraxic" was introduced to designate drugs that produced a state of "detachment" or "indifference."

54. Gaddum, J. H., Serotonin-LSD interactions, *Annals of the New York Academy of Sciences*, 1956, pp. 643–48.

55. Brodie, B. B., and Shore, P. A., A concept for a role of serotonin and norepinephrine as chemical mediators in the brain, in *Annals of the New York Academy of Sciences*, 1957, pp. 631–42.

56. Hasse's "handwriting test" is described by Hans Hippius in Healy, D., *The Psychopharmacologist* (London: Chapman and Hall, 1996), p. 201.

57. The substantia nigra of the brain has a black appearance because of melanin, which is a precursor of dopamine.

58. Carlsson, A., Lindqvist, M., and Magnusson, T., 3,4, Dihydroxyphenylalanine and 5-hydroxytryptophan as reserpine antagonists, *Nature*, 1957, 180, 1200.

59. Hornykiewicz, O., From dopamine to Parkinson's disease: A personal research record, in Samson, F., and Adelman, G., eds., *The Neurosciences: Paths of Discovery II* (Boston: Birkhaüser, 1992), pp. 125–46 (quotation from p. 130).

60. Cotzius, G. C., Van Woert, J., and Schiffer, I. M., Aromatic amino acids and modification of parkinsonism. *New Eng. J. Medicine*, 1967, 276, 374–79.

61. Langley, J. N., The autonomic nervous system, *Brain*, 1903, 26, 1–26.

62. Clark, A. J., *The Mode of Action of Drugs on Cells* (Baltimore: Williams and Wilkins, 1933).

63. Ibid. (quotation from p. 47).

64. Van Rossum, J. M., The significance of dopamine-receptor blockade for the action of neuroleptic drugs, in Brill, H., Cole, J., Deniker, P., Hippius P., and Bradley, P., *Neuro-Psycho-Pharmacology, Proceedings of the Fifth International Congress of the Collegium Internationale Neuro-Psycho-Pharmacologicum* (Amsterdam: Excerpta Medica Foundation, 1967), pp. 321–29 (quotation from p. 327).

65. Seeman, P., Dopamine receptors and psychosis, *Scientific American*, 1995, vol. 2 (September/October), 28–37.

66. For a review of the work of Philip Seeman and his colleagues, see Seeman, P., Dopamine receptors and psychosis, *Scientific American*, 1995, 2, 28–37. Solomon Snyder has presented a clear view of some of this history in Chapter 3 of his book *Drugs and the Brain* (New York: Scientific American Library, 1986).

67. Snyder, S. H., *Brainstorming: The Science and Politics of Opiate Research* (Cambridge, Mass.: Harvard University Press, 1989), pp. 174–75.

68. Amphetamine is often referred to on the street as "speed." The phrase "speed kills" may be justified by the fact that the paranoid delusions and poor judgment of people on high amphetamine doses are likely to lead to behavior that is dangerous to themselves and to others. See Connell, P. H., *Amphetamine Psychosis* (London: Chapman & Hill, 1958).

69. Amphetamine enhances norepinephrine, dopamine, and serotonin by causing these neurotransmitters to be released into the synapse and by prolonging their action by interfering with their reuptake into the neuron that had released them.

70. There were several experiments in which human volunteers given high doses of amphetamine began to hallucinate and have delusional thought processes resembling those seen in schizophrenia. See Angrist, B., and Sudilovsky, A., Central nervous stimulants: Historical aspects and clinical effects, in Iverson, L. L., Iverson, S. D., and Snyder S., eds., *Handbook of Psychopharmacology*, vol. 2, New York and London, Plenum, 1978, pp. 99–165; Janowsky, D. S., El-Yousef, M. F., Davis, J. M., and Sereke, H. S., Provocation of schizophrenic symptoms by intraveous injection of methylphenidate, *Archiv. of Gen. Psychiatry*, 1973, 28, 185–91.

71. Following high doses of amphetamine, laboratory rats, the species most commonly used in these studies, began to move their heads back and forth and sniff continuously at the same spot. The higher the dose of amphetamine the sooner the rats started this "stereotyped behavior" and the longer it persisted. Since it is not possible to demonstrate schizophrenia in animals, "stereotyped behavior" was widely accepted as an experimentally useful model of "amphetamine psychosis," which it was hoped would provide some insight into schizophrenia and the action of antipsychotic drugs. Randrup, A., and Munkvad, I., Stereotyped activities produced by amphetamine in several animal species and man, *Psychopharmacologia*, 1967, 11, 300–304.

72. Rylander, G., Preludin narkomaner från klinisk och medicinsk-kriminologisk synpunkt, *Svenska Lakartidningen*, 1966, 63, 49–73.

73. Ellinwood, E. H., Jr., and Sudilovsky, A., Chronic amphetamine intoxication: Behavioral model of psychoses, in Cole, J. O., Freedman, A. M., and Friedhoff, A. J., eds., *Psychopathology and Psychopharmacology* (Baltimore: Johns Hopkins University Press, 1973), pp. 51–70.

74. The "second messenger" that is suspected of being affected by lithium is phosphatidyl-insitol-bis-phosphate (PIP2).

75. Post, R. M., Weiss, S. R. B., and Chaung, D.-M., Mechanisms of action of anticonvulsants in affective disorders: Comparison with lithium, *J. Clin. Psychopharmacology,* 1992, 12 (Suppl.), 23s–35s.

76. Hans Mohler, working under the auspices of the Roche drug company in Basel, and Claus Braestrup and Richard Squires of the Ferrosan drug company in Denmark performed the basic studies that led to the identification of the benzodiazepine receptors.

77. Essentially, competitive binding studies determine the relative capacity of different drugs to bind to the same receptors by placing them in competition with each other. A given amount of radioactive Drug A will bind to receptors. This can be determined by washing away all the unbound radioactive drug and measuring the remaining radioactive drug bound to membranes in a scintillation counter. After determining a measure of the binding capacity of Drug A, an equal amount of Drug B is mixed in solution with it. If the two drugs have equal strength in binding to the receptors, then the residual amount of radioactive Drug A will be reduced by one-half. In this way, the relative binding affinity of different drugs can be determined.

78. Buspirone has been marketed since 1986 by Meade Johnson under the trade name BuSpar. BuSpar, which has been reported to bind to both dopamine and serotonin receptors, takes longer to alleviate anxiety than the benzodiazepines. It is recommended for chronic anxiety, while the benzodiazepines, which have more abuse potential, are recommended for acute anxiety.

4. A Closer Look at the Evidence

1. Carlsson, A., Trying to understand the brain's chemical language, in Samson, F., and Adelman, G., eds., *The Neurosciences: Paths of Discovery II* (Boston: Birkhaüser, 1992), pp. 107–22.

2. Schildkraut, J. J., and Kety, S. S., Biogenic amines and emotion, *Science,* 1967, 156, 21–30 (quotation from p. 24).

3. Mendels, J., and Frazer, A., Brain biogenic amine depletion and mood, *Arch. Gen. Psychiatry,* 1974, 30, 447–51; see also Janowsky et al., *Lancet,* 1972, 2, 632–35.

4. Bernstein, S., and Kaufman, M. R., A psychological analysis of apparent depression following Rauwolfia therapy, *J. Mt Sinai Hospital,* 1960, 27, 525–30. Note that Bernstein and Kaufman's prospective study included a careful baseline study of the patients before reserpine treatment, and the patients were seen regularly throughout treatment and afterward.

5. Davies, D. L., and Shepherd, M., Reserpine in the treatment of anxious and depressed patients, *Lancet,* 1955, ii, 117–20.

6. David Healy (The psychopharmacological era: notes toward a history, *J. Psychopharmacology*, 1990, 4, 152–67; see p. 154) remarked that it is interesting that the results of an exceptionally well-controlled Davies and Shepherd study were overlooked while reports of uncontrolled observations about reserpine causing depression were repeatedly cited. In the Davies and Shepherd study patients were randomly assigned between drug and placebo control groups, and a double-blind procedure was employed so that neither patients nor staff knew whether drug or placebo had been administered.

7. Alpha-methyl-para-tyrosine (AMPT) selectively depletes the brain of the catecholamines, norepineprine and dopamine, while parachlorophenylalanine (PCPA) blocks the synthesis of serotonin. The basic amino acid building block of the catecholamines is tyrosine, while tryptophan is the amino acid basic to serotonin.

8. The drug levoprotoline (developed by Ciba-Geigy in Basel), for example, was reported to alleviate depression, but it did not have much effect on either serotonin or norepinephrine. See Kuhn, R., *J. of Psychopharmacology*, 1990, 127.

9. Physostigmine and some organophosphate insecticides prolong acetylcholine activity by reducing the enzyme cholinesterase, which breaks down (inactivates) acetylcholine.

10. Hofstatter, L., and Girgis, M., Psychotic depression: The common therapeutic principle, *Southern Medical Journal*, 1980, 73, 870–72 (quotation from p. 872).

11. Willner, P., Dopamine mechanisms in depression, in Bloom, F. E., and Kupfer, D. J., eds., *Psychopharmacology: The Fourth Generation* (New York: Raven, 1995), pp. 921–31.

12. The main metabolite of norepinephrine is MHPG (3-methoxy-4-hydroxyphenylglycol), while 5-HIAA (5-hydroxyindoleacetic acid) is the primary serotonin metabolite.

13. Nuland, S. B., The pill of pills (review of *Listening to Prozac*), *New York Review of Books*, 9 June 1994, XLI. no. 11, 4–8.

14. Wurtman, J., and Suffes, S., *The Serotonin Solution: The Potent Brain Chemical That Can Help You Stop Bingeing, Lose Weight, and Feel Great* (New York: Fawcett Columbine, 1996), quotation from p. 18.

15. See Asberg, J., et al., Serotonin depression—a biochemical subgroup within the affective disorders, *Science*, 1976, 191, 478–81.

16. Coppen, A., Indoleamines and affective disorders, *J. Psychiatric Research*, 1972, 9, 163–71.

17. Asberg, M., Träskman, L., and Thorén, P., 5-HIAA in the cerebrospinal fluid: A biochemical suicide predictor? *Archives of General Psychiatry*, 1976, 33, 1193–97. See also Asberg, M., Thorén, P., Träskman, L., Bertilsson, L., and Ringberger, V., Serotonin depression: A biochemical subgroup within the affective disorders, *Science*, 1976, 191, 478–80.

18. Higley, J. D., Suomi, S. J., and Linnoila, M., A nonhuman primate model of Type II alcoholism? Part 2, Diminished social competence and excessive aggression correlates with low cerebrospinal fluid 5-hydroxyindoleacetic acid concentrations, *Alcoholism: Clinical and Experimental Research*, 1996, 20, 643–50.

19. See, for example, the supplementary issue of *The Journal of Clinical Psychiatry* entitled "New Uses for Antidepressants" (1997, vol. 58, suppl. 14).

20. We know something about some physiological effects of receptor subtypes. For example, it is claimed that certain subclasses of receptors are mainly "autoreceptors," located on the cells that secrete that same neurotransmitter to communicate with other cells. "Autoreceptors" are believed to mainly have an inhibitory effect, slowing the activity of neurons and thus decreasing the amount of neurotransmitter they release. However, we know virtually nothing about the consequences of those physiological effects for behavioral and psychological variables.

21. Most readers have probably heard of "beta blockers," drugs which are given this name to indicate that they block the "beta," rather than the "alpha" noradrenergic (norepinephrine) receptor subtype. The most commonly used "beta blocker" is propranolol, which slows heart rate, especially under conditions of increased demand. Propranolol is prescribed for cardiac arrhythmia, angina pain, and hypertension. Two types of beta adrenergic receptors have been identified: B_1, found mostly in the heart, and B_2, found mostly in smooth muscles.

22. A technique for finding compounds that bind selectively to a particular receptor involves a plate with ninety-six small wells. Each well contains neuronal tissue known to have a particular receptor, for example, dopamine D_2 receptors, and a radioactive drug that binds to these receptors. Different chemical compounds can be put in each well, and if one of them is able to bind to these particular dopamine receptors it will compete with the radioactive drug and reduce the amount of radioactivity bound to the receptors. This reduction can be detected by a "scintillation counter," which can measure the amount of radioactivity bound to the receptors. When a compound that competes at a receptor site is discovered, it can be systematically subdivided (fractionated) until the active ingredient has been identified and chemically characterized. With this method, several hundred thousand compounds can be screened in a six-month period, a task that—if it could be done at all—would have taken many years to accomplish by other methods.

23. The tricyclic antidepressants potentiate the action of the amine neurotransmitters by blocking their reuptake and thereby prolonging their action. Prozac has a similar action, but its action is thought to be restricted to serotonin. Prozac and similar drugs now being marketed are called "selective serotonin reuptake inhibitors" (SSRIs). Prozac was introduced in 1986 and by 1994 it had been prescribed for more than 10 million people (Barondes, S., Thinking about Prozac, *Science*, 1994, 203, 1102–1103). The figures for the sales of Prozac and Zoloft were estimated by I.M.S. America, a market research company based in Plymouth Meeting, Pennsylvania.

24. Flesinoxin is claimed to act as a serotonin agonist at both pre- and postsynaptic serotonin receptors. It is difficult therefore to know what the net effect will be on serotonin activity.

25. The antidepressant amfebutamone drug Nomifensene is claimed to block mainly the reuptake of dopamine and norepinephrine. Also see Kapur, S., and Mann, J. J., Role of the dopaminergic system in depression, *Biological Psychiatry*, 1992, 32, 1–17.

26. Baldessarini, R. J., Drugs and the treatment of psychiatric disorders: Depression and mania, in Hardman, J. G., and Limbird, L. E., eds.-in-chief, *Pharmacological Basis of Therapeutics* (New York: McGraw-Hill, 1996), Chapter 19 (quotation from p. 453).

27. Duman, R. S., Heninger, G. R., and Nestler, E. J., A molecular theory of depression, *Arch. Gen. Psychiatr.*, 1997, 54, 597–606.

28. Hollister, L., *Chemical Psychosis: LSD and Related Drugs* (Springfield, Ill.: Thomas, 1968).

29. Seeman, P., Lee, T., Chau-Wong, M., and Wong, K., Antipsychotic drug doses and neuroleptic/dopamine receptors, *Nature.* 1976, 261, 177–79; Creese, I., Burt, D. R., and Snyder, S. H., Dopamine receptor binding predicts clinical and pharmacological potencies of antischizophrenic drugs, *Science*, 1976, 192, 481–83.

30. Snyder, S. H., *Drugs and the Brain* (New York: Scientific American Books, 1986), p. 80.

31. Seeman, P., Dopamine receptors and psychosis, *Scientific American*, 1995, 2 (Sept./Oct.), 28–37 (quotation from p. 35).

32. Lee, T., Seeman, P., Tourtellotte, W. W., Farley, I. J., and Hornykeiwicz, Binding of ^{3}H-neuroleptics and ^{3}H-apomorphine in schizophrenic brains, *Nature,* 1978, 274, 897–900. To do these receptor binding studies they used a radioactive form of the antischizophrenic drug haloperidol and estimated the amount of radiation in three different brain regions (caudate, putamen, and nucleus accumbens) known to be terminal areas of dopamine pathways.

33. Seeman, P., op. cit.

34. Kornhuber, J., Riederer, P., Reynolds, G. P., Beckman, H., Jellinger, K., and Gabriel, E., ^{3}H-Spiperone binding sites in postmortem brains from schizophrenic patients: Relationship to neuroleptic drug treatment, abnormal movements, and positive symptoms, *J. Neural Transm.*, 1989, 75, 1–10.

35. Carlsson, A., Early psychopharmacology and the rise of modern brain research. *Journal of Psychopharmacology*, 1990, 4, 120–26 (information cited on p. 123). The PET studies were done by injecting living schizophrenic patients with radioactive drugs that bind to dopamine receptors. The PET brain scanner can detect the amount of radioactivity bound to different brain regions.

36. In one study, it was reported that there is a tendency of dopamine neurons to release abnormally high levels of dopamine when challenged by stimulating drugs, such as amphetamine, or by stress. These results suggest that it is not the dopamine receptors that are abnormal, but that too much dopamine is secreted when schizophrenics undergo stress. Here too, the results may be difficult to replicate, as the studies indicate that the tendency to secrete high levels of dopamine may at best be characteristic of less than a third of the schizophrenic patients examined. It is not reasonable to consider a finding that applies to less than one-third of schizophrenics as a cause of the disorder. Breier, A., et al., Schizophrenia is associated with elevated amphetamine-induced synaptic dopamine concentrations: Evidence from a novel positron emission tomography method, *Proc. Natl. Acad. Sci.*, 1997, 94, 2569–74. See also Laruelle, M., et al., *Proc. Natl. Acad. Sci.*, 1996, 93, 9235–40.

37. Sokoloff, P., Giros, M-P., Martres, M-L., Bouthenet, J-C., and Schwartz, Molecular cloning and characterization of a novel dopamine receptor (D_3) as a target for neuroleptics, *Nature*, 1990, 347, 146–51.

38. Some preliminary results reported by Pierre Sokoloff suggested that drugs that activate D_3 receptors tend to increase exploratory locomotor activity in animals, whereas the traditional antipsychotics tend to produce sedation. Targeting schizophrenia: Pierre Sokoloff on dopamine receptors (Interview with Pierre Sokoloff), *Science Watch*. 1994, 5 (July/August), 3–4.

39. The neurological condition called tardive dyskinesia refers to the fact that the motor impairment that characterizes this disorder normally appears after prolonged treatment with antipsychotic drugs. At first, patients exhibit twitches of the face and tongue. With progression the movement disorders include the shoulders, arms, and possibly the entire body. The facial twitches often involve the tongue darting in and out of the mouth in a manner that is both embarrassing and debilitating.

40. Okubo, Y., et al., Decreased prefrontal dopamine D_1 in schizophrenia revealed by PET. *Nature*. 1997, 385, 634–36.

41. Baldessarini, R. J., Antipsychotic agents, in Baldessarini, R. J. ed., *Chemotherapy in Psychiatry: Principles and Practice*, 2d ed. (Cambridge: Harvard University Press, 1985), pp. 14–92. One of the effects of dopamine is to inhibit pituitary gland secretion of prolactin, the hormone that stimulates milk production. One effect of antipsychotic drugs is to block the dopamine inhibition of prolactin, which has been shown to increase long before any psychiatric benefit is achieved. There has been a recent suggestion that a subpopulation of schizophrenics may respond more rapidly to antipsychotic drug treatment. See Garver, D. L., et al., Etiologic heterogeneity of the psychoses: Is there a dopamine psychosis? *Neuropharmacology*, 1997, 16, 191–201.

42. Grace, A. A., *Neuroscience*, 1991, 41, 1–24; Carlsson, M., and Carlsson, A., *Trends in Neuroscience*, 1990, 13, 272–76; Grace, A. A., Bunney, B. S., Moore, H., and Todd, C. L., Dopamine-cell depolarization block as a model for the therapeutic actions of antipsychotic drugs, *Trends in Neuroscience*, 1997, 20, 31–37.

43. Kraepelin, E., Zur diagnose und prognose der dementia praecox. *Allg. Z. Psychiat.*, 1899, 56, 254–64.

44. Only the term *paranoid schizophrenia*—referring to the prevalence of delusional ideas—is used today. *Simple schizophrenia* designated profound withdrawal and lack of interest, initiative, and drive. *Hebephrenia* referred to patients whose behavior seemed "silly"—often giggling inappropriately. *Catatonic schizophrenia* applied to individuals who were generally mute and often rigid, maintaining the same posture for hours. *Dementia* is now used mainly in cases of known (or highly suspected) brain pathology, such as senile dementia, and rarely is it used to refer to schizophrenic thought processes.

45. Bleuler, E., *Dementia Praecox or the Group of Schizophrenics* (New York: International University Press, 1950; originally published in German in 1911).

46. A study headed by the British psychiatrist John Cooper compared the admission diagnoses at two representative London and New York hospitals. The high rate of schizophrenia at the New York hospitals was demonstrated to be com-

pletely due to differences in diagnostic criteria. Cooper, J. E., et al., *Psychiatric Diagnosis in New York and London* (New York: Oxford University Press, 1972).

47. The distinction between positive and negative symptoms was first described in 1974 (Strauss, J. S., Carpenter, W. T., Jr., and Bartko, J. J., The diagnosis and understanding of schizophrenia: Part III, Speculations on the processes that underlie schizophrenic symptoms and signs, *Schizophrenia Bulletin*. 1974, 11, 61–69). More recently psychiatrist Timothy Crow argued that positive and negative symptoms distinguish between two etiologically and prognostically separate schizophrenic subtypes (*British Medical Journal*, 1980, 280, 66–68).

48. Crow, T. J., and Johnstone, E. C., Schizophrenia: Nature of the disease process and its biological correlates, *Handbook of Physiology—The Nervous System V*, ed. Mountcastle, V. (Bethesda, MD: American Physiological Society, 1987), pp. 843–69.

49. For example, it is not clear whether "response stereotypy"—the tendency to repeat certain activities over and over again—should be considered a Type 1 or Type 2 symptom. For evidence of patients having an overlap of Type 1 and Type 2 symptoms, see Sommers, A. A., "Negative symptoms": Conceptual and methodological problems, *Schizophrenia Bulletin*, 1985, 11, 364–79.

50. The problem with the "atypical antipsychotic" clozapine is that it can produce a condition called agranular cytosis (reduced white blood cells) that can sometimes be fatal because of the lowered resistance to infection. Among other adverse side effects of many antipsychotic drugs, in addition to those mentioned in the text, are galactorrhea (spontaneous flow of milk from the nipples) and oligomenorrhea (abnormal menstrual blood flow).

51. The overall effectiveness of psychiatric drug treatment is usually stated to be between 60 and 70 percent, but this figure would be much lower if the 20 to 30 percent of patients who are estimated to improve without drug treatment were taken into consideration.

52. Kane, J., Current perspectives on the pharmacological treatment of schizophrenia, lecture delivered to the Department of Psychiatry, University of Michigan School of Medicine, 2 March 1994.

53. Mathews, S. M., et al., A non-neuroleptic treatment of schizophrenia: Analysis of the two-year post discharge risk of relapse, *Schizophrenia Bulletin*, 1985, 11, 31–42; Rapoport, M., et al., Are there schizophrenics for whom drugs may be unnecessary or contraindicated? *International Pharmacopsychiatry*, 1978, 13, 100–111; WHO, *Schizophrenia—An International Pilot Study*, Chichester, 1979.

54. Carlsson, A., Early psychopharmacology and the rise of modern brain research, *Journal of Psychopharmacology*, 1990, 4, 120–26.

55. Bunney, B. G., Bunney, W. E., Jr., and Carlsson, A., Schizophrenia and glutamate, in Bloom, F. E., and Kupfer, D. J., eds., *Psychopharmacology, the Fourth Generation of Progress* (New York: Raven, 1995), pp. 1205–14. See also Carlsson, A., Early psychopharmacology and the rise of modern brain research, *Journal of Psychopharmacology*, 1990, 4, 120–26.

56. Roth, B. L., and Meltzer, H. Y., The role of serotonin in schizophrenia, in Bloom, F. E., and Kupfer, D. J., eds., *Psychopharmacology, the Fourth Generation of Progress* (New York: Raven, 1995), pp. 1215–27.

57. Snyder, S. H., and Dawson, T. M., Nitric oxide and related substances as neural messengers, in Bloom, F. E., and Kupfer, D. J., eds., *Psychopharmacology, the Fourth Generation of Progress* (New York: Raven Press, 1995), pp. 609–18 (quotation from p. 609).

58. Carlsson, A., Rationale and design of a selective inhibitor of 5-HT reuptake, *British Journal of Clinical Practice: A Symposium,* 1982, 19, 19–22 (quotation from p. 19).

59. Iverson, L., Review of *The Psychopharmacologists, Science,* 1997, 275, 1438–39 (quotation from p. 1439).

60. Healy, D. T., The structure of psychopharmacological revolutions. *Psychiatric Developments,* 1987, 4, 349–76 (quotation from p. 359).

61. Herbert Meltzer quoted in Healy, D. *The Psychopharmacologists* (London: Chapman and Hall, 1996), pp. 449–50.

62. Schou, M., Forty years of lithium treatment, *Arch. of Gen. Psychiatry,* 1997, 54, 9–13 (quotation from p. 12).

63. For a concise critique of the limbic system see Joseph LeDoux's *The Emotional Brain: The Mysterious Underpinnings of Emotional Life* (New York: Simon and Schuster, 1996), pp. 85–103. For other critiques of the limbic system concept see Brodal, A. *Neurological Anatomy* (New York: Oxford University Press, 1982), and Kotter, R., and Meyer, N., The limbic system: A review of its empirical foundation, *Behavioral Brain Research,* 1992, 52, 105–27.

5. The Interpretation of the Evidence

1. Just in case the explanation did not occur to you, in most countries women are much more likely than men to have first names ending in a vowel, and on average, women are shorter. No causal relationship exists. It is not the ending vowels that cause women to be shorter than men.

2. It was found that following amphetamine injections, the dendrites of neurons in the nucleus accumbens and prefrontal cortex had increased significantly in length, and they contained a higher density of spines than did the neurons of animals treated with saline. Robinson, T. E., and Kolb, B., Persistent structural modification in nucleus accumbens and prefrontal cortex neurons produced by prior experience with amphetamine, *The Journal of Neuroscience,* 1997, 17, 8491–97.

3. Antelman, S. M., Eichler, A. J., Black, C. A., and Kocan, D., Interchangeability of stress and amphetamine sensitization, *Science,* 1980, 207, 329–31; Antelman, S. M., Stressor-induced sensitization to subsequent stress: Implications for the development and treatment of clinical disorders, in Kalivas, P. W., and Barnes, C. D., eds., *Sensitization in the Nervous System* (Caldwell, N.J.: Telford Press, 1988), pp. 227–54.

4. Wilcox, R. A., Robinson, T. E., and Becker, J. B., Enduring enhancement in amphetamine-stimulated striatal dopamine release in vitro produced by prior exposure to amphetamine or stress in vivo, *European J. Pharmacology,* 1986, 124, 375–76.

5. Sapolsky, R. M., Krey, L. C., and McEwen, B. S., The neuroendocrinology of stress and aging: The glucocorticoid cascade hypothesis, *Endocrine Reviews,* 1986,

7, 284–301; Sapolsky, R. M., *Stress, the Aging Brain, and the Mechanisms of Neuron Death* (Cambridge, Mass.: MIT Press, 1992).

6. Stewart, J., and Vezina, P., Conditioning and behavioral sensitization, in Kalivas, P. W., and Barnes, C. D., eds., *Sensitization in the Nervous System* (Caldwell, N.J.: Telford Press, 1988), pp. 207–24.

7. Much of the literature demonstrating how experience can modify brain development has been reviewed in Greenough, W. T., Black, J. E., and Wallace, C. S., Experience and brain development, *Child Development,* 1987, 58, 539–59.

8. Kandel, E. R., Cellular mechanisms of learning and the biological basis of individuality, in Kandel, E. R., Schwartz, J. H., and Jessell, T. M., *Principles of Neural Science* (San Francisco: W. H. Freeman, 1991), pp. 1009–31.

9. Jacobs, B., Schall, M., and Scheibel, A. B., A quantitative dendritic analysis of Wernicke's area in humans: II, Gender, hemispheric, and environmental factors, *J. Comparative Neurology,* 1993, 327, 97–111. An excellent review of much of the relevant literature on brain plasticity is presented in Kolb, B., Forgie, M., Gibb, R., Gorny, G., and Rowntree, S., Age, experience and the changing brain, *Neuroscience and Biobehavioral Reviews* (in press).

10. Breedlove, M., Sex on the brain, *Nature,* 23 October, 1997.

11. Schwartz, J. M., et al., Systematic changes in cerebral glucose metabolic rate after successful behavior modification treatment of obsessive-compulsive disorder, *Archives of General Psychiatry,* 1996, 53, 109–13.

12. Rauch S. L., et al., Regional cerebral blood flow measured during symptom provocation in obsessive-compulsive disorder using oxygen 15-labeled CO_2 and positron emission tomography, *Archives of General Psychiatry,* 1994, 51, 62–70.

13. Schachter, S. and Singer, J. E., Cognitive, social, and physiological determinants of emotional state, *Psychological Review,* 1962, 69, 379–99.

14. Carroll, B. J., et al., Diagnosis of endogenous depression: Comparison of clinical, research, and neuroendocrine criteria, *Journal of Affective Disorders,* 1980, 2, 177–94.

15. Albala, A. A., et al., Changes in serial dexamethasone suppression tests among unipolar depressives receiving electroconvulsive treatment, *Biological Psychiatry,* 1981, 16, 551–60.

16. Mullen, P. E., Linsell, C. R., and Parker, D., Influence of sleep disturbance and calorie restriction on biological markers of depression, *Lancet,* 1986, 1051–54.

17. Bignami, G., Disease models and reductionist thinking in the bio-medical sciences, in Rose, S., ed., *Against Biological Determinism* (London: Allison & Busby, 1982), pp. 94–110.

18. Cited in Reichman, D., Guidelines coming on ADD diagnosis, Associated Press, 21 July 1996.

19. Rapoport, J. L., Buchsbaum, M. S., Zahn, T. P., Weingartner, H., Ludlow, C., and Mikkelsen, E. J., Dextroamphetamine: Cognitive and behavioral effects in normal prepubertal boys, *Science,* 1978, 199, 560–63 (quotation from p. 562).

20. For a further discussion of the relation of treatments to causes see Valenstein, E. S., Causes and treatments of mental disorders, in Valenstein, E. S., ed., *The Psychosurgery Debate* (San Francisco: W. H. Freeman, 1980), pp. 314–33.

21. For some examples of *ex juvantibus* reasoning in psychiatry, see Bignami, G., Disease models and reductionist thinking in the biomedical sciences, in Rose, S., ed., *Against Biological Determinism: The Dialectics of Biology Group* (London and New York: Allison and Busby, 1982), pp. 94–110.

22. Endler, N. S., *Holiday of Darkness: A Psychologist's Personal Journey Out of His Depression* (New York: John Wiley, 1982).

23. Although ECT produced dramatic improvement, Endler became alternately manic and depressed afterward. Eventually lithium was prescribed and for the three-year period during which lithium was taken regularly, Endler had no mood swings and functioned as he had before his illness.

24. See criticism of the book *Violence and the Brain* by Vernon Mark and Frank Ervin (New York: Harper & Row, 1970) in Valenstein, E. S., Physical intervention into the human brain: Ethical and scientific considerations, in McCabe O. L., ed., *Changing Human Behavior,* (New York: Grune & Stratton, 1977), pp. 129–50. See also Valenstein, E. S., *Brain Control* (New York: Wiley Interscience, 1973).

25. The drug Yohimbine blocks some norepinephrine receptors, and this leads to an increased firing rate of neurons that secrete norepinephrine and resulting high levels of MHPG, a norepinephrine metabolite. See Charney, D. S., Heninger, G. R., and Breier, A., Noradrenergic function in panic anxiety: Effects of Yohimbine in healthy subjects and patients with agoraphobia and panic disorder, *Arch. Gen. Psychiatry,* 1984, 41, 751–63. The results of a study of the effect of Yohimbine administered to Vietnam veterans was reported by Dr. Dennis Charney in a lecture to the Psychiatry Department of the University of Michigan's School of Medicine on 19 November 1997.

26. Liebowitz, M. R., et al., Lactate provocation of panic attacks, *Arch. Gen. Psychiatry,* 1984, 41, 764–70.

27. Bowden, M. L., and Hopwood, N. J., Psychosocial dwarfism: Identification, intervention and planning, *Social Work in Health Care,* 1982, 7, 15–36.

28. This tale is slightly modified from one described in Kety, S. S., A biologist examines the mind and behavior, *Science,* 1960, 132.

29. Diamond, M. C., *Enriching Heredity: The Impact of the Environment on the Anatomy of the Brain* (New York: The Free Press, 1988).

30. Suddath, R. L., et al., Anatomical abnormalities in the brains of monozygotic twins discordant for schizophrenia, *New England Journal of Medicine,* 1990, 48, 357–61.

31. LeVay, S., *The Sexual Brain* (Cambridge, Mass.: MIT Press, 1993); Ward, L., and Ward, O. B., Sexual behavior differentiation: Effects of prenatal manipulations in rats, in Adler, N., Pfaff, D., and Goy, R., eds., *Handbook of Behavioral Neurobiology,* vol. 7 (New York: Plenum, 1985), pp. 77–98.

32. Alzheimer, A., Beitrage zur pathologischen Anatomie der Dementia praecox, *Allgemeine Z. Psychiatrie,* 1913, 70, 810–12.

33. Plum, F., Neuropathological findings, in Kety, S. S., and Matthysse, S., eds., *Prospects for Research on Schizophrenia, Neuroscience Program Research Bulletin,* 1972, 10, 384–88.

34. Wyatt, R. J., Neurodevelopmental abnormalities and schizophrenia, *Archives of General Psychiatry,* 1996, 53, 11–15.

35. There have also been some studies of the brains of patients with obsessive-compulsive disorder. These studies used positron emission tomography (PET) scans, computerized-tomography (C-T) scans, and computerized averaging of magnetic resonance imaging (MRI) scans. For brief reviews of this literature and references to specific research see Williamson, P. C., Schizophrenia as a brain disease, *Archives of Neurology,* 1993, 50, 1096–97; Taubes, G., Averaged brains pinpoint a site for schizophrenia, *Science,* 1994, 266, 221.

36. Weinberger, D. R., Berman, K. F., and Zec, R. F., Physiological dysfunction of the dorsolateral prefrontal cortex in schizophrenia: I, Regional blood flow evidence, *Archives of General Psychiatry,* 1986, 43, 114–24.

37. Goldman-Rakic, P., Dissolution of cerebral cortical mechanisms in subjects with schizophrenia, in Watson, S., ed., *Biology of Schizophrenia and Affective Disease* (Washington, D.C.: American Psychiatric Press, 1995), 113–27.

38. There are reports that the amygdala, hippocampus, entorhinal cortex, and parahippocampal gyrus in the brains of schizophrenics tend to be significantly smaller than they are in normals. For one example, see Suddath, R. L., et al., Anatomic abnormalities in the brains of monozygotic twins discordant for schizophrenia, *New Eng. J. Med.,* 1990, 62–67.

39. Andreasen, N. C., et al., Thalamic abnormalities in schizophrenia visualized through magnetic resonance image averaging, *Science,* 1994, 266, 294; Taubes, G., Averaged brains pinpoint a site for schizophrenia, *Science,* 1994, 266, 221.

40. A recent article has reviewed a number of the reports of brain anomalies claimed to have been found in schizophrenics and depressed patients. See Andreasen, N. C., Linking mind and brain in the study of mental illness: A project for a scientific psychopathology, *Science,* 1997, 275, 1586–93. See also the study by Eric Hollander of the Mount Sinai Medical Center in New York in the February 1996 issue of the *Archives of General Psychiatry.*

41. Andreasen, N. C., op. cit., p. 1590.

42. There is an eminently readable review of the genetics of mental disorders in Chapter 9 of Steen, R. G., *DNA & Destiny, Nature and Nurture in Human Behavior* (New York: Plenum, 1996).

43. This figure may be on the high side. More recent estimates of the concordance rate for identical twins are between 25 and 29 percent, and an estimate of a maximum of 2 percent (not far from the base rate for the general population) for second-degree relatives (nieces, nephews, aunts, and uncles). Walker, E., and Grimes, K., Genetic counseling for schizophrenia, *Clinical Advances in the Treatment of Psychiatric Disorders* (A KSF Publication), 1991, 5, 1–10.

44. A study had reported that a gene marker had been found on chromosome 11 in a population of Old Order Amish (Egeland, J. A. et al., Bipolar affective disorder linked to DNA markers on chromosome 11, *Nature,* 1987, 325, 783–87). Several other studies failed to replicate these results and several of the original authors retracted their original report. See Steen, R. G., op. cit., pp. 142–46, for references and a more complete discussion of these studies.

45. See Healy, D. T., op. cit., pp. 155–56.

46. Healy, D., Psychopharmacology in the new medical state, in Healy, D., and Doogan, D. P., eds., *Psychotropic Drug Development: Social, Economic and Pharmacological Aspects* (London: Chapman & Hall Medical, 1996), pp. 13–40 (quotation from pp. 30–31).

47. Solomon, A., Anatomy of melancholy, *The New Yorker*, 12 January 1998, pp. 46–61.

48. Shorter, E., *A History of Psychiatry: From the Era of the Asylum to the Age of Prozac* (New York: John Wiley, 1997), p. 296.

49. Szasz, T. S., *The Myth of Mental Illness: Foundations of a Theory of Personal Conduct* (New York: Hoeber-Harper, 1961; revised 1974); Szasz, T. S., *Law, Liberty, and Psychiatry: An Inquiry into the Social Uses of Mental Health Practices* (New York: Macmillan, 1965); Szasz, T. S., *Psychiatric Justice* (New York: Macmillan, 1965); *The Manufacture of Madness: A Comparative Study of the Inquisition and the Mental Health Movement* (New York: Harper & Row, 1970); *Law, Liberty and Psychiatry* (New York: Macmillan, 1963); *Psychiatric Slavery* (New York: Free Press, 1977).

50. Szasz, T. S., What counts as a disease? *Canad. Med. Assoc. Journal*, 1986, 135, 859–60. The views of the psychiatrist Peter Breggin are quite similar to those of Thomas Szasz. Breggin believes that psychiatric institutions and drug treatment are often used to incarcerate and subdue people who are unwanted and inconvenient, rather than for treating people with illnesses. See Breggin, P., *Psychiatric Drugs: Hazards to the Brain* (New York: Springer, 1983), pp. 55–56.

51. Szasz, T. S., *The Myth of Psychotherapy* (New York: Anchor/Doubleday, 1978), Preface, p. xv.

52. Szasz, T. S., What counts as a disease? *Canad. Med. Assoc. Journal*, 1986, 135, 859–60.

53. Clouston, T. S., *Clinical Lectures on Mental Disease*, 6th ed. (London: Churchill, 1904).

54. Moore, J. W., The syphilis–general paralysis question, *Review of Neurology and Psychiatry*, 1910, 8, 259–71; Noguchi, H., and Moore, J. W., Demonstrations of *Spirochaeta pallida* in brain in cases of general paralysis, *J. Exper. Med.*, 1913, 17, 232.

55. Similar arguments can be made from the gradual realization that many people thought to be psychotic early in the century were actually suffering from pellagra (a deficiency of the B vitamin niacin). Idiopathic epilepsy and migraine headaches are disorders whose cause is not known today, but many believe that a physical cause will eventually be found. A similar controversy exists over the cause of autism.

56. Pert, C., quoted in the *Baltimore Evening Sun* (special reprint) 23–24 July 1984, p. 3.

57. Mohl, P. statement made at the 1986 American Psychiatric Association, as quoted in Data accumulating to support concept that psychotherapy is biologic treatment, *Clin. Psychiatric News*, 1986, 14, 1, 28.

58. Szasz, T., What counts as disease? *Canad. Med. Assoc. J.*, 1986, 135, 859–60 (quotation from p. 859).

59. Cartwright, S. A., Report on the diseases and physical peculiarities of the negro race. *New Orleans Medical and Surgical Journal,* May 1851, p. 709.

60. Stover, E., and Nightingale, E. O., eds., *The Breaking of Bodies and Minds: Torture, Psychiatric Abuse and the Health Professions* (New York: W. H. Freeman, 1985).

61. Ennis, B., *Prisoners of Psychiatry: Mental Patients, Psychiatrists, and the Law* (New York: Harcourt Brace Jovanovich, 1972). See pp. vii–viii.

62. Kesey, K., *One Flew Over the Cuckoo's Nest* (New York: Viking Press, 1962).

63. Breggin, P., *Psychiatric Drugs: Hazards to the Brain* (New York: Springer, 1983), pp. 55–56.

64. For an excellent description of Kraepelin's evolving classification system for mental disorders and his influence and his critics, see Shorter, E., *A History of Psychiatry* (New York: John Wiley, 1997), pp. 99–109.

65. Meyer, A., Letter to Samuel Orton, 25 April, 1919. Cited by Grob, G. N., Origins of DSM-I: A study in appearance and reality. *Amer. J. Psychiatry,* 1991, 148, 421–31 (see p. 426).

66. Orton, S. T., On the classification of nervous and mental diseases, *Am. J. Insanity,* 1919, 76, 131–44.

67. The medical historian Gerald Grob has described the events leading up to the publication of the first edition of the *Diagnostic and Statistical Manual: Mental Disorders (DSM-*I) in 1952. Grob, G. N., Origins of DSM-I: A study in appearance and reality, *Am. J. Psychiatry,* 1991 148, 421–31.

68. Cited in Shorter, E., *A History of Psychiatry* (New York: John Wiley, 1997), p. 299.

69. Ibid., p. 297.

70. Kendell, R. E., et al., Diagnostic criteria of American and British psychiatrists, *Archives of General Psychiatry,* 1971, 25, 123–30.

71. Kirk, S. A., and Kutchins, H., "Is Bad Writing a Mental Disorder?" *The New York Times,* 20 June 1994, p. A11. For a fuller discussion of their criticisms of the *DSM,* see Kutchins, H., and Kirk, S. A. *Making Us Crazy: DSM: The Psychiatric Bible and the Creation of Mental Disorders* (New York: The Free Press, 1997).

72. Dumont, M. P., The nonspecificity of mental illness, *The American J. of Orthopsychiatry,* 1984, 54, 326–34 (quotation from pp. 327–28).

73. Goleman, D., "Scientist at Work. Allen J. Frances: Revamping Psychiatrists' Bible." *The New York Times,* 19 April 1994, p. C1.

6. How the Pharmaceutical Industry Promotes Drugs and Chemical Theories of Mental Illness

1. This is the title of a book examining the practices of the pharmaceutical industry in the Canadian province of Manitoba. Klass, A., *There's Gold in Them Thar Pills* (Middlesex: Penguin, 1975).

2. The sales of all pharmaceuticals were extrapolated from the World Health Organization calculation, which listed the pharmaceutical industry market at $43.6 billion in 1976 and $94.1 billion in 1985 (WHO, 1988, 7–15). Also, see *The*

Financial Times (16 March 1995, p. 11) for estimates of the sales of the ten most frequently prescribed psychotherapeutic drugs. Sven Borho, an analyst with Mehta & Isaly, a pharmaceutical securities firm in New York, estimated the 1995 sales of all antidepressant drugs. *The Wall Street Journal* reported that the 1996 sales of the selective serotonin reuptake inhibitors (SSRIs) alone was approximately $4.5 billion. Some of these figures have been provided by I.M.S. America, a market research company based in Plymouth Meeting, Pennsylvania.

3. Greenwood, J., Prescribing and salemanship, *HAI (Health Action International) News*, 1989, no. 48, 1–2, 11.

4. Interview with Frank Ayd in Healy, D., *The Psychopharmacologist: Interviews by Dr. David Healy* (London: Chapman & Hall, 1996), pp. 106–107.

5. Smith, J. A., The treatment of depression with drugs, in Davies, E. B., ed., *Depression: Proceeding of the Symposium Held at Cambridge 22 to 26 September 1959* (Cambridge: Cambridge University Press, 1964), pp. 196–206 (quotation from p. 206).

6. This "marketing blitz" is described in Ann Braden Johnson's *Out of Bedlam: The Truth about Deinstitutionalization* (New York: Basic Books, 1990).

7. Reminiscences of Mr. Charles Bolling and Mr. Frazier Cheston (product manager and director of hospital sales, respectively) of Smith Kline & French given in an interview by Swazey J., op. cit., pp. 202–207.

8. Swazey, J., op. cit., p. 160; Overholser, W., Has chlorpromazine inaugurated a new era in mental hospitals? *J. Clin. Exp. Psychpath.*, 1956, 17, 197–201.

9. Menninger, W. C., Facts and statistics of significance for psychiatry, *Bulletin Menninger Clinic*, 1948, 12, 1–25.

10. Deutsch, A., *The Shame of the States* (New York: Harcourt, Brace, 1948); Ward, M. J., *The Snake Pit* (New York: Random, House, 1946).

11. Fuller, R. G., Expectations of hospital life and outcome for mental patients on first admission (civil state hospitals, New York), *Psychiatric Quarterly*, 1930, 4, 295–323.

12. Johnson, A. B., *Out of Bedlam: The Truth about Deinstitutionalization* (New York: Basic Books, 1990).

13. Shepherd, M., Goodman, N., and Watt, D. C., The application of hospital statistics in the evaluation of pharmacotherapy in a psychiatric population, *Comp. Psychiat.*, 1961, 2, 11–19.; Odegaard, O., Pattern of discharge from Norwegian psychiatric hospitals before and after the introduction of psychiatric drugs, *Amer. J. Psychiat.*, 1964, 120, 772–78.

14. Shepherd, M., The present status of psychopharmacology, *J. Chron. Dis.* 1961, 13, 289–92. In 1992, for the first time, there were more mentally ill in state-financed group homes and apartments than in state hospitals, and in California there were only 3,736 patients in state psychiatric hospitals, while 340,000 state residents were receiving some mental health services in the community. Foderaro, L. W., "Mentally Ill Gaining New Rights," *The New York Times*, 14 October 1995, pp. 1 and 8. In Italy, a law (referred to as Law 180) prohibited the building of any new psychiatric hospitals and encouraged discharging patients and treating them in the community. Patients requiring hospitalization were to be placed in general

hospitals, but for shorter periods. Even though Italy's Law 180 was not passed until 1978, the argument that psychiatric institutions did more harm than good, rather than the availability of drugs, was most important in getting the law passed. See *Psychiatry Inside out: Selected Writings of Franco Basaglia,* Scheper-Hughes and Lovell, A. M., eds., 1987.

15. The word "ALL" was capitalized in the original. The drug desPLEX was marketed by the Grant Chemical Company in New York. The study cited was Canario et al., *Amer. J. Obstet. & Gynecology,* 1953, 65, 1298.

16. Brook, C., editorial, Growth hormone: panacea or punishment for short stature? *British Medical Journal,* 1997, no. 7110, vol. 315.

17. Coste, J., et al., Long-term results of growth hormone treatment in France in children of short stature: Population register based study, *British Medical Journal,* 1997, 315, 708–13. See also discussion of this study by others in Gilbert, S., "Growth Hormone Use in Children Found Ineffective in Large Study," *The New York Times,* 23 September 1997, p. B15.

18. For a more complete account of Genentech's marketing tactics for Protropin and other products, see Marsa, L., *Prescription for Profits* (New York: Scribner, 1997).

19. "Zoloft Maker Warned to Stop Misleading Claims About Drug," *Mental Health Law Reporter,* September 1996, vol. 14, no. 9, p. 66 (Business Publisher, Inc., 951 Pershing Drive, Silver Spring, Md.).

20. Stryer, D., and Bero, L. A., Characteristics of materials distributed by drug companies, *J. of Gen. Internal Medicine,* 1996, 11, 573–83.

21. Strauch, B., "Use of Antidepression Medicine for Young Patients Has Soared," *The New York Times,* 12 August 1997, p. 1. According to this article, pharmaceutical companies were anticipating FDA approval to market these drugs to children and started preparing mint- and orange-flavored liquid versions of the SSRIs.

22. It has been reported that MIT received about $1 million a year from the patent rights, and one-third of that went to Richard Wurtman.

23. See, for example, "Is Marketing of Diet Pill Too Aggressive?" *The Wall Street Journal,* 21 November 1996, pp. B1–B4.

24. Quoted by Kitta McPherson and Edward R. Silverman of the Newhouse News Service in an article entitled "Weighty Matters: Its Side-Effects Disputed, the Redux Diet Drug Has Created a Kind of Scientific Food Fight," *Ann Arbor News,* 13 March 1997, p. D1.

25. Johannes, L., and Stecklow, L., "Early Warning: Heart-Value Problem that Felled Diet Pills Had Arisen Earlier: U.S. Sellers Heard Reports from Belgium but Passed Only Some on to the FDA," *The Wall Street Journal,* 11 December 1997, p. 1.

26. NARSAD was created as an alliance and research arm of three major "support groups" in the field of mental disorders: the National Alliance for the Mentally ill; the National Mental Health Association; and the National Depressive and Manic Depressive Association.

27. Sabshin, M., Turning points in twentieth-century American psychiatry, *American Journal of Psychiatry,* 1990, 147, 1267–74 (quotation from p. 1271).

28. Merrow, J., "Reading, Writing and Ritalin," *The New York Times*, 21 October 1995, p. 16.

29. *The New York Times*, 28 March 1996, p. A13. It is estimated that 6 percent of all school-age boys in the United States are taking Ritalin and about 2 percent of all school-age girls.

30. The ad appeared in the magazine section of *The New York Times* (18 August 1996).

31. Shapiro, S., Skinner, E. A., and Kessler, L. G., Utilization of health and mental health services: Three epidemiologic catchment area sites, *Arch. Gen. Psychiatry*, 1984, 41, 971–78. See also "Dear Colleague" letter (November 1996) written by Beverly Long, president of the World Federation of Mental Health.

32. Spitzer, R. L., et al., Utility of a new procedure for diagnosing mental disorders in primary care: The PRIME-MD 1000 Study, *JAMA*, 1994, 272, 1749–56. The five psychiatric categories the PRIME-MD was designed to diagnose are mood disorders (depression, dysthymia, and so forth), anxiety disorders (generalized anxiety, panic, and so forth), eating disorders, alcohol abuse, and somatoform disorders (hypochondriasis, pain, and so forth). Mood and anxiety disorders constitute the major proportion of psychiatric complaints. Diagnosis of schizophrenia, which is estimated at 1 percent of the population, was not included, presumably because general practioners would generally not be able to treat such patients.

33. Novack, D. H., and Goldberg, R. J., Psychiatric problems in primary care patients, *J. Gen. Internal Medicine*, 1996 11, 56–57.

34. The study of computer-administered PRIME-MD was headed by Kenneth A. Kobak and reported in *The New York Times*, 21 October 1997, p. B11 (Science Watch). See also Kobak, K. A., et al., A computer-administered telephone interview to identify mental disorders, *Journal of the American Medical Association*, 1997, 278, 905–10.

35. Dr. Kurt Kroenke quoted by Goleman, D., "Helping Family Doctors Spot Psychiatric Problems," *The New York Times*, 14 December 1994, p. C12.

36. Marcia Valenstein, personal communication, 7 April 1997.

37. The report, entitled "Length of Antidepressant Therapy: Consensus Conference Statement," has been widely distributed. The report was copyrighted in 1995 by Health Learning Systems, Inc., of Little Falls, New Jersey.

38. Hirschfield, R. M. A., et al., Consensus statement: The National Depressive and Manic Depressive Association consensus statement on the undertreatment of depression, *JAMA*. 1997, 277, 333–40. See also Gilbert, S., "Lag Seen in Aid for Depression," *The New York Times*, 22 January 1997, p. B11.

39. Sheldon, T. A., and Smith, G. D., Consensus conferences as drug promotion, *Lancet*, 1993, 341, 100–102; Skrabanek, P., Nonsensus consensus, *Lancet*, 1990, 335, 1446–47; Lynoe, N., Consensus and consensus conferences, *Scand. J. Soc. Med.*, 1988, 16, 193–95; Bero, L. A., Galbraith, A., and Rennie, D., The publication of sponsored symposium in medical journals, *N. Engl. J. Med.*, 1992, 327, 1135–40.

40. Randall, T., Kennedy hearings say no more free lunch—or much else—from drug firms, *Journal of the American Medical Association*, 1991, 265, 440–42.

41. Rawlins, M. D., Doctors and the drug makers, *Lancet* ii, 1984, 276–78.

42. This estimate was made from the symposia on the preliminary program of the 1996 American Psychiatric Association meeting listed as supported by pharmaceutical companies (*Psychiatric News,* 16 February 1966, vol. 31, no. 4).

43. APA details drug industry support for consumer group, *Psychiatric News,* xxx, 15 September 1995, 1.

44. Office of Technology Assessment, *Pharmaceutical R&D: Costs, Risks and Rewards* (Washington, D.C.: U.S. Government Printing Office, February 1993; OTA-H-522); Pharmaceutical Manufacturers Association of Canada, *1988–1993: A Five-Year Report on the Canadian Brand-Name Pharmaceutical Industry* (Ottawa, 1993).

45. Uchitelle, L., "Companies Reported Spending More on Research," *The New York Times,* 7 November 1997, p. C8.

46. Blumenthal, D., Causino, N., Campbell, E., and Louis, K. S., Relationship between academic institutions and industry in the life sciences—an industry survey, *The New England J. Med.,* 1996, 334, 368–73.

47. Ibid.

48. Blum, A. L., Chalmers, T. C., Deutsch, E., et al., Differing attitudes of industry and academia towards controlled clinical trials, *Eur. J. Clin Invest.,* 1986, 16, 455–60.

49. Davidson, R. A., Source of funding and outcome of clinical trials, *J. of Gen. Intern. Med.,* 1986, 1, 155–58.

50. Davidson, R. A. Source of funding and outcome of clinical trials. *J. of Gen. Intern. Med.,* 1986, 1, 155–58; Goetzsche, P. C., Methodology and overt and hidden bias in reports in 196 double-blind trials of nonsteroidal anti-inflammatory drugs in rheumatoid arthritis, *Controlled Clin. Trials,* 1989, 10, 31–56. An excellent brief review of this literature can be found in Lexchin, J., Is there a bias in industry supported clinical research? *Can. J. Clin. Pharmacol.,* 1995, 2, 15–18.

51. Tollefson, G. D., et al., Olanzapine versus haloperidol in the treatment of schizophrenia and schizoaffective and schizophreniform disorders: Results of an international collaborative trial, *Amer. J. Psychiatry,* 1997, 154, 457–65 (quotation from p. 457).

52. Ross, C. A., Errors of logic in biological psychiatry, in Ross, C. A., and Pam, A., eds., *Pseudoscience in Biological Psychiatry: Blaming the Body* (New York: Wiley, 1995), pp. 85–128 (quotation from p. 111).

53. Kolata, G., "The FDA Approves a Prescription Drug. Then What?" *The New York Times,* 7 October 1997, pp. B9 and B13.

54. Fisher, S., Hanky panky in the pharmaceutical industry, first posted in three parts on the Internet, ASCAP, December 1995, 8, no. 12 (Cumulative no. 97), 12–18. The paper was eventually published under the title Postmarketing surveillance by patient self-monitoring: Preliminary data for sertraline versus fluoxetine, in the *Journal of Clinical Psychiatry,* 1995, 56, 288–96.

55. A recent example of the pressure that may be exerted by a pharmaceutical company concerns Synthroid, a synthetic thyroid hormone pill. The Boots Company, Britain's largest drug retailer, owned the rights to Synthroid, which has the greatest share of the over $600 million annual sales of synthetic thyroid hormone

in the United States. It is estimated that over 8 million people take Synthroid daily to correct hypothyroid conditions.

In recent years, competing pharmaceutical companies have tried to get a larger share of the market by claiming that their pills are bioequivalent and much less expensive. The Boots Company awarded a $250,000 contract to Dr. Betty Dong, a clinical pharmacist at the University of California at San Francisco (UCSF), to study the bioequivalency of Synthroid and three other synthetic thyroid drugs on the market. Dr. Dong must have appeared to the Boots Company to be an ideal person to do this study for them, as she had previously published articles reporting a risk in switching patients from brand-name thyroid pills to generic versions.

Much to the concern of the Boots Company, when the study was nearing completion at the end of 1990 and the results were analyzed, the data indicated that the four synthetic thyroid drugs tested were bioequivalent. When the Boots Company learned of the unfavorable results, it tried to persuade Dr. Dong to water the conclusions down. When this failed, Boots began to discredit the study, pulling out all stops in an effort to block publication of the manuscript. Letters were written to the head of Dr. Dong's academic unit raising objections to the way the study was executed and asserting that "we believe this study, because of its many difficulties, should be terminated." Boots also sent letters to the chancellor and vice-chancellor of the university and to several other department heads. The letters charged that there were all kinds of methodological, procedural, and also possibly ethical problems with the study, even though the company had approved the research protocol in advance. Two university investigations, however, found only extremely minor flaws in the study and they concluded that Boots was trying to harass them and Dr. Dong.

Dr. Dong and her collaborators made several changes in the manuscript, trying unsuccessfully to satisfy Boots without compromising the study. Finally, not wanting to waste all the time and effort invested in the study, they submitted an article to *The Journal of the American Medical Association (JAMA)* in April 1994. Dr. Dong and her colleagues included a covering letter with their manuscript stating that the study had been funded by Boots, which remained critical of the study despite numerous meetings with the authors, and the letter indicated that copies of all the data and the manuscript had been sent to the company. The article received favorable reviews from five outside consultants and was scheduled for publication. In fact, page proofs were already at the printer. In the meantime, the Boots Company had hired consultants, many of whom were people who had previously received fees from the company for lectures or for serving on their Thyroid Research Advisory Council. The information the consultants received about the study and about what had transpired between Boots and Dr. Dong was supplied only by the company. Dr. Dong had no input. The conclusion of the consultants was that the study was seriously flawed and Boots's research director wrote to the editors of *JAMA* citing the conclusions of the consultants and requesting that the study not be published because of its alleged flaws. Moreover, the Boots Company had included a clause in the contract that forbade any publication of the results without the written consent of the company. Dr. Dong had apparently signed the contract thinking that the statement would have no consequences.

The threat of a lawsuit by the company was effective in eliminating virtually all of Dr. Dong's support at her university. Earlier, the UCSF administration planned to back Dr. Dong, but as the threat of an expensive lawsuit became more of a reality, the dean of the Pharmacy School, George Kenyon, explained that while the university considered academic freedom a critical value, "the difficulty here is weighing the right to publish against a likely claim against the university for breach of contract and the possibility of significant damages." A university attorney warned Dr. Dong and her coauthors that they would have to defend themselves in court without any support from the university. The legal costs would have been prohibitive, and after consulting with her coauthors, Dr. Dong telephoned the editors of *JAMA* and instructed them to pull the article. Carter Eckert, a Boots executive, commented at the time that he had "stopped a flawed study that would have put millions of patients at risk." However, others, including Leslie Benet, chairman of UCSF's Pharmaceutical Sciences Department, scoffed at this claim, declaring that "the Boots people did everything they could to make sure this study didn't get published because it was detrimental to their company." Other, "noninvolved" scientists, described the "flaws" as minor, not affecting the outcome, and they stated that it was "extreme hyperbole to question the scientific merit of the study on the basis of those deficiencies."

In March 1995, Boots was taken over by BASF A.G., a German chemical and pharmaceutical company. BASF then started marketing Synthroid through its subsidiary Knoll Pharmaceutical. In May 1995, *JAMA* received a letter from Gilbert Mayer, formerly of Boots and then of Knoll, which was highly critical of Dr. Dong's study. Similar letters were written to the editors of other journals. The letter to *JAMA* stated that the journal should "be concerned about publishing [the paper]." Gilbert Mayer, along with some of his associates, then wrote a sixteen-page critique in which they appropriated Dr. Dong's data and reanalyzed it to argue that the other synthetic thyroid drugs were not equivalent to Synthroid. This was just the opposite of what Dr. Dong and her colleagues had concluded. Gilbert Mayer's critique was published in the *American Journal of Therapeutics,* where he was an associate editor.

Due to a carefully researched article in *The Wall Street Journal,* Knoll began to receive a lot of criticism, and the FDA started looking into the matter. Facing increasing criticism, the president of Knoll, along with some of the company's board members, met in November 1996 with officials of the University of California at San Francisco, including the university chancellor. At this meeting, Knoll agreed that it would not attempt to stop the study from being published, but the company officials continued to insist that the study was flawed. One can only wonder how many flaws would have been found if Dr. Dong and her colleagues had concluded that the other drugs were not as effective as Synthroid. The study was finally published in *JAMA* in April 1997. It has been estimated that if other, less expensive, synthetic thyroid drugs had been used instead of Synthroid, $356 million would have been saved annually. On 29 April 1997, a lawsuit was filed against BASF A.G. and Knoll Pharmaceutical in the federal court of San Francisco, accusing them of suppressing a medical study in an effort to control the American market for thyroid drugs. An excellent account of this whole incident was written by King, R. T., Jr., "Bitter Pill: How a Drug Firm Paid for University Study, Then Undermined It," *The Wall Street Journal,* 12 April 1996, pp. 1 and 6. See also A Cautionary Tale, *Science,* 1996, 273, p. 411; Rennie, D., editorial, The thyroid storm, *JAMA,* 1997, 277, 1238–43; Altman, L. K., "Drug Firm, Relenting, Allows Unflattering Study to Appear," *The New York Times,* 16 April 1997, pp. A1 and A12; Mayer, G. H., Orlando, T., and Kurtz, N. M., Limitations of levothyroxine bioequivalence evaluation: analysis of an attempted study, *Am. J. Therapeutics.* 1995, 2, 417–32: Dong, B. J., Bioequivalence of generic and brand-name levothyroxine products in the treatment of hypothyroidism, *JAMA,* 1997, 277, 1205–13.

The Synthroid experience is not an isolated example of pharmaceutical company influence. Neil Pearce has recently described his experience following a study of the drug fenoterol, a beta adrenergic agonist used in inhalers by asthmatics. Epidemiologists in New Zealand started to notice an increase in cardiovascular-related deaths among asthmatics using bronchodilator aerosols containing fenoterol. The results of a more focused epidemiological study indicated a strong possibility that the use of inhaled fenoterol was responsible for the epidemic of asthma mortality. The authors of this study were not naive and they anticipated that their results might be challenged by the pharmaceutical company that markets fenoterol. Therefore, before submitting their manuscript for publication, they sent a report of the study and its conclusion to New Zealand's Department of Health, which then convened an independent review panel (The Asthma Task Force). The review panel called for some more data, which was supplied by Neil Pearce, and after the authors incorporated a few suggestions by the panel, a favorable report on the study was reached—with one member of the task force commenting that "these are the best data that will ever be available to try to answer this extremely important question."

The fenoterol-asthma manuscript was then submitted to the British medical journal *Lancet,* which accepted it for publication after two external referees approved it with only minor changes in the text. In the meantime, the director-general of New Zealand's Health Department sent a copy of the manuscript to the Boehringer Ingelheim company, the manufacturer of fenoterol. The company immediately sent copies of the manuscript to reviewers it selected, requesting them to "identify important sources of bias" and "to evaluate the importance of each source of error." Many of the responses of these reviewers seemed to have been evoked by the questions asked by the company, and the criticisms were generally unsubstantiated, contradictory, or of the nitpicking variety to which no clinical study is completely immune.

The Boehringer Ingelheim company then convened a "consensus meeting" to which it invited some of the reviewers it had initially hired. The "consensus meeting," which was held in New York in April 1989, concluded that "the study design is seriously flawed and may lead to unjustified policy formulation and prescribing decisions." The report that emerged from the "consensus meeting" was sent to the editors of *Lancet,* who wrote to the authors of the study:

> Some of the commentaries have now been sent to us and they are causing some anxiety.... Three possible courses of action face a journal having second thoughts about a paper accepted but not yet published ... withdrawal ... counter convincingly the critical comments ... publication in the second half of the journal accompanied by a highly critical editorial in the same issue.

The authors refused to back down, writing back that "we can counter convincingly the very critical comments," and they expressed concern that an unconditional acceptance of a paper could be withdrawn "following submissions made by a pharmaceutical company." To their credit, the editors of *Lancet* accepted the authors' response, and a publication date was set. Before publication, staff of New Zealand's Department of Health decided to send an abstract of the paper, accompanied by a cautionary letter, to all doctors in New Zealand. The Boehringer Ingelheim company got wind of this plan and wrote to the department conveying an implicit threat:

> We are concerned at your intended communication with doctors.... Enclosing a copy of the abstract suggests Departmental approval ... unless the Department's approach is modified we are left with no option but to take every steps available to us to protect ourselves.... We have learned that the content and ambiguity in your letter has caused substantial anxiety and confusion among asthma patients and doctors ... the responsibility for the medical and legal consequences rests with you.... We expect [your next] letter to state that therapeutic conclusions cannot be drawn from the Crane et al. study.

The director-general of health then advised the department not to send out the abstract. After further intradepartmental discussion this decision was reversed and copies of the abstract were mailed, but the department's accompanying letter was softened. The asthma death rate in New Zealand dropped markedly after the publication of the study in *Lancet*. When several later studies confirmed the findings, there was overwhelming evidence that implicated fenoterol in the deaths of asthmatics. The drug was finally withdrawn. See: Pearce, N., Adverse reactions: The fenoterol saga, in Davis, P., ed., *For Health or Profit?* (New York: Oxford University Press, 1992), pp. 75–97.

56. Cohen, W., Florida, R., and Goe, W. R., *University-Industry Research Centers in the United States* (Pittsburgh, Pa.: Carnegie-Mellon University Press, 1994).

57. Blumenthal, D., et al., Witholding research results by academic life scientists: Evidence from a national survey of faculty, *JAMA*, 1997, 277, 1224–28.

58. Stolley, P. D., A public health perspective from academia, in Strom, B. L., ed., *Pharmacoepidemiology* (New York: Churchill Livingstone, 1989).

59. Herxheimer, A., Side effects: Freedom of information and the communication of doubt, in Aronson, J. K., ed., *Side Effects of Drugs Annual 19* (Amsterdam: Elsevier, 1996), pp. xix–xxvii. Also published in *Int. J. Risk & Safety in Medicine*, 1996, 9, 201–10.

60. Quoted in Herxheimer, A., op. cit.

61. Hilts, P. J., "Misunderstanding Seen in Journal's Backing of Obesity Drug," *The New York Times*, 29 August 1996, p. C18.

62. Redux increases the level of serotonin in the synapse and, when maintained too long, has been claimed to have a toxic effect on serotonin neurons.

63. Stelfox, H. T., et al., Conflict of interest in the debate over calcium-channel antagonists, *The New Eng. J. of Medicine*, 1998, 338, 101–106. Also Tanouye, E., "Does Corporate Funding Influence Research?" *The Wall Street Journal*, 8 January, 1998, pp. B1 and B6.

64. See Schwartz, H., *Never Satisfied* (New York: Free Press, 1986).

65. Connolly, H. M., et al., Valvular heart disease associated with fenfluramine-phentermine, *The New Eng. J. of Medicine*, 1997, 337, 581–88.

66. Cited by Kolata, G., "The Fearful Price of Getting Thin," *The New York Times*, 13 July 1997, p. E3.

67. Herxheimer, A., Side effects: Freedom of information and the communication of doubt, in Aronson, J. K., ed., *Side Effects of Drugs Annual 19* (Amsterdam: Elsevier, 1996).

68. Rosenberg, S., Sounding board: Secrecy in medical research, *The New Eng. J. Med.*, 1996, 334, 392–94.

69. The effect of journal advertising on market shares of new prescriptions, *Health Care Communications*, 1989.

70. Kessler, D., Editorial: Addressing the problem of misleading advertising, *Annals of Internal Medicine*, 1992, 116, 950–51.

71. Ibid.

72. Wilkes, M. S., Doblin, B. H., and Shapiro, M. F., Pharmaceutical advertisements in leading medical journals: Experts' assessment, *Annals of Internal Medicine*, 1992, 116, 912–19.

73. See "letter to the editors" by John Beary, senior vice-president, Science and Technology of the Pharmaceutical Manufacturing Association. *Annals of Internal Medicine*, 1992, 117, 616.

74. In this study, it was also found that FDA regulations were violated in a number of instances, as when drugs were mentioned for use for conditions for which they had not been approved. Stryer, D., and Bero, L. A., Characteristics of materials distributed by drug companies: An evaluation of appropriateness, *J. of Gen. Internal Medicine*, 1966, 11, 575–83.

75. Wilkes, M. S., Doblin, B. H., and Shapiro, M. F., Pharmaceutical advertisements in leading medical journals: Experts' assessment, *Annals of Internal Medicine*, 1992, 116, 912–19.

76. Wadman, M., Study discloses financial interests behind papers, *Nature*, 1997, 385, 376. The articles selected for the study were written by scientists working at institutions located in Massachusetts.

77. Marsa, L. *Prescription for Profits: How the Pharmaceutical Industry Bankrolled the Unholy Marriage Between Science and Business* (New York: Scribner, 1997).

78. Lately, the pharmaceutical industry has advertised that "the industry is responsible for 90% of all medicines." It is not at all clear how this figure was determined. The 90 percent must include all the drugs that pharmaceutical companies have taken over at some point from researchers who are rarely able to do the clin-

ical trials and all else that is required to market a new drug. Moreover, many of the marketed drugs are essentially duplicates ("me too" drugs) of other drugs. In the United States, 348 new drugs were introduced between 1981 and 1988. The FDA considered only 3 percent (twelve drugs) as having "an important potential contribution to existing therapies," while 84 percent were considered to make "little or no potential contribution." See Randall, T. op. cit., 1991.

7. Other Special Interest Groups

1. The title of the speech was changed when published. See Spitzka, E. C., Reform of the scientific study of insanity, *Journal of Nervous & Mental Disease*, 1878, 5, 201–29.

2. Mitchell, S. W., Address before the Fiftieth Annual Meeting of the American Medico-Psychological Association, *Journal of Nervous & Mental Disease*, 1894, 21, 413–437.

3. "General paralysis of the insane" (GPI) was also called "general paresis." It was not clear during the early part of the twentieth century that GPI was caused by a syphilitic invasion of the brain, and a number of psychiatrists believed it was a "functional disorder." Many patients in mental hospitals were diagnosed as having GPI. In 1913, for example, 103,842 patients in ninety-five public hospitals in England were listed as having GPI. Rollin, H. R., In the footsteps of Wagner-Jauregg, Appendix to Whitrow, M., *Julius Wagner Jauregg (1857–1940)* (London: Smith-Gordon, 1933), p. 207.

4. A history of this period is presented in Valenstein, E., *Great and Desperate Cures: The Rise and Decline of Psychosurgery and Other Radical Treatments for Mental Illness*, New York: Basic Books, 1986.

5. Russell, W. L., The presidential address: The place of the American Psychiatric Association in modern psychiatric organization and progress, *American Journal of Psychiatry*, 1932, 12, 1–18; May, J. V., Presidential address: The establishment of psychiatric standards by the association, *American Journal of Psychiatry*, 1933, 13, 1–15.

6. Rogers, C. R., In retrospect: Forty-six years, *American Psychologist*, 1974, 29, 115–23.

7. Cameron, D. E., Production of differential amnesia as a factor in the treatment of schizophrenia, *Comprehensive Psychiatry*, 1960, 1, 26–34.

8. Ibid., p. 26.

9. Ibid., p. 27.

10. Quoted by Gillmor, D., Morgue psychiatrique: Psychiatric hubris, *Vie à Montréal*, vol. 1, No. 2, January–February 1988, pp. 30–39.

11. Cameron is thought to have left McGill and the Allan Memorial Institute in 1964 because of his concern over the growing French separatist movement in Quebec. He returned to Albany in New York State where he directed a project on aging at the Veterans Administration Hospital until his death three years later from a heart attack.

12. The membership of the American Psychiatric Association reached 39,500 by 1996.

13. The psychologists in the VA program were graduate students studying for their Ph.D.s, and they were provided with clinical experience in the psychiatric wards of Veteran Administration hospitals.

14. Mental Health: Does Therapy Help? *Consumer Reports,* November 1995, 734–39; Seligman, M. E. P., The effectiveness of psychotherapy: The Consumer Reports study, *American Psychologists,* 1995, 50, 965–74.

15. The most common (modal) charge per session by psychiatrists is $110, in contrast to $90 for psychologists, $75 for social workers and marriage/family therapists, and $70 for professional counselors. Source: National Institute of Mental Health, *Psychotherapy Finances.* However, in some geographical areas the charge per session is much higher. In the New York area psychiatrists are estimated to charge (in 1996) between $150 and $300 per session.

16. Klein, D. F., and Wender, P. H., *Understanding Depression: A Complete Guide to its Diagnosis and Treatment* (New York: Oxford University Press, 1993).

17. "The Pendulum Is Swinging," *Financial Times,* 16 March 1995, p. 11.

18. See, for example, a report by Gerald E. Hogarty of the University of Pittsburgh School of Medicine, which appeared in the November 1997 issue of the *American Journal of Psychiatry.*

19. Naber, D., A self-rating to measure subjective effects of neuroleptic drugs, relationships to objective psychopathology, quality of life, compliance and other clinical variables, *Int. Clin. Psychopharmacol.,* 1995, suppl. 3, 133–38; Award, A. G., et al., Patients' subjective experiences on antipsychotic medications: implications for outcome and quality of life, *Int. Clin. Psychopharmacol.,* 1995, suppl. 3, 123–32.

20. The reports on the effectiveness of lithium vary greatly with different studies and different subtypes of bipolar disorders. See Gershon, S., and Soares, J. C., Current therapeutic profile of lithium, *Archiv. Gen. Psychiatry,* 1997, 54, 16–20. Evidence that family therapy improves the recovery rate and reduces hospital stays of manic-depressive patients was presented by Dr. Gabor Keitner of the Brown University Mood Disorder Program. See "Family Therapy May Aid Recovery from Manic Depression," *The New York Times,* 20 May 1997, p. B11.

21. Seligman, M. E. P., The effectiveness of psychotherapy: The Consumer Reports study, *American Psychologist,* 1995, 50, 965–74.

22. Walsh, B. T., et al., Medication and psychotherapy in the treatment of bulimia nervosa, *American J. Psychiatry,* 1997, 154, 523–31.

23. *Consumer Reports,* op. cit.

24. Cullen, E. A., Six-state tour seeks to advance prescriptive authority initiates, *Practitioner, APA Practice Directorate,* February 1997, vol. 10, p. 6.

25. Psychologists suffer setback in prescription privilege battle, *Psychiatric News,* XXX, 15 September 1995, p. 10.

26. The Oprah Winfrey program was shown on 7 March 1994. The guest expert referred to in the text was the psychiatrist Peter Breggin, who is generally opposed to all drug treatment and to all somatic treatments of mental disorders.

27. The "Dear Abby" column appeared in the *Ann Arbor News,* 8 August 1995, p. D2.

8. Reprise, Conclusions, and Reflections

1. Kemker, S. S., and Khadivi, A., Psychiatric education: Learning by assumption, in Ross, C. A., and Pam, A., eds., *Pseudoscience in Biological Psychiatry: Blaming the Body* (New York: Wiley, 1995), pp. 241–77 (quotation from Susan S. Kemker, from p. 246).

2. Carlsson, A., Neuroleptics and neurotransmitter interactions in schizophrenia, *Int. Clin. Psychopharmacol.*, 1995, 10, suppl. 3, 21–28 (quotation from p. 21).

3. For example, see Williamson, P. C., Schizophrenia as a brain disease, *Archives Neurol.*, 1993, 50, 1096–97.

4. Gottesman, I. I., *Schizophrenia Genesis: The Origin of Madness* (New York: W. H. Freeman, 1991), p. 96.

5. Wolfe, S. M., Why do American drug companies spend more than $12 billion a year pushing drugs? *J. of Gen. Internal Medicine*, 1996, 11, 637–39.

6. For a discussion of the increase in pharmaceutical company advertising directly to consumers, see Zuger, A., "Drug Companies' Sales Pitch: 'Ask Your Doctor,'" *The New York Times*, 5 August 1997, p. B9. See also "Too Clever by Half," *The Economist*, 20 September 1997, p. 67.

7. The ad was placed in *The New York Times* (4 July 1997) by Rhône-Poulenc, the company that introduced Largactil (chlorpromazine) in the 1950s.

8. "Drug Firm to Pay $325 Million," *The New York Times*, 25 February 1997, p. A10. The company charged with fraud was SmithKline Beecham. An official of the company stated that there was no intention to violate any law and that a misunderstanding resulted from "ambiguities over regulations and guidelines." It would be hard to find examples when regulatory ambiguities led to a company's receiving less money than it was entitled to.

9. Don Holdsworth, who formerly worked for PepsiCo, was hired as marketing manager by Merck in 1995.

10. Quoted by Rosenthal, E., "Maker of Cancer Drugs to Oversee Prescriptions at 11 Cancer Clinics," *The New York Times*, 15 April 1997, pp. A1 and D4 (quotation from p. D4).

11. Kotulak, R., *Inside the Brain: Revolutionary Discoveries of How the Mind Works* (Kansas City, Mo.: Andrews & McMeel, 1996).

12. Appleton, W. S., *Prozac and the New Antidepressants: What You Need to Know About Prozac, Zoloft, Paxil, Luvox, Wellbutrin, Effexor, Serzone, and More* (New York: A Plume Book, 1997). Quotation from pp. 47–48.

13. See Solomon, A., Anatomy of melancholy, *The New Yorker*, 12 January 1998, p. 58.

14. Interview with Arthur Meltzer in Healy, D., *The Psychopharmacologists: Interviews by David Healy* (London: Chapman & Hall, 1996), p. 506.

15. Leon Eisenberg quoted in *The New York Times*, 10 August 1997.

16. Reiser, M., Are psychiatric educators "losing the mind"? *American J. Psychiatry*, 1988, 145, 158–53 (quotation from p. 151). The speech on which this paper was based was delivered to a meeting of the American Psychiatric Association in Washington, D.C., 10–16 May 1986.

17. Thomas, L., *The Youngest Science* (New York: Viking Press, 1983).

Index